Brexit and Beyond: Nation and Identity

Edited by Daniela Keller and Ina Habermann

SPELL
Swiss Papers in
English Language and Literature

Edited by
The Swiss Association of University Teachers of English
(SAUTE)

General Editor: Ina Habermann

Volume 39

Brexit and Beyond: Nation and Identity

Edited by Daniela Keller and Ina Habermann

Umschlagabbildung und Einbandgestaltung: Martin Heusser, Zürich
Holzstich: Künstler unbekannt, pub. erstmals 1888 in C. Flammarion, L'atmosphère. Météorologie populaire. Bearbeitung Sabina Horber, Zürich

Bibliografische Information der Deutschen Nationalbibliothek
Die Deutsche Nationalbibliothek verzeichnet diese Publikation in der Deutschen Nationalbibliografie; detaillierte bibliografische Daten sind im Internet über http://dnb.dnb.de abrufbar

Publiziert mit Unterstützung der Schweizerischen Akademie der Geistes- und Sozialwissenschaften.

Dischingerweg 5 · D-72070 Tübingen

Internet: www.narr.de
eMail: info@narr.de

CPI books GmbH, Leck

ISSN 0940-0478
ISBN 978-3-8233-8414-4 (Print)
ISBN 978-3-8233-9414-3 (ePDF)

Table of Contents

Ina Habermann and Daniela Keller (Basel)
Introduction: In the Shallows of National Identity 9

Cultural Constructions of British National Identity

Matthias D. Berger (Bern)
2016 and All That: Medievalism and Exceptionalism in Brexit Britain 23

Barbara Straumann (Zurich)
Long Live the Queen! Queen Victoria as a National Icon in Film 41

Brexit Discourses

Martin Mik and Jo Angouri (Warwick)
"My Lords and Members of the House of Commons": Britain and the European Integration Project through the Queen's Speeches 61

Nora Wenzl (Vienna)
"The United Kingdom is a different state": Conservative MPs' Appeals to Britishness before the EU Referendum 99

BrexLit

Harald Pittel (Potsdam)
Ali Smith's 'Coming-of-Age' in the Age of Brexit 121

Michelle Witen (Flensburg)
The Story of Brexit: Nostalgia in Parody Children's BrexLit 145

Christine Berberich (Portsmouth)
BrexLit and the Marginalized Migrant 167

Beyond the Home Counties: Marginal(ized) Identities

Victoria Allen (Kiel)
Retracing, Remembering, Reckoning: Stuart Maconie's Footsteps Narrative of the Jarrow March 183

Ian Goode (Glasgow)
The Cultural Topography of Rural Cinema-Going in the Post-War Highlands and Islands of Scotland 207

Maurice Fitzpatrick (Villanova)
Fractured Identities: How Brexit Threatens an Agreed Ireland 227

Across the Atlantic: Nation and Identity in America

Cécile Heim (Lausanne)
Unsettling Private Property in Linda Hogan's *Mean Spirit* 251

Shelley Fisher Fishkin (Stanford)
Nostalgia for a Fictive Past: Nation and Identity in a Post-Trump, Post-Brexit World 271

Notes on Contributors 295

Index of Names 301

General Editor's Preface

SPELL (Swiss Papers in English Language and Literature) is a publication of SAUTE, the Swiss Association of University Teachers of English. Established in 1984, it first appeared every second year, was published annually from 1994 to 2008, and now appears three times every two years. Every second year, SPELL publishes a selection of papers given at the biennial symposia organized by SAUTE. Non-symposium volumes usually have as their starting point papers given at other conferences organized by members of SAUTE, in particular conferences of SANAS, the Swiss Association for North American Studies and SAMEMES, the Swiss Association of Medieval and Early Modern English Studies. However, other proposals are also welcome. Decisions concerning topics and editors are made by the Annual General Meeting of SAUTE two years before the year of publication.

Volumes of SPELL contain carefully selected and edited papers devoted to a topic of literary, linguistic, and – broadly – cultural interest. All contributions are original and are subjected to external evaluation by means of a full peer review process. Contributions are usually by participants at the conferences mentioned, but volume editors are free to solicit further contributions. Papers published in SPELL are documented in the *MLA International Bibliography*. SPELL is published with the financial support of the Swiss Academy of Humanities and Social Sciences.

Information on all aspects of SPELL, including volumes planned for the future, is available from the General Editor, Professor Ina Habermann, University of Basel, Department of English, CH-4051 Basel, Switzerland; e-mail: ina.habermann@unibas.ch. Information about past volumes of SPELL and about SAUTE, in particular about how to become a member of the association, can be obtained from the SAUTE website at www.saute.ch.

Ina Habermann

Introduction

In the Shallows of National Identity

Ina Habermann and Daniela Keller[1]

After 23 June 2016 when a slight majority decided that Britain should pursue a future outside of the European Union, and several exit deadlines had come and gone, Britain officially left the EU on 31 January 2020. Brexit, however, is still far from 'done' as negotiations between the UK and the EU may continue until 31 December 2020 (when the so-called transition phase is set to end), and possibly beyond that date.[2] Apart from the political and economic consequences likely to ensue, it is equally hard to fathom the cultural reverberations that this cut from the Continent will create. Several critics have argued that Brexit has always been less about the economy than about (national) identity (Bogdanor 18; see also Henderson et al. 643) and culture

[1] The editors would like to thank all contributors to this volume, the peer reviewers, the copy editor Alexandre Fachard, our student assistants Alexandra Grasso and Melanie Löw, the English seminar librarian Mario Piscazzi, and Sabina Horber and Martin Heusser for the cover design.

[2] The EU and the UK are finding it hard to dovetail their interests. As Chris Morris reported on 23 July 2020, trade negotiations will continue up to a point when the "pressure of time" will force both sides to take concrete decisions. A particular challenge is presented by the fact that "[u]sually if trade negotiations fail, things stay as they are. In this case, though, a breakdown in talks will lead to sudden and substantial changes in the economic relationship between the UK and the EU" (Morris). Among the most knotty issues are the Irish border, fishing rights, and the acceptance of standards designed to ensure a 'level playing field' in future trade relations and economic competition.

Brexit and Beyond: Nation and Identity. SPELL: Swiss Papers in English Language and Literature 39, edited by Daniela Keller and Ina Habermann, Narr, 2020, pp. 9-22.

(Donington 129; Eaglestone 1; Habermann, Introduction 2). Despite the many uncertainties, however, it is undisputed that Brexit has not only produced a rift between the United Kingdom and mainland Europe, but that it has also reignited debates about nation and identity *within* the United Kingdom and the British Isles (see, for instance, Bogdanor 20).

There are straightforward legal and political reasons for this. Firstly, Scotland and Northern Ireland voted Remain, whereas Wales and England supported Leave, but because "84% of the United Kingdom's population" live in England, "the vote to leave in England outweighed substantial Remain majorities in Scotland (62.0%-38.0%) and Northern Ireland (NI) (55.5%-44.6%)" (Henderson et al. 631).[3] The referendum, therefore, forces two nations within the United Kingdom to accept an outcome that they did not vote for, which underlines that "Brexit was made in England" (631; see also Kenny et al. 5). This is a fact that the devolved nations, such as Scotland, have not been hesitant to point out, because a second reason why they feel resentful about the Brexit outcome is that they might lose part of their current autonomy. As Neal Ascherson highlights,

> Scottish governments and agencies have spun a dense web of connections to the EU over twenty years of devolution, often to the irritation of Whitehall which constantly reminds Holyrood that only the UK government has the right to conduct negotiations with the Commission. (73-74)

Hence, it is not surprising that Scotland worries over the UK's "Power Grab" (73), as laws and agreements fall back into the hands of the UK Parliament based in London (see also Kenny et al. 11; Keating 44).

Brexit is a highly complex endeavour, not least because the United Kingdom is a union of divided parts much like the EU itself (Keating 40), and has to satisfy its four nations (and its overseas territory, Gibraltar) as well as find a consensus with the EU member states. As we propose to show in what follows, there is a considerable clash between the Leave camp's arguments urging simplicity and homogeneity, and the actual realities of difference, complexity, and chaos. This is reflected

---

[3] Gibraltar should be mentioned here, too, as 95.9% of its population voted to remain (Ballantine Perera 79). Although Gibraltar is a British overseas territory, it faces similarly challenging prospects as Northern Ireland, since it shares a border with an EU nation (Spain). For more information on Gibraltar, which has often been overlooked in Brexit debates, see Habermann, "British-European Entanglements" and "Gibraltarian Hauntologies"; Sanchez.

both in the treacherous banality of the referendum itself as a choice between 'in' or 'out,' and by meaningless, pseudo-clear slogans such as Theresa May's 'Brexit means Brexit.' In fact, Brexit means many things. Among them, as Maurice Fitzpatrick points out in this volume with reference to a Sinn Féin campaign, 'Brexit means Borders.' In October 2019 it was decided that the border between the UK and the EU would run down the Irish Sea and not between the North and South of Ireland. But Prime Minister Boris Johnson has been reluctant to admit that in this case there would have to be border checks between Northern Ireland and Great Britain (O'Carroll), thus elegantly evading – and appearing to downplay – the difficulties that Brexit entails. According to Lisa O'Carroll, Johnson had initially even advised companies that if they were required to "fill in extra paperwork, they should telephone the prime minister 'and I [Boris Johnson] will direct them to throw that form in the bin.'" Another disarmingly simple and straightforward way to 'get Brexit done' – one is inclined to say – in answer to far more complex queries and conundrums. In line with this somewhat cavalier approach, the British Government proposed an Internal Market Bill, accepted in the House of Commons in September 2020, that is designed to go back on the promise of avoiding a hard border in Ireland. Opponents of this bill, including senior Tories, argued that this unilateral change to the withdrawal agreement effectively constituted a breach of international law, while Johnson is suspected widely to have voted for the withdrawal agreement in the first place 'with his fingers crossed.'

Despite such belated and highly controversial attempts at preserving the unity of the United Kingdom, Brexit is driving wedges between its nation-states. This is perhaps discursively compensated for by such bold ideas as building a bridge (or a tunnel) between Northern Ireland and Scotland (BBC).[4] But even a grand symbolic gesture and physical connection such as a bridge between nations cannot mend the far deeper rifts and the challenges to a common identity that are not only defined by physical or geographical circumstances but also, most crucially, by culture. Building such a bridge will not change the fact that a large number of Leave voters, according to a Channel 4 survey conducted in November 2018, were "not at all concerned" if Northern Ireland left the United Kingdom to re-unite with the Republic of Ireland (O'Toole 62), just as the Eurotunnel did not reduce Euroscepticism (see Redford).

---

[4] Although this idea has not been investigated further by the government, it is nevertheless kept on the table by Boris Johnson as he remarked that the bridge is a "very interesting idea" (qtd. in BBC). Others have proposed building a tunnel instead (Carrell).

The English Channel's example shows that the construction of material links such as bridges and tunnels will not automatically overcome borders of the mind. In fact, a focus on the sea highlights the paradoxical and ideological nature of the whole discourse: the existence of the English Channel supposedly proves that the British are separate from continental Europe, while the Irish Sea is no impediment to a United Kingdom that includes Northern Ireland, just as there can be a special friendship with the US across the Atlantic Ocean, and a Commonwealth that spans the Seven Seas. Many advocates of Brexit systematically overstate a selective geographical evidence for separation, at the same time downplaying the fault lines within Britain.[5]

Likewise, they insinuate that 'nation' and 'identity' can be defined in a simple manner – the former as geographical space and the latter as citizenship, for instance. No attempt will be made here to summarize the extensive critical debates surrounding these highly charged terms; for the present purpose it suffices to recall that they are not essentialist and self-evident, but always constructed, mediated, and entangled with "'fuzzy' phenomena such as cultural myths, narratives and images which circulate in literature, travel writing, films and other media" (Habermann, Introduction 2). While Brexit is driving a wedge between the different nations making up the UK, the notion of identity, which comprises a wide range of intersectional social categories such as age, class, ethnicity, or gender, is now employed in a divisive manner to explain the Brexit vote. In her contribution to this volume, Victoria Allen quotes social geographer Danny Dorling, who shows that Brexit was "unfairly blamed on the working class in the north of England" (1) since the majority of voters who endorsed Brexit are actually middle class and live in the south of England. The decision to leave the EU is also strongly associated with the older generation. Craig Calhoun, for instance, reflects on the fact that "[f]ully 75 percent of voters aged 18-24 opted for a future in Europe. Sixty-one percent of those over 65, along with a majority of all those over 45, voted against" and contemplates that "those who will have to live longest with the consequences wanted a different choice" (60). As Harald Pittel's discussion of Ali Smith's Seasonal Quar-

[5] Joanna Rostek and Anne-Julia Zwierlein also point to Conservative rhetorical strategies aiming to hold the UK together. In their introduction to *Brexit and the Divided United Kingdom* they discuss an excerpt of Theresa May's speech on triggering Article 50 where she used the word 'together' several times desperately to underscore the strength of the union in face of a threatening disunity (9). On another occasion, Theresa May "pledged that 'I will always fight to strengthen and sustain this precious, precious Union,' one precious," as O'Toole insists, "clearly not being enough" (63).

tet in this volume illustrates, however, literature can subvert and oppose the danger to cement a counterproductive divide between 'old Leave voters' and 'young Remainers,' because it acknowledges that the 'blame game' is not the way forward. Rather, a dialogue which does not supress difference is key to coming to terms with the challenges that the UK faces. David McCrone and Frank Bechhofer suggest that it is "helpful to get away from 'identity' (as a noun), implying that it is a badge which affixes to people, [...] and treat it more as a verb, 'to identify with,' which implies a more active process of doing, which varies according to context" (17). The contributions to this volume substantiate this by demonstrating that it matters as much *how* constructions of identity are embedded in political or literary narratives, as *who* defines the identities and narratives, and from *where*, from which perspective or political and social position this is done.

The cracks appearing in the myth of seamless national identity have also revived discussions of the so-called English Question, which concerns the uneven distribution of power between the nations of the UK.[6] Devolution, which has provided Scotland, Wales, and Northern Ireland with their own parliament or assemblies, has raised awareness that Scottish or Welsh MPs can vote on laws that might only concern England (which does not have its own government), although England has no say in Scottish or Welsh decisions. As the Brexit vote has shown, however, momentous decisions that affect the whole UK can be dominated by English voters because they make up the majority of the UK's population. The referendum has therefore conflated England and Britain and thus brought the problematic nature of this conflation back to people's attention. In 2006 Robert Hazell could still comfortably claim that "[w]e cannot readily disentangle Englishness from Britishness in our history or in our institutions" (45). The tide has turned since, as Kenny et al. argue in 2018: "[T]he traditional conflation of England and Britain *is* growing harder to sustain, because of the growing politicisation of English national identity and political divergence between the nations of the UK" (5). As the devolved nations become more self-assured in establishing their own national identities,[7] English identity is seeking to

---

[6] As Robert Hazell explains, "[t]he English Question is not a single question, but a portmanteau heading for a whole series of questions about the government of England" (37).

[7] Devin Beauregard, for instance, insists that "[i]f there is one thing, then, that can be said of Scotland's cultural policy since devolution, it is that it has emblemized a sort of (re)awakening of Scotland's sense of culture and identity – one that had, for a long time, sat dormant" (132).

emancipate itself from British identity and growing more confident as, for instance, a political marketing strategy (see Berger in this volume).

Another significant development in the Brexit discourse on identity can be seen in the Conservatives' Leave strategy to replace the broader identity of a 'European Britain' with a 'Global Britain,' which served to imply that the UK will remain a well-connected country after leaving the EU. Instead, "the May government's advocacy of Global Britain only exacerbated widely-held suspicions about the family resemblance between the ghost of empires past and the first rumblings of Brexit futures" (Ward and Rasch 3). UKIP did not shy away from suggesting the Commonwealth as the better alternative for trade relations in their manifesto (Kenny and Pearce 203), nor were supporters of Brexit hesitant to stage 'the Anglosphere' as a far more significant community of "true friends" compared to the member states of the European Union (Baxendale and Wellings 223).[8]

While 'Leavers' have turned their backs on the Continent to look outwards to other global players, they tend to look backward with regard to time. Many critics have highlighted the role of imperial nostalgia in Brexit debates (Donington 122; see also Straumann and Witen in this volume) and the dangers of painting a picture of a continuous and homogenous history (see Berger in this volume) that employs a "calculated forgetting" (see Fisher Fishkin in this volume). There is a significant tension in the ways that the Brexit-affected nations deal with their own history and identity. As Fintan O'Toole aptly summarizes:

> In Ireland, we have been trying to awake from the epic into the ordinary, from the gloriously simple into the fluidly complex, from the once-and-for-all moment of national destiny into the openness and contingency of actual existence, with all its uncertainties and contradictions. In the England of Brexit, on the other hand, this process is working in reverse. The imagined movement is from the ordinary into the epic, from the complex to the gloriously simple, from the openness and contingency of real life in a society of multiple identities into a once-and-for all [sic] moment of destiny: 23 June 2016 as Independence Day, a sacred day of destiny from which a new history begins – a day that cannot therefore be revisited or returned from. (64)

[8] As Eva Namusoke elucidates, the Anglosphere was "sometimes used interchangeably" (224) with the Commonwealth by Leave supporters and often only refers to white settler nations, such as Australia, Canada, and New Zealand.

As Maurice Fitzpatrick's essay elucidates, the European Union was able to create a home for such a crucial state of indeterminacy in the case of Northern Ireland (as it did for Gibraltar). The devolved nations appear to be more aware of a necessary flexibility, as Adam Tomkins, a Member of the Scottish Parliament, remarked that "the Union not only accommodates but requires difference [...] it is not a unitary state with a single seat of power in which the entire land is ruled in a uniform way" (qtd. in Kenny and Pearce 32). Nation and identity, therefore, cannot, and should not, be homogenous and simple. It remains to be seen to what extent the unions of Britain *and* Europe can strengthen their communities by acknowledging and promoting their differences within.

The contributions in this volume are based on papers that were given at the biannual conference of the Swiss Association of University Teachers of English (SAUTE) on nation and identity that took place on 3-4 May 2019 at the University of Basel. In our call for papers, we asked our speakers to respond to the "debates about national identity [that] have received new currency in recent years in a context of demonstrations of national self-assertion." Beyond the introduction of authoritarian measures in some member states of the European Union, these developments produced the Brexit decision in Britain and significant changes in American international policies. The following essays scrutinize these trends, on the one hand by critically analysing the tendencies of political and literary narratives to look back in time and yearn for a nostalgic, distant past and, on the other, by pointing towards their potential to reimagine a future that is 'closer to home' and based on the actual and present condition of the UK. The latter is perhaps both the most challenging and the most pressing, as "the cosmopolitan elites who shaped the new Britain failed to generate a new narrative, a new national self-understanding to make sense of the changes and membership in the transformed country" (Calhoun 60; see also Wenzl in this volume). In any case, the stories of Brexit have not all been told yet and will require continued attention in the next years, perhaps decades, to come.

The first part of our volume begins with 'Cultural Constructions of British National Identity.' Matthias D. Berger elucidates Henderson et al.'s contention that "Brexit was made in England" (631), highlighting the Leave campaigners' strategies of glorifying *English* medieval history in order to promote ideas of a *British* nation forced to fight for sovereignty against an oppressive EU. In particular, the essay scrutinizes "trained historian-turned-politician" Daniel Hannan's portrayal of a continuous and natural British/English history (and national character) in his book *How We Invented Freedom & Why It Matters* (2013). Conflating England and Britain in this way is certainly strategic here, adding a historical dimension to the geographical pseudo-evidence of the English Channel as a firm dividing line between 'Europe' and Britain.

Barbara Straumann similarly identifies continuity and nostalgia as two defining features of national identity, focussing on fictional representations of Queen Victoria in two films from the 1930s (*Victoria the Great* and *Sixty Glorious Years*) and a recent depiction of the queen in *Victoria & Abdul* (2017). The essay explores how Queen Victoria as a national icon serves different purposes at different times. Most recently, in *Victoria & Abdul*, she appears to respect and appreciate the Commonwealth. As the film foregrounds her admiration for her servant Abdul Karim's culture and country, it celebrates a carefully edited glorious imperial past. There is an intriguing parallel between the spectacle of a caring monarch and her subservient admirer and a (supposedly) open and outward-looking United Kingdom that seeks to strengthen its global ties with the Commonwealth, failing, however, to treat all its nations as equal players.

Our second part, 'Brexit Discourses,' addresses the discursive power of political language. Martin Mik and Jo Angouri analyse the representation of the relationship between the UK and the EU in the Queen's Speeches, which provide a political constant throughout the decades. Particular attention is paid to the time leading up to the UK's two referenda on European integration in 1975 and 2016. This idiosyncratic genre showcases the British Government's intentions within a ceremonial framework whose symbolic weight must not be underestimated as it contributes significantly to shaping the public's understanding of the European-British relationship. Nora Wenzl then proceeds to analyse the Leave and Remain discourses within the Conservative party, asking how they construct British identity. Wenzl's study perfectly exemplifies Calhoun's critical stance when he laments that (especially pro-EU) politicians missed the opportunity to create "a new national self-understanding" (60). Basing her argument on a Critical Discourse Analysis of parliamentary proceedings in the House of Commons from May 2015 to June 2016, Wenzl unveils that *both* sides framed Britain as exceptional and in opposition to Europe. Hence, Conservative supporters of the Remain campaign failed to promote EU membership as the better alternative to exceptionalism.

Our third part turns to 'BrexLit' as a type of fiction that contributes to the discourses of Brexit. In 2017, Kristian Shaw coined the term

'BrexLit' to describe literature that in some form responds to the referendum. Ali Smith's novel *Autumn* (2016), famously considered to be the first piece of post-Brexit literature, is part of Smith's so-called Seasonal Quartet, which also includes *Winter* (2017), *Spring* (2019), and *Summer* (2020). Unlike the previous contributions that tackle the political dimension of national identity, Harald Pittel reads Smith's Brexit fiction with a focus on community building, and specifically in light of age. Along with the divisions between the UK's nation-states and such other markers of difference as class, as mentioned above, Brexit has also revealed a gap between an older and a younger generation. But rather than accepting this opposition, Smith's four contemporary novels write back to the stereotypes of old age and ageing. Moving beyond stereotype and also insisting that literary traditions can be rewritten, Smith's Seasonal Quartet challenges dominant perceptions of old age and provides a new post-Brexit myth of communal understanding.

Michelle Witen takes up the issue of nostalgia again in her analysis of parodies of children's literature concerned with Brexit. She argues that such texts as *Alice in Brexitland* or the Ladybird spoof *The Story of Brexit* form a sub-section of BrexLit that is as yet under-appreciated but may be seen as particularly influential because it uses the visceral appeal of children's literature and readers' nostalgic memories of childhood to make a case about Brexit and its relation to English/British identity. The humour of these stories has a double function, since it offers both a satirical stance, and an emotional coping mechanism in the aftermath of a Brexit decision that has turned out to be extremely disruptive and divisive. Christine Berberich then shifts the focus to the role EU migrants play in BrexLit. She finds that contrary to their actual presence in British society and to the somewhat magnified discursive role they played in the Leave campaign, EU migrants are almost invisible in BrexLit, and if they appear at all, they tend to be reduced to cameo appearances of Eastern European cleaners and similar marginal(ized) characters. Over three million people are silenced in this way, and the question remains whether BrexLit mirrors an actual situation or even colludes in perpetuating it.

Our fourth part, 'Beyond the Home Counties,' continues the preoccupation with identities marginal(ized) from a home-counties and London perspective. Victoria Allen reads Stuart Maconie's travelogue *Long Road from Jarrow: A Journey through Britain Then and Now* (2017) as a non-fictional contribution to BrexLit. Maconie produces a footsteps narrative, revisiting the route of the 1936 workers' protest march from Jarrow to London as he reflects on the current condition of England from a Northern working-class perspective. Travelling yet further north, Ian

Goode offers a historical view of cinema-going in the Highlands and Islands of Scotland made possible by the Film Guild and the Screen Machine, which is run by Regional Screen Scotland – an institution that has profited from European financial support for remote areas. Therefore, as also for historical reasons connected to politics and religion, the Scottish ties to the Continent differ markedly from those of England, which goes a long way towards explaining the different referendum result and many Scottish people's annoyance at being forced into Brexit by the English majority – an annoyance also felt in Northern Ireland. In his contribution, which closes this part, Maurice Fitzpatrick explores the unique challenges that Brexit presents for Ireland as well as for Ireland's relations with the UK. In particular, Fitzpatrick emphasizes how Brexit jeopardizes the peace process implemented with the Good Friday Agreement in 1998, because the Irish border threatens to become a 'hard' external EU border. Predictably, although this was downplayed by the Leave campaign, the Irish situation has become a major crux in the Brexit process and related negotiations.

In the fifth part, 'Across the Atlantic: Nation and Identity in America,' we widen the scope of our discussion of national identity to include the United States as a major player within the 'Anglosphere' with which Britain claims to have a special relationship. Both Cécile Heim and Shelley Fisher Fishkin reiterate the claim made in this volume that it is problematic to treat the concepts of nation and identity as stable and homogenous. Heim queries the ostensibly seamless connection between 'nation' as territory and (individual or collective) identity by contrasting the ways in which white settlers and indigenous peoples relate to their land in Chickasaw author Linda Hogan's novel *Mean Spirit* (1990). Heim's contribution invites us to rethink what it means to own, as opposed to belonging to, a plot of land, as she deconstructs the idea of private property as key to shaping a nation. Finally, Shelley Fisher Fishkin revisits the notion of nostalgia, which runs like a leitmotif through current British and US-American discourses of identity. Crucially, as she insists, this is a nostalgia for a past that never was, based on calculated forgetting and the fabrication of false or fragmented memories. Deconstructing notions of splendid isolation and exceptionalism, Fisher Fishkin argues that both the UK and the US have always been multicultural; her analysis of American literature reveals an inherent transnationalism by showing how writers were "influenced by what [they] read and by where they travelled." Fisher Fishkin ends with the clear message that it is illusory to think that national borders are impermeable, and that it is the responsibility of literary and cultural critics to acknowledge and promote writers who celebrate heterogeneous alternatives to hegemonic discourse.

References

Ascherson, Neal. "Scotland, Brexit and the Persistence of Empire." *Embers of Empire in Brexit Britain*, edited by Stuart Ward and Astrid Rasch, Bloomsbury Academic, 2019, pp. 71-78.

Ballantine Perera, Jennifer. "Gibraltar: Brexit's Silent Partner." *Embers of Empire in Brexit Britain*, edited by Stuart Ward and Astrid Rasch, Bloomsbury Academic, 2019, pp. 79-86.

Baxendale, Helen, and Ben Wellings. "Underwriting Brexit: The European Union in the Anglosphere Imagination." *The Anglosphere: Continuity, Dissonance and Location*, edited by Ben Wellings and Andrew Mycock, Oxford UP, 2019, pp. 207-23.

BBC. "Scotland-Northern Ireland Bridge: No Feasibility Study Commissioned." 5 June 2020, www.bbc.com/news/uk-scotland-52935602.

Beauregard, Devin. *Cultural Policy and Industries of Identity: Québec, Scotland, & Catalonia*. Palgrave Macmillan, 2018.

Bogdanor, Vernon. *Beyond Brexit: Britain's Unprotected Constitution*. I. B. Tauris, 2019.

Calhoun, Craig. "Populism, Nationalism and Brexit." *Brexit: Sociological Responses*, edited by William Outhwaite, Anthem Press, 2017, pp. 57-76.

Carrell, Severin. "Build an Irish Sea Tunnel, Not a Bridge, Says Scottish Secretary." *Guardian*, 5 March 2020, www.theguardian.com/politics/2020/mar/05/build-an-irish-sea-tunnel-not-a-bridge-says-scottish-secretary.

Donington, Katie. "Relics of Empire? Colonialism and the Culture Wars." *Embers of Empire in Brexit Britain*, edited by Stuart Ward and Astrid Rasch, Bloomsbury Academic, 2019, pp. 121-31.

Dorling, Danny. "Brexit: The Decision of a Divided Country." *BMJ*, 6 July 2016, www.bmj.com/content/354/bmj.i3697.full?ijkey=Qzh0MvExCSL1BkA&keytype=ref.

Eaglestone, Robert. Introduction: Brexit and Literature. *Brexit and Literature: Critical and Cultural Responses*, edited by Robert Eaglestone, Routledge, 2018, pp. 1-6.

Habermann, Ina. "British-European Entanglements: M. G. Sanchez' *The Escape Artist* and the Case of Gibraltar." *Journal for Literary and Intermedial Crossings*, vol. 2, 2018, pp. 1-20.

——. "Gibraltarian Hauntologies: Spectres of Colonialism in the Fiction of M. G. Sanchez. *Open Library of Humanities*, vol. 6, no. 1, 2020, p. 19. doi: doi.org/10.16995/olh.503.

——. Introduction: Understanding the Past, Facing the Future. *The Road to Brexit*, edited by Ina Habermann, Manchester UP, 2020, pp. 1-14.

Hazell, Robert. "The English Question." *Publius: The Journal of Federalism*, vol. 36, no. 1, Winter 2006, pp. 37-56.

Henderson, Alisa, et al. "How Brexit Was Made in England." *The British Journal of Politics and International Relations*, vol. 19, no. 4, 2017, pp. 631-46.

Keating, Michael. "Brexit and Scotland." *The Routledge Handbook of the Politics of Brexit*, edited by Patrick Diamond et al., 2019, pp. 40-48.

Kenny, Michael, et al. Introduction: English Identity and Institutions in a Changing United Kingdom. *Governing England: English Identity and Institutions in a Changing United Kingdom*, edited by Michael Kenny et al., Oxford UP, 2018, pp. 3-26.

Kenny, Michael, and Nick Pearce. "Churchill, Powell and the Conservative 'Brexiteers': The Political Legacies of the Anglosphere." *The Anglosphere: Continuity, Dissonance and Location*, edited by Ben Wellings and Andrew Mycock, Oxford UP, 2019, pp. 191-206.

McCrone, David, and Frank Bechhofer. *Understanding National Identity*. Cambridge UP, 2015.

Morris, Chris. "Post-Brexit Deal: What's Happening in the UK-EU Talks?" *BBC*, 23 July 2020, www.bbc.com/news/uk-politics-53518641.

Namusoke, Eva. "The Anglosphere, Race and Brexit." *The Anglosphere: Continuity, Dissonance and Location*, edited by Ben Wellings and Andrew Mycock, Oxford UP, 2019, pp. 224-40.

O'Carroll, Lisa. "Brexit Will Mean Checks on Goods Crossing Irish Sea, Government Admits." *Guardian*, 13 May 2020, www.theguardian.com/politics/2020/may/13/brexit-will-mean-checks-on-goods-crossing-irish-sea-government-admits.

O'Toole, Fintan. "Ireland and the English Question." *Embers of Empire in Brexit Britain*, edited by Stuart Ward and Astrid Rasch, Bloomsbury Academic, 2019, pp. 59-69.

Redford, Duncan. "Opposition to the Channel Tunnel, 1882-1975: Identity, Island Status and Security." *History*, vol. 99, no. 1, January 2014, pp. 100-20.

Rostek, Joanna, and Anne-Julia Zwierlein. Introduction: Brexit and the Divided United Kingdom as Areas of Research in British Cultural Studies. *Brexit and the Divided United Kingdom*, special issue of *Journal for the Study of British Cultures*, edited by Joanna Rostek and Anne-Julia Zwierlein, vol. 26, no. 1, 2019, pp. 3-16.

Sanchez, M. G. "Fifty Years of Unbelonging: A Gibraltarian Writer's Personal Testimonial on the Road to Brexit." *The Road to Brexit*, edited by Ina Habermann, Manchester UP, 2020, pp. 234-44.

Ward, Stuart, and Astrid Rasch. Introduction: Greater Britain, Global Britain. *Embers of Empire in Brexit Britain*, edited by Stuart Ward and Astrid Rasch, Bloomsbury Academic, 2019, pp. 1-13.

2016 and All That: Medievalism and Exceptionalism in Brexit Britain[1]

Matthias D. Berger

Since the turn of the century, national exceptionalism narratives underpinned by medieval history have staged a comeback in numerous European countries. Such discursive use of the Middle Ages – so-called medievalism – often operates at the interface of politics and culture. In Britain, national medievalism played a notable role in preparing the ground for the 2016 Brexit vote. Leavers insisted on the obligating nature of constitutional 'precedents' in the deep past. Many of these medievalisms transport notions of an insular exceptionalism that are rooted in the earliest 'English nation' and stress – often to breaking point – the relevance of medieval versions of self-determination and statehood for the present-day polity. This essay explores a set of emotive Brexiteer medievalisms which appeal to a past that makes strong demands on the present. These examples throw into relief the symbolic attractiveness, but also the practical difficulty, of making a medievalist case for a transhistorical Britishness conceived in opposition to the European mainland. For in lionizing overwhelmingly *English* history while purporting to speak for all the United Kingdom, key Brexiteers signal their frivolous attitude towards British cohesion.

Keywords: Medievalism, Brexit, Euroscepticism, English nationalism, St George, Daniel Hannan, Whig history, Norman Yoke, Anglo-Saxonism, politics of autochthony

---

[1] This essay is based on research conducted for my PhD project, "Unique Continuities: The Nation and the Middle Ages in Twenty-First-Century Switzerland and Britain," sponsored by the Swiss National Science Foundation (project no. 165885).

Brexit and Beyond: Nation and Identity. SPELL: Swiss Papers in English Language and Literature 39, edited by Daniela Keller and Ina Habermann, Narr, 2020, pp. 23-39.

Before and since the Brexit vote, Eurosceptics have invoked the medieval past with a frequency that may baffle the casual observer. Such medievalism – the term refers to the highly diverse ways in which the postmedieval world has reconstructed and reimagined the Middle Ages – played a notable role in preparing the ideological ground for Brexit. Simply put, the Middle Ages have been made to conjure both powerful visions of national greatness and the spectre of humiliation by foreign invasion. More specifically, the referendum and the Eurosceptic currents from which the Brexit vote flowed have insisted on a constitutional heritage of obligating 'precedents' in the deep past and the need to stave off a supranational integration that threatens that heritage.

Far from innovating the connection between the Middle Ages and insular nationalism, Brexiteers infuse well-established *lieux de mémoire* or "memory sites" – abstract focal points of cultural memory that co-create the national community (Nora; see also Boer) – with a new militancy. Nor is British medievalism *sui generis*. Medievalism has had a long and colourful history of appropriation by nationalism throughout Europe. The connection between nationalism and medievalism first became salient with the Romantic movement. In Romantic nationalism, the Middle Ages came to be validated as the cultural origin of the modern national self: the foundation, root, or wellspring of a recognizable and distinct body of people. Medievalism carried connotations of the vernacular and 'homegrown'; the Middle Ages were, as Louise D'Arcens and Andrew Lynch put it, "conceptually *local*" (xii). Though internally diverse as a movement, medievalism thus generally stood in contradistinction to the 'universal,' elite, and cosmopolitan cultural model of neoclassicism.

The imagined relationship of deep continuity between the medieval and the modern nation explicitly extended to the realm of politics. Medievalism legitimized the self-determination of existing and emerging nation-*states* (e.g., Evans and Marchal). Philology and the gradually institutionalized study of the Middle Ages acted as a hotbed for political nationalism in many European countries. After its heyday in the nineteenth and early twentieth centuries, however, such legitimation by medieval lineage became all but impracticable following the violent excesses of political nationalism in the two world wars. During the wars, medieval history had often been used for propaganda purposes (Wood). Valentin Groebner notes that as a result, the Middle Ages ended up almost completely forfeiting their usability for identity politics of all stripes between the 1960s and 1995 (125).

More recently, the nexus between the nation and the Middle Ages has become productive once more in a number of Western countries (see for instance Geary; Carpegna Falconieri; Elliott, *Medievalism*). In certain political varieties of such medievalism, constitutional distinctiveness is traced back to some point in the Middle Ages to make the case for a modern-day arrangement that entails, usually, less close involvement with superordinate political bodies. Nationalists in such European countries as France, Switzerland, Italy, and Scotland cultivate medievalist rhetoric and imagery in addressing questions of sovereignty, independence, separatism, and isolationism.

The Brexit process has been punctuated by distinctive forms of national medievalism. As I will show, Brexit medievalism tends to refer overwhelmingly to the *English* Middle Ages. This is revealing because leading Brexiteers have been keen to portray Brexit as a pan-British liberation movement, whereas I see Brexit primarily as a project of an unspoken English nationalism working in tandem with predominantly English ideological traditions of Euroscepticism (see Winder; Cockburn; Williamson).[2] Brexit medievalism thus expresses what many proponents of Brexit cannot, or will not, articulate directly: the desire to liberate an England which is supposedly being oppressed (see O'Toole xvii).

A first, widely publicized pre-referendum example is that of the *Daily Express* crusader figure.[3] Previously confined to the paper's masthead, the crusader became yoked to its campaign for the UK to leave the EU in November 2010 – almost three years, that is, before David Cameron would commit to calling an in/out referendum on the "fundamental reform" he hoped to procure from the EU (Shipman xiv). The *Express* article in question, "Get Britain Out of Europe," explicitly makes the crusader a symbol of an anti-EU campaign that is intended to put pressure on the Prime Minister: "The famous and symbolic Crusader who adorns our masthead will become the figurehead of the struggle to repatriate British sovereignty from a political project that has comprehensively failed." On 8 January 2011, a special edition of the newspaper featured a blown-up version of the crusader standing

---

[2] Fintan O'Toole likewise argues that English nationalism is at the core of Brexit (166). He discusses in passing pro-Brexit invocations of the Middle Ages as part of what he calls "English Dreamtime," a mythical past that serves to resolve the "compromises, complexities and contradictions" (153) that threaten to discredit the young nationalist project.

[3] I would like to thank Andrew Elliott for first drawing my attention to the *Express* campaign. For Elliott's own reading of it, see his "Medievalism, Brexit, and the Myth of Nations" (35f).

watchful on the white cliffs of Dover, saying "[w]e *demand* our country back," beneath the all-caps headline "GET BRITAIN OUT OF THE EU."[4]

In the picture included in the special edition, there is a slippage between referent identities. It turns out that the "we" in the quotation is far from stable. The headline refers to "Britain" and the figure is called an unspecific "crusader," but thanks to a quirk of history, his coat of arms depicting a red cross on white can be read – and indeed is more likely to be read – as belonging to St George, the patron saint of the English. I read this as a visual variant of the still-common conflation of 'British' and 'English.' The tension between the two need not be resolved. They collapse into the 'happy clarity' of myth once described by Roland Barthes that would suggest, in this case, an Englishness that self-evidently merges into the larger collective of Britain (Barthes 252). The *Express* thus lights on the combination of symbolic notoriety and strange invisibility which characterizes the English constituency that would later vote for Brexit.

A post-Brexit example of the slippage between English and British is provided by Jacob Rees-Mogg, the then chairman of the hardline pro-Brexit European Research Group and incumbent Leader of the House of Commons. In this case, a potted constitutional history openly flirts with jingoism. At the Tory Party conference in October 2017, he recited the following best-of listicle of 'British' success stories to rapt supporters. Rees-Mogg's inspirational pre-modern moments turn out to be a familiar litany of English nationalist touchstones passed off as standing for all Britain:

> We need to be reiterating the benefits of Brexit, because this is [...] so important in the history of our country. I mean, this is Magna Carta, it's the burgesses coming at Parliament, it's the great Reform Bill, it's the Bill of Rights. [...] It's Waterloo, it's Agincourt, it's Crécy – we win all these things. [*As a member in the crowd prompts him:*] And Trafalgar, absolutely. [...] This is such a positive thing for our country. It frees us from a failing economic model. This is a liberation, it is a freedom, it is an inspiration. (Channel 4 News)

English constitutional medievalism – Magna Carta of 1215 and Simon de Montfort's Parliament of 1265 – sits side by side with a post-medieval, British, constitutional landmark, just as the English victories in the Hundred Years' War seamlessly merge with the later, British or

---

[4] The front page of the special edition is reproduced in Chapman.

British-led, victories against Napoleonic France. And loosely connecting them all, as well as facilitating the link to Brexit, is again a sketchy notion of 'freedom.'

One of the most substantial constitutional medievalisms produced prior to the referendum both reproduces the English preponderance and elevates the ideology of freedom to the highest rank. This is Brexiteer and Conservative Member of the European Parliament Daniel Hannan's book-length polemic *How We Invented Freedom & Why It Matters* from 2013.[5] Hannan is arguably Brexit's ideologue-in-chief. (Sam Knight refers to him as "The Man Who Brought You Brexit.") A right-wing libertarian, Hannan has been described by some fellow Conservatives as being part of a set of "'grammar-school imperialists'" whose quest is "to reassert what they regard as Britain's lost place in the world" (Knight). He has benefitted from a reputation as the 'thinking man's Brexiteer' while contributing to the infusion of reactionary ideas about historiography, language, culture, and international relations into the political mainstream.

How We Invented Freedom is a cross between a wide-ranging overview of political, legal, and intellectual history and a broadly Thatcherite polemic. For Hannan, "the story of freedom" *is* "the story of the Anglosphere" (12). 'Freedom' here means the rule of law, personal and economic liberty, and representative government (4). The 'Anglosphere' is conceived as those countries with an English-speaking history committed to these freedoms (in Hannan's generous reading, this includes Singapore as much as it does India). The premise of the book, however, is that the Anglosphere has lately disastrously neglected its heritage. Hannan calls on his Anglosphere readers to remember its history, and to take political action against its Europeanization. His remedies include embracing patriotism, especially on the national curriculum; strengthening democracy, the rule of law, and tax-cutting capitalism (322); and curbing the regulatory and welfare state. In the case of Britain, he recommends quitting the EU and instigating an Anglosphere-wide free-trade zone instead (372).

To advocate a libertarian Anglosphere exceptionalism, Hannan consistently looks to the Middle Ages for precedents. Firstly, he asserts the great seniority of the English nation-state, which he dates to the late Anglo-Saxon period. In his view, this was the basis for all the other unique achievements of the Anglosphere. Secondly, the Anglo-Saxon institution of precedent-based law is just as venerable and survived what

---

[5] For a fuller discussion of Hannan's polemic, see my "Roots and Beginnings."

Hannan calls the "calamity of the Norman invasion" (80) at the county-level and its administrative subdivision, "the hundred," only to be codified at the national level by the Normans in the mid-twelfth century (77). Thirdly, he claims that, uniquely, in the absence of a "peasant[ry]," medieval England developed an individualist society (79) that proved singularly predisposed to a capitalist economy (132-35). Finally, Hannan gives ample space to the early "representative institutio[n]" (James Campbell qtd. in *How* 84) of the *witenagemot* (the meetings of the "wise men" who advised the Anglo-Saxon kings [83]), and even more space to the restitution and strengthening of such institutions with the sealing of Magna Carta in 1215 (here presented as leading to a proto-upper house) and Simon de Montfort's parliament in 1265 (as a proto-lower house) (121-22).

All this is strongly based on so-called Whig history, a strand of historiography that was very successful mainly in the second half of the nineteenth century. In broad strokes, the traditional Whig master narrative envisions a linear historical trajectory for England – and its ideological successor, Britain – towards a liberal parliamentary and capitalist democracy. What Mary Spongberg and Clara Tuite call the "'forging' of Britain" in Whig historiography involved weaving into a national destiny such cornerstones of English cultural memory as "the 'ancient constitution' of the Saxons, the unbroken continuity of limited monarchy, the providential role of the Church of England, parliament and the rule of Common Law (and the extension of these institutions into Empire)" (673). Furthermore, as Andrew James Johnston points out, "the rise of the gentry in the later Middle Ages and in the Early Modern Period and that of the bourgeoisie in the eighteenth and nineteenth centuries" have frequently been argued to constitute "the social side of this ideological construct" (37). A distinguishing feature of the Whig narrative is the premium it puts on genealogy, continuity, and, above all, the notion of progress. The Whig historian, as Herbert Butterfield conceived him in an influential critique, studies "the past with one eye, so to speak, upon the present" (31ff.). The past amounts, in teleological fashion, to "the ratification if not the glorification of the present" (v). The main charge later levelled against Whig history was thus that of practicing immoderate, complacent presentism.

Several characteristics of *How We Invented Freedom* stand out and highlight Hannan's indebtedness to Whig history. Firstly, he engages in bald historical revisionism. He reactivates an outdated grand narrative of the nation to interpret earlier events in light of later ones – that is, teleologically. This is a conscious reactivation: according to Hannan, the current historical profession is either cowed or taken in by a strident anti-colonialism and multiculturalism.[6] For much of the second half of the twentieth century, Hannan asserts, historians "flinched" from the "truths" of an English exceptionalism with "roots in pre-Modern England" (15). Hannan therefore explicitly emulates the Whig historians because they had no difficulty in seeing this exceptionalism (84, 117). He combines this historiographical atavism with an attack on the national curriculum, which he faults for failing to instil proper patriotic virtue (17). These attacks are, in turn, part of a wider populist, anti-elite rhetoric that anticipates more recent examples witnessed in political insurgencies and 'establishment' defeats in the Western world and beyond.[7]

Very obviously, Hannan sees one long constitutional continuity from medieval England to the modern Anglosphere. In a typical example, he describes the overthrow of James II in 1688 as the assertion of a parliamentary self-government ultimately derived from "the folkright of Anglo-Saxon freedoms" (238); he also sees William of Orange's accession "foreshadow[ed]" in 1014, when Æthelred was "invited conditionally to the throne" (87). Such vague analogizing converts contingency and historical specificity into 'timeless' principles. In a related rhetorical move, Hannan argues in terms of historical "implications" (e.g., 42) being worked out: for example, he claims an *unaltered* continuity for the common law, which he suggests the "pragmatic [...] Anglosphere peoples" more actually "discovered" than "made" (78). This is very much the old claim of a 'unique continuity' of laws and liberties from medieval England to modern Britain – in contrast, that is, to the rupture-ridden Con-

---

[6] On the subject of slavery, for example, Hannan argues that postcolonialist critics should stop blaming Britain and the US: "Of course, if your starting point is that Britain and the United States were evil and oppressive colonial powers, you will find something or other to complain about. The absurdity of the whole debate, though, is that we are all descended from slaves; from slave owners too, come to that. It could hardly be otherwise, human history being what it is. [...] We are, in other words, all in this together. Everyone on the planet is descended from the exploiters and the exploited" (287). Hannan's facile comment thoroughly naturalizes, and hence comes close to exculpating, *very specific* instances of slavery by explaining them away as part of a more general "human history." In the historiographical equivalent of privatizing profits and socializing losses, the Anglosphere can be credited with having invented freedom, but it cannot be held to account for having robbed others of theirs.

[7] Hannan seems personally to have participated in the disparagement of an opposition declared elitist during the European Union membership referendum campaign: according to Knight, Hannan was behind the prominent Leave campaigner Michael Gove's infamous claim that people were "fed up with experts."

tinent (Utz 105). And since this early English history holds 'lessons,' 'truths,' and 'precedents,' for Hannan it determines what is politically possible and desirable in the present.

Closely linked to this are Hannan's assertions of transhistorical national identity. Although he dissociates these from racial definitions, he claims cultural filiation from decidedly homogeneous medieval origins (the Anglo-Saxons), and even postulates consistent character traits. Hannan indulges in some striking linguistic essentialism and determinism, claiming English has been a "guarantor of liberty down the centuries" (33) and has the "intrinsic propert[y]" of "favour[ing] the expression of empirical, down-to-earth, practical ideas" (29). He contrasts this latter aspect with the pretentious, "stodgy" (29) continental language of a "Hegel or Marx, Derrida, or Sartre" (30). Without irony, Hannan quotes the "intellectually dazzling" (122) nationalist Enoch Powell's description of English as "'the tongue made for telling truth in'" (qtd. 124).[8]

The claim to continuities of both constitution and character are of a piece with Hannan's organic and procreative diction. He refers to the "germs" of liberties brought over the Channel by the Germanic settlers (57), to parliamentary democracy "pulsing in the womb" in the tenth century (75), and to the common law growing "like a coral" over the centuries (30). The coronation oath sworn by King Edgar upon his consecration in 973, Hannan tells us, contained the idea of government by contract "in foetal form" (85). With some ingenuity, Hannan even detects the "roots of [continental European] statism claw[ing] their way deep into the cold soil of the Middle Ages" (141). It is in such rhetorical devices that the idea of 'homegrown' political culture is at its most apparent. I propose to call this a form of the politics of autochthony. A brand of identity politics, the politics of autochthony works to dignify a highly contingent series of events as the 'natural growth' of the nation, which is here very much conceived as an organic *body* politic.

Hannan's Euroscepticism is rooted in precisely this politics of autochthony. In *How We Invented Freedom*, the EU poses a threat to homegrown liberties not just in its current incarnation. Rather, European integration is contrary to the very nature of Britain in the light of normative ancient origins, unbroken continuity, and timeless national identi-

---

[8] This quotation is from a 1961 speech by Powell that Hannan describes as seeking to articulate no less than "the essence of Englishness" (123) – and not, it goes without saying, Britishness.

ties.[9] Furthermore, Hannan supplements the British/European dichotomy with a familiar populist one that pits a patriotic 'people' against EU-friendly domestic 'elites.' Hannan repeatedly criticizes Britain's "multiculturalist establishment" and "intellectual elites" (17) and imputes to Europhilia "connotations [...] of snobbery, of contempt for majority opinion, of the smugness of a remote political caste" (93). Forgetful of their roots, they are, in a word, un-British.

While Hannan's elaborate medievalism is not, at present, representative of a sizeable political movement, there was a notable pre-Brexit parallel to his essentialist neo-Whig version of history. The right-wing "Historians for Britain" pressure group around Cambridge historian David Abulafia and including a handful of high-profile historians and journalists such as David Starkey and Andrew Roberts pushed a similar Eurosceptic agenda.[10] They banded together to make their case for a Britain outside the EU, again based on an exceptionalist reading of English and British history.

The Historians for Britain made their first appearance in a letter to *The Times* in 2013, then went on to set up a website sporting a blown-up image of the 'original Brexiteer,' Henry VIII, and in 2015, Abulafia issued a "manifesto-style proclamation" in *History Today* (Gregor).[11] They were linked to the Eurosceptic think-tank Business for Britain and readily admitted their "ties to businesspeople with similar agendas" (Gregor; see also Mammone). Incongruously, they also claimed to be "independent and nonpartisan" (as per their homepage). Andrew Knapp points out that, tellingly, the Historians for Britain shared their Westminster address with "the Thatcherite Centre for Policy Studies,

---

[9] Likewise, whereas Hannan champions the homegrown "folkright of Anglo-Saxon freedoms" (238) as expressed, for example, in the American Bill of Rights, he has little time for international, universalist human rights charters (117ff., 359). These appeal, as Jonathan Sumption points out, to natural rights "anterior to society itself" (2) and therefore are ill-suited to valorize one particular society or one particular legal system.

[10] Evidence of the Historians moving in the same intellectual orbit as Hannan is provided by the fact that Roberts is quoted as endorsing *How We Invented Freedom* on the publisher's website: "This is a brilliant book [...]. Daniel Hannan has found the key to the success of the English-speaking peoples: the unique political and legal institutions that make us what we are" ("Polemic of the Year").

[11] The website has been given a complete makeover since 2017. Everything points to a domain abandoned and repurposed: the self-description as a "campaign" has been changed to "an independent and non-partisan academic organization," its manifesto-like profile discarded in favour of a handful of soft-focus articles with such titles as "12 United Kingdom Facts That You Should Know" (all apparently authored by one "Brian"), and all references to the Historians for Britain's original leading lights removed.

the Taxpayers' Alliance (opposed to taxes) and the Global Warming Policy Foundation (opposed to tackling climate change)." Although they purported to be constituted of "dozens of Britain's leading historians" (*Historians for Britain*), Gregor noted that their ranks thinned significantly if one sifted out "the journalists and the purveyors of coffee-table history-as-entertainment."

In occupying the conveniently unaccountable twilight zone between academia and journalism, the Historians for Britain bear a remarkable similarity to Hannan. *How We Invented Freedom* too inhabits a curious discursive grey area. While offering no scholarly apparatus whatsoever, Hannan keeps up a pretence of scholarly decorum for much of the book and in his acknowledgements reflects on his status as a trained historian-turned-politician: "It was only several years after being elected to political office that I finally admitted to myself that I would never be a full-time historian" (n.p.). Adopting the popularizing approach of a part-time historian, Hannan strikes the pose of a worldly outsider to, and ostensibly impartial critic of, today's misguided, unpatriotic academic discipline of history. The similarities between Hannan and the Historians for Britain do not end there. The Historians for Britain too were clearly inspired by the old Whig narrative of unique continuity and so told a very similar story of ancient English (then British) exceptionalism as Hannan had. Like Hannan, Abulafia's *History Today* piece skates over anything that could endanger that positive exceptionalism, including the history of British imperialism and colonialism.

It would be adventurous to claim that there is a direct line leading from the endeavours of these politicians, historians, and journalists to the democratic renunciation of EU membership. Neither Hannan nor the Historians for Britain managed to do much more than preach to the converted: Hannan's book was largely ignored by academia and received only scant attention by non-partisan and left-of-centre media outlets, and a number of public rebuttals showed that the Historians for Britain's history of British exceptionalism were up against some robust opposition among fellow historians.[12] And yet, it is conceivable, even likely, that the kind of historically grounded sense of English-British exceptionalism formulated in detail by these parties is shared, in a more diffuse form, by a great many of their compatriots.

---

[12] An open letter entitled "Fog in Channel, Historians Isolated," challenging the interpretation of British history of the Historians for Britain, was signed by roughly three hundred academics.

If the immemorial 'freedom' of England-Britain is rooted in the Middle Ages, the fear of *unfreedom* too finds a ready home in them, specifically in cultural memories of the Norman Conquest of 1066. The idea that Anglo-Saxon freedoms were lost under a hated 'Norman Yoke,' a yoke only gradually shaken off over subsequent centuries, historically has been a powerful myth (e.g., Brownlie). Continuing this tradition, Brexiteer discourse has readily linked the British relationship with the EU to the Conquest. Predictably, the Bayeux Tapestry can be relied upon as a shorthand for this idea. This ready-to-use link led the *Sun* to publish a gleeful "Bye-EU Tapestry" artwork early in 2018, showing Theresa May's anticipated triumph in the Brexit negotiations – represented by a heap of decapitated European leaders – and a Britain freed from "continental shackles" ("Tapestry Is EU-rs"). Nigel Farage, erstwhile UKIP leader and relentless Eurosceptic agitator since the 1990s, made a political fashion statement already in 2014 by sporting a tie depicting the Tapestry in order to recall, he announced, "the last time we were invaded and taken over" (qtd. in Sutherland). In a 2016 campaign sound bite, hard-Brexit frontman Boris Johnson used the (pre-existing) phrase "the biggest stitch-up since the Bayeux Tapestry" to disparage the Remain campaign (qtd. in Chambre). In these examples, the iconic tapestry is interpreted as a monument to foreign oppression.

The language of feudalism serves a closely related function. In December 2017, Johnson, by now Foreign Secretary, worried that Britain might end up adopting EU regulations without having a say in them after exiting. He was quoted as saying that there was a danger of Britain going "from a member state to a vassal state" (qtd. in Stewart). In early 2018, Rees-Mogg repeated the phrase "vassal state" to refer to the prospect of a transitional period between the UK's exit and the negotiation of a new settlement with the EU. Later that year, he condemned the government's strategy White Paper as "the greatest vassalage since King John paid homage to Philip II at Le Goulet in 1200." Johnson, when resigning from the cabinet, spoke of the prospect of "economic vassalage" (both qtd. in O'Toole 157). These post-Brexit statements were echoes of the Leave campaign's pledge to 'take back control' for Britain. That scenario always assumed that a malignant external force was withholding freedom and sovereignty from Britain, whose natural greatness was thus impeded. The language of feudalism is particularly charged in the English context because a common myth has it that this form of imported 'continental' tyranny supplanted an autochthonous, free English social and political order (Leerssen 48).

Notions of ancestral freedom and foreign oppression, then, are two sides of the same coin. Cultural memories of (to borrow Sellar and Yeatman's phrase) "1066 and All That" – specifically, cultural memories of the Anglo-Saxons, the Norman Conquest, and the subsequent forced transformation of English society – are the most powerful vehicle for these twin notions currently at the Brexiteers' disposal. True to his predilection for vague historical analogies, Hannan too is much exercised by the danger that the Norman Yoke is being repeated in the twenty-first century, reincarnated as the British loss of sovereignty under an overreaching, unaccountable EU. Besides *How We Invented Freedom*, journalistic pieces by Hannan highlight the depth of his concern with Norman-style subjugation ("We"; "Norman Conquest").[13]

As these examples suggest, political medievalism has been catapulted to a place of relative prominence in Brexit Britain. In a sense, however, Hannan and his partners in medievalism may have got more than they bargained for. The language of sovereignty inherited from the nationalisms of the last two centuries may have made the Middle Ages an attractive benchmark for the politics of autochthony once again. In the case of Brexit Britain, however, continuity medievalism is full of pitfalls precisely because the 'home' in its 'homegrown history' is so lopsidedly English.

Fintan O'Toole remarks that the "most dramatic evolution of national identity in Britain in the last two decades is the resurfacing of the idea of England as a distinct political community" (185). Yet before the Brexit vote, that resurgence had no national arena. This is an older problem made acute by the increasing strength of English nationalism. As Krishan Kumar suggests, English national identity has for centuries tended to reach outwards to encompass larger, British, Commonwealth, and Anglosphere identities – that is to say, it has latched on to the ambivalent results of former imperial projects (x). Even after Brexit, O'Toole observes, the increasingly powerful English nationalism is a force "that its leaders [...] refuse to articulate" (193). In a 2012 blog post for the *Telegraph*, Hannan himself argued that not Scottish, but rather "English separatism [is] the chief threat to the Union" ("Greater

---

[13] The medievalizing language of foreign conquest and domination comes easily to today's purveyors of 'sovereignty' not just in Britain but across Europe. In Switzerland, for instance, national-conservative political forces warn that sinister "foreign judges" will undermine Swiss autonomy. The phrase harks back to the core Swiss mythical complex of the medievalist liberation tradition and has become a Eurosceptic watchword since the national decision to join the European Convention on Human Rights (ECHR) in 1969 (Kreis 21).

Threat"). In *How We Invented Freedom*, he consequently rejects the idea that his Anglosphere "is somehow just an amplification of England" (244). Yet I would suggest that Brexit medievalism habitually demonstrates where its allegiances truly lie: with a time-honoured English nation, with former English military glory, and even more with former English constitutional achievements. Precisely this kind of lionizing of English history – to the point of eclipsing all but the most recent histories of Scotland, Wales, and Northern Ireland – may yet become a problem for another union, this time closer to home.

References

Abulafia, David. "Britain: Apart from or a Part of Europe?" *History Today*, 11 May 2015, www.historytoday.com/britain-apart-or-part-europe.

Barthes, Roland. "Le mythe, aujourd'hui." *Mythologies*. Éditions du Seuil, 1957, pp. 213-68.

Berger, Matthias. "Roots and Beginnings: Medievalism and National Identity in Daniel Hannan's *How We Invented Freedom and Why It Matters*." *Anglistentag 2016: Proceedings*, edited by Ute Berns, Wissenschaftlicher Verlag Trier, 2017, pp. 119-35.

Boer, Pim den. "*Loci memoriae – Lieux de mémoire*." *A Companion to Cultural Memory Studies*, edited by Astrid Erll and Ansgar Nünning, in collaboration with Sara B. Young, Walter de Gruyter, 2010, pp. 19-25.

Brownlie, Siobhan. *Memory and Myths of the Norman Conquest*. The Boydell P, 2013.

Butterfield, Herbert. *The Whig Interpretation of History*. Norton, 1931.

Carpegna Falconieri, Tommaso di. *Medioevo militante: La politica di oggi alle prese con barbari e crociati*. Einaudi, 2011.

Chambre, Agnes. "Boris Johnson Blasts 'Biggest Stitch-Up Since Bayeux Tapestry' over No 10 FTSE Brexit Letter." *Politics Home*, 17 May 2016, www.politicshome.com/news/europe/eu-policy-agenda/brexit/news/75095/boris-johnson-blasts-biggest-stitch-bayeux-tapestry.

Channel 4 News. ".@Jacob_Rees_Mogg Extolls the Benefits of Brexit at One of the Busiest Fringe Meetings of the @Conservatives' Conference. #cpc17." *Twitter*, 2 Oct. 2017, twitter. com/channel4news/status/914941451615817728?lang=de.

Chapman, Kate. "Daily Express, on the People's Side to Get Britain Out of the European Union." *Daily Express*, 22 Feb. 2016, www.express.co.uk/news/politics/646232/Daily-Express-peoples-side-European-Union-referendum.

Cockburn, Patrick. "Brexit Unleashed an English Nationalism That Has Damaged the Union with Scotland for Good." *Guardian*, 1 Aug. 2018, www.independent.co.uk/voices/brexit-scottish-referendum-english-nationalism-damaged-union-for-good-a7635796.html.

D'Arcens, Louise, and Andrew Lynch. "The Medieval, the International, the Popular." Introduction. *International Medievalism and Popular Culture*, edited by Louise D'Arcens and Andrew Lynch, Cambria P, 2014, pp. xi-xxx.

Elliott, Andrew B. R. "Medievalism, Brexit, and the Myth of Nations."

Politics and Medievalism (Studies), edited by Karl Fugelso, D. S. Brewer, 2020, pp. 31-38.

——. *Medievalism, Politics and Mass Media: Appropriating the Middle Ages in the Twenty-First Century*. D. S. Brewer, 2017.

Evans, R. J. W., and Guy P. Marchal, editors. *The Uses of the Middle Ages in Modern European States: History, Nationhood and the Search for Origins*. Palgrave Macmillan, 2011.

"Fog in Channel, Historians Isolated." *History Today*, 18 May 2015, www.historytoday.com/fog-channel-historians-isolated#sthash.JoDpBeet.dpuf.

Geary, Patrick J. *The Myth of Nations: The Medieval Origins of Europe*. Princeton UP, 2002.

"Get Britain Out of Europe." *The Daily Express*, 25 Nov. 2010, www.express.co.uk/news/uk/213573/Get-Britain-out-of-Europe.

Gregor, Neil. "Historians, Britain and Europe." *Neil Gregor*, 24 March 2018, neilgregor.com/2018/03/24/historians-britain-and-europe/.

Groebner, Valentin. *Das Mittelalter hört nicht auf: Über historisches Erzählen*. C. H. Beck, 2008.

Hannan, Daniel. "The Greater Threat to the Union Comes from England." *Daily Telegraph*, 17 Jan. 2012, web.archive.org/web/20120419055128/http://blogs.telegraph.co.uk:80/news/danielhannan/100130316/the-greater-threat-to-the-union-comes-from-england.

——. *How We Invented Freedom & Why It Matters*. Head of Zeus, 2013.

——. "The Norman Conquest Was a Disaster for England. We Should Celebrate Naseby, Not Hastings." *Daily Telegraph*, 14 Oct. 2016, www.telegraph.co.uk/news/2016/10/14/the-norman-conquest-was-a-disaster-for-england-we-should-celebra/.

——. "We Have Submitted Ourselves to a New Norman Yoke." *Daily Telegraph*, 30 Nov. 2009, blogs.telegraph.co.uk/news/ danielhannan/100018325/we-have-submitted-ourselves-to-a-new-norman-yoke/.

Historians for Britain. www.historiansforbritain.org/about-us/.

Johnston, Andrew James. "'Rum, Ram, Ruf': Chaucer and Linguistic Whig History." *Linguistics, Ideology and the Discourse of Linguistic Nationalism*, edited by Claudia Lange et al., Peter Lang, 2010, pp. 37-51.

Knapp, Andrew. "Historians for Britain in Europe – A Personal History." *Histoire@Politique*, vol. 31, no. 1, 2017, pp. 27-35.

Knight, Sam. "The Man Who Brought You Brexit." *Guardian*, 29 Sept. 2016, www.theguardian.com/politics/2016/sep/29/daniel-hannan-the-man-who-brought-you-brexit.

Kreis, Georg. *Fremde Richter: Karriere eines politischen Begriffs*. Hier und Jetzt, 2018.

Kumar, Krishan. *The Making of English National Identity*. Cambridge UP, 2003.

Leerssen, Joep. *National Thought in Europe: A Cultural History*. Amsterdam UP, 2006.

Mammone, Andrea. "For Britain and Against the EU: Historians for Britain Strike Again." *Historians for History*, 3 March 2016, historiansforhistory.wordpress.com/2016/03/03/for-britain-and-against-the-eu-historians-for-britain-strike-again-by-andrea-mammone/.

Nora, Pierre. "Between Memory and History: *Les lieux de mémoire*." *Representations*, vol. 26, 1989, pp. 7-24.

Nora, Pierre, editor. *Les lieux de mémoire*. 3 vols. Gallimard, 1984-92.

O'Toole, Fintan. *Heroic Failure: Brexit and the Politics of Pain*. Head of Zeus, 2018.

"Polemic of the Year." *Head of Zeus*, 20 March 2014, headofzeus.com/article/polemic-year.

Sellar, Walter Carruthers, and Robert Julian Yeatman. *1066 and All That: A Memorable History of England, Comprising All the Parts You Can Remember, Including 103 Good Things, 5 Bad Kings and 2 Genuine Dates*. 1930. Illustrated by John Reynolds, Methuen, 2009.

Shipman, Tim. *All Out War: The Full Story of How Brexit Sank Britain's Political Class*. William Collins, 2016.

Spongberg, Mary, and Clara Tuite. "The Gender of Whig Historiography: Women Writers and Britain's Pasts and Presents." Introduction. *Women's History Review*, vol. 20, no. 5, 2011, pp. 673-87.

Stewart, Heather. "Boris Johnson Breaks Ranks with Brexit 'Vassal State' Warning." *Guardian*, 17 Dec. 2017, www.theguardian.com/politics/2017/dec/17/boris-johnson-breaks-ranks-with-brexit-vassal-state-warning.

Sumption, Jonathan. "Magna Carta and the Déclaration des Droits de l'Homme et du Citoyen." *The Supreme Court*, 11 June 2015, www.supremecourt.uk/docs/speech-150611.pdf.

Sutherland, John. "Brexit Lit." *Literary Review*, Sept. 2018, literaryreview.co.uk/brexit-lit.

"The Tapestry Is EU-rs." *Sun*, 18 Jan. 2018, www.thesun.co.uk/news/5374638/download-the-sun-bye-eu-tapestry/.

Utz, Richard. "Coming to Terms with Medievalism." *European Journal of English Studies*, vol. 15, no. 2, 2011, pp. 101-13.

Williamson, David. "Brexit May Be Seen as the Moment When English Nationalism Was Uncorked." *Wales Online*, 18 Dec. 2017, www.walesonline.co.uk/news/politics/brexit-seen-moment-english-nationalism-13926889.

Winder, Robert. "After Brexit, England Will Have to Rethink Its Identity." *Guardian*, 8 Jan. 2018, www.theguardian.com/commentisfree/2018/jan/08/brexit-england-rethink-identity-nation#comment-110543929.

Wood, Ian N. "Barbarians, Historians and the Construction of National Identities." *Journal of Late Antiquity*, vol. 1, 2008, pp. 61-82.

Long Live the Queen!
Queen Victoria as a National Icon in Film

Barbara Straumann

How do films about Queen Victoria use the Victorian monarch as a national icon? And how do their representations speak to the present in which they are made? The following contribution focuses on *Victoria the Great* (1937) and *Sixty Glorious Years* (1938) by Herbert Wilcox and Anna Neagle as well as the recent feature film *Victoria & Abdul* (2017), directed by Stephen Frears and starring Judi Dench. Responding to the Abdication Crisis in 1936 and the geopolitical situation in the late 1930s, the first two films construct Queen Victoria as a figure who stands for the stability of the monarchy and, in so doing, unifies the nation as an imagined community. Focusing on the queen's friendship with her favourite Indian servant Abdul Karim, Frears's comedy of manners juxtaposes Victoria's tolerant attitude with the racist bigotry of her royal household. It does so in order to construct the Victorian queen as a benign monarch but, in so doing, promulgates a spirit of imperialist nostalgia. Created in the context of the Brexit debate, Dench's sovereign thus represents a national figure that is inseparable from a problematic longing for an imperial past.

Keywords: Royal biopics, queenship, invented tradition, imagined community, imperialist nostalgia

Sixty Glorious Years (1938), one of many biopics about Queen Victoria, traces the life of the Victorian monarch from her early years on the throne to the Diamond Jubilee celebrations and her death. The narrative framing of her demise is particularly pertinent to a discussion

Brexit and Beyond: Nation and Identity. SPELL: Swiss Papers in English Language and Literature 39, edited by Daniela Keller and Ina Habermann, Narr, 2020, pp. 41-60.

of Queen Victoria as a national icon because it represents her as the symbol of an entire age and hints at her posthumous use as a national figurehead. The sequence shows several subjects of different social backgrounds commenting on the impending death of their queen: a group of individuals anxiously awaiting news regarding the state of her health in front of the gate at Osborne House, urban pedestrians and omnibus passengers in disbelief at what they read in the newspapers, a flower vendor in the streets asserting that the queen will never die, an elderly middle-class couple noting that the queen's death "will be the end – of our world" (01:27:23-26) as well as three Westminster politicians who reminisce about the change and achievements of an entire era and express their pride in having lived in such a significant historical period. For the politicians, the queen embodies an entire age. As one of them puts it, "more than a great queen is passing into history – an era" (01:27:27-31). By showing the response of several subjects, the sequence highlights how individuals of various social backgrounds are united in the shared grief over their monarch's death. By emphasizing the status of the Victorian monarch as a collective figure, the film also seeks to unite its cinematic audience. The sense of pride the politicians express stands for a nostalgic patriotism which *Sixty Glorious Years*, released in 1938, revives shortly before the outbreak of the Second World War. Made at a time of geopolitical crisis, the film points to the remembrance of Queen Victoria and the era she embodied as a source of national unity and pride.

Royal biopics and historical films more generally are marked by a complex relationship between past and present. As James Chapman notes, "a historical feature film will often have as much to say about the present in which it was made as about the past in which it was set" (1). While evoking past periods, historical films simultaneously address contemporary issues. Like historical films, royal biopics invariably straddle two historical periods, which they bring into dialogue. While drawing on historical lives, they also tend to convey cultural concerns, political interest, and attitudes prevalent at the time of their production. Many films about queens reflect changing notions of gender and attitudes to female power in the specific ways in which they represent the relationship between the queen's two bodies, her body politic and her body natural.[1] Yet many royal biopics also use queens as collective figures in

[1] See Ernst Kantorowicz's well-known discussion of the concept of the king's two bodies; the volume edited by Regina Schulte for discussions of how this notion plays itself out in the case of various queens, whose body natural is always highlighted; as well as

order to develop national narratives in response to the times in which they were made.

Queen Victoria has appeared on screen more frequently than any other British monarch. Her life and reign, characterized not least of all by their longevity, have enjoyed an even longer cultural afterlife in film, ranging from early cinema to contemporary television.[2] In the following, I will examine a small cross-section of this afterlife by analysing how Victoria is constructed as a national icon in cinematic representations from two different time periods. My focus will be on two examples from the late 1930s: *Victoria the Great* (1937) and *Sixty Glorious Years* (1938), which were both directed by Herbert Wilcox and which both feature Anna Neagle in the role of Queen Victoria.[3] This will be followed by a discussion of the recent feature film *Victoria & Abdul* (2017), directed by Stephen Frears and starring Judi Dench. What national narratives do these biopics of the Victorian monarch develop? How does their use of Queen Victoria as a national icon speak to the historical moments in which they were made, namely the volatile political climate of the late 1930s in the case of Neagle and Wilcox, and the context of Brexit in the case of Frears? As we shall see, all these examples respond to moments of political crisis but, in so doing, develop different arguments: *Victoria the Great* and *Sixty Glorious Years* attempt to create national unity and cohesion in the face of the 1936 Abdication Crisis and the impending geopolitical conflict, whereas *Victoria & Abdul* can be seen to produce a wishful fantasy of Britannia and, at the same time, support a spirit of imperial nostalgia in the context of the Brexit crisis.

Victoria the Great and *Sixty Glorious Years* are both composed of crucial scenes from Queen Victoria's life that are presented as episodic vignettes and arranged in chronological order. The first film begins with Victoria's accession to the throne, while the second one starts by showing her as a young queen already married to Albert. However, the two films greatly resemble each other in giving much space to the couple's

---

Margaret Homans's analysis of the symbolic power Queen Victoria had as a female monarch. The relationship between Queen Victoria's body natural and her body politic is very much at the centre of two contemporary film productions: *The Young Victoria* (2009) with Emily Blunt, directed by Jean-Marc Vallée; and the current ITV series *Victoria*, produced by Daisy Goodwin and starring Jenna Coleman (2016-).

[2] According to Steven Fielding (67), Queen Victoria appears in over one hundred films and television programmes.

[3] Because of the great success of the first film *Victoria the Great* in 1937, Wilcox and Neagle made a very similar film – *Sixty Glorious Years* – only one year later, this time in colour. Neagle not only played the title role but also part-funded *Victoria the Great* and wrote much of the script (Street 126).

relationship and their joint work in the interest of the common good. In depicting Victoria and Albert as a close and loving couple, the films emphasize not only their private life but above all their public service for the country. For example, we see them support the repeal of the so-called Corn Laws, which benefitted landowners but made food expensive for the common people. Following Albert's painstaking planning, they jointly open the Great Exhibition in order to "promote a better understanding between all the people" (*Sixty Glorious Years* 00:32:40-42). They even conceive of the dynastic alliances of their children with the European aristocracy as a way of promoting international peace. Observing the courtship of their eldest daughter Vicky and Prince Frederick of Prussia, Albert notes: "[F]or those two children, so much can be done for the peace of the future" (00:56:20-33). In contrast to Victoria, whose German roots are hardly explored in the two films, Prince Albert is repeatedly shown to be vilified as a foreigner by the people and the press describing him as "a foreign agent, an avowed enemy of this country" (00:45:28-31). However, both films follow a reverential approach by putting a strong emphasis on the couple's great sense of duty and service to the country. They construct Albert as a 'good German,' characterized by his keen interest in the arts and science as well as his relentless work for the nation.[4] In addition to the peace project underpinning their plan to marry Vicky off to the Prussian crown prince, the couple try to preserve and promote international peace by attempting to avert the Crimean War or by intervening in the Trent Affair in order to prevent Britain from entering the American Civil War on the side of the Confederate States.

At the same time, *Sixty Glorious Years* represents Victoria as a queen who is ready to go to war if necessary. After the Fall of Khartoum and the death of General Gordon, the queen reprimands Prime Minister Gladstone for having avoided a military intervention. She underlines

---

[4] *Victoria the Great* opens with the misgivings of the Archbishop of Canterbury and Lord Conyngham about the accession of an unknown young girl who appears to have no will of her own and is instead dependent on her uncle "King Leopold of Belgium and Stockmar the German" and "that German mother of hers" (00:02:10-33). However, both *Victoria the Great* and *Sixty Glorious Years* depict Victoria as a British queen who no longer speaks German. Albert teaches her German words and corrects her accent, and she instructs him in English. While later biopics such as *The Young Victoria* (2009) or the ITV series *Victoria* (2016-) feature British actors in the role of the Prince Consort, Albert is here played by the homosexual Jewish-Austrian actor Adolf Anton Wilhelm Wohlbrück. A popular theatre and cinema performer in Austria, Wohlbrück moved to England in 1936 and established a career in British cinema under the name of Anton Walbrook, specializing in continental characters.

that there are situations in which war is unavoidable. This is important as the two films can be seen in the context of the volatile geopolitical climate of the late 1930s. Especially the Khartoum episode in *Sixty Glorious Years* makes an argument against appeasement politics towards Nazi Germany. By invoking this particular event in national history, the film calls on the cinema audience to be prepared for armed conflict should this become necessary. The message is all the more persuasive given that Neagle's queen is certainly no war-hawk but ready to resort to military action only after all other means have been exhausted.

As well as preparing the audience for war in *Sixty Glorious Years*, Wilcox and Neagle's portrayal of Queen Victoria responds to another critical moment in recent history, namely the Abdication Crisis of 1936 (Street 130; Chapman 76-78).[5] The intention of Edward VIII to marry the divorced socialite Wallis Simpson caused a constitutional crisis as their marriage was opposed by both the government and the Church of England. Given the choice between remaining on the throne or abdicating in favour of Wallis Simpson, Edward famously decided to marry "the woman I love." Created after the abdication, *Victoria the Great* and *Sixty Glorious Years* both affirm the institution of the monarchy in the context of these contemporaneous events. They do so by placing emphasis on royal duty in their portrayals of the queen and her prince consort. Edward's insistence on his individual desire is juxtaposed with Victoria and Albert's embodiment of "duty, service and sacrifice" (Chapman 78). In *Victoria the Great*, the dutiful monarch decides to cut their honeymoon short because of pressing government business. Albert, who wishes for a longer honeymoon in the scene in question, is later shown to be extremely hard-working despite the strong public opposition he finds himself confronted with. In fact, *Victoria the Great* goes so far as to suggest that it is his tireless hard work for the nation's welfare in producing a diplomatic solution in the Trent Affair that causes his premature death.

Wilcox and Neagle portray Victoria as a dedicated monarch who has led "a long, productive life" (Ford and Mitchell 159). In the deathbed scene in *Sixty Glorious Years*, a close-up of the dying queen is superimposed with scenes of the young queen receiving the news of her accession and taking her oath during the coronation ceremony. Accompanied

---

[5] As Chapman notes, both films by Wilcox and Neagle "assert the need for national unity, but they do so in response to different circumstances: thus *Victoria the Great* is concerned principally to validate the institution of monarchy in the wake of the Abdication Crisis of 1936, whereas *Sixty Glorious Years* is a strident call for national preparedness that was released shortly after the Munich Agreement of 1938" (64).

by the melody of "God Save the Queen," the young queen promises that she will do "my utmost to fulfil my duty to my country" (01:28:36-39). The queen's great sense of duty is also underlined at the end of *Victoria the Great*, which simultaneously highlights her great popularity. The film culminates in the Diamond Jubilee celebrations, with cheering crowds proving how adored this queen is by her people. Travelling in an open carriage as part of the royal procession, the queen is enthusiastically greeted by the masses. During the Thanksgiving service at the steps of St Paul's Cathedral, the Archbishop of Canterbury congratulates her, referring not just to the longevity of her reign but expressing above all that she is "enthroned forever in the hearts of [her] people" (01:42:51-54). Affirming the Archbishop's words, the crowds follow his call "[t]hree cheers for Her Majesty!" by shouting "[h]ip hip hurray!" as if in one voice (01:43:51-01:44:03). Similarly, their collective singing of "God Save the Queen" is reminiscent of Benedict Anderson's comments on the "unisonance" and "unisonality" that is created by songs, especially the joint singing of national anthems, which play a significant role in the formation of national communities (145). As the anthem is fading away, the noticeably moved Queen addresses her beloved dead husband: "Albert, we have done our best" (01:44:43-46). The credit sequence, finally, revisits her long reign one last time as it juxtaposes a young and an old version of the queen, which represent the monarch in the year of her coronation and her Diamond Jubilee. Wearing a glamorous dress and ermine fur coat and a more subdued outfit, respectively, the young and the old queen look at each other approvingly, accompanied by "Land of Hope and Glory," Edward Elgar's first "Pomp and Circumstance March" and one of Britain's quasi-anthems. As well as demonstrating Neagle's remarkable ability to transform herself in keeping with Victoria's long life, the final tableau underscores that her young self seems pleased with what she has achieved and her old self has no regrets, thus reinforcing a sense of continuity.

Following a decidedly reverential approach, Wilcox and Neagle portray a sovereign who is capable of creating national unity and cohesion. An important means are the series of vignettes which the films consist of and which intertwine the Queen's life with national history and present both in the form of a filmic pageant. The queen's biography and the fate of her nation thus become coterminous. From a visual standpoint, however, the use of Victoria as a collective icon becomes particularly palpable at her coronation in *Victoria the Great*. Following the coronation ceremony in Westminster Abbey, we are presented with a series of superimposed images. A shot of Neagle wearing her crown, holding her royal insignia, and sitting on the coronation chair is first blended with Westminster Abbey, followed by ringing bells, firing canons, the procession of the Gold State Coach, and enthusiastic masses of people. The most significant superimposition combines three visual layers: a static frontal shot of Neagle's queen with her royal regalia, the moving Gold State Coach, and the cheering crowds.

Fig. The Queen as a composite collective figure in *Victoria the Great* (00:15:40)

These visual layers suggest that Queen Victoria represents a composite collective figure. The body of this beloved queen is made up by her subjects similar to the way in which the body of the sovereign is composed of the individual bodies of citizens in the frontispiece of Thomas Hobbes's *Leviathan* by Abraham Bosse. Reminiscent of Bosse's famous image, Neagle's Victoria wears and holds the regalia marking her symbolic investiture as sovereign. However, rather than inducing awe and fear as the sovereign authority does in the consenting individuals in Hobbes, this queen is shown to inspire love in her people.[6] The enthu-

[6] A similar layering of images of the queen and her subjects can be found in *Sixty Glorious Years*: as the monarch returns from the Diamond Jubilee service at St Paul's to Buckingham Palace in her carriage, her image is superimposed with the cheering crowds (01:21:10-20).

siasm of the crowds, greeting their new monarch following her coronation, suggests that what is at stake is a politics of the heart – a kind of 'politics' that is typical of celebrities.[7] Rather than her political power, the scene underlines Victoria's symbolic power as a popular monarch. As sovereign, she reigns over her subjects, but she also needs them, their acclamation, applause, and support. The crowd cheering the monarch as if in one voice implies collective unity, while she represents that unity. The series of blended images is followed by the crowds enthusiastically greeting their new queen in front of Buckingham Palace and the queen receiving their homage on the balcony, while the people continue to rejoice into the night.

Not surprisingly, the filmic depiction of the coronation in *Victoria the Great* closely resembles the contemporaneous coronation of George VI, another dutiful monarch devoted to country and family, who assumed his royal mandate following his brother's abdication. In contrast to the historical coronation of Queen Victoria, which was a chaotic affair, the coronation of her great-grandson was an instance of what Eric Hobsbawm and others have called the "invention of tradition." Modern nations in particular tend to use invented traditions in order to create a national identity. They establish seemingly old traditions that are claimed to be rooted in a historic past, instead of being new and constructed. As David Cannadine has shown, the pageantry of the British monarchy, which forms a key element in the creation of national unity in modern Britain, is largely a product of the late nineteenth and twentieth century.[8] Royal rituals with "no exact precedent" (such as Westminster Abbey weddings for royal children or state funerals for dowager queens) creat-

---

[7] As Steven Fielding observes: "Screenwriters like to present Victoria and her successors as the heart of a heartless political world" (79).

[8] Examining the British monarchy and the "invention of tradition" from 1820-1977, Cannadine calls the period between 1877, when Queen Victoria became Empress of India, until the beginning of the First World War, "the heyday of 'invented tradition'" (108). Many of the royal ceremonial rituals generally believed to be ancient and timeless were in fact only invented from the 1870s onwards. "By modern standards," Dorothy Thompson notes, "Victoria's coronation was modest, almost casual" (27). Even though the event attracted large enthusiastic crowds (Ridley 15), the actual coronation ceremony was a chaotic, muddled affair with a lot of confusion and disorder, several gaffes and blunders. For instance, Victoria was given the orb at the wrong moment and did not know what to do with the heavy object; the Archbishop forced the coronation ring onto a wrong finger so that she had trouble removing it later; and the altar in the sacred shrine was covered with sandwiches and bottles of wine (Baird 78-80; Wilson 86-87; Worsley 98-99, 102). As Cannadine remarks, "the majority of the great royal pageants staged during the first three-quarters of the nineteenth century oscillated between farce and fiasco" (117).

ed a seeming continuity with a historic past (Cannadine 151). The coronation of George VI was "an extravagant, imperial re-affirmation of the stability of monarchy after the interruption of the abdication" (152).

The high-profile event took place on 12 May 1937, the date scheduled for Edward's coronation, and just five and a half months before the release of *Victoria the Great* on 28 October 1937. Designed as a public spectacle consisting of numerous royal events, it was the first coronation to be (partly) filmed and broadcast on radio. Because of the media coverage, cinemagoers watching *Victoria the Great* would have been reminded of this recent royal occasion. For them the coronation sequence with Neagle would have evoked newsreel images of George VI being enthusiastically greeted by the crowds as the State Coach drove through the streets of London during the procession from Westminster Abbey back to Buckingham Palace. Like Neagle's Victoria, the royal family showed themselves to the public on the palace balcony, and in the words of one newsreel commentator, whose voice is accompanied by the cheering crowds: "[F]or days to follow the flood-lit palace is the magnet that draws London's jubilating night crowds, and into the glare of the floodlamps steps [sic] our king and queen nightly to receive our homage" (*Coronation of George VI and Queen Elizabeth* 00:04:51-00:05:07). If the historical coronation of George VI is considered to have drawn on the royal pageantry of "invented tradition," *Victoria the Great* projects tradition onto the coronation of the earlier queen, thus producing an imaginary historical continuity.

Yet the exchange between the queen and her subjects in the film's coronation sequence also evokes the relationship between a film star and her admirers. Victoria's subjects cheer her like fans applauding a star, while the queen receives their tribute like a star standing on a stage lit by floodlights. In fact, it was her performance of Queen Victoria that propelled Neagle to national and international stardom. She belonged to a relatively small group of film stars who emerged and established themselves in Britain while many other British film stars rose to fame only after moving to Hollywood.[9] Neagle came to "signify Britain and Britishness" (Street 124) by playing strong iconic British women such as Florence Nightingale, nurse Edith Cavell, Allied intelligence officer

---

[9] See Jeffrey Richards (161-64) on the difficulty of the British film industry in developing its own film stars at the time. Following the success of their two Victoria biopics, Neagle and Wilcox worked in Hollywood for a few years before returning to Britain after their final American film, *Forever and a Day* (1943), a product of the war effort featuring mostly British Hollywood actors and focusing on the history of a London family house until its destruction in the Blitz.

Odette Samson, and pioneering female pilot Amy Johnson. In 1951 a *Picturegoer* reviewer wrote that "she [was] as much a part of Britain as Dover's white cliffs" (qtd. in Street 124).

Interestingly, however, it was Neagle's performance of Victoria that "invest[ed] her with the status of a sort of monarch of the British cinema" (Street 125). The fact that Neagle, who was later declared a dame of the British Empire, posed as Queen Victoria for Madame Tussauds (Ford and Mitchell 160) underlines how closely associated she was with the Victorian queen and vice versa.[10] The two films by Wilcox and Neagle create national cohesion in the context of the Abdication Crisis and the looming war as Neagle plays Queen Victoria as a national figurehead, while simultaneously presenting herself as a performer in the process of achieving national stardom. Casting Neagle in the role of Victoria as dutiful monarch during moments of national crisis, the films provide the nation with a sense of "continuity, community and comfort" (Cannadine 105).

Similar to *Victoria the Great* and *Sixty Glorious Years*, Stephen Frears's *Victoria & Abdul* (2017) owes a great deal to the star charisma of Judi Dench. Like Neagle, Dench became cinematic royalty due to her performance of Queen Victoria. Regarded as "the greatest Shakespearean actress of our day" (McDonald 131), she had long been "an acknowledged queen of the British theatrical world" (Ford and Mitchell 169). She had also started to appear as M, the strict boss in the Bond films. Yet it was her performance of Queen Victoria in John Madden's *Mrs Brown* in 1997 and Queen Elizabeth I in *Shakespeare in Love*, also directed by Madden, one year later that transformed her into a cinematic queen.[11] It is her authenticity and credibility as a long-time professional and as a much-loved public figure that Dench brings to her performance of Victoria in *Victoria & Abdul*. Playing her royal role, Dench can be haughty and imperious, but she also foregrounds the vulnerable and fragile sides of the queen, who still mourns the deaths of Albert and her loyal Scottish servant John Brown and who is in need of intimacy and affection as a human individual.

In contrast to the extensive ground that the films by Wilcox and Neagle cover in their depiction of the queen's biography and the history of her nation, *Victoria & Abdul* focuses on a single revisionist episode,

---

[10] Also note the musical film *Lilacs in the Spring* (1954), in which Neagle plays an actress dreaming she is Queen Victoria.

[11] For a comprehensive discussion of Dench's career, especially on the Shakespearean stage but also in film, see McDonald (103-44).

namely the queen's personal friendship with her favourite Indian servant Abdul Karim (Ali Fazal), who, in a sense, comes to fill the gaps that Albert and Brown have left in her life. As in *Mrs Brown*, the focus is on the queen as an individual subject with her own emotional needs and anxieties. At the same time, the royal biopic, made during another national crisis, namely the Brexit debate, raises the question of how the national past is put to use in the present. In other words, how does the film reimagine the Victorian sovereign at a time when a divided Britain struggles to redefine itself as a nation?

The question concerning the role Queen Victoria plays in contemporary British culture is all the more pertinent given the fact that she shares a number of similarities with Britain's present female monarch. Queen Victoria was the longest reigning monarch until she was overtaken by her great-great-granddaughter Queen Elizabeth II in 2015, which means that the reigns of both queens represent long periods of national history. Like Victoria, Elizabeth II fulfils an important symbolic role as a national figurehead who is seen on parades, visits, and other public occasions. However, in contrast to Victoria, who liked to exert political influence, Elizabeth II remains above politics. This has led to a great deal of speculation about the queen's political position on Brexit. When she wore a blue hat adorned with blue flowers with yellow seed pearls for the State Opening of Parliament in 2017, the media and public assumed that the queen was paying tribute to the European Union flag and making a subtle comment on the recent Brexit vote. Angela Kelly, the queen's personal assistant and senior dresser, who designed her hat and outfit, claims this was not the case: "It was a coincidence" (137).

Elizabeth II does not take any political position, but she does present herself as one of Britain's symbols contributing to national identity constructions. In Danny Boyle's 2012 Olympic Opening Ceremony, she famously makes a humorous cameo appearance as James Bond (Daniel Craig) meets Her Majesty at Buckingham Palace in order to accompany her to the stadium, where she allegedly jumps out of a helicopter with a Union Jack parachute. Her addresses delivered in the far less optimistic times of spring 2020 attempt to reassure the public by recalling Britain's national past: in her speech broadcast during her self-isolation at Windsor Castle during the coronavirus pandemic, she cites Vera Lynn's hopeful wartime song in asserting, "[w]e will meet again" (*The Queen's Coronavirus Broadcast* 4:13-15); and in her speech on the seventy-fifth anniversary of VE Day, she pays tribute to the VE Day speech of her father,

George VI (*The Queen's VE Day Address*).[12] As a national icon, she continues to address her people as a nation although politically that nation is deeply divided.

Stephen Frears's film implicitly refers to Elizabeth II in that it portrays Queen Victoria, another British female monarch playing a key role as a national figure, in her mature years. While *Victoria & Abdul* does not directly comment on Britain's present monarch and her attempt at a neutral handling of the current political crisis, the film responds to the cultural climate surrounding Brexit in an ambiguous fashion. On the one hand, it develops a wishful fantasy of Victoria as an open-minded Britannia, while on the other hand, it supports a spirit of imperialist nostalgia.

Rather than celebrating the pageantry of pomp and circumstance as Wilcox's films do, Frears's film pokes fun at court ceremonials. The plot is set in the context of the Diamond Jubilee in 1897, requiring the queen to attend countless ceremonial occasions, some of which literally send her to sleep. Not amused by her tedious schedule, the tired, listless queen and empress claps eyes on the handsome servant Abdul Karim, who presents her with an Indian mohur, a commemorative gold coin, during an official banquet and a wobbly jelly at a garden party. Injecting her with new life, Abdul has a spectacular career at court, moving from servant to personal footman, spiritual adviser and teacher or munshi. Victoria asks him to teach her Urdu and confides her feelings of grief and loneliness to him. Ultimately, she makes him a member of the royal household with his own servants and a cottage for his family to live in. The court is scandalized by the fact that a Muslim Indian has moved to the very centre of royal power – a position which is highlighted by the fact that he is the only person present while the queen opens her royal red boxes. Members of the royal family and household eavesdrop on their conversations in disbelief.

Presenting itself as a comedy of manners, the film exposes the racist bigotry of the royal household, while depicting Victoria as tolerant. The open-minded attitude of Dench's queen is reminiscent of the speech Neagle's Victoria gives when she is proclaimed Empress of India in *Vic-*

[12] Queen Elizabeth II has also featured in royal biopics. In *The Queen* (2006), directed, like *Victoria & Abdul*, by Stephen Frears, Helen Mirren's Queen Elizabeth II has to reconnect with the public after the tragic death of Lady Diana and, in so doing, fashion a public image that will help consolidate the power of Tony Blair as Prime Minister. In the Netflix series *The Crown* (2016-), which traces the trials and tribulations of the royal family, Elizabeth II (Claire Foy, Olivia Colman) is characterized as a dutiful monarch who stands for tradition and continuity.

toria the Great. Addressing several Indian characters, Neagle's queen emphasizes that "it is my greatest wish to see my new subjects on an equality with the other British subjects of the Crown, happy, contented and flourishing" (01:39:13-24) before adding that she feels not like a queen or empress, but rather like a mother or "the grandmother of a great family" which is to be guided by "its own principles of democracy, tolerance and freedom" (01:39:49-01:40:12). As if translating Neagle's public speech into the queen's personal life, Dench's Victoria shows great generosity in her treatment of her Indian friend. If *Victoria the Great* affirms democratic principles in the face of the rise of fascism in the late 1930s, *Victoria & Abdul* seems to emphasize open-mindedness at a time when xenophobic sentiments were surfacing together with a nationalistic rhetoric in the context of Brexit. By focusing on Victoria's generosity and friendship, the film personalizes Anglo-Indian relations in a sentimental manner, while at the same time, the relationship between the queen and her servant cannot be separated from, and hence remains entangled in, the larger imperialist context.

While the members of the royal household and family are characterized by their racist prejudice, Victoria's friendship with Abdul Karim evokes 'positive' stereotypes. Abdul Karim is the exotic Other who captures her imagination and allows her to dream: he is the one who tells her about the architecture, art, and food of a foreign colourful country she cannot visit; and he gives her private lessons in Urdu, which he tells her is "the most noble" language in India (00:31:27) and thus the language most appropriate for the Empress of India. Mohammed Baksh, the other Indian servant in the film, is far more radical and outspoken with regard to the British Empire. Early on he expresses his wish to return to India, pointing out to Abdul the oppression practiced by the British: "These people are the exploiters of a quarter of all of mankind" (00:23:27-30). Later when the queen's private secretary Sir Henry Ponsonby and her son Bertie try to blackmail him into providing dirty information on Abdul, he tells them that Abdul seeks preferment like everyone else and thus "crawls up the stinking greasy pole of the shitty British Empire" (01:08:20-29).[13] Mohammed is made to pay dearly for his stance – the Prince of Wales makes sure that he dies in England by denying him medical treatment – whereas Abdul advances at court as an Orientalized figure. His handsome and winning appearance means that

---

[13] Towards the end of the same scene, Mohammed tells a haughty Prince of Wales: "[S]tick your stupid British Empire up your stinky royal bottom hole, Mr Bertie Prince, sir" (01:09:00-09).

he primarily serves as an ornament, an object of the queen's gaze, at least initially. In contrast to her son, who threatens to deprive her of her royal power by having her certified insane, Abdul is represented as a devoted servant who idolizes his empress and willingly subjects himself to her, for instance by kissing her feet. The film's exclusive focus on Victoria's emotions means that the individual character of Abdul is left out, receiving no attention whatsoever. Rather than revealing his feelings and thoughts, for instance about his life in England and Anglo-Indian relations, the film treats him as a screen onto which the queen can project her fantasies of the exotic, much like India, the country that he personifies for her.

While Dench's Victoria cannot visit India, Abdul's vivid descriptions allow her to undertake imaginary journeys and encounter Indian culture through his evocative accounts. This becomes particularly palpable in a film scene modelled on a well-known historical photograph which shows Queen Victoria working on her boxes in the presence of one of her Indian servants under a canopy outdoors.[14] Using the same mise-en-scène as the photograph, the film scene is framed by spying members of the household who wonder what the two can be talking about. In contrast to them, we are privy to the queen's questions concerning Abdul's hometown Agra and his descriptions of the history and beauty of the Taj Mahal, the Shalimar Gardens, and the Peacock Throne. Abdul mentions that the large Indian diamond called the Koh-i-Noor was taken from the destroyed Peacock Throne after the Indian Rebellion, to which the empress responds that she is now in possession of the altered diamond. As becomes evident in the course of their conversation, the Empress of India does not know much about the country she rules. In fact, Dench's allegedly enlightened Victoria is completely unaware of the theft and destruction by British soldiers. With the naïve ignorance of Dench's empress, the scene separates Victoria from British imperialism – the aggression, violence, and destruction perpetrated in her name – and instead highlights her enchantment as Abdul tells her about Indian food and spices, thus evoking India as an exotic country that inspires her imagination.[15]

---

[14] According to the homepage of the National Portrait Gallery, the 1893 photograph by Hills and Saunders shows Queen Victoria together with Sheikh Chidda. Sometimes the servant is identified as Abdul Karim, for example by Margaret Homans, who provides a detailed analysis of the image (xxiv-xxv).

[15] Exploring the impact India had on the historical Queen Victoria and the influence she had over political and cultural life in India, Miles Taylor points out that "for much of her reign India was lived in her imagination" (6). In keeping with "the martial and

A later scene illustrates Queen Victoria's identification with, but also her appropriation of, an imagined India. In the scene in question, Dench's queen demonstrates how she has introduced Indian art and culture to her court as she proudly presents her newly created Indian Durbar Room at Osborne House to her Prime Minister. Leading him through the Indian corridor, she points out that it has been decorated with a series of commissioned portraits of several eminent Indians, including a painting of the Munshi. Entering the ornamental Durbar Room, she comments on the carvings and carpet before homing in on the throne, an exact copy of the Peacock Throne at Agra. Taking her seat on the reconstructed artefact and pointing to the Koh-i-Noor in her brooch, she declares that "now I really do feel like the Empress of India" (00:54:26).

The Brexit debate has often revealed a nostalgic longing for a supposedly glorious national and imperial past. In the Leave camp, Europe was denigrated, and it was suggested, or implied, that Britain might strengthen its ties to the Commonwealth again. As argued by Danny Dorling and Sally Tomlinson, "the EU referendum showed up the last throes of empire-thinking working its way out of the British psyche" (41). Elsewhere Dorling and Tomlinson note that "[i]t has taken the British a long time to adjust to their loss of territory, and a great deal of adjustment is still needed" (63). These after-effects of empire in the Brexit debate recall Renato Rosaldo's notion of "imperialist nostalgia." Opening his discussion with films that represent imperialism in nostalgic terms, Rosaldo provides the following definition: "Imperialist nostalgia uses a pose of 'innocent yearning' both to capture people's imaginations and to conceal its complicity with often brutal domination" (108). As a "sentimental discourse" (120), imperialist nostalgia functions as an absolving gesture concealing guilt and complicity. At the same time, imperialist nostalgia serves as a form of mourning and longing for what one has destroyed. In Frears's film, the treatment of Abdul and Indian culture bespeaks a nostalgia for the British Empire, a longing for renewing past imperial connections, but without remembering the ugly underbelly of this supposedly glorious past. Victoria's identification with, and appropriation of, Indian culture are made to look innocent, thus masking the violence of imperialism as the benevolent monarch is

---

evangelical prejudices of her age," Queen Victoria initially wanted to "conquer and convert India" (7). The Indian Rebellion, however, changed her attitude completely, making her "more sympathetic to India and its people, not less, and growing more tolerant and less instinctively racist than her fellow-Britons" (7).

sporting the disputed jewel while sitting on a reconstruction of the destroyed Peacock Throne.

Presenting itself as a seemingly light-hearted comedy, Frears's film proposes an ambiguous argument in the contemporary political crisis. By characterizing the Victorian monarch as a kind and generous person, the film seems to present a wishful fantasy of an open-minded Britannia, thus expressing a longing for an idealized queen who may never have existed in this shape and form. The queen herself takes a stand against racism when she openly criticizes her son Bertie, her private secretary Sir Henry Ponsonby, and Dr Reid for being "racialists" (01:12:38-39). At the same time, however, the film reminds us that the renewal of Commonwealth ties promised by the Leave camp rests on a problematic vision: the relationship is always envisaged as depicted in the film, namely distanced from the real India, and based on British leadership and domination, imagined as benign. Frears's image of the British monarch sitting on the Peacock Throne evokes an imperialist iconography as we know it from visual representations such as Thomas Jones Barker's painting "The Secret of England's Greatness," in which Queen Victoria presents a kneeling East African envoy with a Bible in her audience chamber; or Walter Crane's 1886 British Empire Map, where the 'natives' place their goods and presents at Britannia's feet. In its revisionist construction of Victoria, the film may attempt to articulate and project a wishful fantasy of an unprejudiced broad-minded Britain, but it remains suffused with imperial nostalgia.

The examples discussed in this contribution all use Queen Victoria as a national icon, albeit in very different ways. In *Victoria the Great* and *Sixty Glorious Years*, the queen functions as a unifying figure. On the screen, the popular sovereign can be seen to unite her enthusiastic people, as demonstrated by the crowds cheering at her coronation and the Diamond Jubilee celebrations. Visually this is supported by the superimposition of cinematic images blending the monarch with her subjects, while the soundtrack suggests the unity of the crowds by virtue of their loud cheering and their joint singing of the national anthem. At the same time, Neagle's performance provides her cinematic audience with a sense of comfort at a time of national crisis. By celebrating a dutiful monarch shortly after the Abdication Crisis, the films by Wilcox and Neagle affirm the stability of the British monarchy. Yet they can also be seen to invoke the nation as an imagined community at a time when, due to the rise of fascism in Europe, the geopolitical situation became increasingly volatile.

With Judi Dench's Victoria, Frears also presents a national figure, but in this case the queen is inseparable from her imperial connections. *Victoria & Abdul* could easily be read as a light-hearted comedy of manners, or simply as a tale about a sentimental friendship cultivated by the queen in her idiosyncratic old age. However, the fact that Frears's film was made during the Brexit debate adds an allegorical layer to the queen's cross-cultural friendship with Abdul Karim. The racist views of the royal household – standing in perhaps for the xenophobia unleashed by the Brexit debate – routinely become the butt of the film's jokes. However, the construction of the queen as a benign monarch is firmly rooted in imperialist nostalgia, perpetuating a vision not of equality but of domination. In the closing scene, Abdul, having returned to Agra after the queen's death, kneels down to kiss the feet of the bronze statue of Queen Victoria against the backdrop of the Taj Mahal. Although the film ends with Abdul, it does so from an entirely British perspective. Abdul is depicted as a loyal servant and friend, whose attitude towards British imperialism is never explored. Instead, the film's closing scene evokes a spirit of imperialist nostalgia by having its Indian protagonist pay homage to a reconstruction of the very statue which was removed in 1947 when India gained independence. In *Victoria & Abdul*, Queen Victoria thus embodies a national figure that remains inseparable from a problematic nostalgia for an imperial past.

References

Works Cited

Anderson, Benedict. *Imagined Communities: Reflections on the Origin and Spread of Nationalism*. Rev. ed., Verso, 1991.

Baird, Julia. *Victoria the Queen: An Intimate Biography of the Woman Who Ruled an Empire*. Blackfriars, 2016.

Cannadine, David. "The Context, Performance and Meaning of Ritual: The British Monarchy and the 'Invention of Tradition,' c. 1820-1977." *The Invention of Tradition*, edited by Eric Hobsbawm and Terence Ranger, Cambridge UP, 1993, pp. 101-64.

Chapman, James. *Past and Present: National Identity and the British Historical Film*. I. B. Tauris, 2005.

Dorling, Danny, and Sally Tomlinson. *Rule Britannia: Brexit and the End of the Empire*. Biteback Publishing, 2019.

Fielding, Steven. "The Heart of a Heartless Political World: Screening Victoria." *The British Monarchy on Screen*, edited by Mandy Merck, Manchester UP, 2016, pp. 64-85.

Ford, Elizabeth A., and Deborah C. Mitchell. *Royal Portraits in Hollywood: Filming the Lives of Queens*. The UP of Kentucky, 2009.

Hobbes, Thomas. *Leviathan*. 1651. Penguin, 2017.

Hobsbawm, Eric, and Terence Ranger, editors. *The Invention of Tradition*. Cambridge UP, 1984.

Homans, Margaret. *Royal Representations: Queen Victoria and British Culture, 1837-1876*. The U of Chicago P, 1998.

Kantorowicz, Ernst H. *The King's Two Bodies: A Study in Medieval Political Theology*. 2nd ed., Princeton UP, 1997.

Kelly, Angela. *The Other Side of the Coin: The Queen, the Dresser and the Wardrobe*. HarperCollins, 2019.

McDonald, Russ. *Look to the Lady: Sarah Siddons, Ellen Terry, and Judi Dench on the Shakespearean Stage*. The U of Georgia P, 2005.

Richards, Jeffrey. *The Age of the Dream Palace: Cinema and Society in 1930s Britain*. I. B. Tauris, 2010.

Ridley, Jane. *Victoria: Queen, Matriarch, Empress*. Allen Lane, 2015.

Rosaldo, Renato. "Imperialist Nostalgia." *Representations*, vol. 26, 1989, pp. 107-22.

Schulte, Regina, editor. *The Body of the Queen: Gender and Rule in the Courtly World, 1500-2000*. Berghahn Books, 2006.

Street, Sarah. *British National Cinema*. Routledge, 1997.

Taylor, Miles. *Empire: Queen Victoria and India*. Yale UP, 2018.

Thompson, Dorothy. *Queen Victoria: Gender and Power*. Virago, 1990.
Wilson, A. N. *Victoria: A Life*. Atlantic Books, 2015.
Worsley, Lucy. *Queen Victoria: Daughter, Wife, Mother*. Hodder & Stoughton, 2018.

Films

Coronation of George VI and Queen Elizabeth. Reel 7, 1937, *YouTube*, uploaded by British Pathé, 13 April 2014, www.youtube.com/watch?v=VHRWJgex5r4.
The Crown. Netflix series created by Peter Morgan, performances by Claire Foy, Olivia Colman et al., UK, USA, 2016-.
Forever and a Day. Directed by Herbert Wilcox et al., performances by Anna Neagle et al., USA, 1943.
Lilacs in the Spring (aka *Let's Make Up*). Directed by Herbert Wilcox, performances by Anna Neagle et al., UK, 1954.
Mrs Brown. Directed by John Madden, performances by Judi Dench et al., UK, Ireland, USA, 1997.
The Queen. Directed by Stephen Frears, performances by Helen Mirren et al., UK, USA, France, Italy, 2006.
The Queen and James Bond London 2012 Performance. Directed by Danny Boyle, performances by Queen Elizabeth II and Daniel Craig, UK, *YouTube*, uploaded by Olympic Channel, 27 July 2012, www.youtube.com/watch?v=1AS-dCdYZbo.
The Queen's Coronavirus Broadcast. *YouTube*, uploaded by BBC, 5 April 2020, youtu.be/2klmuggOElE.
The Queen's VE Day Address. *YouTube*, uploaded by BBC, 8 May 2020, www.youtube.com/watch?v=vuEf9xMmYuo.
Shakespeare in Love. Directed by John Madden, performances by Judi Dench et al., USA, UK, 1998.
Sixty Glorious Years. Directed by Herbert Wilcox, performances by Anna Neagle, Anton Walbrook et al., UK, 1938.
Victoria. ITV series created by Daisy Goodwin, performances by Jenna Coleman et al., UK, 2016-.
Victoria & Abdul. Directed by Stephen Frears, performances by Judi Dench, Ali Fazal et al., UK, USA, 2017.
Victoria the Great. Directed by Herbert Wilcox, performances by Anna Neagle, Anton Walbrook et al., UK, 1937.
The Young Victoria. Directed by Jean-Marc Vallée, performances by Emily Blunt et al., UK, USA, 2009.

Images

Barker, Thomas Jones. *The Secret of England's Greatness* (aka *Queen Victoria Presenting a Bible in the Audience Chamber at Windsor*). Oil on canvas, ca. 1862-63, National Portrait Gallery, London, www.npg. org. uk/ collections/search/portrait/mw00071/The-Secret-of-Englands-Greatness-Queen-Victoria-presenting-a-Bible-in-the-Audience-Chamber-at-Windsor.

Crane, Walter. *Imperial Federation Map of the World Showing the Extent of the British Empire in 1886*. Published as a supplement to *Graphic*, 24 July 1866, Cornell University Library, 25 Aug. 2015, digital.library.cornell.edu/catalog/ss:3293793.

Hills and Saunders. *Sheikh Chidda; Queen Victoria*. Carbon print, 17 July 1893, National Portrait Gallery, London, www.npg.org.uk/ collections/search/portrait/mw06521/Sheikh-Chidda-Queen-Victoria.

"My Lords and Members of the House of Commons": Britain and the European Integration Project through the Queen's Speeches

Martin Mik and Jo Angouri

This essay explores the ways in which the relationship with the European Union was framed by British Governments around the time leading to the two UK-wide referenda (1975 and 2016) concerning the British role within the European integration process. Using the Queen's Speeches as our locus, we combine a political-science reading with a linguistic analysis, paying particular attention to the historicity of the relationship between the UK and the EU as constructed in this public discourse context. We argue that the Queen's Speech is an unexplored genre which allows for a diachronic analysis of complex political landscapes and show in our analysis both the stability and plasticity of this genre. Our findings, based on an analysis of twenty-five Queen's Speeches spanning a total period of twenty-six years, shed light on the ways in which membership to the EU is commodified in relation to economic policies. The data illustrate the systematic construction of the EU as an economic union throughout the decades. We discuss and close the essay with the affordances of the Queen's Speech genre for the study of the UK political system.

Keywords: Queen's Speech, Brexit, EU, UK, referendum, genre theory

The use of referenda in the British political system is a relatively recent innovation, dating back to 1973. It is indicative that two of the three UK-wide referenda to take place to date (in 1975 and 2016) concern the British role within the European integration process and they both

Brexit and Beyond: Nation and Identity. SPELL: Swiss Papers in English Language and Literature 39, edited by Daniela Keller and Ina Habermann, Narr, 2020, pp. 61-97.

represent landmark events that have attracted the public eye as well as scholarly attention.[1] The fact that the UK's membership of the European Union is bookmarked by the referenda constituted the motivation for this essay, which is interested in the historicity of the relationship between the UK and the EU as constructed in public discourses. In particular, we focus on the Queen's Speeches, a distinct political genre which has not been researched as yet despite its symbolic role in British politics.

Unlike referenda, other elements of the British political system are deeply embedded in the country's past. The tradition of the State Opening of Parliament was established already by the end of the fourteenth century ("Living Heritage: Offices"). We use here the Queen's Speech as our locus and explore the ways in which Governments framed and commodified the relationship with the European Union around the time leading to the two relevant referenda.[2]

The gap of over forty years between the two referenda poses obvious challenges as the socio-historical contexts have developed and changed dramatically. Socio-economic structures, composition, and focus have all shifted during the intervening period. Uniquely for the UK, however, at both these points of British history there is one constant: the Monarch, Elizabeth II. We are not proposing to scrutinize the Queen's views on the referenda and the UK's part in the European integration project. The Sovereign in the British political system does not share her political views publicly. The Queen's Speeches, however, given their authorship by the Government of the day, provide a unique and

---

[1] The first UK referendum took place in 1973, but was limited to Northern Ireland. The people of Northern Ireland were invited to decide whether they wanted to join the Republic of Ireland or remain in the United Kingdom. Two years later, the UK's population was asked whether they wanted to stay in the European Communities. For further information on all UK referenda to date, see "Referendums."

[2] Evidently, the European Union of today is a result of decades of gradual development. The milestone events are the Treaty of Paris, signed in 1951, which established the European Coal and Steel Community (ECSC) with effect from 1952; the Treaties of Rome, signed in 1957, which established the European Economic Community (EEC); and the European Atomic Energy Community (EAEC or Euratom), with effect from 1958. Although formally independent, these three communities were working jointly. In 1965, this was marked by the so-called Merger Treaty, which rationalized the institutions of the three Communities. *European Communities* therefore refers to all three entities. The European Union was established by the Treaty on European Union (Maastricht Treaty), signed in 1992. Where we discuss elements that cover the European Communities and the European Union, we refer to the European Union as an umbrella term. We refer to the European Communities (or a specific Community) where the references are time-bound, or pertinent to a single body only.

consolidated insight into the unfolding relationship between Britain and the EU.

We focus in particular on *explicit* mentions of Europe and the EU and the ways in which these are framed and commodified. A close reading of direct references to the European Union allows us to highlight differences, developments, and continuity over a long period of time. We do not evaluate whether these references focus on the right areas/messages and we do not compare the speeches to other genres. The Queen's Speech is different from media and campaign speeches as it is a Government agenda enunciated by the Queen. In more detail, although it is the Queen, i.e., the Head of State and – at least in purely formal sense – the most senior actor in the hierarchy of the British political system who delivers the speech, hers is essentially an agentless role. The Queen does not draft the speech; the Government does. Neither does she comment on the societal importance of the content of the speech. However, because of the way the speech is delivered in a highly formalized manner and through the medium of the Sovereign, these speeches differ significantly from other speeches delivered by the Government. We argue that although the event carries ideological significance, this needs to be read in the context of this unique genre and its distinctive power balance between the core stakeholders.

Given the ceremonial and symbolic weight of the Queen's Speech in political discourse, every explicit reference to the EU or Europe holds significant implications with regard to its positioning and contextualization within the speech. To that end, we systematically analyse all the Queen's Speeches delivered around the time of the 1975 and 2016 referenda. Our corpus draws on a detailed analysis of the speeches between 1960-75 and from 2010-19, to identify these elements and the change/consistency in these references over time.

Our analysis confirms that the UK has always approached the EU from an economic perspective but reveals that this is also consistently the case in the context of the Queen's Speech – a ceremonial act and genre that typically attracts a lot of attention from the political arena and is also visible to the public – it would be useful for future research to properly test whether and to what extent this is because of the political content of the Speech. As Peter John and Will Jennings highlight, "[t]he speech provides a high-profile signal, at a particular point in time, of the priorities of the core executive to parliament, to governing and opposition parties, to interest groups, to the media and to the public" (569). The Queen's Speech encapsulates a unique relationship where the presence of the Monarch (whether in person or through representation) is a condition for the Government's set of priorities to be formally announced. It constitutes a political performative for the Government and an opportunity to perpetuate ideological positioning. The Monarch herself, however, has no role to play in the authorship of the text.

The Queen's Speech is an unexplored genre and combining a historical-political science reading with a linguistic analysis allows us to perform a diachronic and concise analysis of a complex political landscape. The essay is organized into three parts and starts with a brief discussion of our core discursive context before turning to the discussion of the referenda. Reviewing the two referenda and providing a comparison between these two key events that bookmark the UK's membership in the European Union, we close the paper with our general findings and suggestions for future research.

The Queen's Speech as a Genre and a Performative

The so-called Queen's Speech outlines key areas of focus for the Government and unveils forthcoming legislative activity. Naturally, therefore, the political content of the speeches reflects the Government and its make-up. It is the Government that decides when the State Opening of Parliament and the Queen's Speech will take place. As stated, the Queen does not approve nor edit the content of the speech.

The structure and function of the Queen's Speech has attracted very little attention in either political science or linguistics despite the rich body of research on political speeches in both fields of study (e.g., Howarth; Wodak, *Discursive*; Angouri and Wodak). While the political implications of the content of the speeches are always in the media headline, and become subject of academic research (e.g., Jennings and John; John and Jennings), the genre itself has not been researched.

Our analysis has shown that the Queen's Speech meets the necessary conditions for being ratified as a political genre. It has a robust format that changes little over the decades and a stable function within an elaborate ceremony, both of which make it instantly recognizable as a Queen's Speech. We consider the resilience of the format and structure of the Queen's Speeches significant and interesting due to the genre's ritualistic character, which however also has enough plasticity for Government to adjust to their political agenda. Political genres play an important role for the construction, dissemination and/or change of political ideologies; it is therefore a suitable genre to analyse. As such the lack of research on the Queen's Speeches is a gap to be addressed because it provides an insight into what the Government decides to include and represent as matters of priority and public interest in those specific moments in time.

A political genre does not denote a simple static, textual architecture; as genre theory has shown (e.g., Bhatia; Swales), a genre approach brings together stable and generalized features of a discourse event with the possibility for dynamic change over time or according to the needs of a community. Although genre theorists have been preoccupied with primarily written texts, the approach is suitable for either spoken genres (e.g., Angouri and Marra) or hybrid events such as the Queen's Speech, which is carefully crafted and must be read out verbatim without the impromptu changes or extempores that usually characterize speeches. One of the core characteristics of genres is that they are recurrent and immediately recognizable by the relevant small or large communities in different socio-political contexts. The Queen's Speech is a case in point. The Queen's Speech has a standardized length of 1,000-1,200 words (with some variation) and is organized in three parts as indicated in Figure 1 (see Appendix 1 for a full speech).

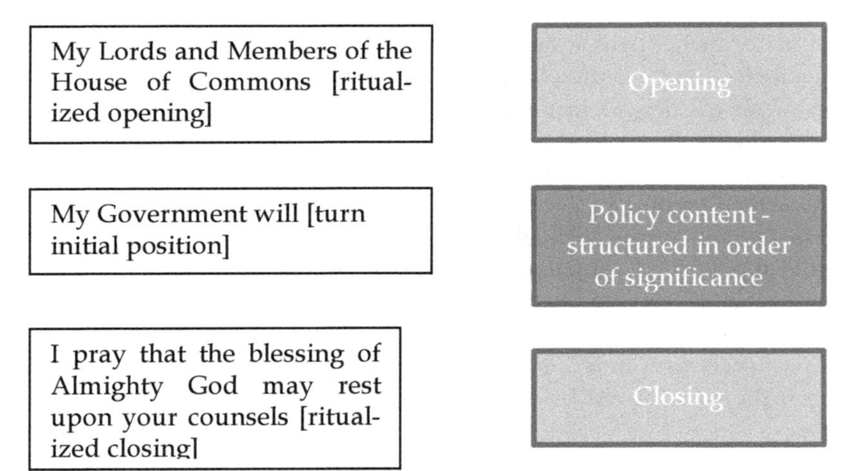

Fig. 1. The Queen's Speech structure

The opening and closing of the speech are stable and perpetuate the unique form of the speech.[3] The Queen's Speech has an established traditional structure and always opens with a standard formula: "My

[3] Genre theorists have used the concept of moves (e.g., Bhatia; Swales) to describe the recurrent and sequentially stable parts of a discourse event.

Lords and Members of the House of Commons." The closing of the speech is similarly formalized: "My Lords and Members of the House of Commons, other measures will be laid before you. I pray that the blessing of Almighty God may rest upon your counsels."[4] These two formulae enclose the main part of the speech, within which the Government presents its priorities. It is in this section of the speech that shifts of topic sequence appear over time. The structure of the main part, however, remains stable, and subjects are always 'My Government' or 'My Ministers,' with a shift to 'My Ministers' in subject position when it comes to specific measures and finances.

The recurrent reference to 'My Government' in paragraph initial position also foregrounds the standing of the Queen as head of state; the sequential design elevates the role of the speech and by extension elevates Government policy. Genres reproduce important aspects of a community's identity and its established processes. This is visible in the Queen's Speech which further perpetuates the role of the Monarchy and the importance of tradition of political systems. It also foregrounds the Governments' positioning in relation to the political reality of the time.

Further, the Queen's Speech as a political genre has a specific function: it formally opens a new session of parliament, either following a general election (and therefore a new parliament), or after the prorogation of an existing parliament.[5] It is only after the Queen's Speech is delivered that the parliament can start working. As such the Queen carries out a clear performative speech act in and through the speech, namely the Opening of Parliament. The Queen's Speech is part of a ceremony which further highlights its role and symbolism. The ceremony of the Opening of Parliament is steeped in tradition and reflects the long history of the monarchy and the parliament, as well as the evolution of their relationship. The ceremony is televised and captured online, often with detailed commentary on the meaning of individual stages, the roles played by various post holders, etc. All the pomp and

[4] In some speeches the closing formula has a slightly different order: "Other measures will be laid before you. My Lords and Members of the House of Commons, I pray that the blessing of Almighty God may rest upon your counsels." See for example: *Queen's Speech, 27 May 2015* (col. 7).

[5] Prorogation is a process of ending one parliamentary session. The term is also used to denote the period between the prorogation of one session and the State Opening of Parliament, which marks the beginning of a new session. Sessions typically run for a year, although not always. For more details see: "Prorogation."

circumstance set the stage for the delivery of the Queen's Speech by the Monarch ("State Opening").[6]

For this essay, we analysed all twenty-five speeches delivered within our focus period for their structure and content. We followed the principles of thematic and interaction analysis (Angouri) and analysed references to the EU in terms of the frequent semantic domains found in the speeches as well as the sequential ordering of reference to the EU compared to the content of the speech.

Our analysis shows the stability and plasticity of the genre. Over the decades, the order in which policy areas appear has changed. This is understandable as different Governments will have different priorities based not only on their political persuasion and their manifesto, but also on domestic and global developments. This fluctuation, which is often subtle and takes place over a number of years/decades, can be illustrated by the positioning of references to the European Union in the Queen's Speeches considered in this essay, i.e., in those delivered 1960-75 and 2010-19 inclusive, as captured in Table 1.

As already mentioned, this essay focuses on *explicit* mentions of the European Union only. Due to the ceremonial and symbolic weight of the Queen's Speech, we consider the positioning of a Europe-related paragraph within the speech a way of underlining its level of importance. With the exception of speeches delivered in 2017 and 2019, the EU tended to be mentioned explicitly only once. This may be surprising given the number of policy areas within which the EU has a considerable control. It must be noted, however, that the Queen's Speech sets out business the Government intends to present to Parliament for consideration so that the majority of topics will be in areas where the EU does not play a role – at least directly for people's daily reality. The speeches thus foreground domestic priorities, whether ad hoc or long-term, or areas such as foreign and security policies.

As Table 1 illustrates, the positioning of EU-related items fluctuates over time. From 1960-75 these mentions appeared in the first half of the speech and even among the first ten substantive items in every speech from 1962-75, fluctuating between item number 2 and item number 9. The situation changes dramatically when we re-engage with the speeches from 2010. Between 2010 and 2016 inclusive, explicit mentions of the EU appear in the second half of the speeches, often towards the very end. 2013 is the only year within our focus with no ex-

[6] Since her accession to the throne in 1952, Queen Elizabeth II delivered all Queen's Speeches bar two: 1959 and 1963 (due to pregnancies).

plicit mention of the EU whatsoever. This may be surprising seen out of context, but less so when taking into consideration the extent to which the EU agenda has been embedded in the British political system since the early 2000s. For example, one need only look at the many areas in which EU legislation would have been automatically transposed into the British legislative system. It would therefore only be extraordinary EU matters that would merit specific mention in the Queen's Speech. And these would have to compete with remaining domestic items for 'newsworthiness,' and therefore a more prominent position in the speeches. The situation changes dramatically after the 2016 referendum, when EU-related items rocket to the top of the Queen's Speech. EU membership has never been straightforward in the UK as we will show below.

The sections containing EC/EU mentions are typically structured as distinct paragraphs preceded or followed by references to other alliances, e.g., the North Atlantic Alliance. The detailed analysis of these parts of the speeches shows that the EU is commodified with reference to two concepts, namely economy and security, with the former clearly dominant in the sub-corpus and hence our focus.

The structure of the paragraphs is equally robust. There is consistent use of 'My Government' in initial subject position and use of the active voice in those paragraphs although the passive voice is found in other parts of the speech. Finally, we note a systematic use of verbs indicating action and effort. Taken together, these points foreground the agency of the Government and place them in control of the agenda. This is particularly prominent given that the speech is delivered by the Monarch, who is otherwise agentless. This is the case with other genres (e.g., religious or judicial) for which power is vested upon an orator. Orators are a key felicity condition for the act but they do not have the authority to intervene.

This will be illustrated in the following sections which include excerpts from all speeches delivered between 1960-75 and then again 2010-19.

Year	Overall number of substantive paragraphs	EC/EU Mention Position
1960	30	13
1961	30	13
1962	31	9
1963	25	5
1964	24	6
1965	36	4
1966	30	6
1967	39	6
1968	38	6
1969	38	4
1970	33	3
1971	23	2
1972	29	2
1973	34	2
1974.i	33	3
1974.ii	31	3
1975	37	3
2010	38	28
2012	37	28
2013	39	0
2014	41	37
2015	31	17
2016	40	35
2017	32	1, 2, 3 & 24
2019	19	1 & 2

Table 1. Position of EC/EU mentions in the Queen's Speech by year

Fig. 2. The fifty most frequent terms used in the Queen's Speech in association with the European Union

Our deliberate engagement with all speeches allows us to position the semantic domains of 'economy' in the wider societal context of the speeches. As mentioned above, 'security' is one of the key consistent messages, but 'economy' is far more pronounced. We show how the relationship between Britain and the EU, enacted in and through the speeches, has been consistently about specific domains of economic activity and not broader European values, although the continuity and relative stability of the genre would be suitable to strengthen European identification, if the Governments over the years had decided to foreground a strong pro-European stance (see *Declaration*). EU membership, however, has always been a contentious issue on political agendas regardless of which political party was in Government. Through the cases and the excerpts below we illustrate core patterns in the data and demonstrate how the primary relationship between Britain and the EU is constructed as an economic agreement rather than a, more broadly, political one. Let us start with the first referendum.

The 5 June 1975 Referendum

The United Kingdom, although invited to participate, refused to take part in the European Coal and Steel Community (ECSC) as well as the European Economic Community (EEC) and the European Atomic Energy Community (EAEC, or Euratom) in the initial stages of the post-WWII integration process in Western Europe. Although supportive of the integration process, the UK did not regard itself as a part of this process. This position was clearly set out by Winston Churchill in his Zurich speech in September 1946. Not in an elected office at the time, Churchill strongly advocated for a close cooperation between France and Germany in particular, and the rest of Europe more broadly, while

> Great Britain, the British Commonwealth of Nations, mighty America – and, I trust, Soviet Russia, for then indeed all would be well – must be the friends and sponsors of the new Europe and must champion its right to live. Therefore I say to you "Let Europe arise!"

Over seventy years later, Dinan (306) put it more directly: "For a variety of cultural, economic, historical, and political reasons, British public and political opinion was largely uninterested in the country's membership in Europe's first supranational organizations." It is important to remember the context. Europe (and indeed the rest of the world) had only just emerged from a protracted global conflict that had cost millions of lives, seen the invention and use of a nuclear weapon, attacked the foundation of world organization, and for many raised concerning questions about humanity. With European countries exhausted by years of war effort, with a challenging recovery ahead, there was no indication how a project aiming to bring together the two key enemies, Germany and France, would end.

Britain had its Commonwealth with long-standing political and economic ties, connecting Britain tightly to markets across the globe. Britain emerged victorious from WWII, which helped to maintain its fading global power status – in the eyes of some at least. Nevertheless, Britain participated in various European endeavours in the post-WWII period, e.g., the foundation of the Council of Europe, or the formation of the North Atlantic Treaty Organization (NATO), which was to play a key role in securing peace in Europe during the Cold War. However, Britain's engagement was limited to developments based on an intergovernmental approach; projects with supranational elements, necessitating at least partial surrender of national sovereignty, did not appeal. It is easy, with the benefit of hindsight, to blame the then-contemporary leaders for their short-sightedness, but it is important to remember the picture of the day. Subsequent developments within the European project, namely the idea of a common market, but also agricultural policy, would be considered a threat to British trade with the Commonwealth (at the time more significant than British trade with European countries). Britain attempted to create a counter to the European Communities (EC) by negotiating the European Free Trade Association (EFTA), which came into existence in 1960, but without the EC member states and on a much looser footing. In the Queen's Speech delivered on 1 November 1960, the situation was captured very briefly as follows:

> [My Government] will continue to cooperate with their partners in consolidating the European Free Trade Association. At the same time they will work towards the political and economic unity of Western Europe, on a basis satisfactory to all the Governments concerned. (col. 3)

It was the British businesses whose calls led to the British Government's change of approach and the decision to apply for EC membership. The first application for membership, submitted in 1961 by the Government of Harold Macmillan (Conservative), was based on an expectation of retaining a preferential relationship with the Commonwealth and, ideally, expanding this preferred status to existing members of the European Communities. This was not an easy negotiating position to have at the beginning of accession talks. The Queen's Speech of 31 October 1961 presented the item with hope, but even in this formal statement the complexity of the task is made clear by references to both the Commonwealth and the EFTA:

> My Government will make every effort to bring to a successful conclusion the negotiations which they are undertaking with the European Economic Community and will at all times maintain close consultation with the interests involved in the United Kingdom and with the other members of the Commonwealth and of the European Free Trade Association. (col. 3)

Just one year later, on 30 October 1962, the Queen's Speech provided an update on the on-going negotiations, which again highlighted the importance of accession, but also the challenges in reaching a deal that would work for the UK, the Commonwealth, and the EFTA:

> My Ministers recognise the great political and economic importance of the development of the European Communities and the opportunities which

> British accession to these Communities would bring. In close consultation with the other members of the Commonwealth and of the European Free Trade Association, and having full regard for those interests in the United Kingdom which are particularly concerned, they will use every effort to bring the current negotiations to a conclusion acceptable to Parliament. (col. 3)

To make matters more complicated, there were strong personalities that played a key role in the negotiations. Most notably, the President of France, Charles de Gaulle, who eventually vetoed the first British membership application in January 1963 (see Milward for a detailed discussion of the initial stages of the British approach to the European integration process). The veto was reflected in the Queen's Speech in October 1963,[7] which also outlined the Government's subsequent steps in light of unsuccessful accession negotiations:

> My Government deeply regretted the interruption of the negotiations for the accession of the United Kingdom to the Treaties of Paris and Rome. They have continued to work for a wider European unity. They have proposed that the work of the Western European Union and the Council of Europe should be further developed, and have continued their efforts to strengthen the European Free Trade Association. (*Prorogation* col. 1296)

In the following years, until the re-opening of negotiations in 1967, the Queen's Speeches included limited references to cooperation on the Continent. Thus on 3 November 1964, the Queen's Speech included a statement announcing that "[m]y Government will continue to play a full part in the European organisations of which this country is a member and will seek to promote closer European co-operation" (col. 10). A year later, on 9 November 1965, a more specific statement featured with an emphasis on trade and the economy:

> My Government will continue to work for the greater unity of Europe. They will seek to strengthen the European Free Trade Association and to promote co-operation between the Association and the European Economic Community, and the establishment of a wider European market. (col. 2)

Finally, on 21 April 1966, the Queen's Speech included a clear indication of preparedness for renewed entry negotiations:

---

[7] This speech is the only one within our focus not delivered by Her Majesty the Queen but by the Lord Chancellor, on her behalf. The format of the speech, however, remains unchanged.

> My Government will continue to promote the economic unity of Europe and to strengthen the links between the European Free Trade Association and the European Economic Community. They would be ready to enter the European Economic Community provided essential British and Commonwealth interests were safeguarded. They will work for tariff reductions under the General Agreement on Tariffs and Trade and for an expansion of Commonwealth trade. (col. 10)

The Queen's Speech delivered on 31 October 1967 heralded the new negotiations of membership following the second British application:

> My Government look forward to the early opening of negotiations to provide for Britain's entry into the European Communities. The closest consultation will be maintained with Commonwealth Governments, the Governments of the European Free Trade Association and the Republic of Ireland. (col. 2)

However, this anticipation was cut short just a couple of weeks later in November 1967 by President de Gaulle, who vetoed the second British application, submitted by the Labour Government under Harold Wilson. The Queen's Speech delivered on 30 October 1968 included a simple statement showing the Government's determination to continue with the application, when the circumstances are more positive: "My Government will maintain their application for membership of the European Communities and will promote other measures of co-operation in Europe in keeping with this" (col. 2). British accession negotiations to the Communities had to wait until after de Gaulle's resignation in April 1969 and his replacement by Georges Pompidou. This turn of events was reflected in the Queen's Speech of 28 October 1969: "My Government will maintain their application to become full Members of the European Communities and desire an early commencement of negotiations. They will take a full part in promoting other measures contributing to European unity" (col. 4). However, the negotiations did not start until after the EC member states finalized the Common Agricultural Policy arrangements and pledged to work towards deeper integration, namely through possible monetary policy and common approaches to foreign policy.

The enthusiasm behind the opening of accession negotiations under a Conservative Government led by Edward Heath, as well as the importance of the step, were reflected in the Queen's Speech of 2 July 1970:

> My Government have welcomed the opening on the 30th of June of negotiations for membership of the European Communities. In these negotiations they will seek to reach agreement on terms fair to all concerned and will remain in close consultation with our Commonwealth and EFTA partners and with the Irish Republic. (col. 9)

The statement appeared as the third item in the speech, immediately after a list of planned state visits and Britain's key international objectives. This marks the highest ranking of an item related to the European Communities since 1960. Such items tended to make their appearance halfway through the speeches in the early 1960s, rising to the top ten from 1963 onwards (appearing fourth to sixth out of over thirty items on average, as illustrated in Table 1). From 1970 to 1975 inclusive, items related to the European Communities appear in either the second or third paragraph of the speeches.

This announcement of opened negotiations preceded a comment on the importance of maintained security via NATO structures and a specific comment on the Commonwealth. However, it maintains its references to the key issues that had marked the UK's relationship with the Communities in earlier periods: the Commonwealth, the European Free Trade Association, and specifically the relationship with the Republic of Ireland.[8] This brief statement in the 1970 speech also refers to a number of difficult areas the UK would need to negotiate, such as the Common Agricultural Policy and the Fisheries Policy. However, the negotiations – opened in 1970, a decade after the first UK application was submitted – benefited from a number of developments that positively impacted on the process. Over a ten-year period, countries of the Commonwealth were able to take steps to prepare for the anticipated accession of the UK to the European Communities and the potential impact on their trading relationships. Equally, EFTA member states had time to find a way of cooperating with the Communities. A number of EFTA members joined the UK in applying for EC membership too. Of the founding EFTA member states, apart from the UK, Denmark and Norway were also negotiating membership.[9] The Republic of Ireland, which enjoyed a privileged relationship with the UK, also applied for member-

---

[8] The Republic of Ireland negotiated EC entry previously, but did not complete the process due to the French veto of the UK application.

[9] Although Norway concluded its entry negotiations successfully, the people of Norway rejected accession in a referendum. The United Kingdom and Denmark, together with the Republic of Ireland, eventually joined the EC without Norway.

ship, removing a possible obstacle to the UK's accession. The importance and complexity of the UK-Republic of Ireland relationship was such that it was mentioned in the 1967 Queen's Speech as a crucial element of the accession negotiations. A scenario in which UK application would be successful whereas an Irish application declined would present challenges similar to the issues surrounding exit arrangements during Brexit talks.

The optimism of entry negotiations was shown again in the Queen's Speech delivered on 2 November 1971, which heralded the signing of the Instrument of Accessions in the second paragraph of the speech (immediately after the list of forthcoming state visits, traditionally the first topic):

> In their external policies My Government will protect and advance the nation's interests. They hope, following the successful conclusion of negotiations, shortly to sign an Instrument of Accession to the European Communities after which legislation will be laid before you. It will be their purpose to maintain the North Atlantic Alliance, sustain the Commonwealth association and uphold our other friendships and alliances through-out the world, while continuing their efforts to achieve international agreement on arms control and disarmament. (col. 1-2)

The Government was careful to mark their continued commitment to both NATO and the Commonwealth, but the positioning of the European Communities at the beginning of the speech suggests this was indeed the primary focus.

This was further underlined during the next Queen's Speech, delivered on 31 October 1972. The European Communities, and the UK's forthcoming membership, again occupy the second position (immediately after the state visits) and use wording that makes clear that the Government wanted to play a major role in the Communities:

> My Government will play a full and constructive part in the enlarged European Communities. They look forward to the opportunities membership will bring, for developing the country's full economic and industrial potential, for working out social and environmental policies on a European scale, and for increasing the influence of the enlarged Community for the benefit of the world at large. (col. 1)

The Government outlined the key areas it wanted the UK to benefit from and to participate in at the European level. Its focus on economic, social, and environmental areas was stated explicitly. The Communities' role in the world arena, however, was left ambiguous: was the UK allowing the Communities to increase their influence in the world, or was the UK benefiting from joining the Communities to increase (or maintain) its world influence?

Following the accession of the United Kingdom on 1 January 1973, the Queen's Speech of 30 October 1973 gave the Communities not only a very prominent position (second only to overseas visits), but also a level of detail regarding the Government's focus:

> In co-operation with other Member States My Government will play their full part in the further development of the European Community in accordance with the programme established at the European Summit in October 1972. This programme includes progress towards economic and monetary union; measures for the establishment of a regional development fund; and co-operation in foreign policy between Member States. My Government's objective throughout will be to promote the interests of the individual, whether as citizen or as consumer. (col. 1-2)

This segment of the Queen's Speech dedicated to the UK's role within the Communities – most extensive so far – suggests the Government's active commitment within the Communities, taking on board agreements reached before its accession and highlighting areas of particular interest. The Economic and Monetary Union and the Regional Development Fund occupy a prominent place in the speech, followed by foreign policy and the rights of an individual as a close third. The fact that these particular aspects of membership are highlighted through the speech illustrates the British focus on the economic aspects of the integration project and reservations towards integration in other areas, often presented as a loss of sovereignty, a theme present in the UK-EU relations since the 1960s all the way through to the 2016 referendum and beyond (for a full discussion of the UK-EU relationship see for example: George; Wall; Young).

1974 saw two Queen's Speeches delivered following a change in Government, with Labour led by Harold Wilson taking office in March 1974, and another one taking place in October of the same year following a snap election that also returned a Labour Government. Both speeches mark a change in the standing of the European Communities item – the international arena takes precedence over Europe. More importantly, the new Government signals its dissatisfaction with the membership deal. This reflects the Labour Party's stance, which was more critical at the time than that of the Conservative Party (with, however, significant differences of opinion within each party). The original membership conditions negotiated by the Conservative Government of Edward Heath made the UK a net contributor to the Communities' budget. The Common Agricultural Policy, agreed before the accession of the UK, was tailored to the needs of the original member states and not suited to the UK. These are just two of the issues the original accession conditions presented. Harold Wilson, leader of the Labour Party, was critical of these membership conditions, deemed detrimental to the UK; and Labour election manifestos in 1974 included a promise of a membership conditions renegotiation.

The first speech was delivered on 12 March 1974 and announced the Government's intention to renegotiate the UK's terms of entry to the European Economic Community: "My Government will seek a fundamental renegotiation of the terms of entry to the European Economic Community. After these negotiations have been completed, the results will be put to the British people" (col. 7). The speech also held a promise of a first-ever nation-wide referendum in which the people would decide whether the UK should remain in the Communities or not. The second speech was delivered on 29 October 1974 and confirmed this pledge. The UK's role in international attempts to address inflation and high oil prices, its dedication to the United Nations, and the importance of the Commonwealth – all came before the European Communities:

> My Government will energetically continue their renegotiation of the terms of the United Kingdom's membership of the European Economic Community. Within twelve months the British people will be given the opportunity to decide whether, in the light of the outcome of the negotiations, this country should retain its membership. (col. 7)

There is an indication of optimism and hope that renegotiations can be concluded successfully and swiftly. The negotiations did take place, but changes to the membership conditions were minimal. The renegotiated conditions, however, were presented as a success to the British electorate. The promise of a new regional policy, pushed for by the UK (already under the Conservative Government of Edward Heath) and agreed by the EC, was the most tangible success as it targeted poorer areas of the Communities, a number of them in the UK, securing direct EC funding. This new policy ensured a tangible route of EC finances back to the UK. However, despite suggestions of an improved situation, the issue of British contributions to the EC budget remained high on the agenda even beyond a 'rebate' negotiated by Margaret Thatcher.

The referendum on the membership of the European Communities took place on 5 June 1975. The people were asked the following question: "Do you think that the United Kingdom should stay in the European Community (the Common Market)?" (*Referendum* 2986). The wording of the question is peculiar as the United Kingdom joined European Communit*ies*. This is captured in the Act of Parliament that marks the accession, the *European Communities Act 1972*: "'the Communities' means the European Economic Community, the European Coal and Steel Community and the European Atomic Energy Community" (Part I). By a 67.2% majority, the voters decided that the UK should stay in ("Living Heritage: Parliament"). Although Government ministers were allowed to express publicly their preferences – collective responsibility was suspended for the referendum, whereas in normal circumstances cabinet ministers are expected to defend an agreed Government position, whatever their personal stance – the support from Prime Minister Wilson and other pro-European ministers was prominent. The 'Yes' camp was supported by a majority of the Conservative Party and other UK parties too (Miller).

A return to a more positive messaging can be detected in the Queen's Speech delivered on 19 November 1975, just over five months after the referendum: "My Government will play their full part in the European Economic Community, devoting particular attention to the achievement of a common approach to the world's political and economic problems" (col. 2). However, the Communities are referred to after both the United Nations and the Commonwealth, and the Government indicates that "the world's political and economic problems" and ways of addressing them are the Government's priority now. The speech also specifically refers to the European Economic Community, rather than the European Communities as a whole. This further shows the importance of the economic unity over political cooperation aspirations. Together with the wording of the referendum question (and the direct mention of the Common Market) it suggests that the matter was regarded as a primarily economic agreement.

A close look at the concept of unity specifically in the speeches is quite indicative of changes during the years leading to the 1975 referendum. The summary below shows these conceptual shifts:

> political and economic unity of Western Europe (1960) → wider European unity (1963) (followed by reference to efforts to strengthen the European Free Trade Association) → greater unity of Europe (1965) (followed by efforts to strengthen the European Free Trade Association and to promote co-operation between the Association and the European Economic Community, and the establishment of a wider European market) → economic unity of Europe (1966) → European unity (1969 – last reference to unity).

Although the referendum turnout was 64%, the outcome did not resolve the issue once and for all; divisions on the topic have survived (Dinan). The challenging context of the British accession, i.e., having to accept the Common Agricultural Policy as a *fait accompli*, budgetary contributions, the Common Fisheries Policy, combined with deep divisions on the topic within the British political elites before and after the first referendum, resulted in a perpetual state of questioning the membership, its benefits, and the European Communities as a whole. This unease is present from the 1970s to this day and forms a context to the next UK-wide referendum on the topic of the European integration project and the British role within it.

The 23 June 2016 Referendum

The next UK-wide referendum on the country's membership in the (now) European Union did not take place until 2016. However, already in the maiden Queen's Speech of the Cameron coalition Government in May 2010, there is a clear nod to Eurosceptics: "My Government will introduce legislation to ensure that in future this Parliament and the British people have their say on any proposed transfer of powers to the European Union" (col. 6). This arrangement, the European Union Act 2011, put in place by a coalition Government of Conservatives (with a significant number of Eurosceptic MPs) and largely pro-EU Liberal Democrats, did not diminish voices criticizing the EU and questioning the benefits of British membership.

The UK's membership in the European Union is not specifically mentioned in the Queen's Speeches again until 4 June 2014. The Queen's Speech of 9 May 2012 makes a reference to the forthcoming EU enlargement only:[10] "My Government will seek the approval of Parliament on the anticipated accession of Croatia to the European Union" (col. 3). In the 2014 speech, the Queen states the Government's determination to "promote reform in the European Union, including a stronger role for member states and national parliaments. My Ministers will also champion efforts to secure a global agreement on climate change" (col. 4). The 2014 speech is an example of the EU item being bundled up with a policy development in another area, in this instance climate change. The wording is ambiguous as to whether the Government desired to champion these efforts within the EU, or whether this

[10] There was no Queen's Speech in 2011.

was an entirely independent topic. Both courses of action can be found elsewhere in Queen's Speeches.

In the 1970s mentions of the European Communities competed with international matters for the top place in the opening paragraphs of the Queen's Speeches (always behind state-visit announcements). In the 2014 speech, the European Union remark precedes the state visits, but both appear towards the very end of the speech. The state-visit announcements now conclude the main body of the Queen's Speech and are followed by a ritualized closing. The EU mention appears in penultimate position in the speech. This trend is apparent through the Queen's Speeches since 2010. Whereas in the 1960s and the first half of the 1970s mentions of the European Communities tended to be among the top ten items, in the early 2010s mentions of the European Union appear in the second half of the Queen's Speeches. The situation changes in 2017 and 2019 when European-Union-related items jump to the top of the speech (1-3 and 1-2 respectively) as Brexit dominates British politics.[11]

Following the May 2015 general election and the creation of a Conservative Government led by David Cameron, the European Union featured two thirds into the Queen's Speech delivered during the State Opening of Parliament ceremony on 27 May 2015:

> My Government will renegotiate the United Kingdom's relationship with the European Union and pursue reform of the European Union for the benefit of all member states. Alongside this, early legislation will be introduced to provide for an in/out referendum on membership of the European Union before the end of 2017. (col. 6)

It shared a message with the people that the United Kingdom would prefer to renegotiate its membership rather than leave the European Union. Furthermore, it not only promised to conduct this in the interest "of all member states" but also the British people, as they are given the opportunity to vote Leave or Remain. The Cameron Government mirrored many of the approaches taken by the Wilson Government in relation to the 1975 referendum. For example, they offered a specific timeline for the referendum and although both Governments formally supported Britain staying in, the Queen's Speeches attempted to balance the pro-European and Eurosceptic tensions on both occasions; instead, the principle of collective cabinet responsibility had been suspended

[11] There was no Queen's Speech in 2018.

(Scott; Cameron). The Cameron Government initiated negotiations with the European Union without delay and the outcomes were announced in February 2016.[12] However, the final 'deal,' although presented positively by the Government, was far from what the Conservative manifesto promised and – crucially – what the Eurosceptics within the party wanted.

On 18 May 2016, the Queen's Speech limited itself to a brief announcement, towards the end of the speech, that "[m]y Government will hold a referendum on membership of the European Union" (col. 3). With just over a month until the referendum and significant differences within the Government and the Conservative Party, the brevity and the neutral tone of the announcement are perhaps not surprising. Although the Government formally supported the Remain outcome, there were a number of key personalities within the Conservative Party opposed to continued membership and the Government, namely the Prime Minister, did not have sufficient control over the Party to enforce a clear and unified stance without risking an internal rift that could have destabilized the entire Government. The strength of the 'rebels' can be illustrated by the fact that the principle of cabinet collective responsibility had been suspended by the Prime Minister in relation to the referendum. The referendum date was set for 23 June 2016, just over a year after the general election and the pledge in the 2015 Queen's Speech. In the referendum, the voters were asked to answer the following question set out in the *European Union Referendum Act 2015* (Chapter 36): "Should the United Kingdom remain a member of the European Union or leave the European Union?" 72.2% of all eligible voters took part in the referendum and, as is well known, 51.9% to 48.1% voted in favour of the United Kingdom leaving the European Union (Electoral Commission).

A year later, on 21 June 2017, the topic of the European Union soared to the top of the Queen's Speech, prepared by a Conservative Government led by Theresa May. Arrangements to be put in place to enable Brexit dominate the entire speech:

---

[12] The Cameron Government managed to secure an agreement that the Treaties would stipulate that the UK was not obliged to partake in further political integration. The agreement also included a provision for national parliaments to be able to mount a challenge to EU legislative proposals. There was an acknowledgement that cooperation of Eurozone countries should not disadvantage non-participating EU states. Additional agreements were reached, amongst them the EU agreed to address the burden of regulation on competitiveness and the single market. (*Best of Both Worlds*; European Council).

> My Lords and Members of the House of Commons, my Government's priority is to secure the best possible deal as the country leaves the European Union. My Ministers are committed to working with Parliament, the devolved Administrations, business and others to build the widest possible consensus on the country's future outside the European Union.
>
> A Bill will be introduced to repeal the European Communities Act and provide certainty for individuals and businesses. This will be complemented by legislation to ensure that the United Kingdom makes a success of Brexit, establishing new national policies on immigration, international sanctions, nuclear safeguards, agriculture and fisheries.
>
> My Government will seek to maintain a deep and special partnership with European allies and to forge new trading relationships across the globe. New Bills on trade and customs will help to implement an independent trade policy, and support will be given to help British businesses export to markets around the world. (col. 5)

The reference to the *best possible deal* and to *business* and *markets* indicates, yet again, the interest in framing the country's future outside the EU in specific economic terms.[13] There is little reference to other possible connections with the EU in terms of values or common heritage. The framing of the relationship between Britain and the EU at this time balances a commitment to 'exiting' with maintaining, or attempting to maintain, involvement with the EU's financial character.[14]

A further mention of the referendum result appears towards the end of the same speech in a reference to one of the key elements discussed during the 1970s accession period: "My Ministers will ensure that the United Kingdom's leading role on the world stage is maintained and enhanced as it leaves the European Union" (*Queen's Speech, 21 June 2017* col. 6-7). The turn to the *world* may be read as Britain resuming a role that had been constrained within the context of the EU or even an indirect reference to the potential impact for the EU given Britain's self-perception of the strength of its historical ties with the Commonwealth and other Alliances.

---

[13] In the Queen's Speech, throughout the years, membership to the EU has been commodified in relation to economic policies. The EU is constructed as, primarily, an economic union. This is a consistent thread in the speeches of core politicians during the Brexit years (see Wodak, *Politics*).

[14] We have written elsewhere that the implications of associating the 'economy' with "essentialised common-sense inferences of monetary resources, fiscal policies and simplified representations of institutions and transactions between countries, banks and supranational bodies" (Angouri et al.) feeds into the micropolitics of fear and discourse of populism that we observe to be on the rise in Europe and elsewhere in the world.

Overall, Brexit has dominated British politics since the 2016 referendum. It remained at the top of the agenda during internal British discussions before the UK formally triggered Article 50 and exit negotiations, during the negotiation process with the European Union, as well as during a protracted process of considering deals reached by the UK Government. During the process, Britain saw another change of Prime Minister, this time in 2019 when Boris Johnson replaced Theresa May. It was following the December 2019 general election that the last Queen's Speech to date was delivered.

The 19 December 2019 Queen's Speech retained the focus on Brexit, as it opened the speech:

> My Lords and Members of the House of Commons, my Government's priority is to deliver the United Kingdom's departure from the European Union on 31 January. My Ministers will bring forward legislation to ensure the United Kingdom's exit on that date, and to make the most of the opportunities that this brings for all the people of the United Kingdom.
>
> Thereafter, my Ministers will seek a future relationship with the European Union based on a free trade agreement that benefits the whole of the United Kingdom. They will also begin trade negotiations with other leading global economies. (col. 7)

The future relationship with the EU is again defined in terms of trade but, unlike the speech in 2015, it states that the agreements should lie in the interest of "the whole of the United Kingdom." This continues the emphasis and interest in maintaining some relationship with the EU's financial policies but with a clearly inward-looking perspective.

The genre of the Queen's Speech will continue to balance form stability and content agility according to the needs it serves. As such it provides the academic community with a robust live corpus for capturing the nuances of a relationship which, so far, has been firmly positioned on economic priorities in an ideologically significant domain. Despite differences in the wider socio-political context, the speeches are consistent in that they frame the UK-EU relationship in economic terms and not on other grounds, such as shared European values. A linguistic analysis of the text has provided evidence of these patterns while a historical-political approach has provided the context within which this is significant.

A relationship between historical and linguistic approaches is not new for discourse analysts. The Discourse Historical Approach (DHA) in particular, developed over decades by Ruth Wodak and others, is exactly built on the need systematically to analyse the relationship between the historical trajectory of texts and contexts. This, however, often remains within the remit of critical-discourse analysts. An interdisciplinary reading such as the one we provide here equips us to access different layers of complex phenomena such as the UK-EU relationship. Although linguists could say more on the texts and political historians could say more on the context, it is the synergy of disciplines that has enabled us to show the robustness of patterns in micro (textual-linguistic) and macro (historico-political) terms. The historical-political approach here has been successful in contextualizing the speeches. The linguistic perspective has shown the genre's distinctive nature and symbolic role in perpetuating the delicate relationship between ceremonial speech and political manifesto; it is a performative act which can be carried out only by the Queen while the Government retains the power of authorship. More broadly the analysis adds to our understanding of performative acts and provides evidence of the significance and stability of economic ideologies that have been associated with EU membership diachronically and frame current pro- and anti-European discourses in the UK. The genre offers fertile ground for further investigation from this perspective. We have made a start in this essay and hope that further studies will follow.

Appendix 1: *Queen's Speech, 31 October 1961*

The QUEEN, being seated on the Throne, and attended by Her Officers of State (the Lords being in their robes), commanded the Gentleman Usher of the Black Rod, through the Lord Great Chamberlain, to let the Commons know, "It is Her Majesty's pleasure they attend Her immediately in this House."

Who being come, with their Speaker:

Her Majesty was pleased to speak as follows:

1,004 words – typically standardized length

My Lords and Members of the House of Commons

ritualized opening

'My Husband and I": standardized preface

"My Husband and I look forward to our coming journey to West Africa.

consistent reference to future visits

"It gives Me much pleasure that My Husband is to visit the countries of Latin America next year and that Princess Alexandra is on her way to South-East Asia and the Far East.

"I shall be glad to welcome President Sukarno of Indonesia on a State visit to this country.

standardized

"My Government will continue to

change of subject

give resolute support to the United Nations. They believe it to be essential for the future of the world that the authority of this organisation should be sustained, and that it should be enabled to carry out the tasks assigned to it under its Charter.

consistent reference to the support to the United Nations after change of subject

"The improvement of relations between East and West remains a primary object of My Government's policy, and they will continue to seek peaceful co-operation with all countries.

"My Government will seek, in conjunction with their allies, to achieve by negotiation a settlement of the Berlin question which will preserve the security and freedom of the people of West Berlin.

consistent reference to the North Atlantic Alliance early in the speech

"The North Atlantic Alliance is now more than ever essential for the continued safety of Europe and the world. My Government will continue to play their part in keeping it and the other regional pacts to which we belong strong and united. The close friendship between this country and the United States will be maintained and, in co-operation with My allies, My armed forces will continue to contribute to the prevention of war. Legislation will be proposed giving power to retain for an additional six months certain National Servicemen who are serving full-time, and to recall for a similar period National Servicemen who have a liability to part-time service. In addition, the reserve organisation of My army will be reviewed.

"My Government will continue to work for the success of the Geneva Conference on Laos and for the maintenance of peace in South-East Asia.

"Guided by the principles agreed upon between the Prime Ministers of the Commonwealth countries at their last Meeting, My Government will do their utmost to achieve general and complete disarmament under effective international control. In spite of the action of the Soviet Union in continuing to conduct nuclear tests on a massive scale in defiance of world opinion, My Government will persevere in their endeavour to promote an international agreement on the discontinuance of tests of nuclear weapons.

"A measure will be laid before you to amend the law to accord with the new status of South Africa.

"Legislation will be introduced to enable Southern Rhodesia to be granted a new Constitution.

"Bills will be introduced to provide for the independence of Tanganyika and of Uganda and for constitutional changes in the West

Indies.

'My Government" in initial subject position + active voice when topics are associated with the EU/EC

"My Government will make every effort to bring to a successful conclusion the negotiations which they are undertaking with the European Economic Community and will at all times maintain close consultation with the interests involved in the United Kingdom and with the other members of the Commonwealth and of the European Free Trade Association.

indicates action + effort

reference to other alliances precedes or follows reference to Europe

'Members of the House of Commons

"Estimates for the public services will be laid before you in due course.

standardized phrase in the middle or towards the end of the speech

"My Lords and Members of the House of Commons

'My Ministers" in subject position when there is reference to "policies" (opposite) or "expenditure" (two paragraphs below)

"My Ministers will continue to direct their policies towards maintaining the stability of sterling. They will seek to strengthen the balance of payments by the measures already announced, including especially the vigorous promotion of exports. Legislation will be laid before you to raise the limits of the liabilities to be assumed by the Export Credits Guarantee Department.

"My Ministers will continue to seek the co-operation of both sides of industry in the better co-ordination of the national effort with a view to promoting faster economic growth, while maintaining stability in prices and a high and stable level of employment.

"They will seek to keep public expenditure within limits justified by the national resources. Continuing efforts will be made to secure a better relationship between increases in incomes and in national productivity.

"My Government will introduce a Bill to give effect to the proposals already submitted to you for the re-organisation of the undertakings under the control of the British Transport Commission.

"A Bill will be introduced to ensure the orderly development of privately-owned industrial pipelines.

"Proposals will be laid before you to amend the law relating to teachers' salaries, school-leaving dates and the award of grants to students.

"My Government are resolved to maintain a stable, efficient and prosperous agricultural industry. They will lay before you a Bill to implement their proposals on the Report by the Committee on the Fishing Industry and on drift netting for salmon.

"Legislation will be proposed to amend local government financial arrangements in Scotland; to secure better distribution of Scottish housing subsidies and amend the law relating to housing in other respects: and to make certain amendments in the licensing law of Scotland.

"Proposals will be laid before you for improving the machinery for administering criminal justice with a view to securing greater expedition and efficiency.

"Legislation will be introduced to control the immigration to the United Kingdom of British subjects from other parts of the Commonwealth, and to give powers for the expulsion of immigrants convicted of criminal offences.

"A Bill will be introduced to improve the provision for supplementing workmen's compensation and to make certain alterations in the administration of the schemes for family allowances, national insurance and industrial injuries.

"Plans will be laid before you for the development of the hospitals over the next decade, within the framework of the National Health Service as a whole.

"Authority will be sought for the establishment of national training councils for health visitors and social workers.

invitation to take a decision	"You will be invited to approve a measure designed to promote greater safety on the roads.	
	"Other measures will be laid before you in due course.	*standardized phrase preceding closing*
	"My Lords and Members of the House of Commons	
	"I pray that the blessing of Almighty God may rest upon your counsels."	*ritualized closing*

References

Angouri, Jo. *Culture, Discourse, and the Workplace*. Routledge, 2018.

Angouri, Jo, et al. "From Grexit to Brexit and Back: Mediatisation of Economy and the Politics of Fear in the Twitter Discourses of the Prime Ministers of Greece and the UK." *Language@Internet*, vol. 16, 2018, www.languageatinternet.org/articles/2018si/angouri.

Angouri, Jo, and Meredith Marra. "Corporate Meeting as Genre: A Study of the Role of the Chair in Corporate Meeting Talk." *Text & Talk*, vol. 30, no. 6, 2010, pp. 615-36. doi:10.1515/text.2010.030.

Angouri, Jo, and Ruth Wodak. "They Became Big in the Shadow of the Crisis: The Greek Success Story and the Rise of the Far Right." *Discourse & Society*, vol. 25, no. 4, 2014, pp. 540-65. doi.org/10.1177/0957926514536955.

The Best of Both Worlds: The United Kingdom's Special Status in a Reformed European Union. UK Government, Foreign and Commonwealth Office, Feb. 2016, assets.publishing.service.gov.uk/government/uploads/system/uploads/attachment_data/file/502291/54284_EU_Series_No1_Web_Accessible.pdf.

Bhatia, Vijay. *Worlds of Written Discourse: A Genre-Based View*. Continuum, 2004.

Cameron, David. "EU Referendum." Letter to Ministerial Colleagues, 11 Jan. 2016, assets.publishing.service.gov.uk/government/uploads/system/uploads/attachment_data/file/491181/EU_Referendum_PM_Minute.pdf.

Churchill, Winston. *Address Given by Winston Churchill (Zurich, 19 September 1946)*. Council of Europe, 6 May 2014, www.cvce.eu/obj/address_given_by_winston_churchill_zurich_19_september_1946-en-7dc5a4cc-4453-4c2a-b130-b534b7d76ebd.html.

Declaration on European Identity (Copenhagen, 14 December 1973). European Union, 18 Dec. 2013, www.cvce.eu/content/publication/1999/1/1/02798dc9-9c69-4b7d-b2c9-f03a8db7da32/publishable_en.pdf.

Dinan, Desmond. "A Special Case: The United Kingdom and the European Union." *Origins and Evolution of the European Union*, edited by Desmond Dinan, 2nd ed., Oxford UP, 2017, pp. 305-26. doi:10.1093/hepl/9780199570829.003.0014.

The Electoral Commission. "Results and Turnout at the EU Referendum." 25 Sept. 2019, www.electoralcommission.org.uk/who-we-are-and-what-we-do/elections-and-referendums/past-elections-and-referendums/eu-referendum/results-and-turnout-eu-referendum.

European Communities Act 1972. UK Government, The Stationery Office, c. 68, www.legislation.gov.uk/ukpga/1972/68/contents.

European Council. General Secretariat of the Council. *European Council Meeting (18 and 19 February 2016) – Conclusions*. 19 Feb. 2016, www.consilium.europa.eu/media/21787/0216-euco-conclusions.pdf.

European Union Referendum Act 2015. UK Government, The Stationery Office, c. 36, www.legislation.gov.uk/ukpga/2015/36/contents.

George, Stephen. *An Awkward Partner: Britain in the European Community*. Oxford UP, 1998.

Howarth, David. *Discourse*. Open UP, 2000.

Jennings, Will, and Peter John. "The Dynamics of Political Attention: Public Opinion and the Queen's Speech in the United Kingdom." *American Journal of Political Science*, vol. 53, no. 4, 2009, pp. 838-54. doi:10.1111/j.1540-5907.2009.00404.x.

John, Peter, and Will Jennings. "Punctuations and Turning Points in British Politics: The Policy Agenda of the Queen's Speech, 1940-2005." *British Journal of Political Science*, vol. 40, no. 3, 2010, pp. 561-86. doi:10.1017/S0007123409990068.

"Living Heritage: Offices & Ceremonies." UK Parliament, www. parliament.uk/about/living-heritage/evolutionofparliament/parliamentwork/offices-and-ceremonies/overview/state-opening/.

"Living Heritage: Parliament & Europe." UK Parliament, April 2013, www.parliament.uk/about/living-heritage/evolutionofparliament/legislativescrutiny/parliament-and-europe/overview/britain-and-eec-to-single-european-act/.

Miller, Vaughne. *The 1974-75 UK Renegotiation of EEC Membership and Referendum*. House of Commons Library, Briefing Paper no. 7253, 13 July 2015, researchbriefings.files.parliament.uk/documents/CBP-7253/CBP-7253.pdf.

Milward, Alan. *The United Kingdom and the European Community. Vol. I: The Rise and Fall of a National Strategy, 1945-1963*. Frank Cass, 2003.

"Prorogation." UK Parliament, www.parliament.uk/about/how/occasions/prorogation/.

Prorogation: Her Majesty's Speech, 24 October 1963. UK Parliament, House of Lords, The Stationery Office, Hansard Online, vol. 252, col. 1295-99, hansard.parliament.uk/Lords/1963-10-24/debates/6cc606f3-c595-48b1-bf29-5eecb79ce6c9/ProrogationHerMajestySSpeech.

The Queen's Speech, 1 November 1960. UK Parliament, House of Lords, The Stationery Office, Hansard Online, vol. 226, col. 1-5, hansard.parliament.uk/Lords/1960-11-01/debates/36424013-c33f-420a-8dbb-fe0525c124fd/LordsChamber.

—, *31 October 1961*. UK Parliament, House of Lords, The Stationery Office, Hansard Online, vol. 235, col. 1-5, hansard.parliament.uk/Lords/1961-10-31/debates/90f98e26-134f-4cce-94b7-28b9f8d5313e/LordsChamber.

—, *30 October 1962*. UK Parliament, House of Lords, The Stationery Office, Hansard Online, vol. 244, col. 1-5, hansard.parliament.uk/Lords/1962-10-30/debates/303b09ef-aa61-478c-951b-2069d6b522ea/LordsChamber.

—, *3 November 1964*. UK Parliament, House of Lords, The Stationery Office, Hansard Online, vol. 261, col. 9-13, hansard.parliament.uk/Lords/1964-11-03/debates/a63d8d5c-7161-4d99-9379-d78faefdc616/LordsChamber.

—, *9 November 1965*. UK Parliament, House of Lords, The Stationery Office, Hansard Online, vol. 270, col. 1-5, hansard.parliament.uk/Lords/1965-11-09/debates/3f7e2c7e-f52e-4081-9ef9-f30d2fb7e728/TheQueenSSpeech.

—, *21 April 1966*. UK Parliament, House of Lords, The Stationery Office, Hansard Online, vol. 274, col. 9-13, hansard.parliament.uk/Lords/1966-04-21/debates/9d29e354-7804-4433-9f58-8bafe497213d/TheQueenSSpeech.

—, *31 October 1967*. UK Parliament, House of Lords, The Stationery Office, Hansard Online, vol. 286, col. 1-5, hansard.parliament.uk/Lords/1967-10-31/debates/a2fd72a3-392d-4d6f-8add-6423e4c4191c/TheQueenSSpeech.

—, *30 October 1968*. UK Parliament, House of Lords, The Stationery Office, Hansard Online, vol. 297, col. 1-5, hansard.parliament.uk/Lords/1968-10-30/debates/0aede8aa-b84d-4ab8-a693-0bb9271ebbc1/TheQueenSSpeech.

—, *28 October 1969*. UK Parliament, House of Commons, The Stationery Office, Hansard Online, vol. 790, col. 4-7, hansard.parliament.uk/Commons/1969-10-28/debates/becde04b-0c83-4258-bf19-e2b64ef8e475/QueenSSpeech.

—, *2 July 1970*. UK Parliament, House of Lords, The Stationery Office, Hansard Online, vol. 311, col. 9-12, hansard.parliament.uk/Lords/1970-07-02/debates/14bdc69b-c8aa-4680-a49e-63ea7d79e870/TheQueenSSpeech.

—, *2 November 1971*. UK Parliament, House of Lords, The Stationery Office, Hansard Online, vol. 325, col. 1-4, hansard.parliament.uk/Lords/1971-11-02/debates/ac8d3e45-2027-4ce1-a1c6-3ab0f3187a22/TheQueenSSpeech.

——, *31 October 1972*. UK Parliament, House of Lords, The Stationery Office, Hansard Online, vol. 336, col. 1-5, hansard.parliament.uk/Lords/1972-10-31/debates/da0f77cd-6275-460d-8b17-40a0d347d729/TheQueenSSpeech.

——, *30 October 1973*. UK Parliament, House of Lords, The Stationery Office, Hansard Online, vol. 346, col. 1-5, hansard.parliament.uk/Lords/1973-10-30/debates/51ba7806-8fad-4c5c-bc72-eddbb2d15a73/TheQueenSSpeech.

——, *12 March 1974*. UK Parliament, House of Lords, The Stationery Office, Hansard Online, vol. 350, col. 7-12, api.parliament.uk/historic-hansard/lords/1974/mar/12/the-queens-speech.

——, *29 October 1974*. UK Parliament, House of Lords, The Stationery Office, Hansard Online, vol. 354, col. 7-11, hansard.parliament.uk/Lords/1974-10-29/debates/e5bc02c3-1825-46fc-99f3-24d167ef1372/TheQueenSSpeech.

——, *19 November 1975*. UK Parliament, House of Lords, The Stationery Office, Hansard Online, vol. 366, col. 1-7, hansard.parliament.uk/Lords/1975-11-19/debates/8a6dd8e7-a49d-466f-aceb-48ce7c3f69cf/TheQueenSSpeech.

——, *25 May 2010*. UK Parliament, House of Lords, The Stationery Office, Hansard Online, vol. 719, col. 5-7, hansard.parliament.uk/Lords/2010-05-25/debates/1005255000153/QueenSSpeech.

——, *9 May 2012*. UK Parliament, House of Lords, The Stationery Office, Hansard Online, vol. 737, col. 1-3, hansard.parliament.uk/Lords/2012-05-09/debates/6b477cad-edb7-418c-8d55-5178c6f411ff/LordsChamber.

——, *8 May 2013*. UK Parliament, House of Lords, The Stationery Office, Hansard Online, vol. 745, col. 1-3, hansard.parliament.uk/Lords/2013-05-08/debates/f3cb7026-2d90-4331-8672-495a7fd85e1b/LordsChamber.

——, *4 June 2014*. UK Parliament, House of Lords, The Stationery Office, Hansard Online, vol. 754, col. 1-4, hansard.parliament.uk/Lords/2014-06-04/debates/14060430000173/Queen%E2%80%99SSpeech.

——, *27 May 2015*. UK Parliament, House of Lords, The Stationery Office, Hansard Online, vol. 762, col. 5-7, han-

sard.parliament.uk/Lords/2015-05-27/debates/15052714000178/Queen%E2%80%99SSpeech.
——, *18 May 2016*. UK Parliament, House of Lords, The Stationery Office, Hansard Online, vol. 773, col. 1-4, hansard.parliament.uk/Lords/2016-05-18/debates/E021E4C9-7D94-4A00-9A84-8BC81A8221A1/QueenSSpeech.
——, *21 June 2017*. UK Parliament, House of Lords, The Stationery Office, Hansard Online, vol. 783, col. 5-7, hansard.parliament.uk/Lords/2017-06-21/debates/b9469547-092d-4d80-8eaa-bc715993dd5d/LordsChamber.
——, *19 December 2019*. UK Parliament, House of Lords, The Stationery Office, Hansard Online, vol. 801, col. 7-9, hansard.parliament.uk/Lords/2019-12-19/debates/0ef0ff35-f8b8-4de5-bb2f-e35347eaee7f/LordsChamber.
The Referendum (Welsh Forms) Order 1975. UK Government, The Stationery Office, no. 841, www.legislation.gov.uk/uksi/1975/841/pdfs/uksi_19750841_en.pdf.
"Referendums Held in the UK." UK Parliament, www.parliament.uk/get-involved/elections/referendums-held-in-the-uk/.
Scott, Edward. *Ministerial Collective Responsibility and Agreement to Differ: Recent Developments*. House of Lords Library Note, LLN 2016/012, 4 March 2016, researchbriefings.files.parliament.uk/documents/LLN-2016-0012/LLN-2016-0012.pdf
"State Opening of Parliament." UK Parliament, www.parliament.uk/about/how/occasions/stateopening/.
Swales, John. *Research Genres: Explorations and Applications*. Cambridge UP, 2004.
Wall, Stephen. *The Official History of Britain and the European Community, Vol. II: From Rejection to Referendum, 1963-1975*. Routledge, 2012.
Wodak, Ruth. *Discursive Construction of National Identity*. Edinburgh UP, 2009.
——. *The Politics of Fear: What Right-Wing Populist Discourses Mean*. Sage, 2015.
Young, Hugo. *This Blessed Plot: Britain and Europe from Churchill to Blair*. Macmillan, 1998.

"The United Kingdom is a different state": Conservative MPs' Appeals to Britishness before the EU Referendum

Nora Wenzl

This essay presents findings from a corpus-assisted critical discourse analysis of Conservative discourses on Brexit. Building on Stephen Reicher and Nick Hopkins's argument that political actors can mobilize voters to act by creating a vision of the nation and the national population that makes this "action seem self-evidently in their interests" (48), this study compares Conservative Leave and Remain discourses with regard to their constructions of Britishness. To this purpose, a corpus of Hansard transcripts of oral parliamentary proceedings in the House of Commons between May 2015 and June 2016 is examined.[1] The focus lies on occurrences of the phrases "we are" and "Britain/the UK/the United Kingdom is" involved in relational processes (Halliday and Matthiessen 210-48) that characterize or identify the nation. The study shows that both sides of the debate mobilize inherently Eurosceptic narratives in their depiction of Britishness, although the Remain side does so to a lesser degree. The findings suggest that, while Leave successfully constructed a vision of Britishness that was incompatible with EU membership, the Remain side did not construct a British identity that encouraged voters to opt for Remain.

Keywords: Brexit, British identity, corpus linguistics, Critical Discourse Studies, national identity, parliamentary discourse, transitivity

---

[1] The Hansard transcripts constitute the official representation of parliamentary proceedings and are therefore an important channel of communication between MPs and the British public. While they are slightly edited (Slembrouck; Mollin), the changes made are mostly pragmatic in nature and therefore unlikely to affect my findings.

Brexit and Beyond: Nation and Identity. SPELL: Swiss Papers in English Language and Literature 39, edited by Daniela Keller and Ina Habermann, Narr, 2020, pp. 99-120.

1 Introduction

While political commentators and scholars have identified a number of partial explanations for the outcome of the UK's EU referendum, from demographic factors (Goodwin and Heath) to dissatisfaction with the political status quo (Bourne), the only consensus seems to be that a plethora of reasons led to the referendum result. Based on Stephen Reicher and Nick Hopkins's argument that political actors strategically use identity constructions to mobilize voters, this essay examines how appeals to Britishness were used by Conservative Leave and Remain speakers in parliamentary proceedings.

To this purpose, I perform a corpus-assisted critical discourse study (Baker; Baker et al.) of Hansard transcripts covering the period between the 2015 General Election and the 2016 referendum. I focus on Conservative Members of Parliament as they were allowed to support either side of the debate, thus enabling me to compare Remain and Leave discourses of speakers with otherwise similar ideological backgrounds. Moreover, the relationship between English, Welsh, Scottish, Irish, and British identities is complex, with Britishness being an Anglo-centric construct (Colley). Thus, examining Britishness in the utterances of an overwhelmingly English party has the advantage of reduced tension with individual national identities.

In what follows, I outline the conceptual framework of Critical Discourse Studies (CDS) and clarify the connections between discourse, identity, the nation, and politics. Section 3 discusses the method, data, and tools of analysis. The analysis presented in section 4 centres on concordance lines for "we are" and "Britain/the UK/the United Kingdom is." It examines all occurrences where the British in-group is involved in what M. A. K. Halliday and Christian Matthiessen (210-48) term "relational processes," that is, where the in-group is identified or characterized. Following Reicher and Hopkins's logic, politicians campaigning for Leave should have constructed a vision of Britishness as fundamentally incompatible with membership, while the Remain side should have done the opposite. My findings show, however, that this was only partly the case. While the Leave side mobilized historical narratives of Britishness as exceptional and incompatible with the EU, Remain employed similar narratives in its conceptions of British identity. I therefore conclude that the Remain side's vision of Britishness was at odds with continued EU membership and therefore, by extension, also with its goal to motivate voters to ensure the country remained a member.

2 Conceptual Framework

Critical Discourse Studies (CDS) sees 'discourse' as "language in speech and writing" and as a "social practice" (Fairclough and Wodak 258). Due to the dialectical relationship between discourse and its contexts of production, discourse is both influenced by the situational, institutional, and social contexts that frame it and has the power to influence non-linguistic and linguistic social practices in those contexts. Discourse can thus reproduce and transform a societal status quo. Taking an explicitly 'critical' stance indicates a commitment to exposing power structures and ideologies underlying discourse while also signalling an awareness of the complex relationships between the investigated data, its context of production and reception as well as society in general (Wodak 9). Critical analysts therefore aim to embed the discussion of text-immanent features in the wider "social and political relations, processes and circumstances" in which a discourse is embedded (Reisigl and Wodak 33). This essay, therefore, looks beyond the "text-internal co-text" of the investigated terms and incorporates the "broader socio-political and historical contexts" (41) of the UK's self-conception and relationship to the EU into the analysis wherever pertinent.

2.1 National Identity and Discourse

In line with previous studies on identities and discourse (Hall and Du Gay; Koller; Mole; Wodak et al.), this essay takes a constructivist approach which states that identities are constructed, relational, and context-dependent and individuals may foreground different aspects of an identity at different times. The nation, in turn, is defined as "imagined community" (Anderson): a mental construct that exists to the extent and in the form that individuals believe in and identify with (Wodak et al. 22). Discourse, then, is the element connecting the complex of beliefs about the nation with the believing individuals. This means that the nation "is constructed and conveyed in discourse, predominantly in narratives of national culture" (22).

The importance of (political) appeals to national identities becomes clear when viewing them through the lens of Social Identity Theory (Tajfel; Tajfel and Turner). According to SIT, individuals derive part of their self-image from their membership in groups and each group entails specific values and norms. Additionally, individuals strive to preserve or improve their own sense of self-worth (Islam 1781), which they do by endowing their in-group with positive evaluations (e.g., by favourable comparison to an Other), while also ensuring that their actions benefit it (Tajfel).

Appeals to national identity, therefore, are potent political motivators because identification with a group provides individuals with a set of values that indicate a group's goals, and individuals wish to be able to positively evaluate their group. Moreover, *different* definitions of a nation's identity, or the foregrounding of different national characteristics, will result in *different* goals being in the nation's interests. Reicher and Hopkins thus conclude that "the way to get people to act in a given way is by providing a definition of the self that makes such action seem self-evidently in their interests" (48). They note, however, that those constructions are more successful that build on already existing and widely disseminated narratives of the nation.

Crucially, these appeals to national identities are not the exclusive domain of fringe parties or 'extreme' political groups, but are instead ubiquitous in everyday (political) discourse. The use of deictic expressions (e.g., 'us' vs. 'them') or appeals to 'the people' can be seen, Michael Billig argues, as instances of "banal nationalism" which subtly and implicitly call upon and reinforce specific interpretations of a given national identity in everyday discourse.

3 Method and Data

To base the qualitative analysis in empirical evidence, I employ methods from corpus-assisted Critical Discourse Studies (Baker; Baker et al.) and combine a quantitative overview of large amounts of data with a qualitative discussion of pertinent or frequent examples. Moreover, aspects of transitivity analysis (Halliday and Matthiessen 230-78), a method often used in CDS, are employed in the analysis. This essay is based on a corpus of Hansard transcripts of oral parliamentary proceedings in the House of Commons, spanning the period from 7 May 2015 – the first relevant sitting after the 2015 General Election – to 15 June 2016 – the last relevant sitting before the referendum on 23 June 2016. The 'relevance' of proceedings was established by referring to the title of the transcript, with all titles referring explicitly to the UK-EU relationship being chosen. Transcripts were downloaded from the Hansard webpage as text files and mark-up was performed in Notepad++ (Ho). Sub-corpora consisting of all utterances by members of each party were extracted using the Multilingual Corpus Toolkit

(Piao). The Conservative sub-corpus was further marked up with information regarding each speaker's stance on Brexit,[2] and the Conservative Remain and Leave corpora were created. Corpus analysis was conducted using AntConc (Anthony).

The Brexit corpus comprises 1,104,324 tokens (running words after mark-up), with the Conservative sub-corpus accounting for 62% (674,413 tokens). Of these, the Conservative Remain corpus makes up 56% (379,939 tokens) and the Leave corpus accounts for 44% (293,241 tokens).

The investigation of transitivity aims to discover, in crude terms, "who did what to whom and in what circumstances" (Thompson 32). While Halliday and Matthiessen distinguish between six process types (169-305), the focus of this essay is on relational processes, as these are of particular relevance to the question of how Britishness is portrayed in the data. Relational processes "serve to characterize and to identify" (259) an actor or thing by assigning either class membership or identity to it. There are three subtypes – intensive, possessive, and circumstantial – all three of which may be realized as *attributive* – assigning a category – or *identifying* – assigning a unique identity. Table 1 provides an overview.

	(i) Attributive "a is an attribute of X"	(ii) Identifying "a is the identity of x"
(1) Intensive "x is a"	Sarah is wise	Sarah is the leader; the leader is Sarah
(2) Possessive "x has a"	Peter has a piano	the piano is Peter's; Peter's is the piano
(3) Circumstantial "x is at a"	the fair is on a Tues-day	tomorrow is the 10th; the 10th is tomorrow

Table 1. Overview of relational processes (Halliday and Matthiessen 265)

Most notable in the context of my data are non-reversible intensive attributive relational processes realized with an adjective, such as "we are not powerless" or a noun, as in "we are a leading player in climate change diplomacy." Additionally, there are some notable occurrences of reversible intensive identifying relational processes, which are realized

[2] Speaker stance on the EU as of 22 June 2016 was taken from the BBC's databank (BBC).

with a definite article and noun, such as "we are the fifth largest economy in the world." Lastly, attributive circumstantial relational processes, realized with a prepositional or adverbial phrase, as in "Britain is outside the EU," also occurred several times. The focus of this essay will thus be on these three sub-categories of relational processes. Since the number of possessive relational processes in the data is negligible, these will not be discussed here.

For the analysis, concordance lines were generated for the phrases "Britain/the UK/the United Kingdom is" and "we are." Regarding the latter, only concordance lines where the pronoun was interpreted to stand for the entire UK or the British population were analysed.[3] In a last step, all concordance lines where the search queries were part of future constructions were excluded. Table 2 shows the number of concordance lines taken into consideration for each search query, as well as the final number analysed once future constructions were excluded.

	Leave	**Remain**
we are	375	678
Britain is	13	46
the UK is	16	35
the United Kingdom is	6	17
	407	776
future constructions	-37	-83
concordance lines analysed	**370**	**693**

Table 2. Number of concordance lines generated and analysed

[3] The referential range was determined, in line with Jane Mulderrig's similar study, by taking into account textual anchors, while excluding those instances where logic dictated that the referential range did not include the wider public. See also Wenzl ("This").

4 Analysis

4.1 Quantitative Analysis of Process Types

For the analysis, a five-word span to the right of the search queries was initially considered, but extended to ten words where necessary. Of the 693 concordance lines for Remain, 364, or 53%, depicted the country as involved in a relational process, while the number was slightly lower for the Leave side with 181 lines, or 49%. While the dominance of relational processes is partially explained by the nature of the search queries – this type of process is frequently realized with a form of 'to be' – the number also suggests that characterizations and identifications of the nation played an important role in the run-up to the EU referendum.

Regarding the Leave data, 65% of relational processes were intensive attributive, realized with adjectives or nouns. In contrast, only 11% of relational processes could be categorized as intensive identifying. Approximately a quarter of analysed Leave concordances for relational processes was accounted for by attributive circumstantial processes. With 71%, the Remain data contains more intensive attributive relational processes, but only 7% of the remaining relational processes are made up by intensive identifying ones. Lastly, slightly less than one fifth of relational processes are categorized as attributive circumstantial. In other words, the dominance of intensive attributive relational processes shows that Leave, and to an even greater extent Remain, exhibit a preoccupation with classifying the in-group by describing what sort of country the United Kingdom is with a noun phrase or ascribing characteristics to the we-group with adjectives. The smaller numbers of intensive identifying processes, which are all realized with noun phrases, by contrast, suggest that there is less interest in ascribing a unique and fixed identity to the nation, although Leave does this slightly more than Remain. Additionally, the sizeable number of circumstantial relational processes reveals that both sides characterize the nation or its population by – usually metaphorically – positioning them in spatial or temporal terms. Table 3 presents an overview of the occurrences of the various sub-types of relational processes. The following section will now move on to a discussion of pertinent topics in the data. In the following sections, an analysis of dominant themes in the Leave and Remain data is presented, beginning with a quantitative overview and moving on to a qualitative analysis. Due to the negligible number of possessive processes, they will be disregarded.

		Leave	Remain
intensive	attributive	68 (adjective) 49 (noun)	180 (adjective) 79 (noun)
	identifying	20 (noun)	28 (noun)
circumstantial	attributive	41	69
	identifying	0	0
possessive	attributive	3	8
	identifying	0	0
		181	364

Table 3. Number of concordance lines of relational process sub-types

4.2 Qualitative Analysis of Dominant Themes

When considering how the nation is characterized and described in the Leave and Remain data, three general themes emerge. Firstly, 43% of all characterizations, both in the Leave and in the Remain data, portray Britain in terms of its strengths and positive attributes. In contrast, only 9% of Leave data and 7% of Remain data highlight British weaknesses. While the numbers and concrete contents of these two categories do diverge slightly between the two sides of the debate, the third topic shows the most notable differences. This third topic, which accounts for 50% and 44% of analysed data in the Leave and Remain corpus, respectively, defines Britishness in terms of its international connections and memberships. The remaining 6% of Leave and 3% of Remain data are categorized as "other." It must be noted that the category of "connections," unlike the other two, is neither clearly positive nor negative. Instead it contains data that portrays the nation as strong and connection as positive, as well as utterances that see connections as burdensome or even threatening and the nation as powerless. The decision not to incorporate these data points into the other two categories was made due to the centrality of the topic of EU membership and other international connections to the topic under investigation. Moreover, by coincidence more than by design, it is this category that displays some of the most pertinent differences between the two sides. Tables 4 and 5 present a quantitative overview of the occurrence of topics and sub-topics for Leave and Remain. The following will now discuss relevant patterns for the two dominant topics – British strengths and connections – in some detail, beginning with Leave. For reasons of scope and clarity, the analysis will be a synthesis of themes in all relational processes according to topic.

	strengths						**weak-nesses**		**connection**					**oth er**
total occur-rence of topic[4]	**77**						**16**		**90**					**10**
realized with:	self-confidence	determination	fortune	leadership	economy	progress	worry	misfortune	memberships	freedom/opt-outs/disconnect	better off in	entrapment	connection (gen-eral)	
adjec-tives	8	14	3	0	0	0	5	0	0	4	8	28	11	2
nouns	4	0	0	13	23	0	2	0	17	5	0	0	0	5
prepo-sitions	0	0	0	2	1	9	9	0	9	8	0	0	0	3
	12	14	3	15	24	9	16	0	26	17	8	28	11	10

Table 4. LEAVE – topics and sub-topics

[4] Note that this number exceeds the number of concordances because of occurrences with more than one adjective within the five-word span of the node.

	strengths						weak-nesses		connection					oth-er
total occur-rence of topic	157						26		161					12
realized with:	self-confidence	determination	fortune	leadership	economy	progress	worry	misfortune	memberships	freedom/opt-outs/disconnect	better off in	entrapment	connection (gen-eral)	
adjec-tives	35	33	8	0	0	0	14	0	0	12	46	7	18	7
nouns	5	0	0	31	20	0	3	0	19	19	0	0	7	3
prepo-sitions	0	0	0	9	0	16	0	9	10	16	0	0	7	2
	40	33	8	40	20	16	17	9	29	47	46	7	32	12

Table 5. REMAIN – topics and sub-topics

4.2.1 Leave

4.2.1.1 Britain as Exceptional

Of the concordance lines investigated for Leave, 43% highlight Britain's strengths. Thus, analysis of adjectives shows that the country is described, amongst others, as "strong," "able," "fair," "bold," and "proud." The noun phrases used to describe the nation grant even more insight, as they show a preoccupation with British leadership as well as the nation's economic power. Regarding the latter, speakers consistently highlight the nation's economic strength to underline the argument that the UK cannot only prosper outside the EU, but that it will also have no difficulty in negotiating trade deals with other nations. Thus, the country is defined in terms of its ability to acquire capital and export goods, being described as "a trading nation," "a prosperous country," or "a thoroughly investable economy." Moreover, Britain's position as "the fifth largest economy in the world" receives particular stress, and is mentioned nine times. The relative size of Britain's economy is referenced as inspiring optimism in the respective speakers, who cite it as a reason why other nations should be more than willing to trade with the UK post-Brexit. This argument is also expressed by referring to the UK's status as a "customer" [3] to other European nations, thereby implying that those nations exporting to the UK need the country more than it does them.[5] There is thus an underlying sense of the supremacy of Britain in these utterances that mobilizes traditional conceptions of the British as trading nation (Colley). Although never voiced explicitly, celebrations of British commerce as the key to prosperity post-Brexit play with visions of the country returning to its former glory during the days of Empire.

With regard to leadership, elements of British exceptionalism emerge as the nation is positioned as superior to the rest of the world by highlighting that it is "a key player" or "Europe's leader." Moreover, descriptions of the country as "a great country" and "a big hitter in its own right," "a self-confident, successful nation," and a "healthier democracy" now than it used to be play into what is termed the "Whig" interpretation of British history.[6] This long-established Anglo-centric narrative celebrates the country as being on an inexorable path towards greater enlightenment, liberty, and democracy and constructs Britain in contrast to mainland Europe (Spiering 54). Reiterations of these historical and widely disseminated narratives thus always entail implicit conceptions of the UK as un-European.

The Whiggish idea of a nation on the constant path to progress becomes even more evident when regarding circumstantial relational processes. Nine times, the nation is (metaphorically) positioned as being either at the beginning or in the midst of a process of change and transformation. Much as in the example above, the idea is expressed – explicitly and implicitly – that circumstances have changed since the EU began, and once-beneficial aspects of membership are no longer necessary in the "new" or "different world" in which the UK finds itself now.

Lastly, depictions of the we-group as "determined" [2] to resist the EU and "not prepared" to adhere to (supposedly) unjust EU rulings portray the British as rebellious and just. Although this topic only occurs fourteen times in the data examined here, analysis of the portrayal of "the [British] people" (Wenzl, "There") has shown that drawing on associations of Britishness with justice and rebellion was a potent mobili-

---

[5] Numbers in square brackets indicate more than one occurrence. No numbers are given for single occurrences.

[6] See also Matthias D. Berger's contribution in this volume.

zation tool employed by Leave speakers. Menno Spiering highlights the long tradition of this narrative by arguing that the British island nation story entails the idea that islanders must defend their separate status and freedom with particular ferocity (30-43). Reiterating narratives of British rebellion against the yoke of European tyranny thus allows speakers to mobilize not only a narrative of positive self-portrayal for the population, but also to offer a vote for Brexit as the 'natural' enactment of traits ascribed to the British.

4.2.1.2 Britain as Connected but Trapped

The category of "connections," which makes up half of all Leave data analysed, is also the most fuzzy, as it contains representations of connections both as strengthening and as threatening the nation. Since a key argument against EU membership brought forth by Leave was the fact that the UK is sufficiently important on the world stage to make the EU unnecessary for the country's success, there are frequent enumerations of the inter- and supra-national organizations that the UK is a member of in the data. Thus, Britain is described as being "a member of many prominent international organisations" and indeed, "a member of more international organisations [...] than any other country." On two occasions, a wealth of organizations is listed to bolster the argument of the country's international influence. In these cases, membership of supranational organizations is presented as strengthening the country. Additionally, the emphasis on the sheer number of organizations and the explicit mentions of the fact that the UK is member of an especially large number of them also serve to highlight the country's exceptional role on the world stage. Despite the Remain side's argument that the EU lends influence to the UK, it is suggested, the country is, in fact, influential and connected *without* the EU.

When EU membership is mentioned in the Leave data, it is often connected to restrictions imposed by the EU. The argument is made that, far from giving the UK influence in the world's largest trading bloc, EU membership is in fact meaningless as the country only represents "one vote out of 28" on European issues. On another occasion, the Remain argument that membership of the largest single market in the world is beneficial to the UK is refuted by arguing that the EU is, in fact, only this powerful *because* Britain is a member. According to this logic, it is the UK that endows the rest of Europe with trading power, and not the other way around, reinforcing the narrative of the British trading nation.

A striking aspect of the Leave side's depiction of British connections surfaces in relation to the adjectives the nation is associated with. While there are three occurrences where connection is described in positive terms, with the nation positioned as "not alone," "connected," and "engaged" in co-operation, a staggering twenty-eight adjectives depict connection to the EU with adjectives that have very negative connotations. Thus, words of entrapment such as "locked into" [2], "barred," "bound," "captive," or "trapped" portray the nation as powerless in the face of the EU (Wenzl, "This") while simultaneously mobilizing the common metaphor of the EU as a prison that has also been traced in right-wing newspaper discourses of the EU (Islentyeva).

Lastly, 8% of the data in the "connections" category for Leave shows the country as *dis*connected or free by mentioning the UK's opt-outs from Schengen, the Euro, and ever-closer union. Since these three projects are central to the EU, Leave speakers generally express their relief at not participating in them and use the opt-outs to emphasize British difference from continental Europe. On a few occasions, however, the prospect of being forced to join the Euro or the nation's inability to escape from growing political integration are constructed as consequences of remaining that present a threat to the nation's well-being.

4.2.2 Remain

4.2.2.1 Britain as … Exceptional, Too!

Of the investigated Remain data, 43% highlight British strengths, and the country's current state seems to inspire optimism in Remainers as much as in Leave speakers. The adjectives describing the nation construct it as a self-assured country that is "able" [15], "proud" [3], "right" [2] in its decisions, and "tough" [2] in their implementation, as well as "confident," "great," and "successful." Additionally, words like "fortunate" [3], "happy," or "grateful" point to the UK's positive role in the world and construct being British as a stroke of good fortune. By stressing that the UK's population is "privileged to live in a country where anyone […] can […] achieve their dreams" and "fortunate to live in a country in which politicians do not direct the legal process," the democratic process is highlighted and the country represented as a meritocracy. On two more occasions, speakers label the country "fortunate" for its excellent international relations, while another professes national pride in the NHS. All of these portrayals, apart from perhaps the last, show clear traces of the Whig narrative and thus betray some inherent Euroscepticism.

Like Leave speakers, Remain supporters portray Britain as determined, although they do so not to signal rebelliousness but to express plans for the country's future. This is done by stating that the we-group is "clear" [13] about its wishes or "keen" [5] and "ready" [2] to do something as well as "committed" [6] and "determined" [3] to reach its goals. The country (standing in for its leaders) is thus represented as strong-willed and clear-minded; a nation that knows what it wants and takes steps to achieve its goals. Nonetheless, the depiction of a nation of pragmatists that pursue their goal with logic instead of passion also mobilizes narratives of the rational Brit, familiar from Leave discourses.

British determination is expressed even more clearly on occasions where the nation is positioned as a leader in international politics. Descriptions of Britain as a "world leader," a "leading player in climate change," and as "at the forefront" [4] of various developments explicitly assign this role. Even more frequently, however, the nation's leading position is not mentioned explicitly, but implied by emphasizing that Britain is "the first" or "only" to implement environmental policies or donate a promised amount to the Syrian aid effort. Furthermore, the we-group is identified as "the ones in the vanguard" regarding conflict in the Ukraine, "the ones making the argument" concerning sanctions against Russia, or, five times, as "the second biggest bilateral donor." Throughout these utterances, the UK is positioned not only at the forefront of global events, but also singled out as different and apart from the rest of the world. British accomplishments are highlighted, and they often relate to topics such as security, climate change or international aid, and the eradication of poverty. Thus, the country is indirectly branded as progressive and charitable, contributing to causes which might be interpreted as morally good. By implication, Britain is therefore positioned not merely as a world leader, but as a *moral* leader, using its wealth to do good deeds around the world. This vision of Britain can be traced back to interpretations of the British Empire that not only represented a process by which British virtues, liberty, and wealth were transmitted to deprived foreign regions (Parkeh 35), but which was also portrayed as benign enterprise, spread by trade and not armies (Armitage 8).

In addition to positioning the country as a moral leader, depictions of Britain as "the fifth largest economy in the world" [3] and a "powerful and growing economy" as well as a "massive recipient" [3] of foreign direct investment in the EU also highlight its role as an economic leader. Thus, the vision of Britain as a powerful trading nation with a glorious future is also mobilized in Remain discourses. But despite the parallels to Leave discourses, there is an essential difference in the representation of the country's economic situation: its well-being is frequently tied up with the EU. Thus, two of the three iterations of "the fifth largest economy in Europe" question whether this is a convincing reason to leave the EU – as the Leave side makes it out to be – and instead suggest that British economic success might be caused by EU membership. Similarly, the large amount of direct investment that the country is receiving is twice attributed to the fact that the UK is part of the European customs union.

And yet, even in the Remain data, there are counter-examples where speakers do not connect economic success to EU membership and therefore argue that the UK should *not* remain a member merely for economic reasons. The third occurrence of "the fifth largest economy," for instance, is used by the speaker to stress that they "will never argue that Britain could not survive outside the European Union" because its economic power means that it could well do so. Similarly, a speaker highlighting the UK's "massive" receipt of investment states that, despite others' arguments, uncertainty over a potential Brexit would not cause investors to take their money elsewhere. To sum up, therefore, Remain speakers put strong emphasis on the country's role as an international leader, both in moral and in economic terms. Opinions diverge, however, on whether there is a connection between the country's strong economic standing and EU membership.

4.2.2.2 Britain as a Reluctant and Pragmatic European

While the Remain side utilized many of the same Eurosceptic narratives that the Leave side did, it is in the category of international connections, which accounts for 44% of the analysed Remain data, that the most striking differences between the two sides become apparent. Before discussing those, however, one parallel must be mentioned. Of the nineteen occasions where the nation is assigned the category of "member," "part," or "signatory" of an international group or project, only ten position the nation explicitly as EU member. Similarly, half of the ten circumstantial processes that spatially position the nation "in" something actually portray the country not unequivocally as member but as being hypothetically in limbo between being "in or out." Like Leave speakers, Remainers thus frequently question the country's membership, while enumerating its many connections to other international organizations. Implicitly, the importance of membership for the nation is thereby lessened (Wenzl, "This").

While Leave seems preoccupied with the metaphor of the EU as a prison, the Remain corpus contains only seven occurrences of similar language of entrapment. Although the nation is depicted as "bound" [2] and "tied," the use of the more benign "required" and particularly "compliant" [2] suggests at least a measure of voluntary co-operation. Moreover, several more adjectives depict connection in more neutral, even positive, terms, with words like "involved" [3], "engaged" [2], and "supportive" [2] suggesting wilful participation of the British in international projects. A similar spirit of co-operation is apparent in circumstantial representations, where the UK is positioned as "there for" various aspects of the EU [4]. Moreover, the argument is made twice that being "around the table" of EU members enhances British international influence, while the opposite is the case when Britain is "not around the table" or "not at the heart of what is going on."

Another noticeable pattern in the Remain data that is almost absent in the Leave corpus is the use of the comparative forms "better," "safer," or "stronger" in connection with EU membership, as in "we are safer, stronger and better in the European Union." In all, there are forty-six occurrences of one or all of these words (or similar formulations), and more than half are accounted for by a statement to the effect that the UK is "better (off)" inside the European Union. This is partially explained by the fact that "better off in" was one of the Remain side's campaign slogans, with the official campaign being called "Britain stronger in Europe." Remarkably, however, closer examination shows that these phrases entail relatively few unequivocal embraces of membership. Instead, the phrase mostly occurs attributed to non-British heads of state or as part of a neutral 'in-or-out' question (Wenzl, "This").

In an even more striking difference to Leave discourses, Remain speakers explicitly position the UK and its citizens as "free" [3], while also evaluating British opt-outs not as threats, but as opportunities to make membership work for the UK. Nonetheless, the nation's opt-outs from EU regulations are emphasized with an astounding frequency and speakers stress that the UK is "carved-out" [3] of certain processes, "not compelled" to join Schengen, "not involved" in the Eurozone or "blocked off" from routes to further integration with Brussels. This pattern becomes even more distinct when the country is positioned as "not part of" or "not a member of" the group of Schengen countries [12], the Eurozone [2], ever-closer union [2], Frontex [2], and the European quota system to deal with refugees. Unlike the Leave side, which claim that the UK's numerous opt-outs are evidence of the country's unwillingness to remain in Europe, Remain speakers often construct opt-outs as a reason to stay. On several occasions, for instance, the opt-out from Schengen is cited to refute the Leave argument that the country needs to 'take back control,' and is linked to a vision of Britain as un-bound and self-determined.

Despite the positive framing of opt-outs, emphasis on them defines the nation in terms of what it is not part of – and what it is not part of are, in fact, key European Union projects. The Remain side's view on EU membership is thus revealed to be that of a pragmatic union that is meant to serve its members and not the other way around. Oliver J. Daddow terms this neither decidedly Europhile nor passionately Eurosceptic view "revisionist" and traces it throughout discourses on the Union since 1945 (114). It must be noted, however, that although this view holds that EU membership should be the result of a thorough cost-benefit analysis instead of passionate sentiment (Gibbins 22), the portrayal of the British as supremely rational actually stems from cultural narratives that contrast British 'common sense' with continental irrationality and amorality (Spiering 55, 56). In short, the pragmatic interpretation of membership, which at first glance appears neutral, is in fact steeped in Eurosceptic narratives of the British. Furthermore, by stressing British opt-outs, speakers highlight Britain's positions on the – metaphorical and geographical – margins of the Union and inadvertently portray the nation as, at best, "reluctant" Europeans (Riihimäki).

Although these formulations emphasize British exceptionalism, the EU is painted in a more friendly light than in the Leave data. By stressing that the country is "not bound" [2] by certain treaties and "not obliged" to do what other members do, speakers portray the EU as an institution that is a "non-radical Other" (Gibbins 17), allowing its members freedom, instead of 'imprisonment.' The sense of co-operation is strengthened by speakers stating that the country is now "far more immersed in Brussels" and thus more influential, "committed to cutting red tape" to improve the bureaucratic situation on an EU level and "proud to be part of the discussion" on the circular economy. Nonetheless, emphasizing the need to reform the EU for membership to be beneficial also betrays dissatisfaction with the current state of the Union (see also Wenzl, "This"). To sum up, while Remain depictions show that one can co-operate with the EU, a clear division between the UK and other members is created by the emphasis on opt-outs and Britain's exceptional leadership role. Thus, while the EU and its members might be a benevolent Other, they must remain, irrevocably, Other.

5 Conclusion

A (brief) transitivity analysis of concordance lines for "we are" and "Britain/the UK/the United Kingdom is" shows a clear dominance of relational processes in both data sets, suggesting a preoccupation of Conservative Members of Parliament on both sides with characterizing or identifying the nation. By (re)defining the nation while making their case for or against EU membership, speakers have the chance to create a vision of Britishness that enforces their argument by constructing leaving or remaining, respectively, as in line with the national character and in the nation's best interest.

My analysis shows, however, that only the Leave side was truly successful in this endeavour. Leave speakers consistently constructed the UK as exceptional and superior to other nations by emphasizing its leading role in the international community as well as its economic strength. A nation as successful and internationally connected as Britain, they argue, does not need the crutch of EU membership to remain prosperous. Visions of Britain as a thriving trading nation post-Brexit enable Leave speakers to hint at the possibility of reliving the glory of Empire. Additionally, Leave discourses generally convey a sense of optimism regarding post-Brexit Britain and mobilize Whig narratives of the nation on an inexorable path to liberty and prosperity, and away from Europe. The EU itself is characterized as a prison that diminishes the country's international significance. The positioning of the British as rebellious and unwilling to tolerate injustice, moreover, is perfectly aligned with the Leave side's goal to motivate the population to vote against EU membership.

Somewhat surprisingly, the difference from Remain discourses is one of degree and not of kind. Remainers, too, mobilize narratives of Whiggishness and Empire by stressing the nation's exceptional role in the world and positioning Britain as a moral leader. Although some speakers argue that EU membership is the reason for Britain's economic success, opinions on the necessity of the EU diverge within the Remain camp and the representation of Britain as self-confident and strong does not always easily lend itself to bolstering pro-European arguments. Regarding the UK-EU relationship, a spirit of co-operation is evident in the relative absence of a language of entrapment as well as the emphasis on the willingness to work together. However, British opt-outs from EU projects are highlighted with striking frequency. While they are generally depicted as positive, the pragmatic view of membership as the result of thorough cost-benefit analyses and the positioning of Brits as supremely rational portrays the nation as reluctant Europeans. Moreover, the renewed emphasis on British exceptionalism betrays a lack of enthusiasm for the EU on the part of Remainers and positions the nation firmly as different and apart from the Continent. Needless to say, these constructions of Britishness, combined with conflicting representations of the necessity of the EU, do not encourage passion for the EU project. In fact, they do not even suggest that membership is in the nation's best interest.

References

Anderson, Benedict R. O. *Imagined Communities: Reflections on the Origin and Spread of Nationalism*. Revised ed., Verso, 2006.

Anthony, Laurence. *AntConc*. Waseda U, 2017, www.laurenceanthony.net/software.

Armitage, David. *The Ideological Origins of the British Empire*. Cambridge UP, 2004.

Baker, Paul. *Using Corpora in Discourse Analysis*. Continuum, 2006.

Baker, Paul, et al. "A Useful Methodological Synergy? Combining Critical Discourse Analysis and Corpus Linguistics to Examine Discourses of Refugees and Asylum Seekers in the UK Press." *Discourse & Society*, vol. 19, 2008, pp. 273-306.

BBC. "EU Vote: Where the Cabinet and Other MPs Stand." 2016, www.bbc.com/news/uk-politics-eu-referendum-35616946.

Billig, Michael. *Banal Nationalism*. SAGE, 1995.

Bourne, Ryan. "Why Did the British Brexit? What Are the Implications for Classical Liberals?" *Economic Affairs*, vol. 36, 2016, pp. 356-63.

Colley, Linda. *Britons: Forging the Nation, 1707-1837*. Pimlico, 2003.

Daddow, Oliver J. *Britain and Europe since 1945: Historiographical Perspectives on Integration*. Manchester UP, 2004.

Fairclough, Norman, and Ruth Wodak. "Critical Discourse Analysis." *Discourse as Social Interaction*, edited by T. A. van Dijk, Sage, 1997, pp. 258-84.

Gibbins, Justin. *Britain, Europe and National Identity: Self and Other in International Relations*. Palgrave Macmillan, 2014.

Goodwin, Matthew J., and Oliver Heath. "The 2016 Referendum, Brexit and the Left Behind: An Aggregate-Level Analysis of the Result." *The Political Quarterly*, vol. 87, 2016, pp. 323-32.

Hall, Stuart, and Paul Du Gay. *Questions of Cultural Identity*. SAGE, 2003.

Halliday, M. A. K., and Christian Matthiessen. *Halliday's Introduction to Functional Grammar*. 4th ed., Taylor and Francis, 2014.

Ho, Don. *Notepad++*, 2015, notepad-plus-plus.org/.

Islam, Gazi Nazrul. "Social Identity Theory." *Encyclopedia of Critical Psychology*, edited by Thomas Teo, Springer, 2014, pp. 1781-83.

Islentyeva, Anna. "The Europe of Scary Metaphors: The Voices of the British Right-Wing Press." *Zeitschrift für Anglistik und Amerikanistik*, vol. 67, no. 3, 2019, pp. 209-29.

Koller, Veronika. "How to Analyse Collective Identity in Discourse: Textual and Contextual Parameters." *Critical Approaches to Discourse Analysis Across Disciplines*, vol. 5, 2012, pp. 19-38.

Mole, Richard C. M. "Discursive Identities/Identity Discourses and Political Power." *Discursive Constructions of Identity in European Politics*, edited by Richard Mole, Palgrave Macmillan, 2007, pp. 1-21.

Mollin, Sandra. "The Hansard Hazard: Gauging the Accuracy of British Parliamentary Transcripts." *Corpora*, vol. 2, 2007, pp. 187-210.

Mulderrig, Jane. "The Hegemony of Inclusion: A Corpus-Based Critical Discourse Analysis of Deixis in Education Policy." *Discourse & Society*, vol. 23, 2012, pp. 701-28.

Parkeh, Bhikhu. "Being British." *Political Quarterly*, vol. 78, 2007, pp. 32-40.

Piao, Scott. *Multilingual Corpus Toolkit*, 2002, sites.google.com/site/scottpiaosite/software/mlct.

Reicher, Stephen, and Nick Hopkins. *Self and Nation: Categorization, Contestation, and Mobilization*. SAGE, 2001.

Reisigl, Martin, and Ruth Wodak. *Discourse and Discrimination: Rhetorics of Racism and Antisemitism*. Routledge, 2001.

Riihimäki, Jenni. "At the Heart and in the Margins: Discursive Construction of British National Identity in Relation to the EU in British Parliamentary Debates from 1973 to 2015." *Discourse & Society*, vol. 30, 2019, pp. 412-31.

Slembrouck, Stef. "The Parliamentary Hansard 'Verbatim' Report: The Written Construction of Spoken Discourse." *Language and Literature*, vol. 1, 1992, pp. 101-19.

Spiering, Menno. *A Cultural History of British Euroscepticism*. Palgrave Macmillan, 2015.

Tajfel, Henri. "Experiments in Intergroup Discrimination." *Scientific American*, vol. 223, 1970, pp. 96-102.

Tajfel, Henri, and John Turner. "An Integrative Theory of Intergroup Conflict." *The Social Psychology of Intergroup Relations*, edited by William G. Austin and Stephen Worchel, Brooks/Cole, 1979, pp. 33-47.

Thompson, Geoff. *Introducing Functional Grammar*. 3rd ed., Taylor and Francis, 2013.

UK Parliament. Hansard Online. hansard.parliament.uk/.

Wenzl, Nora. "'There is a wonderfully contrary spirit among the British people': Conservative MPs' (Un)successful Branding of the British Nation in the Brexit Debate." *Language and Country Branding Research Companion*, edited by Irene Theodoropoulou and Johanna Woydack, Routledge, forthcoming.

——. "'This is about the kind of Britain we are': Discursive Constructions of National Identities in Parliamentary Debates About EU Membership. *Discourses of Brexit*, edited by Veronika Koller et al.,

Routledge, 2019, pp. 32-47.

Wodak, Ruth. "What CDA Is about – A Summary of Its History, Important Concepts and Its Developments." *Methods of Critical Discourse Analysis*, edited by Ruth Wodak and Michael Meyer, SAGE, 2001, pp. 1-14.

Wodak, Ruth, et al. *The Discursive Construction of National Identity*. 2nd ed., Edinburgh UP, 2009.

Ali Smith's 'Coming-of-Age' in the Age of Brexit

Harald Pittel

Ali Smith's celebrated Seasonal Quartet – *Autumn* (2016), *Winter* (2017), *Spring* (2019), and *Summer* (2020) – has often been hailed as an epitome of "Brexit fiction." There has been less focus so far on the fact that the cycle also addresses ageing as a social and cultural issue. This essay argues that Smith's engagement with old age should be read in close relation with these novels' larger cultural and political strategies, amounting to a complex intervention in a post-referendum discourse which tends simplistically to present the situation in terms of an antagonism between age groups. More specifically, Smith unfolds a distinctive un-ideological view of ageing, placing it at the heart of an elaborate communicative and political ideal aimed at reinvigorating a sense of open culture and reclaiming history in solidarity. Also insisting that literary traditions can be rewritten, the Seasonal Quartet challenges dominant perceptions of old age and provides a new myth as antidote to Brexit.

Keywords: Ageing, Ali Smith, Brexit, Brexit fiction, myth, Northrop Frye, old age

In social-media discussions concerning the state of the nation in the wake of the 2016 referendum, commentators have drawn stunning parallels to Terry Gilliam's short film *The Crimson Permanent Assurance Company*. Some will remember this pre-movie to Monty Python's *The Meaning of Life* (1983) about the elderly employees of this "Permanent Assurance Company" – a dull and dusted London firm which has recently been taken over by ruthless yuppies in charge of "The Very Big Corporation of America." Tormented like galley slaves by their much

Brexit and Beyond: Nation and Identity. SPELL: Swiss Papers in English Language and Literature 39, edited by Daniela Keller and Ina Habermann, Narr, 2020, pp.121-44.

younger corporate masters, the ageing employees start to rebel after one of them is sacked. Doing their best to emulate swashbuckling movies from the 1940s and 1950s, they turn their huge Edwardian office building into a pirate ship (of sorts) to cross an oceanic desert and take on the monumental corporation's glass tower. The bloodthirsty crew make all the yuppies walk the plank; they celebrate their glorious victory and keep on sailing the Seven Seas, only to fall eventually off the edge of the world – which, sadly enough, they still take for a disc.

This dramatization, once created as a satire of neo-liberal capitalism as facilitated by Margaret Thatcher in the 1980s, can easily be adapted to fit a prevailing mentality in referendum times, in which a common stereotype constructs 'old' Britain as essentially non-European and the comparatively young European Union as a hostile economic power. This is why iconic images commenting on the Brexit situation can be drawn from the film that would seem to illustrate the often-made, blunt association of the older generations with archaic values, stubbornness, and nationalism. Correspondingly, the young are blamed for shunning their elders, and for being always already too deeply involved in globalization, which in this light would seem clearly marked as an inhuman capitalist project.

Gilliam's film also reflects a more general trend in British culture to present younger and older generations as antipodes, a clash that has often been amplified by youth cultures, as most memorably expressed in The Who's 1960s Mod anthem, "My Generation" (which includes the line "Hope I die before I get old"). While such a rigid opposition reflects a questionably romantic and heroic ideal of youth, it is important to note, regarding the present predicament, that not all representations of social divisions in terms of an age conflict must necessarily be simplistic, stereotypical, or myth-ridden. On the contrary, various researchers have confirmed that looking at different age groups indeed offers one key to understanding the contemporary crisis. Age difference, though, must be grasped not so much as a natural difference but as arising from the social conditions and cultural implications of life phases and generational gaps. The fact that citizens over forty-five largely voted Leave in the referendum, while those below that age preferred to Remain, is in tune with a generational divide regarding stances on immigration and security, reflecting disparate preferences for either cultural openness or nationalism (Clarke et al. 146-74; Norris and Inglehart 385-94). Moreover, as in many other Western societies, age segregation effects "the division of individuals within society on the basis of their age" (Kingman 5), often related to housing conditions which manifest themselves in increasing country-city and inner-urban divides (Sabater et al.). To put it plainly, in times of rapid population ageing, the old and the young no longer share the same worlds; they live separate lives with little intergenerational contact (Umunna).

No wonder that a growing number of programmes, initiatives, and platforms in today's Britain pursue various strategies to overcome age segregation socially, culturally, and politically. The creation of shared sites for young and old, as well as integrative approaches to childcare, student housing, and care for the elderly are advocated by specialized think-tanks and realized by many regional and local projects (United for All Ages; All Party). Such practical strategies, while advancing change at many interrelated levels, might not be sufficient to raise awareness for the depth of the trenches, the actual dimensions of intergenerational misunderstandings. One might think of art and literature as having a vital function here when it comes to recording – and thereby helping to understand – the age-related "structure of feeling" (Williams, *Marxism* 128-35) of the conflicted present.

The Scottish author Ali Smith, long known for exploring the deeper and complex interdependencies that constitute identity and reality in works such as *There but for the* (2011) or *How to Be Both* (2014), has reacted to the present crisis by creating the Seasonal Quartet, a political kind of fiction that captures and chronicles the post-referendum climate. The novels that constitute the series – *Autumn* (2016), *Winter* (2017), *Spring* (2019), and *Summer* (2020) – have often been referred to as landmarks of "Brexit fiction" or "BrexLit," as they use a literary style of multi-perspectivity and intertextuality to paint not only a picture of the extent of social estrangement marking today's Britain, but also to suggest an ideal of dialogic communication and political solidarity to overcome this state of paralysis (see for instance Rau; Tönnies and Henneböhl). However, I would suggest a more specific reading of Smith's Seasonal Quartet, arguing that her analysis of the present predicament, as well as her approaches to overcome it, are most closely associated with representations, myths, and traditions related to the social experience of old age and the cultural process of ageing. This essay aims to show that Smith thoroughly subverts established ideas about the condition of old age as well as intergenerational relations, suggesting better alternatives. This is not to imply that Smith, now writing in her fifties, is *exclusively* interested in old age and ageing; however, it is a vantage point from which the novels' more general critical and political ambitions can be elucidated adequately.

Five interrelated aspects are particularly worth looking at: (1) the Seasonal Quartet presents old people as embodied ideals, serving as antitheses to social reality which is marked by nationalism, estrangement, and disorientation; (2) the novels feature ageing characters as 'changers,' able not only to redefine the direction of their lives but also to embody larger perspectives of social transformation and political solidarity; (3) this view of ageing implies that history, with the elderly figuring as the most qualified bearers of historical knowledge and wisdom, can be made productive to animate such political change in the present that fundamentally questions one-sided and nationalist perceptions of identity and reality, making visible many deeper and more complex connections; (4) such a transformative view of history is also manifest in how the novels engage with the Western *literary* tradition. In the way they undermine and revise long-standing literary myths or meta-narratives, they challenge old-age-related assumptions on an even deeper level which problematically associates ideas around age with the cycle of seasons. More specifically, the circularity of the Seasonal Quartet implies that although some traditions appear to be more stable than others, such as the fact that autumn precedes winter, there is nevertheless hope for a transformation of those traditions that can potentially be changed and rewritten. By revisiting the literary myths of romance, tragedy, comedy, and irony/satire, Smith's engagement with old age and ageing shows that even key narratives at the heart of Western culture can be freed from ideological implications. (5) Moreover, by circling around the idea that young and old can reunite ever anew in solidarity, the Seasonal Quartet comes close to a new myth as antidote to Brexit – the myth of a joint 'coming-of-age,' so to speak.

1 Revising Representations of Old Age

In the most general terms, the representations of old people in Smith's quartet are targeted at fighting cultural stereotypes that link ageing with bodily and mental decline, unproductivity, and social invisibility. Following Andrew Blaikie, it was only in the earlier twentieth century that "modernity produced an enhanced awareness of stigma via the growing administrative classification of older people as a chronologically determined social group with a fixed identity" (111). However, even in our own days of ageing societies, positive ideas and cultural forms to realize the 'third age' in diverse and meaningful ways are less highly developed and widespread than one might think. The danger of challenging the 'decline' narrative of old age is naively to embrace the exact opposite and cling to the ideology of infinite progress, the belief that death can be conquered and kept at bay virtually forever (Gullette 18-19; Gilleard and Higgs 59-89). These opposing views hark back to a long cultural history in which longevity was either ignored and condemned or associated with wisdom and hence seen as worth aiming for (Parkin 37; Minois 303-07).

How does Smith's take on ageing deal with the multiple demands and pitfalls in this ideology-fraught territory? To begin with, positive figurations of old age feature prominently in the Seasonal Quartet. These depictions of preferable and/or successful ways of getting old often have a clearly idealizing tendency, which is balanced, however, by a note of social realism. The most obvious example of this would be Daniel Gluck in *Autumn*, who befriends eleven-year-old Elisabeth Demand when he is long past retirement age, emerging as a kind of mentor and thus taking a significant influence on the young girl's coming-of-age. An affinity towards idealizing is evident when Daniel appears larger than life to her, "like a magician" who is "always just too far ahead" (39, 38). By sharing with Elisabeth whatever is generated in some "fruitful place in his brain" (29), "the cave of [Daniel's] mouth becomes the threshold to the end of the world as she knows it" (36).

While these sublime perceptions of Daniel, conveyed through the perspective of Elisabeth's childhood amazement, partly verge on the otherworldly sphere of myth, fairy tale, or romance, it would seem difficult to figure his peculiar presence from a more conventionally grounded point of view. To begin with, Daniel does not meet expectations that old age goes together with bodily decay: "He wasn't old. [Elisabeth] was right. Nobody truly old sat with their legs crossed or hugged their knees like that. Old people couldn't do anything except sit in front rooms as if they'd been stunned by stun guns" (50).

Figured as a young man in an old body, Daniel somehow fails to hit the mark and effectively subverts common assumptions about old people. No wonder then that Elisabeth's mother – although at first charmed by Daniel's voice, which reminds her of "old films where things happen to well-dressed warplane pilots in black and white" (48) – retains a queer impression of him overall. She stigmatizes Daniel's influence as "[u]nnatural" and "[u]nhealthy" and takes him for gay or perverted or worse, using a register that is apt vaguely to remind some readers of anxious late-Victorian reactions to decadent aesthetes like Walter Pater or Oscar Wilde (77-83). An even more blatant allusion to the sexually monstrous is made in passing when Elisabeth is promised a video of the Disneyfied *Beauty and the Beast* as a reward for *not* meeting Daniel (231). It is for the young girl to counter all these allegations from her mother regarding sexual unorthodoxy by declaring bluntly: "Daniel's not gay. He's European" (77).

If being "European" in this context implies 'un-stranging' the strange, Elisabeth's remark would seem to entail that there is nothing "[u]nnatural" and "[u]nhealthy" (83) about what Daniel has to impart: namely, a richer life that is open to more authentic forms of communication, to making significant contacts with others, and, by the same token, to getting in touch with the deeper, more complex and inherently social dimensions of the self. "European" in this sense can be understood as a political metaphor signalling, in Brexit times, a more socially and culturally interdependent sense of self than a narrow codification of identity in terms of 'Britishness,' let alone 'Englishness,' would imply. This is why the novel takes meticulous care not to let Daniel's otherworldly loftiness indicate a point of yearning for a deep-set, purely original, and mysterious self in terms of the romantic genius. Rather, what makes Daniel so attractive is closely related to his French and German background, countries that were often constructed as Britain's cultural and political Other. Retroactively identifying in *Summer* as the son of a "German Englishman" (155), hybridity would seem to constitute Daniel's sense of self from the beginning. Imagining himself in *Autumn* as "shut in the trunk of a Scots pine" (89) in a dream, "a tree that can last for centuries" as it "doesn't need much soil depth" (90), perfectly sums up Daniel's identity in terms of a 'more-than-English' migrant self that can belong to a place without the guarantee of having exclusive ancestral ties to the land.[1]

While embodying these complex connections, Daniel is not simply a mental construct, an implanted idea, symbol, or 'utopian container' of a culturally and socially 'better' personality. Rather, the novel presents Daniel as an interactive agent, encouraging Elisabeth to share her reading experiences and freely co-create in joint storytelling, and thereby work towards a more authentic expression of identity and reality so as to "bagatelle it as it is" (121): "I [Daniel] can make up something useful, entertaining, perspicacious and kind. We have this in common, you [Elisabeth] and I. As well as the capacity to become someone else, if we so choose" (51-52). And as Daniel's teachings help Elisabeth find a

---

[1] There is also a darker note as Daniel is associated with the European Jews and the Holocaust, which is discussed further below in the context of the Seasonal Quartet's engagement with history.

sense of self along with an aesthetic vision of her own, she soon discovers that Daniel's sense of particularity is not about standing apart from others, rather implying a deep awareness of the collective dimension of reality as "[n]obody spoke like Daniel. Nobody didn't speak like Daniel" (148). Despite his idiosyncrasy he shares a common 'language' with people that goes beyond speaking a specific national language such as English, which further underlines a sense of borderless and therefore European communication. And even beyond, as Daniel explains to Elisabeth, his "unexpected queen of the world" (52) that her last name "Demand" really means "du monde," revealing his will to share his deep-seated cosmopolitan outlook with his soulmate (50).

Society, however, marked as it is by social pathologies, its unquestioned clinging to arbitrary borders and regulations, is depicted as immune to such modes of contact and channels of communication. By conventionally locating old people at the margins, dominant ways of seeing fail to understand people like Daniel and his uncommon friendship with Elisabeth. Rather than recognizing the third age as a phase of self-determination and vitality – Daniel remains fit at an age far beyond seventy, and he is able to run his household all by himself until well into his nineties (113, 157) – society associates old age with a fourth age instead and generalizes it as mental and bodily decline. However, when the novel shows Daniel spending his final days in a care facility in what Smith abstains from ever directly referring to as 'deathbed,' it amounts in more general fashion to a complex critique of how society frames and treats its elderly: old people are left alone while their individuality and citizenship are denied. Daniel, willing to pay for the understaffed care facility himself, can no longer do so because he did not receive any compensation for the use of his song "Summer Brother Autumn Sister" in a recent TV commercial. Elisabeth's active solidarity-in-friendship forces her to intervene, to pose as a lawyer claiming the song's rights for Daniel, and thus to beat the system at its own game (233-38).

Old people thus suffer most in an alienated society as their status as a subject of rights is impaired and their contributions to culture no longer count. In short: they are prone to become dehumanized. Yet while old age receives an added cultural meaning here as it represents the extremes of marginalization and misrecognition, the novel's idealizing strategy very much deploys Daniel as an embodiment of hope, aimed at overcoming that unwholesome climate. Daniel retains his creativity even during his fourth age; his dreams are not set apart from but reflect the political reality of a world in which, in times of precarious migration, dead bodies are found on beaches (12); he is still temporarily able to share his thoughts with Elisabeth and even bonds with his care assistants (170-71) – another glimpse of hope in this sterile environment. All this helps to revise stereotypical views of ageing as it unfolds a radically alternative image to the extreme perspective of senescence and care dependency. Associating the active life of the mind and communicative ethos of a 101-year-old man with being "European" creates a visionary outlook against the Brexit climate because it revokes the assumption of elderly people's supposed Euroscepticism.

Iris Cleves from *Winter* similarly undermines the idea that older generations abandon their relations beyond Britain. Iris, well into her seventies, has been a socialite and socialist all through her adult life, fighting, among others, for peace, the environment, and open borders for refugees. Described by her conventionally grounded sister Sophia as both "brilliant" and "trouble" from childhood days (23), Iris in this light would seem to inhabit a different plane of reality, as Sophia alternately calls her a "mythologizer" (155, 173) and laments her proclivity to "disenchant" (211). There is a parallel to Daniel Gluck, as Iris makes an inspiring connection in conversation with her nephew, encouraging him to tell her "something real" (170). This reiterates Daniel's tenet to "bagatelle it as it is" (Smith, *Autumn* 121), which would suggest a sense of authenticity in storytelling. Her character embodies the history of left-wing protest culture and alternative life forms in Britain and elsewhere, and thereby clearly counters the prejudice often heard throughout the Brexit-related state-of-the-nation debates which, in a simple manner, associates the older generations with political conservatism and falsely registers progressive tendencies as movements exclusively initiated by the young. And Iris's energy remains undaunted in *Summer*, when she supports homeless immigrants during the Covid-19 pandemic (341-42), thus setting a towering example for younger generations of activists.

Daniel Gluck and Iris Cleves are not the only elderly people in the four novels who are surrounded by an air of the extraordinary and retain an open-minded political attitude. Patricia Heal, aka Paddy from *Spring*, conspicuously associated with the power of healing, is a vivid depiction of a charismatic, wise, self-reliant, and cultivated woman who dies at the age of eighty-seven. Her close friend, the documentary film director Richard Lease – younger by seventeen years – finds her, a former scriptwriter, extraordinarily "*good*" (20) at what she does; echoing Daniel's and Iris's calls for authentic storytelling, her scripts make "*something real*" (21) happen, thus animating Richard's own work and self-understanding with a sense of realism that is both social and imaginative. Paddy is widely read in European literature and history, and deeply affected by the present socio-political situation, not losing her sense of anger until very late in her life. This is partly due to her Irish heritage, as Paddy remembers the times when anti-Irish racism was virulent in England. Identifying as a migrant, she comes to reject the discourse around a "migrant crisis" claiming that migration should be accepted more generally as a condition that constitutes identities (67-68). Richard admires Paddy for knowing "everything about everything" (39) – a naively idealizing way of seeing which she modestly ridicules. Impressed with her aura, Richard believes that she will "never die," but Paddy warns him not to fall for the "modern fantasy and malaise" of "sailing the ship into the sunset forever" (32). For Richard, Paddy embodies a combined ideal of friend, lover, colleague, and mother at the same time. At one point in their friendship, they have a one-night stand, and at another, they giggle together like schoolchildren. Richard reckons that "[t]hey were bigger than sex," but unlike Daniel, Paddy is by no means completely aloof from the sexual: she likes "a good fuck as much as the next person" (63-64).

All in all, Paddy is a passionately energetic and determined woman who has had it all in a competitive and male-dominated world: marriage, twins, and a job, all of which have made her appear "even more carefree" to Richard (62). However, while Paddy represents a creative, independent, and professionally successful woman with a migration history – quite unlike Daniel, an outsider – her depiction also implies a critique of certain ideologies about ageing. While Paddy, just like Daniel, complicates the standard association between old age and bodily/mental decline from the outset, her character explicitly takes issue with the idea of ageing as infinite progress, namely the widespread belief in the "ship of the liberal world" (32) which promises that you can be whatever you like regardless of both social conventions and nature.

Following Margaret M. Gullette, it is precisely between these two ideological extremes of negative and positive stereotypes around ageing – based on decline and progress, respectively – that a more unbiased discourse regarding old age should emerge (21-39). This is very much what Smith's presentation of a free and independent Paddy amounts to. Paddy is successful and happy at an advanced age, but she is *not* larger than life, as she accepts the natural fact of dying with pride and equanimity. This dignified ideal of ageing, a sense of greatness that remains existentially down-to-earth, is summarized in Richard's formulation that Paddy belongs to the "uncategorizable sort" (62): extraordinary, but still a "sort"; not aloof from the everyday world, nor a romantic mystery. The presentation of Paddy thus underwrites a persisting myth about

Irishness, or more generally, Celticness, in terms of an unexpected 'third' position subverting the binary oppositions that construct hegemonic culture (Pine).

The unconventional friendship between Paddy and Richard, just like the one between Daniel and Elisabeth, testifies to relationships between people that defy any categorization in terms of appropriate behaviour concerning age and gender. However, if we compare these relationships, it seems that Smith's strategies of representing old age more adequately have shifted a bit from the "uncategorizable" to the "sort," so to speak, presenting Paddy, unlike Daniel, as a more earthbound and socially integrated embodiment of the extraordinary, with a sexual side and a higher psychological complexity. It is only fitting, then, that Daniel is retroactively ascribed a sex life (with men and women) and biological fatherhood in *Winter* (248-76) and *Summer* (185), while his spiritual presence remains unbroken.

From this first survey of figurations of old age in the Seasonal Quartet, it is clear that Smith complicates any straightforward stereotypical associations, constructing ageing as neither unequivocal decline nor unquestioned progress, and depicting a range of old characters as neither unproductive nor politically conservative. While this 'ideal' cast of elderly people is diverse and undermines the sweeping perception of old people as a homogenous or indigenous group, the following section discusses a further set of older characters that is not so ideal but shows a readiness to reflect seriously on their existence, thus allowing them to change and develop at a late stage in their lives in order to arrive at a new self-understanding and political attitude.

2 Never Too Late: Learning to Change

Looking at the earlier novels, *Autumn* and *Winter*, it would seem at first sight that processes of change are mainly attributed to the adult protagonists in their thirties. Both Elisabeth Demand in *Autumn* and Art Cleves in *Winter* feel a need to question and revise ready-made conceptions of identity so as to overcome a certain extent of alienation, as is manifest in Elisabeth's longer coming-of-age story and in Art's more acute state of confusion and disorientation over his broken-up relationship. Even a character like Brittany "Brit" Hall in *Spring*, who works as a security guard in a detention centre and is wholly absorbed in hegemonic logic, is not immune to change. This becomes clear as deeper and more complex levels of the self are temporarily awakened in

Brit when she encounters the novel's miraculous child, Florence, who engages her in a joyful conversation about her favourite things and makes her "remember the more-than-one meaning of a word like cell" (183). The established ways of seeing nevertheless eventually get the better of Brit (319-29). In all of these relatively young adults, Elisabeth, Art, and Brit, maturing is connoted with an important phase of reorientation, typically associated with a new project such as Elisabeth's decision to write her doctoral thesis on Pauline Boty against the explicit will of her tutor (Smith, *Autumn* 154-56), or Art's resolution to turn his blog on nature observation into a co-written project (Smith, *Winter* 318).

But change is not exclusively ascribed to the younger generation in the Seasonal Quartet, as some of the older characters, too, undergo such significant processes. A thorough kind of transformation is evident in Elisabeth's conventionally grounded mother, Wendy Demand, who, having been stuck in her house for ages, is now in her mid-fifties yet not too old to start her first lesbian relationship and turn into a political protester (Smith, *Autumn* 213-21, 254-55). Likewise, Richard, well past retirement age, comes to cut his ties with the alienating culture industry and funds his own solidarity project for a refugee support network (Smith, *Spring* 269-77).

As already indicated, a crucial dilemma deplored by Gullette in her seminal *Aged by Culture* is that a fundamental change of one's outlook regarding the cultural meaning of old age is often bound to shift from the blunt extreme of decline to a progress narrative, with little in between (143-47). However, the transformations presented by Smith are at once subtler and deeper, implying not an unthinking break with one's past but, first and foremost, a thorough change in making sense of one's memories. Wendy is suddenly able to see that her nostalgic passion for collecting antiques was actually aimed at preserving bits of hope that a better society might have been possible in the past, or may be possible in the future. Throwing the collectibles at an ominous fence that may well belong to a detention centre is thus a plausible step from passive to active resistance against a *zeitgeist* perceived as thoroughly dehumanizing.

Similarly, Richard gains unexpected recognition from Alda for his documentary films made in the seventies (Smith, *Spring* 254-60), which is a crucial reminder for him that he had always been creative and independent, and that there is no reason not to build on that former sense of self and establish a new political relation to it. Ageing, then, is not simply about decline or progress, but about inventing new ways of making the past cause the present, which the novels present as a social and political act.

It is also clear from these examples that Smith sees expressions of political solidarity, and commitment in terms of political activism, as the highest forms, the ultimate goals, and most important dimensions of transformation. Change as such has no age, and authentic decisions to change, as the novels make clear, are neither bound to any specific phase of life nor overly 'path-dependent' in terms of a previous orientation or occupation that may have been far removed from any serious political awareness or commitment. But how can one work towards such transformation? A key factor would be an ideal of communication that is implicitly and explicitly advocated in the novels to overcome the deplorable state of society with its real and arbitrary divisions. 'Communication' here is not to be simply understood as pertaining to technology or a national language; rather, communication is centred around a collective dimension of existence that opens up an authentic dialogue with others, thus overcoming the restrictions of the overly atomized, privatized, or even national self (Williams, *Keywords* 36-37). This is obvious in Daniel Gluck's Europeanness, as discussed above, and in former chain-store owner Sophia Cleves in *Winter*, who, far over seventy, is able to overcome the barriers of identity which have led her to Scrooge-like isolation in a state of paralytic nostalgia. What seems most important in *Winter* is that one should never attempt to bypass what Sophia registers as "the pitfalls of human exchange" (36). Rather, one should accept arguing as something liberating, which is what eventually breaks the ice between 'capitalist' Sophia and her 'political' sister, also implying that the referendum gap between Leavers and Remainers might be overcome in this way (205-14, 229-36). At any rate, a real, more authentic sense of self, grounded in recognizing and accepting one's true social relations with significant others, is something one needs and can achieve regardless of age if one does not wish to feel haunted, like Sophia in the novel's opening pages, by ghosts from the past (7-32).

However, the idea of 'communication' put forward here exceeds the level of immediate intersubjectivity. It entails cultural forms and media practices that may be shared as points of departure for larger strategies to change the social climate (Williams, *Marxism* 36-37; Eldridge and Eldridge 63-64, 75-95). What one should therefore carefully consider are the various forms of communication that, as Smith suggests, play a role in overcoming the restrictions of identity to arrive at a more socially grounded sense of self. Generally speaking, as we have seen between Iris and Sophia, the sharing of memories, exposing one's experience and judgments to the views of the other, and engaging in the free play of perspectives, may well help to challenge cemented individual outlooks.

At a higher level, there are the more cooperative approaches of joint imagining and storytelling as co-practiced by Daniel and Elisabeth in *Autumn*. Their common construction of a shared way of seeing is bigger than any individual outlook but nonetheless bears the signum of true individuality (72-76, 116-21).

Other forms of communication function over longer distances in both time and space. Smith is not blind to the innovative connections offered by digital forms of communication such as the collective blog initiated by Art in *Winter*; however, the use of email in *Spring* would suggest a certain amount of scepticism regarding the cultural dominance of new media, foregrounding their aseptic side (when Paddy's sons coldly inform Richard about her funeral, 73-76) and manipulative potential (when a big-headed scriptwriter sends an obtrusive email to Richard's superiors, pretending to speak in the film director's name while really ignoring his opinion and making it hard for him to intervene, 103-05).

By contrast, the exchange of picture postcards, apt to communicate moments of one's life to others while allowing them to co-imagine what these moments may be like, becomes the prime channel of communication between Richard and Paddy (76-81). And little wonder that he thinks of this type of communication when looking for a way to transform a novel about the impossible encounter between Katherine Mansfield and Rainer Maria Rilke into a film (95-99). In more general terms, literature offers itself as a more complex medium that allows a similar degree of shared intensity in objectified form, which is made clear as Richard discovers Paddy's final message to him as an addendum to her volume of Mansfield's *Collected Stories* (278-85), which now bears an added dimension of personal significance for him.

Smith thoroughly explores all these channels of communication as they help to work on a desirable 'old-and-new culture,' offering many forms to relate to each other in unrestricted, diverse, and authentic contacts, also implying the creation of new networks of political solidarity. All this happens regardless of any specific associations with age, but because it invites the sharing of memories and experiences, it especially welcomes the participation of older people as they not only have a wealth of memories and experiences to look back to, but also are potentially considerably wiser than the younger generations and, as I argue below, can relate their own past to a broader understanding of history. They thus ensure that key events, such as the world wars and the Holocaust, or important developments in art, are not forgotten.

3 Reclaiming History

It is in this sense that the political consciousness and commitment of the old taps into history. In fact, history offers a very concrete explanation for Daniel's interest in Elisabeth, as she would seem to remind him of his long-lost beloved sister, Hannah, who was deported in Nazi-occupied France, probably to be killed in a concentration camp (Smith, *Autumn* 63-66, 181-93). Historical and personal dimensions converge here as the complex whole of the twentieth century, centred around the persecution of the European Jews and the Holocaust, crystallizes in Daniel, who had a German-Jewish mother (Smith, *Summer* 155). He was also interned together with his German father by the British Army during the Second World War, which gives rise to a whole network of British-continental historical relations. As *Summer* specifies, Daniel and his father were eventually transported to Hutchinson camp, in which German academics and artists were safeguarded from the Nazis (144-46, 168-92). This facility, which became famous for its high level of intellectual exchange and production, was located on the Isle of Man in the geographical centre of the British Isles, at roughly equal distances from the English, Scottish, Welsh, and Irish mainlands. This setting symbolically locates the joint creativity of displaced artists and intellectuals at the very heart of twentieth-century Britain and thus implicitly challenges unilinear accounts of overly 'national' history-writing.

A sense of ethical commitment arising from historical awareness becomes evident from Richard's concern with the popularity of extreme right-wing views, which remind him of "[t]errible times, easily resurrected" as too many people play history "on repeat" rather than learning from it (Smith, *Spring* 241) – an insight he has probably gained while working with Paddy. The more demanding potential of history to animate commitment becomes clear by looking at yet another character from *Spring*, namely, the seemingly weird woman identified as "Alda Lyons." She is a librarian in her fifties from the Scottish town of Kingussie, who first appears in an absurd setting in front of the town's train station, operating a coffee truck that has no coffee, nor anything else, to sell (50-55). When she gives Richard a ride up north to Inverness and they pass the site of the 1745 Battle of Culloden, she is easily able to substantiate Richard's simplistic idea of this event as the "[l]ast battle of the English against the Scots" by explaining the conflict's historical complexities (232-37). It becomes clear that Alda is probably just as knowledgeable as Paddy, though she lacks the scriptwriter's glamour and charisma.

Despite these similarities with Paddy, the depiction of their old age is different, since Alda's character complicates the simple categorization of either being a social insider or outsider. As a local librarian, Alda would seem to lead an 'ordinary' and quiet everyday life, with a stable and respectable position in an accessible public institution. At an advanced age, such constant and modest lives may well bear the stigma of unproductivity in a society focused on staying competitive and career-oriented regardless of age – a condition well known to Richard, who was not offered a job in nearly four years. In fact, the ridiculous introduction of Alda as spending her day off in a coffee van without coffee epitomizes this stereotype of unproductivity and social dysfunctionality. In meritocratic societies, lives like Alda's are therefore likely to be belittled as marginal and insignificant, a condescending view that ties in with often-heard negative expectations regarding Scottish independence. This cliché is corrected by Alda, whose preference for books and films reflects the desire to really understand the collective past and present – a humanist will to knowledge that not only empowers her to read the traces of a historical conflict in the landscape but also informs her involvement in the "Auld Alliance" programme – a project of active solidarity (370-77).

The "Auld Alliance" – an underground railroad for refugees – unites committed people of all ages, based on a radical vision of political equality in which everybody involved is called by the Guy-Fawkes-style universalizing signifier "Alda" or "Aldo Lyons." This once again undercuts the clichéd perception of political movements in terms of youth culture by reimagining the bonds of solidarity in the sign of old age (270). Furthermore, the "Auld Alliance" alludes to a literally 'old' alliance between Scotland and France. Originally formed in 1295 as a treaty that lasted till the sixteenth century, this military defence agreement stipulated that if either Scotland or France were attacked by England, the other country would invade English territory. In Smith's appropriation of the term, this historical "antidote to the English" (Macdougall) is reanimated to undermine England's dominance in times of Brexit. In the light of this allegory, England would be always already known for its hubris, prone to impose its rule and expand its sovereignty at the cost of others. However, the borders constituting England's cultural and political identity in the first place are more porous than they would seem, and its false sense of stability might be challenged more easily than expected. The old and the young acting in concert in this "countrywide" (270) network for unrestricted migration and open borders thus becomes the obvious expression for a 'good repetition' in terms of a transformative understanding of history, in which the "Auld Alliance" is not simply a thing of the past, but remains "to come" (Derrida 81) as a tentative realization of even stronger alliances in the future.

4 Transforming Literary Tradition

The transformative approach to history in terms of a 'good repetition' is also enacted in the quartet at the self-reflexive level of *literary* form. This is most evident in the novels' seasonal cycle and the often-cited postmodernist aspects of Smith's writing (see, for example, Wood). Ripe with intertextual references across the ages and media, including paintings, film, songs, and much else, the novels present their material from cultural registers high and low in multiple perspectives, their non-linearity also allowing for shifts in narrative voice.

Also, stylistic elements like puns, and the sustained allegorizing of names as in Elisabeth Demand or Paddy Heal, would suggest a systematic-yet-instable view of language: everything is connected, while words nonetheless lend themselves to multiple, even oppositional readings and/or spawn diverse associations that go beyond a narrow (English) meaning. Hence Daniel suggests that Elisabeth really wants to go to free-spirited "collage" rather than stifling college (Smith, *Autumn* 71), while the Cleves family name would evoke the word 'to cleave' (to break apart) but also the French 'clé' (key, old spelling 'clef') in terms of a possible opening-up and connection. Multi-perspectivity thus even exists at the level of signifiers, as meaning is typically 'more-than-English' and refuses to let itself be unambiguously pinned down to a pure, monocultural signified. However, in our context it is especially interesting that the decentring of a privileged viewpoint thus effected goes together with a more specific strategy that exposes literary tradition itself as dynamic and not immune to change. Avoiding a conservative view that overemphasizes the coherence and distinct qualities of certain traditions, Seasonal Quartet demonstratively destabilizes their borders and paves the way for an unrestricted transformation of the literary past.

This comparatively 'young' approach to writing, with its proclivity for popular culture, is nonetheless fascinated with the 'old' inventory of tradition as it actualizes Shakespeare, revises Dickens, and draws on Ovid – 'classic' writers whose works provide Smith with a rich repertoire of literary elements around the idea of unexpected, even impossible change. However, Smith's novels show an even deeper investment in literary history, fully acknowledging tradition's importance for shaping today's consciousness but nonetheless emphasizing its transformative potential. Smith's engagement with the literary canon goes beyond exploring a few selected poets or works of the past, as it also shows a more wholesome – though somewhat hidden – understanding of the *systematic* aspects of tradition, which by no means stand in the way of transformative appropriations or reinterpretations. More specifically, her overall approach to writing a comprehensive set of texts, respectively identified in terms of different seasons, can be plausibly related to the literary prominence of the seasonal cycle as a systematic structure pertaining to the logic of genre at a fundamental level.

The best-known example of this approach (though not exactly *en vogue* with present-day scholars) is Northrop Frye's theory of modes as presented in his *Anatomy of Criticism* (1957). Frye's theory is centred around four literary modes or "mythoi," including romance, tragedy, comedy, and irony/satire. These modes act as meta-genres – one could also say: meta-narratives – organizing the traditional space of (Western) literature, reflecting its historical development from more myth-bound (romance) towards more secular outlooks (irony/satire), with the "high-mimetic" mythos of tragedy and the "low-mimetic" mode of comedy negotiating between these radically opposed horizons (131-239, 33-67).

Frye's system thus provides traditional coordinates by which literary works can be described in most general terms. Each of these modes implies vague yet fundamental assumptions in terms of existential and social outlooks, which Frye sees attuned to the natural cycle of seasons. According to this view, a cosmology has marked literature from ancient times on, to crystallize fully in the works of Dante and Milton, according to which the order of nature is somehow embedded between heaven and hell, with the cycle of seasons serving as a prime analogy for human life thus conditioned. This exceeds an understanding of life phases attuned to the seasons. More specifically, the seasonal cycle reflects, on the one hand, the upward movement (spring to summer) of human aspiration towards transcendence, and on the other it implies a corresponding downward movement: humanity's fall (autumn to winter) to chaos (158-62). Thus tragedy as the mythos of autumn is traditionally understood in terms of the fate of the tragic hero, who is somewhere between the "divine" and the "all-too-human" and comes to face sordid reality (206-23). At the cold and wintry end of secularity, the brutal realism of irony and satire conveys a modern disillusioned outlook of existential thrownness, reflecting a desperate state of humanity in which fixed, metaphysical coordinates for orientation are no longer available (223-39). On a more optimistic note, comedy's 'spring' is about the desire of the young to go beyond what is taken for granted, whose urge to rejuvenate and transform society is typically "blocked" by the old, the usurping keepers of the established order (163-86). And the 'summer' of romance celebrates the heroic struggles of the pure and innocent forces of good against evil – aloof from the everyday world and verging on the fantastic; aspiring towards a sense of victory that overcomes previous failure (186-206).

It is obvious from this brief summary that such a systematic approach can easily be criticized for a number of reasons, most importantly, perhaps, because it gives an air of universality to a narrow Eurocentric canon whose underlying norms it reconstructs. However, Frye's theory is useful for raising awareness of the unconscious determinism that comes with naively accepting the implicit assumptions enshrined in the logic of a given literary mode. And once this determinism is recognized, it becomes evident how absurd it is to assume that human beings can never change their customs and conventions. Moreover, Frye's theory implies that every work of literature can in principle be rewritten so as to be liberated from the logic of any particular mode; it can be transposed from one mode to another, and – to continue the train of thought beyond Frye's own reflections – be amalgamated with any other form of narrative, across the boundaries of cultural conventions or media limitations. It is in this sense that Hayden White, arguing that the logic of modes also underlies the development of historical criticism over the centuries, has emphasized that even wilder combinations of modes, with all sorts of genres and narratives, do actually occur (267-80). However, it would be wrong to assume that the traditional outlooks of the mythoi, and the ways they are defined against and interrelated with one another, have completely lost their authority.

Smith's Seasonal Quartet seems to be informed by a similar mythical horizon. In each of the novels, the author does not hesitate subtly to evoke a general outlook that comes close to the logic of Frye's modes, but such a ground note is no sooner struck than subverted, as Smith seems highly aware of tradition's transformative potential. In *Autumn*, the downward movement from the lofty summer of romance to wintry realism as implied by Frye's mode of tragedy is clearly visible in Daniel Gluck. As a romantic artist figuring as an old extraordinary man, still vibrant with uncommon memories and an elevated sense of connectedness, he comes to a fall as he sees his final days in a health care facility, running out of money in an estranged and privatized culture. However, the tragic thrust is successfully countered as Daniel's border-overcoming communicative ethos is continued by others, namely Elisabeth and Wendy Demand. Together, they generate the golden harvest of a new faith and an attitude of political resistance – a glimpse of hope in an increasingly fractured society.

Winter, a season that Frye associates with secularity and brutal realism as nature is perceived at a standstill, most conspicuously distances itself from its opposite, stating explicitly on the first page: "Romance is dead. Chivalry is dead" (2). Indeed, the novel evokes a bleak outlook of everyday life verging on the ice-cold irony of the absence of higher levels of meaning, as reflected, for instance, in the ridiculous bureaucracy and false friendliness that Sophia Cleves has to face when unsuccessfully attempting to withdraw money from her bank account (36-38). However, it seems that a sense of romance eventually returns to the land – helped by the almost magical light-bearer Lux, who makes the ice melt between Sophia and Iris, culminating in a Christmas-time family reunion and a new understanding of political solidarity in Art/art, who feels this revitalization as a divination that also refers to the novel as a whole: "Art will never die. Art will live forever" (307).

In *Spring*, the logic of the comedy mode, associated by Frye with the endeavours of the young to rejuvenate society being barred by the old, is both evoked and inverted; the young block the old when a careerist representative of the culture industry temporarily gets the better of Richard's creativity, demanding that he render the speculative encounter between Rainer Maria Rilke and Katherine Mansfield in such a way that allows for inclusion of a "comedy fuck" scene: the two writers having sex in a Swiss Alps cable car, making bystanders wonder why it is shaking so much (35-36, 83-87). By contrast to such marketable nonsense, it is for Richard not to let himself be 'fucked' any further by the black comedy of commercial exploitation, breaking away from the absurdity of the system in order to realize his own independent, historically sensitive, and solidarity oriented project.

It is for *Summer*, eventually, to both affirm and complicate the corresponding mode of romance, which has some special implications. It should be noted that romance is the narrative most closely associated by Frye with the political, which might sound surprising considering the more commonly apolitical associations of the romance mode with wish-fulfilment in a dream-like atmosphere. By contrast, Frye also ascribes to romance a "genuinely 'proletarian' element," seeing in figures like the unknown chivalric hero, with his fight against evil effecting the transformation of society, the manifestation of the hopes of a subdued class

(186). Accentuating the political dimension of romance somewhat differently, White even considers an anarchist outlook reflected in the mode – an interpretation that is not implausible considering that heroic interventions challenging, and helping to transform questionable foundations of culture and society are, in principle, possible always and everywhere (22-29).

A slightly amended quote from *David Copperfield* opens a discussion that is very much at the heart of *Summer*, regarding the question of what political heroism means today: "Whether I shall turn out to be the heroine of my own life" (7). More specifically, Seasonal Quartet's conclusive volume would seem to conjure the heroic ideal of chivalric romance at several points, for example, when young Sacha Greenlaw, a Greta Thunberg fan, posts a self-ironizing "knight in shining armour emoji" (41) to a friend. However, when her mother remembers an old rhyme about "the days of old when knights were bold," this would seem to question the patriarchal implications of a bygone age in which "women weren't invented" (291). Rather than subscribing to an all-too-straightforward understanding of romance with its outmoded and chauvinist ideas of heroism, the overall design of *Summer* corresponds to the mode's less conventional *penseroso* variant, which, according to Frye, typically unites a group of congenial people in a homely storytelling round and which "marks the end of a movement from active to contemplative adventure" (202). This adequately describes what happens in *Summer* when Art and Charlotte (his ex-girlfriend-turned-political-ally) from *Winter* initiate the Greenlaws into an unexpectedly open and sympathetic exchange of views. It all reads like a deepened and extended conversation scene in which the bars that separate the inner life from expression and collective reflection are no longer in place. Yet this shift towards a shared act of contemplation, in which the characters easily drift between the present and their memories, does not simply entail that the world no longer needs heroes; rather, *Summer* seems to underwrite Sacha's faith that "the modern sense of being a hero is like shining a bright light on things that need to be seen" (246). While this outlook de-centres heroism so as to make it plural and democratic, it also implies that contemplation is not just for its own sake: rather, it should exercise and fortify the mind in order to make things visible, which is the primary aim that art shares with political commitment. It is therefore only fitting that the *penseroso* romance of *Summer* prominently revisits Daniel Gluck and Iris Cleves, thus giving centre stage to old and wise people with a clear and steady vision rather than celebrating the heroic cliché of the knightly dare-devil.

5 Conclusion

All in all, in Smith's Seasonal Quartet cycle, history and tradition, in terms of the flexible logic of literary modes, provide an antidote to the determinism and one-sidedness of dominant narratives. The ideal of inspirational communication and political solidarity animating Smith's novels is, to a large extent, a romance of the old, though the cultural constructs around old age are simultaneously revised, without ever succumbing to the false optimism of a simplistic progress narrative. By returning to the 'ideal old,' Daniel and Iris, *Summer* also provides a sense of closure to the cycle as a whole, pointing back to its beginning in *Autumn* but also suggesting, by nonetheless introducing new characters and drawing surprising connections, that the cycle's prospected repetition will entail difference. In an article for the *Guardian* on the occasion of Seasonal's completion, Smith characterizes the quartet as a whole as "a kind of experiment sourced in cyclic time but moving forward through time simultaneously" (Smith, "Before Brexit"). This experiment, both aesthetic and philosophical, is said to be facilitated by the novel form itself, praised by Smith as "ever-evolving, ever-communal, ever-revolutionary, and because of this, ever-hopeful to work with, whatever it formally does." As such an outlook implies unexpected transformations of generic expectations, it would not appear too far-fetched to read these works more specifically as amended and partly transvalued variants of the coming-of-age novel, in which processes of maturation, implying a ripening sense of collective awareness and responsibility, are presented as independent from biological age.[2] In *Summer*, the coming-of-age of the teenagers Sacha and Robert (her disoriented-yet-brilliant brother) – whose evolving ways of seeing have much in common with Iris and Daniel, respectively (which is also true for Charlotte and Art) – thus reiterates a process of awakening and change that the earlier volumes in the series have attributed to characters of *all* ages, including older people like Wendy Demand and Richard Lease. This sense of an ending, with its revised understanding of family and kinship in terms of wider reaches of

---

[2] *Summer* mentions in passing the violence a school teacher recently had to experience from a fanaticized father when insisting that the word "Bildungsroman" does not simply signify a "foreign" literary tradition but has long entered English culture as the general term for a "story of a person's personal development," "about learning how to live and maturing into adulthood" (97). By contrast to such anti-intellectual rancour, the 'coming-of-age' conducted in Smith's Seasonal cycle would expose a careful revision of the Bildungsroman tradition, freeing it from gendered, elitist, and age-related assumptions.

connectedness, would indicate the hope for a new generation that is eager to engage with and learn, rather than to seek distance, from the old. Adapting the expression more generally as a metaphor for Smith's political writing in hard times, 'coming-of-age' as a shared experience in the Seasonal Quartet would suggest a new empowering myth of an ongoing and infinite process, like the change of seasons, that continuously and ever anew unites old and young in empathy, creativity, and solidarity.[3]

[3] While the Seasonal Quartet shares with Yuri M. Lotman's seminal definition of myth a sense of cyclical time attuned to natural processes (151-53), the novels' repetitions of the central 'coming-of-age' theme also generate something new, thus constituting an enlightened and political myth of change that does not impair, but actually encourages, human agency.

References

All Party Parliamentary Group (APPG) on Social Integration. *Healing the Generational Divide. Interim Report on Intergenerational Connection*, socialintegrationappg.org.uk/wp-content/uploads/sites/2/2019/05/Healing-the-Generational-Divide.pdf.

Blaikie, Andrew. *Ageing and Popular Culture*. Cambridge UP, 1999.

Clarke, Harold D., et al. *Brexit. Why Britain Voted to Leave the European Union*. Cambridge UP, 2017.

"The Crimson Permanent Assurance Company." Directed by Terry Gilliam. *The Meaning of Life*. Directed by Terry Jones and Terry Gilliam, Celandine Films, Monty Python Partnership, and Universal Pictures, 1983.

Derrida, Jacques. *Spectres of Marx. The State of the Debt, the Work of Mourning and the New International.* Translated by Peggy Kamuf, Routledge, 2006.

Eldridge, John, and Lizzie Eldridge. *Raymond Williams. Making Connections*. Routledge, 1994.

Frye, Northrop. *Anatomy of Criticism. Four Essays*. Princeton UP, 1957.

Gilleard, Christopher, and Paul Higgs. *Cultures of Ageing. Self, Citizen and the Body*. Pearson, 2000.

Gullette, Margaret M. *Aged by Culture*. Chicago UP, 2004.

Kingman, David. *Generations Apart? The Growth of Age Segregation in England and Wales*. The Intergenerational Foundation, 2016, www.if.org.uk/wp-content/uploads/2016/09/Generations-Apart_Report_Final_Web-Version-1.pdf.

Lotman, Yuri M. *Universe of the Mind. A Semiotic Theory of Culture*. Translated by Ann Shukman, I. B. Tauris, 1990.

Macdougall, Norman. *An Antidote to the English. The Auld Alliance, 1295-1560*. Tuckwell, 2001.

Minois, Georges. *History of Old Age. From Antiquity to the Renaissance*. Translated by Sarah Hanbury Tenison, Polity, 1989.

Norris, Pippa, and Ronald Inglehart. *Cultural Backlash. Trump, Brexit, and Authoritarian Populism*. Cambridge UP, 2019.

Parkin, Tim. "The Ancient Greek and Roman Worlds." *A History of Old Age*, edited by Pat Thane, Thames and Hudson, 2005, pp. 31-70.

Pine, Richard. *The Thief of Reason. Oscar Wilde and Modern Ireland*. Gill and Macmillan, 1995.

Rau, Petra. "*Autumn* After the Referendum." *Brexit and Literature. Critical and Cultural Responses*, edited by Robert Eaglestone, Routledge, 2018, pp. 57-71.

Sabater, Albert, et al. "The Spatialities of Ageing: Evidencing Increasing Spatial Polarization between Older and Younger Adults in England and Wales." *Demographic Research*, vol. 36, 2017, pp. 731-44.

Smith, Ali. *Autumn*. Hamish Hamilton, 2016.

——. "Before Brexit, Greenfell, Covid-19... Ali Smith on Writing Four Novels in Four Years." *Guardian*, 1 Aug. 2020, www.theguardian.com/books/2020/aug/01/before-brexit-grenfell-covid-19-ali-smith-on-writing-four-novels-in-four-years.

——. *How to Be Both*. Hamish Hamilton, 2014.

——. *Spring*. Hamish Hamilton, 2019.

——. *Summer*. Hamish Hamilton, 2020.

——. *There but for the*. Hamish Hamilton, 2011.

——. *Winter*. Hamish Hamilton, 2017.

Tönnies, Merle, and Dennis Henneböhl. "Negotiating Images of (Un-)Belonging and (Divided) Communities: Ali Smith's Seasonal Quartet as a Counter-Narrative to Brexit." *Literatures of Brexit*, special issue of *Journal for the Study of British Cultures*, edited by Anne-Julia Zwierlein et al., vol. 26, no. 2, 2019, pp. 181-93.

Umunna, Chuka. "When You See How Different Generations Voted in the Brexit Referendum, You Realise How Important It Is to Change Perspectives." *Independent*, 25 June 2018, www.independent.co.uk/voices/politics-generation-uk-brexit-labour-conservatives-young-vote-a8416271.html.

United for All Ages. *Mixing Matters. How Shared Sites Can Bring Older and Younger People Together and Unite Brexit Britain.* docs.wixstatic.com/ugd/98d289_8e6302f601be4e70942a1d3909a7d2bd.pdf.

White, Hayden. *Metahistory. The Historical Imagination in Nineteenth-Century Europe*. Johns Hopkins UP, 1975.

Williams, Raymond. *Keywords. A Vocabulary of Culture and Society*. New ed., Oxford UP, 2015.

——. *Marxism and Literature*. Oxford UP, 1977.

Wood, James. "The Power of the Literary Pun." *New Yorker*, 22 Jan. 2018, www.newyorker.com/magazine/2018/01/29/the-power-of-the-literary-pun.

The Story of Brexit: Nostalgia in Parody Children's BrexLit

Michelle Witen

This essay examines the children's literature parodies *Five on Brexit Island* (by Bruno Vincent, 2016), *Five Escape Brexit Island* (by the same, 2017), *Alice in Brexitland* (by Leavis Carroll, 2017), and the Ladybird spoof *The Story of Brexit* (by Jason A. Hazeley and Joel P. Morris, 2018) through the lens of 'BrexLit,' focusing on the politicization of these texts whose originals each capture an idealized British past. Beginning with a juxtaposition of the pastiches with their original counterparts, this essay moves through the different facets of Enid Blyton's Britain as Brexit's Britain, and the subversion of Lewis Carroll's Wonderland into a delusional Brexitland, before focusing on *The Story of Brexit.* Paying particular attention to the publication and reception history of the Ladybird series, this essay engages intertextually with the parody's reproduced illustrations of the allegedly simpler life pictured in formative Ladybird books of the 1960s and 1970s and performs a close reading of the accompanying text. In each case, the parodies function as humorous coping mechanisms for a Brexit reality, but they also expose how the nostalgia associated with the charm of the originals becomes a political and social commentary for the 2016 Brexit campaigns.

Keywords: Brexit, nostalgia, Ladybird books, children's literature, BrexLit, parody

In his introduction to *Brexit and Literature: Critical and Cultural Responses*, Robert Eaglestone writes, "Brexit grew from cultural beliefs, real or

Brexit and Beyond: Nation and Identity. SPELL: Swiss Papers in English Language and Literature 39, edited by Daniela Keller and Ina Habermann, Narr, 2020, pp. 145-66.

imaginary, about Europe and the UK; the arguments before, during and after the referendum were – and are – arguments about culture" (1). Connecting this to a specifically literary culture that has emerged after Brexit, Kristian Shaw, in the same collection, addresses how Brexit "revealed the inherent divisions" within Britain (16), and questions "the purpose of 'national' literature in a divided cultural landscape" (18). For Shaw, "BrexLit" is post-2016 fiction that "engage[s] with emergent political realities" (16). In his words, it is a term that encompasses fictions that "directly respond or imaginatively allude to Britain's exit from the EU, or engage with subsequent socio-cultural, economic, racial or cosmopolitical consequences of Britain's withdrawal" (18). While it is a commonplace to consider novels such as Ali Smith's *Autumn* (2016), Anthony Cartwright's *The Cut* (2017), Sarah Moss's *Ghost Wall* (2018), Melissa Harrison's *All Among the Barley* (2018), or the works of Bernard Cornwell as examples of BrexLit, there nevertheless exists another category of fiction that also engages with Britain's new political reality, namely, the parodies of Enid Blyton's *Famous Five*, Lewis Carroll's *Alice in Wonderland*, and the Ladybird series. Although these humorous books tend to be dismissed critically because they are political spoofs, this essay considers *Five on Brexit Island*, *Alice in Brexitland*, and *The Story of Brexit* as BrexLit, first by differentiating them from other politically explanatory Brexit non-fiction, and then by examining each text in turn to show how these "quintessentially British" (Zeegen 7) children's literatures reveal deep-seated elements of nostalgia that are then critiqued and dismantled. This essay pays particular attention to *The Story of Brexit* and its relationship to the relatively underexplored original Ladybird series, demonstrating how this pastiched BrexLit exposes the underlying issues that helped generate and propagate narratives and slogans such as 'Take Back Control,' the roots of which can be found in classic nostalgic images of the allegedly simpler life of the 1960s and 1970s pictured in formative Ladybird books.

Almost as soon as the referendum result to leave the EU was announced, the British public began trying to make sense of the EU, what leaving it meant, and what it was they had voted on in the first place. Amid this confusion, seemingly helpful 'guides' began to pop up, many of them parodies, humorous histories, and satires that fit seamlessly alongside more serious tomes. Some, in keeping with the many portmanteaux that emerged from the word 'Brexit,' provided historical 'brexplanations': what is the EU; why the vote happened; what trends can be detected, etc. Recent examples of these include Danny Dorling and Sally Tomlinson's critique of the British post-empire mentality in

Rule Britannia: Brexit and the End of Empire (2019) and Kevin O'Rourke's *A Short History of Brexit: From Brentry to Backstop* (2019), where he explains the history of the EU and how it shaped British/European relations, with a particular emphasis on the Irish border as integral to the European project.

In addition to texts that try to locate Britain's changing place on the world stage, much Brexit-based non-fiction has been devoted to particular politicians who shaped the Remain and Leave campaigns: Steve Bell's *Corbyn the Resurrection* (2018), Channel 4's Dominic Cummings biopic *Brexit: The Uncivil War* (2019), and Tim Shipman's *All Out War: The Full Story of How Brexit Sank Britain's Political Class* (2016) come readily to mind. The latter, published within six months of the 2016 referendum, reconstructs the daily activities of the two campaigns with a focus on Boris Johnson, Michael Gove, George Osborne, Nigel Farage, and Dominic Cummings. Some politicians also took to writing self-help books in the wake of Brexit, ranging from George Walden's prescient *Exit from Brexit: Time to Emigrate* (written before Brexit and revised in 2016) to Nick Clegg's somewhat self-serving *How to Stop Brexit (and Make Britain Great Again*) (2017).

Amid these burgeoning genres, there also emerged four Brexit-based pastiches of well-loved British children's literature that can be seen as both a 'brexplanation' but also, arguably, as an example of 'BrexLit': namely, *Five on Brexit Island* (2016), its sequel *Five Escape Brexit Island (*2017), *Alice in Brexitland* (2017), and the Ladybird spoof *The Story of Brexit* (2018). Though similar in purpose to the above-mentioned non-fiction, these four texts nevertheless operate as reimaginings of classic children's literature, treading a fine line between fiction and fact. The first two of these are a reinterpretation of Enid Blyton's classic *Five on a Treasure Island* (part of the *Famous Five* series). The original story, strongly influenced by Robert Louis Stevenson's *Treasure Island*, concerns the adventures of Julian, Anne, Dick, and their tomboy cousin George (and, of course, Timmy the dog). After surviving a brutal storm on "George's Island" (officially known as Kirrin's Island), they are the first to uncover a box from a shipwreck revealed by the storm, which contains a treasure map of the island. When the discovery is made public, the island is invaded first by reporters, then by prospective real estate buyers, and finally by these same procurers, but this time as trespassers and thieves, before foreclosure of the property. The sale is blocked when the treasure is discovered; George's family becomes wealthy again; and ownership of George's Island is returned to her, later to be divided equally amongst her cousins.

First published in 1942, *Five on a Treasure Island* led to twenty-one more books in the *Famous Five* series, all of them elevating the courage of the protagonists as well as extolling the value of exploring England and Wales. In the context of World War II (including "Operation Pied Piper"), this idealization of the British countryside, in the form of intrepid English schoolchildren and their adventures, encapsulates British insularity and moral rectitude. Many of the novels involve the investigation of suspicious persons and question notions of property and ownership, with the villains of the series being categorized as "'gypsies,' 'tinkers,' swarthy-looking strangers, people who work for the circus, people with non-RP accents, people who don't speak English, [and] foreigners in general" (Risbridger). However, the xenophobic Othering of the villains aside, Blyton also captures an idyllic Britain that matches the slogan of the Leave campaign. As Eleanor Risbridger puts it:

> Brexit Blighty is Blyton's Blighty. It's white socks, rock cakes, church bells. It's cricket pitches, jolly hockey sticks, high tea and home for the holidays. It's Victoria sponge, cucumber sandwiches, and four kinds of fork. It's pounds, shillings and pence; it's poles, perches and rods; it's the boy stood on the burning deck whence all but he had fled; it's thinking that the Empire wasn't all bad, come on, what about the trains and the post office? [...] It's about Britain – domestic, green, leafy little Britain – as the centre of the universe. That's what people want when they say "give us our country back": they want to take it back to Blyton's Britain.

Given this snapshot of 'Blyton's Britain,' it is no wonder that in 2017, one year after the Brexit vote, the Great Western Railway (GWR) chose to repurpose the Famous Five as emblems of adventure, exploration, and Britishness in their marketing campaign, "Five go on a Great Western Adventure." Featuring the GWR as the fastest and most efficient way to travel, the TV spots show the unsupervised Famous Five witnessing stunning views of South West England and Wales while pursuing a swarthy villain, an unruly Timmy, and madcap inventor, Uncle Quentin.

In another unexpected afterlife, Enid Blyton's Famous Five grow up and continue to have more adventures, this time negotiating the perils of modern-day living by "giving up the booze," "going Gluten-free," getting "beach body ready," and, apparently, joining in the Brexit debate. Picking up on the earlier issues of property, ownership, and borders in *Five on a Treasure Island*, *Five on Brexit Island* presents George and Julian going head-to-head in "another referendum" (21) to decide the ownership and independence of Kirrin's Island in the wake of Brexit and its ultimate fate to become a haven for shell companies. In this first of the classic British children's literature parodies, both sides of the political debate are represented, and it is arguably less partisan as compared to its sequel, *Five Escape Brexit Island*, where the intrepid bunch are trying to escape Cousin Rupert's independent island to reach mainland Europe. Presenting a full parody of the Leave and Remain campaigns, the text stays true to the "didactic Blyton texts that have 'edified' generations of child readers" (Berberich 156), providing a fictional outlet for factual content that adds an element of humour absent both in Blyton's original and in the two campaigns. If 'Brexit Blighty' is 'Blyton's Blighty,' then this pastiche serves the purpose of holding up a humorous, but non-partisan, mirror to the British idealization of an imaginary past.

By contrast, Leavis Carroll's *Alice in Brexitland* is much more overtly partisan. Following the original storyline of Lewis Carroll's *Alice in Wonderland*, the spoof begins with a tired, bored, modern-day (yet still somehow explicitly Victorian) Alice sitting with her sister and finding the non-picture books unappealing: "[W]hat is the use of a book without pictures or conversations?" both Lewis and Leavis Carroll ask (Carroll 7; Leavis Carroll 1). Alice is then distracted from her imaginings by a white rabbit named David Camerrabbit, who is muttering about being late, but this time, his lateness is linked to 23 June. In following the Camerrabbit, Alice thus begins her adventures "[d]own the Brexit-hole" (Leavis Carroll 5). The fantasies of consumption – "DRINK ME" and "EAT ME" (Lewis Carroll 10, 12) – are subverted into the consumerist "READ ME" with reference to the *Daily Murdoch* (Leavis Carroll 7), a clear parody of the *Sun*, known for propagating fear and Euromyths. As she reads, Alice's fury makes her grow; and she only returns to her normal size by reading the *Gordian* (aka the *Guardian*), though it too is criticized for its "tiny" print and "smug" tone (11-12).

In her adventures, she encounters various topsy-turvy, nonsensical, yet recognizable political figures, including the hookah-smoking "Corbyn-pillar"; the "Cheshire Twat" (Farage), who, along with his smile, disappears after the referendum; "Tweedleboz" and "Tweedlegove" (Johnson and Gove); "The Queen of Heartlessness" (Theresa May); and three playing cards in judges' periwigs – meant to represent Lord Chief Justice Baron Thomas of Cwmgiedd, Head of Civil Justice Sir Terence Etherton, and Lord Justice of Appeal Sir Philip Sales – blocking the road to Article 50. She is also literally cat-apulted by the Cheshire Twat over the Atlantic Ocean, where she meets "Trumpty-Dumpty" on his golden wall and his mad Tea Party supporters, wearing their "Make

America Great Again" baseball caps (until they don KKK headdresses). Even the caucus race occurs in the form of a bizarre conversation with forest animals – with the exotic animals of John Tenniel's illustrations and the original text conspicuously replaced by animals indigenous to Britain, such as the cock, the hedgehog, the fox, and the duck – where Alice is accused of being an illegal immigrant who has swum to their forest and is now "on benefits" (18). As in the original, *Brexitland*'s Alice attempts to anchor herself in her knowledge by trying to recite basic rhymes and failing, and by continually asking other characters the way.

Within its Victorian context, Lewis Carroll's Wonderland is a magical, nonsensical realm that also encapsulates a kind of Britishness in its representation of tea-drinking, imperialism, class-values, and childhood education – albeit in a disordered way. As Gillian Avery writes, "[h]owever far Alice wanders through Wonderland or Looking-Glass Country, she is constantly reminded of things she has learned, but always in a gloriously muddled way, which makes the real subjects seem equally nonsensical" (325). In so doing, imagination makes the inconceivable conceivable, but there is no lesson to be learned from waking up. However, in the case of its parody, while real subjects remain nonsensical, imagination in the form of delusion is the cure, making *Alice in Brexitland* a moral tale in a way that the original is not. Upon awakening, Alice now seeks to educate herself, asking her sister: "May I read your book? [...] The one about the EU? At first I thought it looked horribly dull, for it had no pictures or conversations, but now I realise I should like to understand the subject" (99).

There is an even further departure in Leavis Carroll's text, because Alice's delusions are presented as realities when she awakens. Rousing herself with a yell, Alice returns to her own sensible world, where Remain has prevailed at 99% of the vote; Hillary Clinton is President; and neither Prince, Alan Rickman, nor David Bowie has died (98-99). Alice realizes "she had been wrong to wish away facts and figures, for [...] [t]hat road led to Brexitland, and [...] to live there permanently would be a nightmare" (99). However, as she wanders away, Alice sees the smiling Cheshire Cat in her alleged reality, leaving Alice to wonder: "Am I in a sane world dreaming of madness, or a mad world dreaming of sanity?" (100). This conclusion presents a bleak contrast to the charming original, where Alice's sister half dreams herself in Wonderland while gazing at the sleeping Alice – "[s]o she sat on with closed eyes, and half believed herself in Wonderland, though she knew she had but to open them again and all would change to dull reality" (Lewis Carroll 98) – since Alice's dreams in Brexitland were clearly a nightmare, and "dull reality" is, in fact, topsy-turvy. In Lewis Carroll, there is a clear line drawn between the fictional wonderland and the adult world; however, Leavis Carroll represents this madness and Alice's helplessness as a Leaving reality that is disorienting for adult and child alike. In this sense, he subverts the nostalgia for childhood – "for little Alice and all her wonderful Adventures" (Lewis Carroll 98) – and dismantles it into a delusion, a "struggle to engage," and "impoten[ce]" (Leavis Carroll 101).

Just as *Alice in Brexitland* and the Brexit version of the *Famous Five* represent parodies of two different types of British literary mythologies, so too does *The Story of Brexit* appeal to a very particular audience because of the special place occupied by the Ladybird series within the British psyche. Of the three, the Ladybird series is likely the least well-known outside of Britain, so the following paragraphs will address the publication and reception history of the original series in order to bring the parody into sharper relief.

Lawrence Zeegen – author of *Ladybird by Design*, one of only two monographs on the Ladybird phenomenon and a respected expert in the field – describes the special place attributed to the Ladybird books by the British reading public:

> Now undeniably considered a national treasure, Ladybird Books have a place in the nation's psyche; our collective memories hold dear the influence of these charming books. A Ladybird book evokes strong feelings; deep-rooted memories of a time and a place when a simply designed and cheaply produced book could resonate across generations of readers. (8-11)

The "simply designed" Ladybird book is a well-known trademark, and the Ladybird parodies take full advantage of the nostalgia associated with its familiar format. Measuring 11.5 cm by 8 cm, the 52-56-page hardcover book features a colour illustration on the recto and, on the verso, text in a sans-serif font that closely resembles very neat handwritten (non-cursive) print. This typeface is particularly fitting, considering the Ladybird's publication and reception history, where the *Key Words Reading Scheme* series (colloquially known as the "Peter and Jane books") were even used as elementary school primers in the 1960s.

Although the first book in the series was a Beatrix Potter-esque story called *Bunnikin's Picnic Party* (1940), the Ladybird books had their heyday in the 1960s and 1970s, with series titles such as "Historical Figures," "How it Works," "People at Work," "Keywords," "The Ladybird Book of," and "The Story of." The books were, and still are, a staple in British and Commonwealth households and are often "credited with [having] introduc[ed] reading skills to millions of children worldwide" (Duthie).

In fact, by the time Wills & Hepworth, the original Loughborough-based publishers of the series, was sold in 1972 to Penguin Random House, "about 500 different Ladybirds had been published, observing everyday life in postwar Britain and demystifying it with words and pictures that anyone could understand. In 1946, annual sales were 24,000; by 1971 they had reached 20m" (Day, "How Ladybird").

The aforementioned "deep-rooted memories" of "time and place" (Zeegen 8-11) are also firmly entrenched in nostalgia and represent the deeply ideological nature of the series. As Malcolm Clark writes, "[f]or anyone under the age of 50, a glance at an old Ladybird book is a peek into a lost age of innocence" (40). However, for those who lived during the peak popularity of the Ladybird books, they also voiced what Zeegen refers to as an "overtly British view of the world" based on its status as an empire:

> At a time when the British empire had yet to decline and the combined colonies still represented one-fifth of the world's population, Ladybird's overtly British view of the world was one that reflected a nation growing in confidence and prosperity following the end of the Second World War. If a Ladybird book were to have had a voice, it would most likely have sounded like a radio or TV Presenter from the 1950s or 1960s, with every syllable articulated precisely, every expression nuanced perfectly and every sentence grammatically impeccable. (Zeegen 216)

Given that the time after the Second World War is often seen as the death knell of the British Empire, Zeegen's categorization of this time as its zenith is confusing for a non-British reader. However, further nationalistic statements about their status as a symbol of British prosperity pepper Zeegen's complete history of the imprint in *Ladybird by Design* as well as his interviews with Britain's leading newspapers. Some striking examples of Zeegen's nationalism include his description of the tone of the books as "that of a friendly teacher, an older guiding brother or sister, a knowledgeable uncle or aunt: never patronizing, always optimistic and forever British" (216); the declaration that the "editorial approach" of the books "reflected the views that the nation had of itself: proud to be British, and proud to entertain and educate children" (217); or his description of the "quintessentially British" tone of the books:

> The Ladybird tone of voice was authoritative, but never condescending. Ladybird language was open and honest, nurturing and caring, down-to-earth, yet also aspirational. Quintessentially British, but with truly global ap-

> peal, Ladybird was a trusted British brand akin to the BBC, Rolls-Royce and Marks & Spencer. (7)

A large part of the overall image attached to the Ladybird books which made it such a "British brand" was the use of artwork from "the top commercial artists and illustrators of their day" (42). For example, Harry Wingfield, who was the artist behind the Peter and Jane series, was known for having created the "distinctive look" of the series: "bright primary colours, blue skies, cotton-wool clouds and children running around, limbs akimbo, when they weren't trying to mend kites or conduct wide-eyed experiments on miniature pulleys" (Clark 40). These images have grown to encapsulate this readership's nostalgic image of a simpler time.

As for the subject matter of the Ladybird books, the project was intended to spark the curiosity of a young reader and inspire them to pursue easily digestible knowledge in literary form. As Clark phrases it:

> [O]nce you had learned to read, you could move on to a panoply of different subjects, each featured in its own dedicated little tome, from the lives of biographical figures such as Captain Scott or Robert the Bruce, to significant moments in history, such as the civil war. (41)

Importantly, these significant moments are firmly rooted in British history and, more specifically, in the glorification of Britain. Looking at the Ladybird history of *Captain Cook*, for example, in the treatment of the indigenous peoples, the text accompanying a picture of 'peace-loving' Captain Cook and his men brutally shooting and killing the Maoris reads:

> Unfortunately, [the Maoris] were also hostile when Cook went ashore, and the first landing resulted in a skirmish. Cook tried again, with a similar result. When he had himself rowed round the bay to look for a place where they could land unopposed, they were attacked by warriors in canoes and had to open fire in self defence. (Humphris 29)[1]

[1] This 1980 version of *Captain Cook* is a revision – both in text and in illustration – of the 1958 version, which pictures an even more violent altercation, and the caption reads: "Here he [Captain Cook] was attacked by some of the natives, called Maoris, and was obliged to fire on them in self defence. Cook always treated natives well, and it was unfortunate that he was on this occasion forced to take such action" (qtd. in Orestano 15-16).

This is the second of three images of indigenous peoples being fired upon: earlier in the book, Cook and the British also kill First Nation Canadians (15) and again the shooting that led to Cook's death in Hawaii is pictured (50). The other representation of the relations between the British and indigenous peoples is shown in Cook's reception in Maui as an accidental god (49), which is also featured as the first page's titular image of the book (1). In terms of tone – alleged to be "authoritative, but never condescending […] open and honest, nurturing and caring, down-to-earth, yet also aspirational" (Zeegen 7) – these violent conflicts are watered down to diminishing descriptors such as "skirmish" (Humphris 29) and "scuffle" (50).

Critics such as Caroline Lowbridge have acknowledged some of these problems in the Ladybird books for a twenty-first-century readership, which persist even though the images were updated in the 1970s in view of their noticeable sexism:[2] as Lowbridge states, one would think that "women do all the housework"; "men do the important work"; "only Britain shaped the world"; "everyone in Britain is white"; British children played pretty dangerously; "mini computers are the size of a room"; Richard III was unilaterally a villain; nuclear power and oil are definitely good things (published pre Chernobyl); and, as seen from the "Travel Adventure" series, "the USA is full of 'Cowboys and Indians'" (Lowbridge). Clark also gestures to the fashion of seeing Wingfield's Peter and Jane as "politically suspect": "Supposedly, their passion for exercise as well as school uniforms has a little too much of the Teutonic, if you get my drift. Jane, smiling till her face ached, with a thatch of blonde (yes blonde) hair, is supposed to be nothing less than Riefenstahl for infants" (40). Zeegen counters these critiques with the *zeitgeist* defence:

> Ladybird's portrayal of the wider world up until the 1970s was one that chimed with the views and thoughts of most people in Britain at the time.

---

[2] Despite its status as a "national treasure," the Ladybird series has received little critical attention. Aside from Zeegen's *Ladybird by Design*, there is only one other monograph on the series, Lorraine Johnson and Brian Alderson's *The Ladybird Story: Children's Book for Everyone*, which focuses primarily on the "rise, decline, and fall" of Wills & Hepworth Publishing (x). Outside of this, there are entries in the *Oxford Encyclopedia of Children's Literature* ("Easy Readers," "Ladybird Books") and some cultural critiques in newspapers and blogs (see Clark; Armistead; Lowbridge; Day). Other engagements are primarily labours of love devoted to curating collections and historical background (i.e., Helen Day's *Ladybird Fly Away Home* blog and Facebook pages), cataloguing the series (i.e., Nicole Else's *List of Standard-Sized Ladybird Books*), and particular artists (i.e., Frank Hampson and Martin Aitchison).

> Whilst with the benefit of hindsight we might be tempted to re-enter Ladybird's world and critique the values of the day through the lens of the 21st century, it is worth remembering that just a few decades ago information on and empathy towards different cultures was not widely known [...] Britain's understanding of the world in the early 1960s was still resolutely based upon the notion of the British Empire. (173)

As Lowbridge also bluntly points out, "it's fair to say that if you only learnt your history through Ladybird books, you had a very British view of the world that pretty much said that Britain shaped it."

Like the Famous Five, the Ladybird series has also experienced a comic afterlife in the form of the "Ladybird Books for Grown Ups." The series pokes fun at aspects of adult life – such as *The Ladybird Book of the Hangover*, *Dating*, *The Hipster*, and *Mindfulness* – and are very clearly satires, with *The Story of Brexit* falling under this umbrella, despite its intention of functioning as a "stand-alone title" (Fox-Leonard). Also similar to *Five on Brexit Island*, the latter diverges from the subject matter of its other parodies (i.e., as opposed to *Five Give up the Booze*) by focusing on a political event rather than lifestyle choices. Adopting the original Ladybird tone of trying "to make the world easy-to-understand and unshocking" (Armistead), *The Story of Brexit* treads the fine line between escapist mockery and a genuine attempt, through humour and irony, to make sense of and come to terms with Brexit. This ambiguity is encapsulated by the juxtaposition of satirical text with original Ladybird artwork from the pictorial archive, to which the TV comedy writers Jason Hazeley and Joel Morris had full access. These latter-day images become their own instrument of pastiche: the acerbic content that matches the images make the pictures speak in a way that is completely other from their original context, while also highlighting the irony of the explanations: "The once cutting-edge illustrations ha[ve] become a gift for pastiche [...]. The fun of the series lies in the relationship of mid-20th-century iconography aimed at children to 21st-century comedy for adults" (Armistead).

While there is much fun to be had in reading texts like *The Story of Brexit* – and there are certainly points where the little volume is laugh-out-loud hilarious – the remainder of this essay is devoted to a close reading of this parody in light of its publication and cultural history. At the risk of dissecting the humour and moving away from the authors' stated intention of "just want[ing] people to have a giggle" (Fox-Leonard), I will examine the illustrations – the seemingly generic images of everyday life from the 1960s and 1970s that idealize Britain,[3] which are still relevant when providing a political and social commentary of the 2016 campaign in *The Story of Brexit* – both in their original contexts and alongside Hazeley and Morris' text, showing that the nostalgia that has made these books bestsellers can also reveal the roots of the 'Take Back Control' nostalgia that led to the Leave vote.

Despite Hazeley's insistence that "it's actually not that political" (Fox-Leonard), *The Story of Brexit* presents the stereotypes of the Brexit Leave campaign, using a deceptively simple tone that could either be seen as stark criticism or as a further propagation of the types of statements that infused the Leave campaign, depending on the reader. The first page of the "story" begins by assuring us that "Britain is a proud island. For centuries we stood alone. Now we stand alone again. Other countries, like Croatia and Spain, need to be part of Europe, because they are clearly cowards. But our country is special [...]. This is the future" (6). The second half of this statement is blatantly disingenuous, yet the 'Britain stands alone' and 'being part of the EU indicates weakness' mentality was omnipresent in the Leave campaign. Read alongside the archival illustrations, however, the irony becomes clearer: pictured next to this as a vision of the 'future' is an image of a sparsely populated early modern village, replete with thatch-roofed cottages, a steepled church, verdant fields dotted with sheep, and a horse-drawn carriage. By foregrounding their rootedness in a romanticized idyllic past, this image problematizes statements about the future and demonstrates the incongruity of envisioning the future as the past.

The apposition of the more recent past (the 1960s) with the realities of 2016 can also be seen in the following statement: "The British are known all over the world for keeping calm and Carry On films" (10). While very popular in the 1960s and 1970s, the *Carry On* franchise would not be considered the primary cinematic export of Britain today, though harkening to them matches the heyday of the Ladybird books. The other reference is most certainly to the 1939 "Keep Calm and Carry On" motivational poster: although it was not actually used during World War II (Hughes), its (re)discovery in 2000 has led to an intense meme afterlife which, though separate from the original stiff upper lip in the face of the Blitz message, is nevertheless one about keeping calm in the face of adversity. After lauding the British "sense of humour" and its

[3] For a perspective on how faded British imperialism in the 1960s and 1970s affected childhood education (i.e., the imperial pink of the map) and the attitude towards the commonwealth, see Sally Tomlinson's *Education and Race: From Empire to Brexit.*

"common sense," this segment of the book concludes with the following ambiguous line, "Brexit has been Britain at its best" (10). Read in the ironic tone that was intended, this is clearly a self-deprecating statement; however, as seen in the 'The People Have Spoken' post-referendum headlines, Leave voters genuinely claimed that Brexit was British democracy at its best. Nevertheless, to make the irony clearer, facing this passage and its conclusion is a seemingly non-sequitur image of an English bulldog – known for its stubbornness and selective deafness – which is also a well-known image for representing British nationalism.

Often, the Ladybird books in "The Story Of" series present particular modes of British achievement, as can be seen with titles such as *Our Land in the Making*, *Homes and Houses*, and *The Story of the Railways: A Ladybird 'Achievements' Book*. Thus, it is worth pointing out that the spoof *The Story of Brexit*, which appears as a parody continuation of this series, is missing the "Achievements" component (on the title page or anywhere else in the book – an omission which is itself a comment), and in fact, the alleged British achievements that are mentioned are hilariously diminished into, for example, statements about a singly-run, booming British jam industry:

> Evelyn makes lots of jam. The jam is sold all over the world. British jam is very popular. Brexit has made Evelyn's job much easier. She can put whatever she likes in her jam and sell it to whomever she pleases. Without Evelyn's jam, the British economy would collapse. (30)

This statement about Evelyn's jam as the backbone of the British economy recalls the misinformed argument that voting to leave the EU was a way of supporting small, local businesses and circumventing unreasonable regulations from Brussels. Likewise, "[s]he can put whatever she likes in her jam" also highlights the removal of the EU regulations regarding health and safety, which is a common concern of Remain rhetoric. However, the content becomes more overtly caustic when read alongside the image of "Evelyn" making a large pot of jam that will fill five bottles as her son and daughter gaze on with a hazy mixture of joy and trepidation. The original image comes from *Uncle Mac's ABC* (1950), and its context is "J is for Jam. We like Jelly better" (McCulloch 22-23).[4] Jam is not even the preferred condiment in this

---

[4] I am grateful to Helen Day of ladybirdflyawayhome.com for identifying the original sources of the images from *The Story of Brexit* (here and elsewhere in this essay).

situation! The jam/jelly debate aside, these images of a simpler past are clearly incongruous and delusional relative to Britain's future.

Small businesses are not the only aspect of the Brexit Leave campaign and the proliferation of Euromyths addressed. In addition to the restrictions placed by EU regulations on consumer products, *The Story of Brexit* also mentions "freedom bananas" (12), "[p]roject fear" (16), buses as a way of communicating important and reliable information to the masses (48), the disconnected financial backers behind the Leave campaign (26), the voter demographic and their belief that "foreign workers" are taking away desirable jobs from British people (36), the EU's "red tape" (34), and the deceptively simple ballot phrasing: "Being in the European Union is terribly complicated. Leaving it is terribly complicated too. Luckily the choice on the ballot paper did not look very complicated at all" (12). The authors also comment on the short-term aftermath of Brexit: the stockpiling of water "in the weeks leading up to the Brexit deadline" (48), "the Prime Minister's shed" (20), the corporate and market response to Brexit (38), the disillusion of Remainers (24, 28, 50), Leaving packages (here jokingly called "Concrete Brexit" [42]), concerns about dual nationality (44), and all this being "the will of the people" (18).

The references to the campaign are fairly clear and the accompanying images either serve to disrupt the text or highlight ironies. As shown above, one does not necessarily need to know the original source of the illustrations – and perhaps the average reader would not be able to recognize the images on sight and might even assume that it is new artwork in the style of the original Ladybirds (Day, "How It Works") – in order to read the image as a commentary on the text. However, knowing the source of the pictures provides additional intertextual insights. For example, on one page, the authors blandly point out the issues with the ballot and the information provided by the media: the choice to remain or leave "was something about freedom and bananas" (12). The corresponding image is a newspaper and magazine kiosk featuring advertising boards for the *Daily Telegraph*, the *Daily Express*, and the *Daily Mirror* as well as a man in a business suit reading *The Times*. The illustration can be traced to *The Story of Newspapers* (1969), and the accompanying text from within that story is the following: "As we have seen, different newspapers appeal to different types of reader. A popular paper appeals to the majority of people, while a quality paper appeals to a more specialised reader" (Siddle 30). This statement acts as a conclusion to the stereotypes surrounding the readership attracted to each type of paper: according to Ladybird,

> [o]ur national papers fall into two groups. Papers like the "Daily Express" are popular papers. They present their news in a bright, lively fashion, with easy-to-read articles and many photographs. Papers like "The Times" and "The Daily Telegraph" are called "heavy" or quality, papers. They emphasise the more serious subjects, and print longer articles about them. (6)

The *Daily Mirror* was originally "a paper for gentlewomen, written by gentlewomen" but due to lack of success, "was changed to a popular one" with equal prominence given to photographs and the news, making it "the first illustrated, halfpenny, daily newspaper" (24). By contrast, *The Times* is "a national institution" (20). As "the oldest national paper in Britain," it has garnered "a reputation for accurate, unbiased reporting of news, and for thoughtful, unsensational comments. It is world-renowned for its excellent news services, particularly of foreign news" and is therefore the newspaper of choice for "leaders of opinion and other influential people" (20). This division between "heavy" and "popular" newspapers and the type of news covered was very clear in the lead-up to Brexit, with blatant partisanship voiced in the *Daily Mail* and the *Daily Express*. Given that the Euromyth regarding the curvature of bananas can be traced to "popular" newspaper, the *Sun*, and that Boris Johnson during his stint with the "heavy" *Daily Telegraph* was also responsible for propagating many Euromyths, the role of newspapers in the lines "it was something about freedom and bananas" (Hazeley 12) extends beyond Euromyths to the media itself (see Evans and Ferguson).

Likewise, the divide between "heavy" and "popular" newspapers was also at the root of representations of the EU to the British voting public, with most of the Leave-leaning newspapers such as the *Sun* and *Daily Mail* appealing to "working class newspaper readers and those in casual or no employment" (Deacon et al.). Given that post-referendum coverage attributes the Leave victory to the unprecedented influence of the daily press and the misinformation contained therein (Martinson), the choice of an image from *The Story of Newspapers* enables a reading of the two texts alongside each other. This highlights that the problems of class readership and partisan politics long predate 2016, and can be traced all the way back to the advent of the newspaper. Thus, an analysis of the illustration from *The Story of Newspapers* reveals that the underlying Leave/Remain problems could even be more clearly discerned in the 1960s.

One of the many retractions that the *Daily Mail* and the *Sun* had to publish was regarding the misrepresentation of European immigration into the UK (Martinson). However, the issue of European workers taking away jobs from hard-working British citizens was one of the prejudices that informed the Leave campaign, and is reflected in *The Story of Brexit* as follows:

> Vernon is not worried about foreign workers leaving. "British people can mop up in hospitals and supervise veterinary conditions in abattoirs and stand in fields picking beans," he says. Vernon will not be doing those jobs himself, of course. He is 63. (Hazeley and Morris 36)

Supplemented by an image of a pipe-smoking man wearing a sports jacket and flat cap from *The Story of Cricket* (1965), we have a series of confused messages: the assumption that "foreign workers" in Britain only have unpalatable jobs like janitorial work, slaughterhouse inspection, or farm labouring; a contradictory narrative regarding the foreign workforce that is stealing supposedly 'good jobs' from British citizens; an odd understanding of the British economy; an account that is devoid of any mention of the EU; a statement on the voting demographic. On this one page alone, the volume addresses almost every issue at stake in a one-sided "story of Brexit."

Another such example can be seen in the arrangement of a commentary about the "exciting new words" spawned by Brexit:

> Brexit gave us lots of exciting new words, like brextremist, remoaner, bremoaner, remaybe, breprehensible, remaintenance, brexorcist, remaidstone, brex-girlfriend, remange, brextortion, remayhem and bregret. The new words make it harder for foreigners to understand what we are saying. In a tough, new international business world, small advantages such as this can be crucial. (Hazeley and Morris 22)

To complement a series of words that were mostly *not* in fact Brexit neologisms, *The Story of Brexit* illustrates the above text with an image from the "Ladybird Keywords Reading Scheme Series," *4C: Say the Sound* (1965). The original purpose of the "Keywords Reading Scheme" was to introduce early readers to "commonly used words" in English, as is elaborated in the introduction to the keyword reader:

> *Reading skill is accelerated if these important words are learned early and in a pleasant way.* The Ladybird Key Words Reading Scheme is based on these commonly used words. Those used most often in the English language are introduced first – with other words of popular appeal to children. All the Key Words list is covered in the early books, and the later titles use further word lists to develop full reading fluency. The total number of different words

which will be learned in the complete reading scheme is over one thousand. The gradual introduction of these words, frequent repetition and complete 'carry-over' from book to book will ensure rapid learning. (Murray 2-3)

The Peter and Jane illustrations that match these keywords are intended "to create a desirable attitude towards learning – by making every child *eager* to read each title" (3). Thus, in contrast to the stated purpose of easing children into reading with commonly used keywords that become the building blocks of communication, which is also one of the more recognizable uses of the original Ladybird books, *The Story of Brexit* showcases the absurdity and alienation of Brexit and its language.

Echoing the first page of the book's "Britain is a proud island. For centuries we stood alone. Now we stand alone again" (6), *The Story of Brexit* ends with the same discourse of 'Britain stands alone,' as taken within the context of World War II, but this time, in contradistinction to its previous confidence, the story ends with a question:

When the Nazis flew over the white cliffs of Dover, Britain fought back bravely, with nobody to help except lots of pilots from Eastern Europe, Canada, Africa, the USA and the Caribbean. When we cracked the secrets of the Nazi Enigma code machine, we needed nothing but British ingenuity and a Nazi Enigma machine stolen for us by some Polish spies. We stood alone before. We can do it again – can't we? (52)

The text draws upon archetypal images of empire by mentioning current and former colonies, the geopolitical borders of the white cliffs of Dover, and revealing the hypocrisy behind declarations of singlehanded wartime victories. These same inconsistencies are also present in the 1968 Ladybird *Kings and Queens, Book 2* – from which the adjacent image is taken – in the write-up on George VI taking the throne after Edward VIII's abdication and therefore Britain's role in World War II. The passage reads:

During [George VI's] reign, the evil dictator of Germany, Adolph [sic] Hitler, broke all the promises which Germany made after the First World War, and treacherously invaded Poland. Germany had been secretly training an army and air force, and soon Hitler had conquered all western Europe. A British army was forced to retreat, and return to England from Dunkirk.

For a year Britain, inspired by one of the greatest men in our history, Winston Churchill, fought alone against Hitler's Germany. London and many cities in England were heavily bombed. [...] Later, Russia became involved in the war against Germany, and also the United States of America

> came in on our side – and so final victory was certain, though not without great suffering to many millions of people. (Du Garde Peach 48)

This idea of standing alone against oppression during World War II is often yoked to the British nostalgia which fuelled the Leave campaign:

> From the phrase "take back control" to UKIP's adoption of the Trump-esque "make Britain great again," the call for Britain to leave the EU has been saturated with nostalgia. These slogans invoke a sense of our past so familiar that it seems to need no dates or references: they bring to mind the late-Victorian/Edwardian period, when most of the atlas was pink; they celebrate Britain's courage and fortitude in the Second World War and its alliance with the US and USSR – the "other" superpowers at the time. In this story, membership of the EU emasculates Britain by rendering it equal to the European nations it liberated and defeated, affronting its hard-won status as a global power. (Newbigin)

The Story of Brexit revises the notion that the British army stood alone by also including members of the Commonwealth and Eastern Europe in its accounting. The writers seem to be aware that

> this view of Britain's past is a fantasy, not history. Brexiteers are nostalgic for something that never existed: a time when Britain was both a wartime hero and a powerful global force. The reality, however, is that Britain's contribution to the allied war effort came at the price of its empire. (Newbigin)

Thus, this history, this achievement, is revealed to be a story of many fictions, with a very clear narrative slant. On the one hand, there is the Remain accusation that the Leave campaign pushed a nostalgic agenda "where passports were blue, faces were white and the map was coloured imperial pink" (Barber, quoting Vince Cable), while those who voted Leave argue that "what motivated Brexit voters was the belief that 'we have watched our sovereignty systematically eroded in virtually every area of our national life,' especially since the EU's 1992 Maastricht treaty" (Barber, quoting Ian Moody). Both stories are represented in *The Story of Brexit*, and the parody of Ladybirds and the repurposing of archival illustrations dismantles generational assumptions about British national identity. Ending with this particular event ultimately hints at a view of British history and life that is devoid of achievement, where the people are presented as petty, bewildered, divided, and uncertain.

The authors of *The Story of Brexit* claim that their pastiches are "a love letter to the Ladybird books of our childhood, which might seem a strange thing to say when you're writing about hangovers and mid-life crises, but it works because, visually, it's a very colourful, happy, simplistic version of life" (Fox-Leonard). However, this simplicity encapsulates the disjunct between the nostalgic Britain of the Ladybird classics of the 1960s and 1970s, and the realities of 2016 highlighted by the juxtaposition of text and image. By examining the Ladybird series as a cultural phenomenon that is explicitly rooted in the British psyche as a 'national treasure,' or even a collective memory of a non-existent time, one can see ways in which the Leave campaign exploited this sense of nostalgia. As Dominic Cummings's character in *The Uncivil War* says: "So much of our understanding of who we are comes from this nostalgic view we have of our past. These stories, these myths we tell each other [...] the idea that we want to return to a time when we knew our place, when things made sense, fictional or not" (51:19-38). While they represent very different segments of reading for children, very different times, brows, and trajectories, the hypotexts of each of these Brexit parodies offer specific loci for this romanticized past: in *Alice in Wonderland*, published at the height of British imperialism; in *Five on a Treasure Island*'s function as an escapist fiction of a pre-Blitz Britain; and in the cotton-candy 1960s "notion of the [allegedly still-thriving] British Empire" (Zeegen 173) of the original Ladybird books. By identifying the source of nostalgia in childhood fantasy, and thus collapsing individual nostalgia into collective memory, these very different texts allow Brexit parodies to get at the visceral, affective level, on which many people made their referendum decision. By satirizing these texts and having them engage with "emergent political realities" (Shaw 16), they cross over into BrexLit and demonstrate how "the arguments before, during and after the referendum were – and are – arguments about culture" (Eaglestone 1). Thus, while *Five on Brexit Island*, *Alice in Brexitland*, and *The Story of Brexit* use humour to cope with the results of the 2016 referendum, they also demonstrate the ways in which nostalgia for an idealized past, as seen in the intertextual relationship of each of the parodies to their originals, gave rise to, and sustained, "the stories" and "the myths" of the Leave campaign.

References

Armistead, Claire. "The Ladybird Phenomenon: The Publishing Craze That's Still Flying." *Guardian*, 21 Feb. 2017, www.theguardian.com/books/2017/feb/21/ladybird-phenomenon-publishing-craze-books-for-grown-ups.

Avery, Gillian. "Fairy Tales for Pleasure." *Alice's Adventures in Wonderland* by Lewis Carroll, edited by Donald J. Gray, Norton Critical Edition, 2nd ed., W. W. Norton, 1992, pp. 324-27.

Barber, Tony. "Nostalgia and the Promise of Brexit: Leavers Dispute British Imperial Past Has Shaped Their Mental Picture of World." *Financial Times*, 19 July 2018, www.ft.com/content/bf70b80e-8b39-11e8-bf9e-8771d5404543.

Bell, Steve. *Corbyn the Resurrection*. Guardian Faber Publishing, 2018.

Berberich, Christine. "Our Country, the Brexit Island: Brexit, Literature, and Populist Discourse." *Literatures of Brexit*, special issue of *Journal for the Study of British Cultures*, edited by Anne-Julia Zwierlein et al., vol. 26, no. 2, 2019, pp. 153-65.

Blyton, Enid. *Five on a Treasure Island*. Hodder & Stoughton, 1942.

Brexit: The Uncivil War. Directed by Toby Haynes. Channel 4, 2019.

Carroll, Leavis (alias Lucien Young). *Alice in Brexitland*. Ebury Press, 2017.

Carroll, Lewis. *Alice's Adventures in Wonderland*, edited by Donald J. Gray, Norton Critical Edition, 2nd ed., W. W. Norton, 1992.

Clark, Malcolm. "Age of Innocence: Easy Reading." *New Statesman*, 15 April 2002, pp. 40-41.

Clegg, Nick. *How to Stop Brexit (and Make Britain Great Again)*. Bodley Head, 2017.

Day, Helen. "How It Works: The Ladybird Pastiche." 29 June 2016, ladybirdflyawayhome.com/how-it-works-the-ladybird-pastiche/.

——. "How Ladybird Books Taught Children to Love Nature." *Financial Times*, 9 Aug. 2019, www.ft.com/content/e6948878-b394-11e9-b2c2-1e116952691a.

Deacon, David, et al. "Hard Evidence: Analysis Shows Extent of Press Bias towards Brexit." *Conversation*, 16 June 2016, theconversation.com/hard-evidence-analysis-shows-extent-of-press-bias-towards-brexit-61106.

Dorling, Danny, and Sally Tomlinson. *Rule Britannia: Brexit and the End of Empire*. Biteback Publishing, 2019.

Du Garde Peach, L. *Kings and Queens, Book 2*. Illustrated by Frank Hampson, Wills & Hepworth, 1968.

Duthie, Peggy Lin. "Ladybird Books" *Oxford Encyclopedia of Children's Literature*, edited by Jack Zipes, Oxford UP, 2013.

Eaglestone, Robert. Introduction: Brexit and Literature. *Brexit and Literature: Critical and Cultural Responses*, edited by Robert Eaglestone, Routledge Taylor & Francis Group, 2018, pp. 1-6.

Evans, Margaret. "Tall Tales about Bananas: How 'Euro-myths' Haunt the U.K. Brexit Debate." *CBC News*, 21 June 2016, www.cbc.ca/news/canada/brexit-euro-myths-1.3645183.

Ferguson, Donna. "From Epic Myths to Rural Fables, How Our National Turmoil Created 'Brexlit.'" *Guardian*, 27 Oct. 2019, www.theguardian.com/books/2019/oct/27/brexlit-new-literary-genre-political-turmoil-myths-fables.

"Five Go on a Great Western Adventure." *Great Western Railway*, 2020, www.gwr.com/adventuresstarthere.

Fox-Leonard, Boudicca. "Hipsters, Mindfulness and Brexit: The Authors Behind the Hit Ladybird Books for Grown-Ups Series on Why They Are Quitting While They're Ahead." *Telegraph*, 12 Nov. 2018, www.telegraph.co.uk/family/life/hipsters-mindfulness-brexit-authors-behind-hit-ladybird-books/.

Hazeley, Jason A., and Joel P. Morris. *The Story of Brexit.* A Ladybird Book for Grown-Ups, Ladybird Books, 2018.

Hughes, Stuart. "The Greatest Motivational Poster Ever?" *BBC News*, 4 Feb. 2009, news.bbc.co.uk/2/hi/uk_news/magazine/7869458.stm.

Humphris, Frank. *Captain Cook*. Illustrated by Frank Humphris, Ladybird Books, 1980.

Johnson, Lorraine, and Brian Alderson. *The Ladybird Story: Children's Books for Everyone*. The British Library, 2014.

Lowbridge, Caroline. "Ladybird Books: The Strange Things We Learned." *BBC News*, 6 March 2015, www.bbc.com/news/uk-england-leicestershire-30709937.

Martinson, Jane. "Did the Mail and Sun Help Swing the UK towards Brexit?" *Guardian*, 24 June 2016, www.theguardian.com/media/2016/jun/24/mail-sun-uk-brexit-newspapers.

McCulloch, Derek. *Uncle Mac's ABC.* Illustrated by Septimus E. Scott, Wills & Hepworth, 1950.

Murray, W. *Book 4C: Say the Sound.* "The Ladybird Key Words Reading Scheme." Illustrated by J. H. Wingfield, Wills & Hepworth, 1965.

Newbigin, Eleanor. "Brexit, Nostalgia, and the Great British Fantasy." *Open Democracy*, 15 Feb. 2017, www.opendemocracy.net/en/brexit-britain-and-nostalgia-for-fantasy-past/.

Orestano, Francesca. "Children's Literature, History, Cultural Memory:

Intersections." *Cultural Perspectives: Journal for Literary and British Cultural Studies in Romania*, vol. 19, 2014, pp. 7-21.

O'Rourke, Kevin. *A Short History of Brexit: From Brentry to Backstop*. Pelican, 2019.

Risbridger, Eleanor. "How the Famous Five Sold Us a Myth of Britain – And Set the Stage for Our Brexit Fantasies." *Prospect*, 27 Oct. 2017, www.prospectmagazine.co.uk/arts-and-books/how-the-famous-five-sold-us-a-myth-of-britain-and-set-the-stage-for-our-brexit-fantasies.

Shaw, Kristian. "BrexLit." *Brexit and Literature: Critical and Cultural Responses*, edited by Robert Eaglestone, Routledge Taylor & Francis Group, 2018, pp. 15-30.

Shipman, Tim. *All Out War: The Full Story of How Brexit Sank Britain's Political Class*. William Collins, 2016.

Siddle, W. D. *The Story of Newspapers*. A Ladybird Achievements Book, illustrated by R. Embleton, Wills & Hepworth, 1969.

Tomlinson, Sally. *Education and Race: From Empire to Brexit*. Policy Press, 2019.

Vincent, Bruno (as Enid Blyton). *Five Escape Brexit Island*. Enid Blyton for Grown-Ups, Quercus Editions, 2017.

——. *Five on Brexit Island*. Enid Blyton for Grown-Ups, Quercus Editions, 2016.

Walden, George. *Exit from Brexit: Time to Emigrate*. Revised ed., Gibson Square Books, 2016.

Zeegen, Lawrence. *Ladybird by Design*. Penguin, 2015.

BrexLit and the Marginalized Migrant

Christine Berberich

This essay assesses the role that EU migrants play in current British BrexLit literature. While the growth in this particular new genre that tries to engage with the ramifications of the 2016 EU referendum in Britain is laudable, the essay contends that most BrexLit actively appears to *ex*clude the voices of EU migrants. They might have cameo roles – generally as East European cleaners or Romanian plumbers – but they do not have vital roles to play in these works of fiction. Paying particularly close attention to Cynan Jones's *Everything I Found on the Beach* (2011), Jonathan Coe's *Middle England* (2018), and Linda Grant's *A Stranger City* (2019), the essay contends that this appears to reflect contemporary British society where the voices of over three million EU migrants, many of whom have been resident in the UK for most of their lives, have been entirely silenced. BrexLit either attempts to mirror this situation or, more worryingly, to actually perpetuate it.

Keywords: BrexLit, migrant voices, Euroscepticism, Cynan Jones, Jonathan Coe, Linda Grant

Since the Brexit referendum in June 2016, a new genre has begun to emerge: the BrexLit novel. These novels, written in a predominantly realist mode, deal with the impact of the referendum on contemporary British society, the toll it has taken on individual families and local businesses. They include Ali Smith's Seasons novels *Autumn* (2016), *Winter* (2017), and *Spring* (2019); Anthony Cartwright's *The Cut* (2017); and Sam Byers's *Perfidious Albion* (2018), among others. Some, such as John Lanchester's *The Wall* (2019), have adopted a dystopian tone, offering a futuristic tale of a country affected by both climate and

Brexit and Beyond: Nation and Identity. SPELL: Swiss Papers in English Language and Literature 39, edited by Daniela Keller and Ina Habermann, Narr, 2020, pp. 167-82.

political change, entirely surrounded by a high wall built specifically to keep incoming Others out. The focal point of this essay will be on Cynan Jones's novel *Everything I Found on the Beach* (2011), which preceded the Brexit referendum by five years; Jonathan Coe's *Middle England* (2018), to date one of the most obviously Brexit-themed novels; and Linda Grant's *A Stranger City* (2019), a multivocal novel celebrating London's multiculturalism. Specifically, it will focus on the depiction of EU migrants living and working in the UK in these novels, rather than looking at the depiction of Brexit in general. In addition to critically assessing their representations, the essay will argue that there is currently a dearth of literary representation of EU migrants in BrexLit novels. Although the over three million EU migrants living in the UK form a sizeable part of the population, they have not been granted a voice or a say in either the initial EU referendum nor the ensuing official Brexit negotiations. Accordingly, EU citizens living and working in the UK are also largely marginalized, if not silenced altogether, in the cultural works produced to date. Much has been said in the press and on social media about the situation of EU nationals in the UK after the referendum. The organization "The 3 Million," campaigning for EU citizens to retain all their existing rights post Brexit, is the main group that tries to give a voice to EU migrants who feel that the referendum and the ensuing political debate have left them disenfranchised and silenced, merely treated as convenient bargaining chips. This essay argues that much cultural production on Brexit follows a similar – and worrying – trend of silencing the voices of those who have come to live in the UK from the EU, be they newly arrived highly educated professionals, or fully integrated and low-skilled yet vital labourers. Most Brexit literature has shied away from offering voices to them. While this could, potentially, be read as a critique of the existing real-life silencing of these voices, the essay argues that, instead, it reinforces the migrants' position as marginalized and disenfranchised outsiders in British society.

The road to Brexit should not have come as a surprise. Euroscepticism has a long history in the UK, particularly in England, and is simply too deeply entrenched in everyday life. Many critics, among them Fintan O'Toole, have convincingly argued that the roots of Brexit lie in English post-war disillusionment. O'Toole outlines English disappointment in the wake of the Second World War:

> It was by no means ridiculous to feel that Britain [...] had deserved much [after the war] but received little. It had lost its empire, become virtually bankrupt, suffered economic stagnation and, in the Suez Crisis of 1956 [...] had its pretensions as a world power brutally exposed. To make matters

> much worse, the former Axis powers of Japan, Germany and Italy were booming, as were France and the Benelux countries, all of whom had been rescued from the Nazis in part by the British. Who could avoid a sense of disappointed expectations? (4)

This disappointment, as O'Toole continues to discuss, led to self-pity, but also to an inflated sense of self. Despite having lost its empire, Britain could not shake off a sense of imperial grandeur and superiority – and with it a sense of entitlement. Post-war Britain felt *entitled* to special treatment – and bitter about the fact that it did not receive it. And rather than self-critically reflect on this, there was a national quest for a scapegoat. In the late 1940s, the 1950s, and the 1960s, scapegoats were those who were visibly different: immigrants from the former colonies in Asia, Africa, the Caribbean. The first post-war decades in Britain were full of xenophobia and not even thinly veiled racism, and this has found representation in literature and culture: in Sam Selvon's *The Lonely Londoners* of 1956, for instance, or, more recently, in Andrea Levy's prize-winning novel *Small Island* (2004). "England in the 1960s and 1970s," as O'Toole explains, "was flagrantly racist. There was a ready and visible target for those looking for someone to blame for the country's economic and social ills – black people, who had themselves replaced Jews in the role" (16). However, openly and blatantly racist politicians such as Enoch Powell soon – and mercifully – lost public support. But rather than this putting an end to racism, racism changed track and went into hiding. Instead of being out in the open it became more subtle – and looked for a different target. This target became the EU, as Richard Weight has outlined in his study *Patriots*, which precedes the Brexit vote by a good fourteen years. He explains that "when scapegoating black Britons for the UK's problem became less morally acceptable, the EEC made a useful substitute. In short, Brussels replaced Brixton as the whipping boy of British nationalists" (514).

From the day Britain joined the EEC in 1973, Eurosceptics from across the political spectrum have helped stoke a fire of anti-European sentiment within Britain. This was, to a large extent, aided and abetted by parts of the mainstream press, in particular the tabloids, which have revelled, over decades, in perpetuating anti-EU myths and scapegoating Europe or certain groups of EU migrants. In response, and as early as the 1990s, the European Commission set up a website with the sole aim of "debunk[ing] the myths they saw as being propagated by the British press" (Levy et al. 10): the notorious "straight EU bananas," for instance. Wikipedia, not normally a website renowned for its academic rigour, should be mentioned here anyway as it has an entertaining page dedicated to the most outrageous "Euromyths" that includes stories about EU rules allegedly banning British barmaids from showing a cleavage, demands that British fish and chips be sold using Latin terminology, and plans to ban mince pies ("Euromyth"). The European Parliament's more sober "Liaison Office in the United Kingdom" has its own page engaging with those myths, highlighting – and debunking – particularly misleading tabloid headlines ("Euromyths"). These stories could be seen as harmless and entertaining, brushed aside as funny, and not to be taken seriously. However, Dominic Wring has shown that "one of those journalists most associated with propagating [...] baseless 'Euro-myths' designed to undermine [the EU's] credibility" was, in fact, Boris Johnson (12) – and this immediately gives the "Euromyths" a far more sinister and overtly political context. Johnson actively supported and even campaigned with the help of another "Euromyth": the claim, prominently splashed across the Leave campaign's now infamous red bus, that Britain had to pay the EU £350 million a week, money that ought to be better spent supporting the NHS. And while Brexit-sceptic newspapers tried to debunk this myth, alongside others, at the time – see, for instance, Jon Henley's measured article in the *Guardian* in the run-up to the referendum in May 2016 – its claim stuck, addressing deep-seated anxieties about the pressure of migration on, for instance, the National Health Service.

This also illustrates that it was a small step from blaming the EU for restricting British traditions (the barmaids! The fish and chips!) to demonizing those people who had come to live in Britain via another EU law: Freedom of Movement. The European Parliament's website explains that "[f]reedom of movement and residence for persons in the EU is the cornerstone of Union citizenship, established by the Treaty of Maastricht in 1992" (Marzocchi). It is something that the UK of course subscribed to and seemed to support – after all, hundreds of thousands of Brits of all ages have similarly made other EU countries their home. Yet, anti-EU-immigrant headlines became a fundamental part of pro-Brexit propaganda. As Levy et al.'s study *UK Press Coverage of the EU Referendum* shows, and as I have discussed further elsewhere (Berberich), there was a clear shift towards the issue of immigration at the end of the Brexit campaign that even mainstream politicians and Remain campaigners such as David Cameron were prone to slip into. EU migrants, in particular those from Eastern Europe, were scapegoated and blamed for the country's ills: the shortage in housing, the pressure on schools and the NHS. A recent study by researchers at Oxford University's Centre on Migration, Policy and Society (COMPAS), the Budapest Business

School, and the European Journalism Centre at Maastricht has investigated different approaches to media reporting across Europe and has found that, in particular on the subject of "migration," there is vastly different reporting across the Continent. The UK media, in particular, are singled out by the study for their particularly negative approach towards migration; while a Swedish journalist has stressed that, for him and his colleagues, "[g]lobalisation is a positive force. We rarely write something negative. Labour force migration is positive," his British counterpart has admitted that his focus will always be "more likely to be [on] people who are a burden to society than those who are a benefit to [it]" (qtd. in McNeil). McNeil points out that "the culture within UK media – particularly within newspapers – is focused on winning political victories," and this has, of course, become especially apparent in the run-up to the Brexit referendum. The Leave campaign, in fact, was entirely founded on negative images, on 'Othering' – on setting Britons apart, and in more prominent and entitled position. As O'Toole highlights,

> [o]n the one hand, Brexit [was] fuelled by fantasies of "Empire 2.0" [...]. On the other, it is an insurgency and therefore needs to imagine that it is a revolt against intolerable oppression [in this case by the EU and non-British bureaucrats]. It therefore requires both a sense of superiority and a sense of grievance (3).

With all this political, social, and media focus on immigration, it is surprising – to put it mildly – to see that migration does not play a wider role in the most prominent form of cultural production on Brexit to date: literature. BrexLit does engage with the current situation in Britain – but does so by predominantly foregrounding the British perspective. While it could, of course, be argued that Brexit is an issue that affects the British more than anybody else, it seems short-sighted to silence those many EU citizens who have made their lives in the UK and who are such an important factor in British life, commerce, and industry. As Kristian Shaw has outlined, BrexLit "concerns fictions that either directly respond or imaginatively allude to Britain's exit from the EU, or engage with the subsequent socio-cultural, economic, racial or cosmopolitical consequences of Britain's withdrawal from the EU" (18). But how is this possible without hearing the actual voices of Europe? After all, and as many cultural commentators have written about, literature has traditionally always played – and still does play – an important role in forming and shaping public opinion; silencing so many voices might then give credence to those polemicists who say that migration is not important, and that migrants, regardless of their background, should not be given voices. As Baroness Young of Hornsey has said so astutely, "[t]here's a role for literature, so adept at humanising big questions and creating emotional and cultural landscapes, in metaphorically poking us all in the ribs and urging us to start thinking critically and becoming politically active again" (xviii). Brexit itself has mobilized tens, if not hundreds of thousands, both in support but, predominantly, in protest and opposition. It is therefore important that its literary representation similarly engages in the political activism and shows the very real struggles and arguments of day-to-day life in Brexit Britain. BrexLit, more so than other kinds of literature, ought to humanize an often purely political and in many cases lamentably vague debate, in particular when it comes to showcasing the *personal* cost it has on the lives of both the British and migrants alike.

A look at the recent history of the British novel shows that this absence of migrant voices is all the more astonishing because, as Bryan Cheyette has convincingly argued, "a migrant's perspective is at the heart of English literature, [...] of English cinema, [...] of English theatre, [...] of English art," citing Joseph Conrad, Karel Reisz, Arnold Wesker, and Lucian Freud as just a few examples. Yet, as he also shows, most of these immigrants' "stories are little known as our national story still dominates" (70). Maybe it is a lack of interest on the part of the reading public or the publishing industry. Maybe an effort on the part of the immigrants to show how much they have become 'anglicized' or assimilated. Whatever the reason, the effort to showcase and emphasize a sense of 'unified' national identity, a white Anglo-Saxon Englishness, seems to have outweighed efforts to highlight the stories of minorities. And now, this is becoming a real problem. As Cheyette has argued, "Brexit means that our national straightjacket – Englishness, not even Britishness – becomes much tighter and the value of a migrant's perspective becomes increasingly discounted and devalued" (69). This is where BrexLit *should* play a more active role – by highlighting more stories of migrants – but where, so far, it has fallen short. The following section will look, in more detail, at the three very different novels highlighted in the introduction and assess how they represent EU migrants – and what the potential effects of this representation could be.

Cynan Jones's novel *Everything I Found on the Beach* predates the referendum by five years. But its early focus on the experiences of Polish migrant worker Grzegorz is quite remarkable and, to date, virtually unique. The novel consists of two parallel narrative strands. On the one hand, it tells the story of Grzegorz, his wife Ana, and their two children, in a house shared by many migrant workers and provided – at high rent – by the very agency that brought them to Britain in the first place. The second narrative strand focuses on the British character Hold, his battle against poverty and his desperate efforts to provide for his dead friend's wife and child. Grzegorz's and Hold's stories interlink when, one early morning on the beach, Hold finds the dead Grzegorz and several kilos of cocaine in an inflatable. He tries to get rid of the body by pushing the boat back into the sea, and keeps the cocaine to try and sell it and create a better life for himself. Given that the dead Pole is found early on in the novel, as readers we do not get to hear much of Grzegorz's actual voice. But the novel does provide ample context for how he came to be where he was found.

Everything I Found on the Beach starts with Grzegorz and several of his Polish co-workers waiting for a special job that will see him alleviate the financial dependence from the migrant agency that he has to endure. It becomes clear very quickly that he has signed up for a special task that is going to be illegal. The novel makes no excuses for this; but it also does not condemn this illegal activity. Instead, it shows that his regular job, at a slaughterhouse, is one where he works extra-long hours for a minimum wage that does not allow him to move his family out of the shared accommodation they have been in for a year. Grzegorz describes the house he and his family share with many other Polish migrant workers as a "no-man's-land between Poland and what they had held as an ideal new world" (10). The reality of England – the poor living conditions in the house, the "Polish out" graffiti on the outside wall, the "dullness of the buildings, the latent fatigue of the place, colourless shops with broken signage" (9, 11) do not fit the image of England he had held. He – and all his fellow migrant workers – had come to England full of hope to be able to work hard and forge a better future for themselves. Instead, they find that they are all reliant on the migrant agency. He explains:

> Because of the break when they'd laid them off for three weeks, he hadn't quite clocked up the twelve months' unbroken work that would make him eligible for benefits, so he couldn't move out of the house yet, not on the money he had. There was talk that the agency had organised this break deliberately so they didn't have a choice but to accept the work and the stoppages in their pay cheques – the deductions for rent, for the transport to work that was laid on, for house cleaning, though none of them had ever seen a cleaner. (11)

This passage shows clearly how limited the freedoms of the migrant workers and how prescribed their lives really are. It defeats the *Daily Mail* headlines shouting about migrants coming to the UK for instant benefits. Grzegorz realizes that "I didn't come here for this" but is also adamant that, despite the disappointment, Britain is "the land of choice" (9, 11). He wants a different future for his two sons and begins to resent the Polish sounds, traditions, superstitions, and influences around them in the house. Although he is aware that "with all the Polish around him, nothing had really changed" (13), his memories of Poland begin to fade – before he has had a chance to create new and positive ones of his new life in the UK. The result is that Grzegorz feels uprooted and fragmented, trying to leave life in Poland behind him, yet unable to make sense of what he experiences in his new life. He desperately tries to shed his 'Polishness' and become more assimilated to an Englishness he cannot grasp yet: "We can't move on while there is all of this [meaning the house full of fellow Poles speaking Polish and cooking Polish foods], we can't become anything new" (19). This highlights the migrants' dilemma: the belief that, in order to fit into their new world, they need to give up their sense of who they were in the past. The result is that their sense of self, their identity becomes confused and shadowy – no longer one thing, not yet another. Grzegorz concludes: "This is where we are now. [...] And we have to move on. Here. Poland has nothing for us" (20). Grzegorz convinces himself to willingly suppress and attempt to forget his Polish roots, his traditions, and his memories in order to "become" English as soon and as smoothly as possible – and this is an experience shared by so many migrants these days: the pressure to, potentially, suppress personal identity and traditions in order to fit in better and more quickly. In contemporary Britain, both in pre- but particularly in post-Brexit years, assimilation is considered more important than bringing different cultural outlooks. Cheyette contrasts this contemporary trend unfavourably to the 1980s, when "[a]ssimilationism was being challenged by compelling voices such as Salman Rushdie and his generation of writers" (68). He concludes that "this was a time [...] when the history and place of migrants in Britain was being understood from a positive perspective and other options, rather than mere assimilation or disappearance, were being voiced" (68). For Grzegorz, a mythical Englishness becomes the be-all, end-all: "We want more now. [...] We're not so simple. We can't be happy living the old way any more. It is better to be here. Poland can rot" (50).

Grzegorz's story ends pretty much as soon as Hold finds his body on the little boat. As readers we find out that he had agreed to pick up some smuggled drugs from a ship in the Irish Sea, that his compass had given out on him and that he had lost his bearings at night. Hold does not know who Grzegorz is; all he can do is judge him by his facial features, the "high cheekbones and wide face of a Slav" (82). But the faceless victim becomes much more personal to him once he listens to the meaningless Polish voice messages on Grzegorz's mobile phone, the increasingly desperate and sad messages left by a woman he cannot understand but who nevertheless touches his heart. "He listened as with each message the woman broke up into smaller and smaller pieces into the useless, unanswered phone. When he sat down, he felt he had killed the man" (107). As such, a nameless body becomes much more personal to Hold, his left-behind family almost an additional responsibility for him. For Hold, finding Grzegorz's body means establishing a personal connection to the plight of just one immigrant – and this is, maybe, what literature can help us all do.

By comparison, though, this is exactly where Jonathan Coe's much lauded *Middle England* (2018) fails. The novel focuses too much on stereotypes – admittedly maybe in an attempt to showcase the stereotypes and clichés that had been tapped into by the referendum Leave campaign. In *Middle England*, to date the heftiest and most obviously Brexit-themed of all BrexLit novels, there are, virtually, *no* EU migrants. The focus is very much on white, middle-class English characters – which also silences out the voices from the British margins: the Scottish, the (Northern) Irish, the Welsh. The one exception is a young Lithuanian woman, Grete, who works, predictably, as a cleaner for one of the novel's several elderly characters. Grete becomes the victim of racist abuse in the village store, when a drunk man turns on her and starts shouting abuse for her speaking Lithuanian in public:

> He shouted, "Get off your effing phone," and then just as we were both outside the door he grabbed me by the arm and said, "Who are you speaking to?" and "What language were you speaking?" I shouted, "Let go of me," but he just repeated, "What effing language were you speaking?", and then "We speak English in this country," and then he called me a Polish bitch. I didn't say anything, I wasn't going to correct him, I'm used to people thinking that I'm Polish anyway, I just wanted to ignore him, but he didn't stop there, now he grabbed my phone and took it off me and threw it on the ground and started stamping on it. [...] He kept saying Polish this and Polish that – I can't repeat the actual words he used – and told me "We don't have to put up with you ... people any more" [...] and then he spat at me. Actually spat. (381)

This scene does not only stand out for its violence that is perpetrated towards an entirely innocent woman, out to do her weekend shopping in a small village, but also for the denial of identity that immigrants so often have to suffer: the Lithuanian becomes a Pole just because it is easier; because the abuser cannot differentiate between Polish and Lithuanian; because it is easier to conflate an entire region, that of Eastern Europe. This dialogue between the novel's protagonist, Sophie, and Grete, which stretches over a mere six pages, is the longest appearance of the Lithuanian in a novel that is 421 pages long. Coe uses her to compress all the negative experiences of EU migrants in post-referendum England. So much more could have been done with her character – but she remains on the sidelines, marginalized due to her background and her socio-economic standing as a cleaner. Both she and her husband reappear at the very end of the novel – they have left the UK as a direct result of Brexit and have settled in France as live-in housekeeper and handyman to the novel's other British protagonists Benjamin and Lois Trotter in their new French B&B. While Grete and her husband seem to end the novel in a seemingly safer and friendlier environment, they are still banished to the margins, not quite of the same standing as their British employers Benjamin and Lois, and this despite the fact that the Trotters themselves have now also acquired migrant status. Some migrants are more equal than others: the British migrant Trotters in France assume a higher place in the hierarchy than the Lithuanians Grete and Lukas.

To add insult to injuries, Grete's erstwhile elderly British employer Helena Coleman, a Brexiteer and ardent quoter of Enoch Powell slogans, is given considerably more space in the novel, especially more space to speak and distribute her questionable views. Helena considers herself as living "under a tyranny," specifically the tyranny of "an idea," in this case the "idea of political correctness" (212-13). She believes that political correctness prevents her from expressing her views or ideas and thinks that the country has become divided into "our people" and "others" who, for her, are all those people with different options, backgrounds, or skin colours. Helena, very problematically, does not speak up for or support Grete after she has been subjected to verbal and physical abuse in the village, despite having witnessed it first-hand. Instead she suggests that "on the whole, it would be better if you and your husband went home" (383). Coe certainly does not take sides in his novel; he does not give his readers the feeling that he is more in support of one group of characters than another. He merely shows a country that is deeply divided between unquestioning supporters of the left and liberal ideas of multiculturalism, and a right that feels aggrieved and abandoned, betrayed by its own politicians and left alone to fight for their mythical ideas of a once-great England. As Ian, Helena's son, deftly summarizes, "this was basically how she'd been living her whole life. In a state of undeclared war" (385). Helena's "undeclared war" goes back full circle to O'Toole's statement of "disappointed expectations" (4) that I quoted at the beginning of this essay. For Helena, life in post-war Britain had been one disappointment after another, a country seemingly selling out on its own ideals – no matter how misguided they might have been – to accommodate the changing times. It is this seething, underlying anger and vitriol that Coe masterfully draws out in his novel. But it is a shame that this has to come at the expense of more migrant voices.

By contrast – and finally! – these migrant voices abound in Linda Grant's *A Stranger City* of 2019. In fact, hers is a multivocal novel with a large number of different protagonists from various backgrounds: the native and passionate Londoner, policeman Pete, and his wife Marie who, in turn, starts to support UKIP and dreams of a less complicated and more 'English' life in the Lake District, far away from multicultural London; the documentary filmmaker Alan and his wife Francesca, of Persian-Jewish background; Francesca's family, with special focus on her immigrant grandparents Younis and Amira; the highly educated German family, Caspar, Elfriede, and their little girl Gaby; Mrs Simarjit Kaur Khalistan and her best friend, the Jewish widow Audrey Shapiro; the Irish nurse Chrissie and her pretentious flatmate Marco who has traded in his suburban family background, Lebanese heritage, and birth name "Neil" for the allegedly more interesting and potentially safer Italian-sounding "Marco" to accelerate his career in PR; the Greeks from the local deli; Alan's Hungarian business partner Johanna; and Alexandru Radu, the Romanian plumber. The novel consequently cannot be accused of a lack of 'migrant' voices; in fact, it offers a perfect blend of migrant and 'native' voices. What it does investigate, through a narrative as diverse as its voices, is the uncertainty that has been created in the country through the Brexit referendum. Characters no longer feel at home, are uncertain about their future, feel frightened about the continuation of the very existence they have laboriously built for themselves over years or even decades, and are worried about showing their 'difference' outside the safety of their own houses. Grant expertly showcases instances where migrant characters forcibly deny or hide their difference by no longer speaking their own language outside the confines of their own homes. Francesca's Persian grandparents, for instance, not EU migrants but caught up in the maelstrom that is post-Brexit xenophobia, hardly leave the house anymore. "Only when Younis was dressed in his pyjamas and Amira in her nightgown lying under pink sheets and rabbit-coloured waffle blankets, a fringed lampshade casting a rose-coloured flush to their old faces, did they whisper to each other in Farsi" (105). This homely scene – the old couple in their cosy bedroom, clearly at ease with each other after a long life together – stands in stark contrast to Younis's life after Amira's death, when "the widower [...] had no one left apart from his son to whom he could speak his native language with fluency and intimacy" (261). With the loss of native language comes a loss of self, a loss of identity; a big part of Younis's life, his simple enjoyment of his mother tongue, is literally being silenced. Similarly, the German family make a conscious decision to "talk a little less German in the house and [...] no longer chat in German outside" after daughter Gaby, post referendum, is asked in school, "why are you still here, aren't you going home now?" (216-17). For Younis and Amira, as well as Caspar, Elfriede, and Gaby, the referendum impacts on their sense of belonging; it is not only their ability to speak freely in their own languages that is being affected, but also their physical well-being. Already before Amira's death, Younis is told that they should not

> leave their building, except for the few steps from the front door to his Audi. [Their son] did not want them loose on the streets, pleading in painful English, without a phone in their pockets. Groceries were delivered now by van. Walks were restricted to the rear garden. Amira missed her visits to the hairdresser, her son said it was safer to try to manage herself. (257)

This well-meant advice by a concerned son effectively turns his parents into prisoners in their own home, depriving them of the pleasure they had previously found in exploring the city and feeling part of their adopted country. This imposed house arrest leads to their physical and mental decline, especially for Amira: "It took only two months of house arrest for her to die" (257).

The German family have a near-death experience when Gaby is attacked and nearly drowned by two girls on the towpath close to her home (296). Towards the end of *A Stranger City*, Grant's narrative turns positively dystopian when she depicts a London that is, literally, haemorrhaging people, predominantly migrants. Alan observes trains full of detained migrants passing along the tracks behind his house, with "deportees [...] pleading at the glass"; he also comments on "prison ships [that] had appeared in the Thames estuary confining illegal immigrants before they were floated back to mainland Europe" (254-55). But it is not only those anonymous strangers that preoccupy him. His own friends, acquaintances, and neighbours leave: his business partner Johanna has returned to Hungary and sends him updates and advice via Skype (256); the Greeks from the local Delicatessen have left overnight, "slid away without farewells" (209). The German family are leaving "voluntarily, with smiles and dignity and farewell presents and exchanges of email addresses," explaining that "[w]e won't take the risk, our safety is too important" (314-15). Post-referendum Britain, Grant predicts, is no longer a welcoming and safe place for resident migrants.

What Grant's novel consequently does, and in a way so far unachieved by other BrexLit novels, is show a country that has, indeed, turned into the "hostile environment" advocated by former Prime Minister Theresa May in her previous incarnation as Home Secretary (see, for instance, Yeo). Her increasingly dystopian narrative thus shows how perilously close contemporary Britain is to a dystopian future. While ex-policeman Pete ponders that "[y]ou couldn't have London without foreigners, it wouldn't be the same place, would it?" (302), Grant conjures a country that is, indeed, prepared to go further to get rid of immigration: "The country was being emptied of its unwanted population. Paperwork must be in scrupulous order to avoid being picked up and forcibly removed" (257). In *A Stranger City*, Grant effectively gives her foreign migrants a voice – only to show that the right to speak is, slowly but steadily, eroded and taken away from them again: in short, she empowers her migrant characters to illustrate how they are being disempowered in post-Brexit Britain. This is neatly summarized after the departure of the Greek family: "Believing they were of this country they were not, or in not quite the right way. They had come too early or too late, it was all opaque, but their status was wrong, and could not be fixed easily" (209). In this respect, there are many parallels between the migrants' experiences in *A Stranger City* and Grzegorz's experience in *Everything I Found on the Beach*: like Grzegorz, Grant's migrants arrive full of hope and eager to blend in, and then go through the various stages of disillusion when they find that their hopes and expectations are not matched by reality in post-Brexit Britain, to finally arrive at utter dejection and loss of self. Jake Arnott, reviewing *A Stranger City* for the *Guardian*, notes that "[a]t a time when dangerous inert notions of national identity are on the rise once more, Grant reminds us that humanity is a migrant species: we are all strangers." *A Stranger City*, with its many vignettes of different migrants' experiences, thus succeeds in humanizing the very migrants marginalized or silenced by the tabloid press, populist politicians and, sadly, also many other BrexLit novels. It allows its readers to connect with these characters, to share in their hopes and dreams but also in their experiences and frustrations.

In conclusion, it is clear that BrexLit has a responsibility: it has the responsibility to not only address British concerns with regards to England, but also to address the situation of the EU citizens living and working and making homes for themselves in England. Over three million voices should not be neglected or sidelined in such prominent cultural production. Instead, BrexLit could and should be used to speak up for these marginalized groups and make a stronger case for their integration. Every migrant has their own story to tell – and if we had more opportunity to listen to them, to read about them, to see them presented on stage or screen, then maybe there would be that little bit less ignorance, and that little bit less vitriol against them.

References

Arnott, Jake. "*A Stranger City* by Linda Grant Review – Lost in the Labyrinth of London." *Guardian*, 4 May 2019, www.theguardian.com/books/2019/may/04/a-stranger-city-by-linda-grant-review.

Berberich, Christine. "Our Country, the Brexit Island: Brexit, Literature, and Populist Discourse." *Literatures of Brexit*, special issue of *Journal for the Study of British Cultures*, edited by Anne-Julia Zwierlein et al., vol. 26, no. 2, 2019, pp. 153-65.

Byers, Sam. *Perfidious Albion*. 2018. Faber & Faber, 2019.

Cartwright, Anthony. *The Cut*. Peirene Press, 2017.

Cheyette, Bryan. "English Literature Saved My Life." *Brexit and Literature. Critical and Cultural Responses*, edited by Robert Eaglestone, Routledge, 2018, pp. 66-72.

Coe, Jonathan. *Middle England*. Viking, 2018.

"Euromyth." *Wikipedia*, 2019, en.wikipedia.org/wiki/Euromyth.

"Euromyths." *European Parliament*, 31 July 2017, www.europarl.europa.eu/unitedkingdom/en/media/euromyths.html.

Grant, Linda. *A Stranger City*. Virago, 2019.

Henley, Jon. "Is the EU Really Dictating the Shape of Your Bananas?" *Guardian*, 11 May 2016, www.theguardian.com/politics/2016/may/11/boris-johnson-launches-the-vote-leave-battlebus-in-cornwall/.

Jones, Cynan. *Everything I Found on the Beach*. Granta, 2011.

Lanchester, John. *The Wall*. Faber & Faber, 2019.

Levy, Andrea. *Small Island*. Tinder Press, 2004.

Levy, David A. L., et al. *UK Press Coverage of the EU Referendum*. Reuters Institute for the Study of Journalism, 2016.

Marzocchi, Ottavio. "Free Movement of Persons." *European Parliament*, Nov. 2019, www.europarl.europa.eu/factsheets/en/sheet/147/free-movement-of-persons.

McNeil, Rob. "Migrants and the Media: What Shapes the Narratives on Immigration in Different Countries." *Conversation*, 29 April 2019, theconversation.com/migrants-and-the-media-what-shapes-the-narratives-on-immigration-in-different-countries-116081.

O'Toole, Fintan. *Heroic Failure. Brexit and the Politics of Pain*. Head of Zeus, 2018.

Selvon, Sam. *The Lonely Londoners*. 1956. Penguin, 2006.

Shaw, Kristian. "BrexLit." *Brexit and Literature. Critical and Cultural Responses*, edited by Robert Eaglestone, Routledge, 2018, pp. 15-30.

Smith, Ali. *Autumn*. Hamish Hamilton, 2016.
——. *Spring*. Hamish Hamilton, 2019.
——. *Winter*. 2017. Penguin, 2018.
Weight, Richard. *Patriots. National Identity in Britain, 1940-2000*. Macmillan, 2002.
Wring, Dominic. "From Super-Market to Orwellian Super-State: The Origins and Growth of Newspaper Scepticism." *EU Referendum Analysis 2016: Media, Voters and the Campaign. Early Reflections from Leading UK Academics*, edited by Daniel Jackson et al., Centre for the Study of Journalism, Culture and Community, 2016, p. 12.
Yeo, Colin. "Theresa May's Immigration Legacy." 2019, www.freemovement.org.uk/theresa-mays-immigration-legacy/.
Young of Hornsey, Baroness. Preface. *Brexit and Literature. Critical and Cultural Responses*, edited by Robert Eaglestone, Routledge, 2018, pp. xvii-xviii.

Retracing, Remembering, Reckoning: Stuart Maconie's Footsteps Narrative of the Jarrow March

Victoria Allen

This essay reads Stuart Maconie's travelogue *Long Road from Jarrow: A Journey through Britain Then and Now* (2017) through the lens of memory studies to contextualize Maconie's peregrination as his way of contemplating and grappling with Brexit. Maconie retraces the iconic Jarrow March on the occasion of its eightieth anniversary, revisiting the past in order to gain a perspective on the social and political state of present-day Britain. This essay introduces the public persona of Maconie and provides background information on the Jarrow workers' 1936 protest march, drawing on the concept of cultural memory both to determine what the Jarrow March signifies today and how the book functions as a product of cultural memory. As Maconie revisits the route of the Jarrow protest march shortly after the Brexit vote in June 2016, the two historical events become intertwined through his account. Approaching both the journey and the book as cultural memory projects highlights how the Jarrow March retains its mythical resonance in the present. Consequently, Maconie's social snapshot of the current condition of England is analysed as his personal narrative negotiation of the reasons for the referendum, and of Brexit as a pivotal socio-political event.

Keywords: Cultural memory, Jarrow March, Brexit, Stuart Maconie, Nigel Farage, working-class, myth, footsteps narrative, travel writing

Stuart Maconie's footsteps narrative *Long Road from Jarrow: A Journey through Britain Then and Now* (2017) is analysed in terms of constructions

Brexit and Beyond: Nation and Identity. SPELL: Swiss Papers in English Language and Literature 39, edited by Daniela Keller and Ina Habermann, Narr, 2020, pp. 183-205.

of cultural memory to show how the myths and memories surrounding the Jarrow March and its working-class protesters are projected onto the present day in an attempt to explain the Brexit vote.[1] Maconie's book adopts the Jarrow March's iconic status within the discourse of working-class struggles purporting to use his retracing of the march as a means to examine present-day class issues in England.

Long Road from Jarrow joins a recent trend in travel writing of following in the footsteps of previous travellers, but unlike the typical footsteps narratives, or what Maria Lindgren Leavenworth refers to as "second journeys" (Youngs 184), Maconie's itinerary is based on an actual protest march rather than an earlier travelogue. His narrative is organized in twenty-two chapters named after the Jarrow marchers' overnight stops on the route from the north to the south of England, each chapter providing additional socio-historic background to the march and the various locations. The author interweaves social and media commentary with encounters and incidents during his own 'march' in which he apprehensively reflects on the recent Brexit referendum as the "seismic shock of the summer" (Maconie, *Long Road* 299). Though Maconie does not explicitly set out to discuss Brexit, each chapter-passage forms an integral part of his own reckoning of the outcome and his attempts to assuage the associated animosity propagated by neo-populist interests. His 'second journey' therefore does not merely "imitate" the march but "reinforce[s] the natural distance between past and present," thus creating something new and relevant to the contemporary (Leavenworth, *Second Journey* 192; see also Youngs 185). However, although Tim Youngs sees this as a "way of neutralising nostalgia" (185), Maconie still taps into a yearning for his own working-class background and thereby unveils "not only the first traveller, but [...] also him[self]" (Leavenworth, *Second Journey* 192).

Stuart Maconie as Social and Popular Cultural Commentator

In order to understand Maconie's incentive and his references to Brexit, it is necessary to consider his role as author-narrator and popular commentator on British culture. Well known as a music journalist, Maconie notably was the editor for *New Music Express* (NME) and wrote articles for prominent music magazines including *Mojo*, *Q*, and the *Radio*

[1] For more information on the conflation of Britain with England, see Davey 6; Habermann 3-8; Kumar.

Times. A renowned advocate for the 1980s and 1990s Manchester music scene, he developed his public persona as a radio DJ, co-hosting shows with Mark Radcliffe on BBC 2 (2007-11) and 6 Music (2011-present), and more recently with his own Sunday set "Stuart Maconie's Freak Zone" (6 Music, 2017-present) ("Stuart Maconie"). This has established him as a popular culture critic in Britain. In his columns and article contributions to newspapers such as the *Guardian* and the *New Statesman*, Maconie proclaims his Marxist political stance (Maconie, "I'm a Marxist") – political views that can be traced back to his northern, working-class upbringing, his study of politics and history, and his work as a teacher of English and sociology.

Maconie has published a range of books, often written from a biographical perspective or based on his expertise in popular British culture and music. Examples of his music interests include the autobiographical *Cider with Roadies* (2005) and *The People's Songs: The Story of Modern Britain in 50 Records* (2013). His writing tends to mix social observations with personal anecdotes and reflection, contextualized with historical background information and delivered in a mild, wry style to comment on contemporary cultural issues. This is the formula for his popular piece on the north-south divide, *Pies and Prejudice: In Search of the North* (2008) and the sequel *The Pie at Night: In Search of the North at Play* (2015), as well as the travel account *Adventures on the High Teas: In Search of Middle England* (2009). These three books illustrate Maconie's preoccupation with the cultural, social, and economic differences and delineations between the north and the south of England, a major component of the contemporary discourse on Englishness (Kumar 10, 17). His most recent publication, *Long Road from Jarrow* (2017), is a continuation of this north-south exploration and an attempt to capture the 'condition of England.' Although Maconie marches from the north to the south of *England*, he tends to conflate England and Britain by suggesting – with his book title – that his writing is a consideration of the 'condition of Britain.' This conflation is both quite common in discourses of national identity, and politically problematic, especially considering that Brexit was made largely in England, and it is predominantly English identity that is at stake.

In his writing Maconie notably draws on a number of renowned works which have established this type of travel writing: H. V. Morton's *In Search of England* (1927, followed by other *In Search of* volumes), J. B. Priestley's *English Journey* (1934), and George Orwell's *Road to Wigan Pier* (1937). Documenting their encounters with 'ordinary' people, these writers were commended for their perceptions of the *zeitgeist*, despite the marked difference in their agendas and political visions. Maconie draws on these texts, particularly those by Priestley and Orwell, in order to exemplify the living and working conditions of people from the north of England around the time of the Jarrow March. More than merely paying homage to these two celebrated left-wing social commentators, his self-stylization and referencing of Priestley and Orwell place Maconie's *Long Road from Jarrow* in this tradition.[2]

In his latest work, Maconie pursues his personal interests such as food and drink, music, sports, media, literature, local history, and politics – well recognized topics in his previous books and commentaries. Employing these themes as foci, he juxtaposes historical events with contemporary issues. The travelogue format of this book project, in particular, showcases him "as a keen walker and advocate of walkers' rights" ("Stuart Maconie Named").[3] For his travelogue *Long Road from Jarrow*, he puts his own advice of "exercise and experiences" ("Stuart Maconie Named") into practice by following in the footsteps of the Jarrow marchers.

Incentive for Maconie's March from Jarrow

Pies and Prejudice (2008), *Adventures on the High Teas* (2009), and *The Pie at Night* (2013) illustrate Maconie's penchant for using his travels as inspiration for his writing. All three travel texts conform to Youngs's description of the travel-writing genre as "predominantly factual, first-person prose accounts of travels that have been undertaken by the author-narrator" (3). The incentive for Maconie's *Long Road from Jarrow* was the eightieth anniversary of the Jarrow March. In tribute, he retraces the route of the protest marchers who set off from Jarrow to

---

[2] In *Myth, Memory and the Middlebrow*, Ina Habermann illustrates how Morton's (61-80), Priestley's (80-95) and Orwell's (95-104) English journeys engaged in creating a mythological sense of Englishness in the interwar period. Maconie's account can be read as a contemporary middlebrow attempt of writing back to Morton and echoing Priestley and Orwell, revisiting Englishness as a 'symbolic form' at the present political conjuncture. An in-depth comparison of these works is beyond the scope of this essay.

[3] Indeed, just prior to the publication of *Long Road from Jarrow*, Maconie was appointed president of the Ramblers – an organization whose mission is to encourage outdoor pursuits on foot. As he explains, the Ramblers organization "works to help people get access to the great outdoors in Britain, to encourage you to walk, to encourage you to get out there and enjoy both the exercise and the experiences that putting one foot in front of the other in the Great British countryside can give you" ("Stuart Maconie Named").

Westminster. Using the journey as a way of engaging directly with the people, he asks those he meets along the way if they have heard of the 1936 Jarrow March. These *en route* encounters enable him to include personal impressions and memories of witnesses in his documentation.

Along with Maconie's intention "to compare the England of now and then, to see if the shadow of 1936 really did fall across 2016," he also wants "to get to the heart of England today first-hand" (*Long Road* 17), indicating his physical experience of the journey – an attempt to re-embody and, thereby, re-activate memory, allowing him to evince more considerate and reflective responses than those that dominated the debate in the public discourse of Brexit. This is evoked through the imagery of the heart and its association with a sense of care combined with having a more profound understanding and relationship with the people of contemporary England. This physical tie is strengthened in the use of "first-hand," which evokes a sense of authenticity through lived experience.

The suggestion of authenticity is pertinent in relation to the footsteps genre where "second journeys illustrate a contemporary search for the authentic" (Leavenworth, *Second Journey* 13) since the second traveller is compelled to "use, recycle and emphasise the first texts, which originate in a past in which authenticity is believed to be attainable" (14). Aligned with this is his emphasis on sensorially experiencing England in 2016, accentuated by slow travel and taking the time to 'savour' the journey: "I wanted to see, to hear, smell even what England was like close up by walking it, moving along its length at a speed where I could look it in the eye, shake its hand, maybe buy it a drink" (Maconie, *Long Road* 17). The many descriptions of meals suggest that he is literally eating his way through England and his consumption of culture and cuisine is framed as engagement with the country's most staple elements. The humanizing narrative strategy of feeling England's pulse or tasting it underlines that he actually meets and interacts with its inhabitants as equals, 'eye to eye.' This is a feat he promises to achieve with the open, inquisitive, and transient friendship of a traveller who captures his own experience and provides an authentic and accurate snapshot of the English people.

Despite Maconie's attempts to capture the 'real' north of England, as if it could be grasped in the shape of a (homogenous and tangible) person with whom one is able to 'shake hands' and 'have a drink,' his encounters are nevertheless filtered by his personality. He does not reflect upon his own role as traveller-narrator or his editorial power but appears to enjoy the limelight as popular cultural commentator, which is masked to a certain extent by Maconie's self-deprecating humour and his asserted allegiance with the disaffected working-class, typical for conservative left-wing sentimentalism.

Maconie positions himself as well-suited to comment on the working class of the north of England as a 'professional northerner' with a working-class background. His route from the north to the south of England allows him to trace a national cultural and political dichotomy – an established trope within English socio-political and media discourse which has a far reaching socio-economic and cultural impact (see Russell; Kirk; Ehland). After the referendum result, it was commonplace to think that the majority of the working-class population had voted Leave and that the north of England fundamentally contributed to the Brexit outcome. This myth has been undermined by scholars such as Danny Dorling, who commented that "[t]he outcome of the EU referendum has been unfairly blamed on the working class in the north of England" (1; see also Jorgenson-Murray). He elucidated further that "most people who voted Leave lived in the south of England [and that] of all those who voted for Leave, 59% were in the middle classes (A, B, or C1)." Leave voters, nevertheless, constituted a majority in almost all northern counties and Maconie's footsteps narrative aims to explore and create an understanding for the marginalized English region that is commonly known as the former industrial and working-class heartland.

Jarrow and the 1936 Protest March

Jarrow is a once-industrial town in the north-east of England situated in the Great Durham Coalfield along the River Tyne, located between Newcastle and Sunderland. By 1930, the majority of those employed in Jarrow worked for Palmer's Shipbuilding & Iron Company Ltd. or in the various trades linked to the local shipbuilding industry (Robinson and Waller). The company closed in 1933, putting 80% of Jarrow town out of work (Morton; Maconie, *Long Road* 23-24). A similar fate befell thirty-seven other British shipyards. Therefore, as a nationwide measure to rein in the excess capacity in British shipbuilding and to keep ship production low and profitable, a decree by the National Shipyards Security Ltd. (NSS), the government, and other still-operating shipyard owners was issued. The decree determined that once yards such as Palmer's were closed and dismantled, none could be re-established on those sites for forty years (Maconie, *Long Road* 24).

The socio-economic effects on Jarrow's inhabitants were harrowing as no alternative employment was secured for the workers whose skillset was specialized in shipbuilding and steelworks. These grim conditions were noted in detail by J. B. Priestley when he passed through Jarrow during his research for *An English Journey* (1934). Published two years before the march, this book included impressions that reflected the state of the town just after the closure of Palmer's:

> Wherever we went there were men hanging about, not scores of them but hundreds and thousands of them. The whole town looked as if it had entered a perpetual penniless bleak Sabbath. The men wore the masks of prisoners of war. A stranger from a distant civilisation, observing the condition of the place and its people, would have arrived at once at the conclusion that Jarrow had deeply offended some celestial emperor of the island and was now being punished. He would never believe us if we told him that in theory this town was as good as any other and that its inhabitants were not criminals but citizens with votes. (314)

At the time, the Labour MP for Jarrow, Ellen Wilkinson, illustrated Jarrow's dire situation following the effects of the shipyard closure.[4] She articulates, more explicitly than Priestley, the sense of the town being let down, or even punished by the government and the NSS, as expressed in the evocative title to her book *The Town That Was Murdered: The Life-Story of Jarrow* (1939). Wilkinson's description of the town gives an overview of the ebb and flow of different waves of capitalism and industrialization, which also saw the coming and going of the pits and mining life in Jarrow (Maconie, *Long Road* 22). She rebuked Sir Charles Palmer, owner of the Jarrow shipyards and steelworks, for the exploitative working conditions and lack of care for his employees who were working in unsanitary and intolerable living conditions, which further deteriorated once this branch of his business had been closed (Wilkinson in Maconie 23).

The Jarrow March was organized as a protest in 1936 as one of the numerous hunger and unemployment marches and was also known as the Jarrow Crusade. Calling it a crusade demonstrates the organizer's reluctance to aggravate political powers and industrial stakeholders that they relied on for employment infrastructures in Jarrow. Labelling their protest with a religious term framed the marching petitioners as "god-

---

[4] The activist, journalist, communist, trade unionist, and feminist Ellen Wilkinson, also named Red Ellen "because of her fiery auburn hair and politics to match" (Maconie, *Long Road* 21), was one of the first female Labour members of Parliament.

fearing citizens," rather than demanding, "bolshy" workers which at the time would have been perceived as part of a communist threat (Maconie, *Long Road* 215).

Two hundred men, on certain stretches accompanied by Wilkinson, marched three hundred miles from Jarrow to London to request government support for a new steelworks to be built (Maconie, *Long Road* 26). Carrying a wooden box containing an estimated 10,000 signatures, it took over three weeks for the Jarrow marchers to reach The Houses of Parliament in Westminster (343). The march gained national attention through the national press, radio, and newsreels, partly due to two journalists being amongst the marchers, which helped them garner support in the form of food and shelter at their various overnight stops along their route to Westminster. However, upon their arrival in London the then Prime Minister, Stanley Baldwin, refused to meet the men. Instead, they were invited on a boat trip along the River Thames "ostensibly as a reward for their efforts, but actually to avoid any ugly scenes in the House [of Parliament]" (347-48). Afterwards, they were informed that their petition had been presented and discussed in their absence. The whereabouts of the petition – a particularly notable piece of people's history – is still unknown (Picard; Maconie 348).

The way the petition was ignored by the Houses of Parliament indicates a contempt for working-class voices and causes by political institutions. Nevertheless, as Matt Perry posits in *The Jarrow Crusade: Protest and Legend* (2005), the march memorializes working-class struggle, solidarity, unity, pride, tenaciousness, perseverance, and peaceful protest. Despite, or because of, parliament's casual treatment of the protesters' concerns, the event has captured the popular imagination, and different versions of the tale have been reincarnated in various forms of popular art and culture (see Perry, *Jarrow Crusade*). It is, therefore, crucial that Maconie chose to record and retrace the route of the Jarrow March eighty years later as the year 2016 can be notionally considered the transitional moment when first- and second-hand memories become entrusted to cultural memory. Cultural artefacts, such as Maconie's book, are therefore required in order to retain meaning in contemporary culture and shape today's understandings of the historical event.

Mythologization of the Jarrow March in Cultural Memory

The Jarrow March is on the verge of shifting from "communicative" to "cultural memory," as the people who witnessed the event and who were still able to 'communicate' what occurred in order to generate a sense of identity and belonging are ageing and gradually passing away (Jan Assmann 113-14).[5] Their communicative memories thus become cultural memories after eighty to one hundred years (111, 117). According to Jan Assmann, once this period of time has passed, cultural memory is retained and functionalized by a community or a collective through the production of culture or cultural artefacts. Drawing on his joint research with Aleida Assmann, he posits that

> [o]n the social level, with respect to groups and societies, the role of external symbols becomes even more important, because groups which, of course, do not "have" a memory tend to "make" themselves one by means of things meant as reminders such as monuments, museums, libraries, archives, and other mnemonic institutions. This is what we call cultural memory (111).

Regarding the concept of cultural memory, it is important to question when, by whom, and why events are deemed worthy of remembrance. This is particularly the case in commissioning public artefacts such as monuments and statues, where the question of funding, potential political and ideological motivations, or desired effects of such an institutionalized form of remembering should also be taken into consideration (see Aleida Assmann; Erll and Nünning; Erll et al.). The fact that Maconie's re-enactment occurs on the cusp of these two types of memory throws into relief the relevance of *Long Road from Jarrow* for inquiries into what Aleida Assmann terms "cultural functional memory" (127-28) at the conjuncture of remembering and forgetting.

The predominantly oral communicative memory within families and communities finds new ways of remembering the march, which then become institutionalized as collective and cultural memory. Furthermore, the various forms of retelling and remembering articulate different nuances of the same event with different meanings for different audiences, so that narrating the Jarrow March feeds into ideological processes of myth-making. Indeed, Maconie claims of the march: "It has attained the status of a national myth akin to the stories of Robin Hood or King Arthur, and like those, has become negotiable, malleable, debatable. While its status is unarguable, its details are anything but" (*Long Road* 5-6). Maconie's recourse to folkloric legends that have been used

---

[5] For a comprehensive overview of memory studies see Olick et al. For further reading on the concept of cultural memory which has informed my approach, see Aleida Assmann, as well as Erll and Nünning.

to narrate and establish a sense of Englishness illustrates his awareness of the political potency of how the Jarrow March has come to represent the voice of the 'ordinary' working-class people of England.

In *The Jarrow Crusade: Protest and Legend*, Perry traces how this historical event has become a collection of potent myths, and, as part of his analysis, he has compiled a selection of poems, paintings, songs, and novels inspired by the memory of the Jarrow March and popular cultural references to the event in radio, film, and television shows. These show the breadth and variety of cultural artefacts which, in diverse ways, help to recall and retain the memory of the march on a regional, national, and global level. Perry's work highlights the reification of the Jarrow myth, arguing that its construction should be understood as processes active in chronological phases with specific geographical domains, driven by individual initiative, institutional receptiveness, and cultural production ("Myth" 130). Maconie, also, observes that "[p]opular art has kept the name of Jarrow and its complex associations – struggle, hardship, heroism, failure even – alive down the decades" (*Long Road* 28).

Two such cultural memory artefacts are displayed in Jarrow today. The first of these is the mural at the Jarrow metro station designed by Vince Rea, eponymously called *Jarrow March* (1984). The low-relief sculpture was adapted from photographic footage of the marchers to give a sense of having captured the actual event; the use of recycled steel from a scrapped ship is a poignant, material reference to the closure of the Jarrow shipyards and its aftermath ("Jarrow March"). Placed prominently along the Tyne and Wear metro line at the metro stop of Jarrow, the mural is the first icon of local and national history that presents itself to visitors entering the town. It marks the place as noteworthy for its working-class history, symbolizing a pride in the past that is linked to social prestige and is of cultural value to Tyne and Wearside – a region characterized by its recent de-industrialization.

The second exhibit is based on a similar motif of an assembled group depicting a collective of flat-capped men holding a banner, along with a woman holding a child, and a dog alongside them. The collective emerges from the hulk of a ship. It is designed by Graham Ibbeson and located outside of the Jarrow branch of Morrisons supermarket. The life-size bronze sculpture, named *The Spirit of Jarrow* (2001), was commissioned by the supermarket to mark the sixty-fifth anniversary of the march. In a similar manner to the metro mural, the statue of a collective representing the marchers, erected outside a heavily frequented shopping centre, stands as a reminder for the ongoing symbolic relevance of the crusade for the self-identification and representation of the town.

The choice to depict a group including men, women, and children signifies how this event is remembered as affecting the entire working-class community of the town, which no longer thrives on the ship- and steel-building industries.[6]

Such representations only partially retell historical events, or perhaps only capture a vague sense of memory and, therefore, become mythologized (see Barthes). As Jonathan Bignell explains, "[w]hat myth does is to hollow out the signs it uses, leaving only part of their meaning, and invests them with a new signification which directs us to read them in one way and no other" (22). To evade contributing to a myth-making that seeks to channel one particular signification through the more complex picture, Maconie assures us that he is aware of the multitude of "takes" the march has created:

> Jarrow has its own murky legacy of half-truth, partial truth and downright falsehoods. The old northern term "romancing" seems appropriate here as most of these myths are attempts to appropriate the teary romance and sentiment of the Crusade. (*Long Road* 328)

This demonstrates Maconie's awareness of how the memory of the march is utilized to evoke a certain myth: "It resonates down the years and like all good myths you can bend it to your own ends in any era" (11). In recent years, the march has been sentimentalized in working-class nostalgia with Maconie again cautioning the reader that "it's wise to remember that you're working on hallowed ground and dealing with emotive, if not entirely accurate, memories" (8). The myth of the Jarrow March has, thus, not only found various forms of expression, but has also been appropriated to serve different functions.

How the cultural memory of the Jarrow March is functionalized on a local and national level is exemplified in Alan Price's folk-pop homage to the protest march against unemployment and poverty, which reached number 6 in the 1974 May Music charts ("Jarrow Song") and was written in relation to the 1972 and 1974 UK miners' strikes. Price's *Jarrow Song* (1974) epitomizes how the memory of the Jarrow March is recalled and rearticulated in cultural memory artefacts at specific moments in time when the past is employed to comment on the present. In "The

---

[6] The effects of unemployment that affected the whole family were also institutionally constructed because, as Christine Collette elucidates, "[t]he wages of all family members, and any household assets, were taken into account when deciding whether or not relief should be paid. This meant that in some cases redundant men were dependent on their daughters or wives, a situation that did not fit in with the mores of the time."

Myth of the Jarrow Crusade and the Making of a Local Labour Culture," Perry demonstrates how memory and myth have on several occasions been politically appropriated and revived by the local Labour party of Jarrow as a means of "regenerating the distinctively local labour culture in the area" (137). Analysing Jarrow memorials, such as the aforementioned statues and additional place names, Perry concludes that these cultural memory artefacts have "afforded the local party the opportunities to insinuate the Crusade into the brick, tarmac and asphalt of Jarrow," which has contributed to Labour's sustained political and "cultural hegemony" in Jarrow since the time of the march (137). It was not until the march's fortieth anniversary, in conjuncture with mass unemployment in the 1970s, that the myth attained national resonance and became institutionalized, primarily through the efforts of the BBC and the Labour Party (142).[7]

A more recent example of how the proletarian iconography of the Jarrow March myth has been appropriated for political and ideological means on a national level is the *March to Leave* led by Nigel Farage as a part of the *Leave Means Leave* campaign promoting the newly formed Brexit Party.[8] Setting off from Sunderland in the north-east of England, only fifteen kilometres south from Jarrow, the "Brexit betrayal march" was scheduled to take place over two weeks, culminating in an organized demonstration in London's Parliament Square on 29 March 2019 (Parkinson). The city of Sunderland was chosen as the starting point for the *March to Leave* as the traditional, 'safe' Labour city was the first to announce the outcome of their vote to leave the European Union on the 24 June 2016 referendum broadcast by a majority of 61% to 39%, which resulted in the media-produced notoriety of Sunderland as 'Brexit City' (Rushton 3-4). While it was not explicitly stated that the *March to Leave* was a re-enactment of the Jarrow March, choosing the march, which has iconic status for the Labour Movement (see O'Neill and Roberts), combined with starting from Sunderland, a city known for its historic Labour allegiance, the *March to Leave* becomes a statement for the disintegration of both the new and old Labour Party after Brexit.

---

[7] For the fiftieth anniversary, a repeat march was staged from the north-east to London to raise awareness of the high rates of unemployment, where the "context of Thatcherism, deindustrialisation and industrial conflict combined to make 1986 the most powerful anniversary" (Perry 142).

[8] Much of the coverage on social media and in the left-wing press focused on the small turn-out of marchers in the wet weather conditions and Farage's noticeable absence from various legs of the journey, despite being the poster face of the event (Drury; "March to Leave"; "Nigel Farage").

The Jarrow myth is evoked to form a narrative that is purportedly sympathetic to English working-class needs which builds on the cultural memory of unemployment marches, tapping into inter-generational fear of poverty and neglect exacerbated by the decade-long implementation of austerity after the financial crisis in 2008. In this instance it is used to garner support and legitimize the political agenda of the *Leave Means Leave* campaign. In a BBC 4 radio feature on the *March to Leave*, Maconie remarks on the temptation to compare the Jarrow March with what he describes as Farage's publicity stunt:

> By the time it [the *March to Leave*] arrives in Parliament Square, Nigel claims that 20 million people will have joined them [marchers] in spirit. Quite what he means by this is hard to fathom, but if by spirit he means ghosts, well, the ghosts of the Jarrow marchers are clearly still with us, still clattering these roads, a spirit army that can be pressed into service by any side it seems and its opinion we will never know. (*World This Weekend*)

Maconie again points out how the malleable memory of the original marchers is open to political and ideological appropriation by the political right and left. This exemplifies clearly that while memory is an account of something that has occurred in the past, its power lies in generating resonance with the present. In that sense, it is important to treat *Long Road from Jarrow* as a cultural memory artefact that, as such, helps to retain the memory of the Jarrow March, but has its own agenda as well – an agenda that deserves further exploration.

Maconie's Narrative Negotiation of Brexit

As is indicated in the subtitle "A Journey through Britain Then and Now," Maconie's commentary on his commemorative journey attempts to navigate the past and present. His travelogue, through both the rural and urban areas of England, appears as an anthropological quest to collate and balance contemporary opinions regarding the Brexit vote, markedly because he only begins his walk about three months after the referendum. Since travel writing not only provides the reader with "impressions of the travelled world" but also lays bare the travelling subject (Korte 6), *Long Road from Jarrow* needs to be read in terms of the author-narrator's personal "culture-specific and individual patterns of perception and knowledge" (6). This allows us to then situate Maconie's book project as a personal reckoning with his current and erstwhile class status, where his metropolitan outlook is contrasted with the provincial towns he visits; towns that are reminiscent of his own upbringing in Wigan, a former industrial town, imbuing his political and social appraisal of Brexit and the changing socio-cultural construction of the country with a nostalgic notion of an England conflated with Britain.

The walk through the de-industrialized, agricultural regions – predominantly in the north-east of England – to the more urban areas in the south-west, reflects a perceived political divide along which the fronts of Leave and Remain gradually became entrenched during the referendum campaigns (Rostek and Zwierlein 7-8, 10). Since the announcement of Britain's intention to leave the EU, these oppositional views have become more hardened (Asthana et al.). This is evident in the national and social media debates aiming to clarify what Brexit actually means and its social, political, and economic implications.[9]

Maconie is openly apprehensive about the Brexit referendum, and the sojourns, the conversations he has with people he meets, along with his contemplations of them, read as an attempt to reconcile an apparently divided country with an ever-widening rift in terms of class inequality. Comparing the times of the Jarrow Marchers and the England he encounters on his journey, he states, "[d]espite a genteel nervousness about it these days, class supplied the great splintering fault line through British life in 1936 and the crack is still wide. As I ventured further south, I and the men of Jarrow, would feel it between our feet" (*Long Road* 278). Maconie, hereby, claims the now-dead marchers as comrades in both his wrangling with the present and the continued struggles of the working class. It may also be suggested that by embedding himself in an alternative temporally distanced context, Maconie creates the sense of Brexit Britain as a foreign land which allows him to journey 'abroad' experiencing "[t]he foreignness of a travelled country" through "an act of construction on the part of the perceiver," and defining Brexit Britain's "otherness against his or her own sense of identity, his or her own familiar contexts" (Korte 20) where "the observing self and the foreign world reverberate within each work" (Blanton xi).

Throughout, Maconie's weighty socio-political assessments are buoyed by humorous reflections on his own persona and class status. This is epitomized in his purchase of a flat-cap for the journey – the symbol of working-class masculinity; the irony of buying it in Fenwick's – Newcastle's answer to Harrods – is not lost upon Maconie. However,

---

[9] For a snapshot of the divisive post-Brexit media discourse at the time of Maconie's Jarrow journey and to date, see Cosslett; Erlanger; Kensington et al.; Taylor; and Wallace.

it does serve as a symbol for Maconie's 'donning' the working-class voice in his writing, while in open acknowledgment that although his roots were working-class he is now middle-class – a recognition of his own navigation between classes. It is interesting to note that Farage also wore a flat-cap when launching the *March to Leave* – an equally arch recognition of the symbolic power of artefacts in creating contemporary resonance. In Farage's case, however, it is evident that this is a calculated choice within a larger appropriation, with a more explicit political aim, of a prior protest movement myth, using it as a vehicle to express, or create, a contemporary sense of disenfranchisement. However, whether openly acknowledged or not, both Maconie and Farage doff their respective caps to the power and mythology of the Jarrow March.

While neither the title nor the blurb hint at Brexit, post-referendum Britain is heavily referenced in Maconie's descriptions of the current state of the country. Indeed, his discussion of Brexit begins in his prologue where he asserts: "In truth whether England is little or large and whether you want its borders iron clad or porous. Brexit proved that one thing is not in doubt: we are a divided country, chiefly along the lines of geography and class" (*Long Road* 12). Maconie perceives the referendum vote as exacerbating an already existent social fault line in Britain. He openly states his own position as a 'remainer' in the Brexit referendum debate, but emphasizes that he does not write against those who had voted to leave the European Union:

> That's the walkabout that took us away from Brussels, and whilst I don't agree with that decision, I can understand it. In the three months between the seismic shock of the Brexit vote and me setting out from Jarrow, I read and heard countless leftist commentators and writers airily, and I think snobbishly, waving away some of the concerns of older, non-metropolitan working-class voters as racism and bigotry. (81)

Rather than voicing his displeasure with those who voted against his political views and opinions, Maconie criticizes the social and media discourse following the referendum from peers and, indeed, people who share his political position. Through both his walking and writing he appeals for more understanding for the rationale of a particular demographic of Leave voters, who come from different, often less privileged backgrounds, to echo his own footsteps and consideration of opposing views. This is to foster acceptance for their reasons to opt out of the EU, rather than simply categorize their vote as uninformed and motivated by racism or xenophobia.

Rather, Maconie argues that austerity is the fundamental factor in the increasing social divide in Britain, which he sees as having culminated in the referendum. An instance of this transpires in Maconie's visit to the Quaker House pub in Darlington. Talking to the landlady, Stella, he follows on from her account of how Darlington was affected by austerity, stating:

> Here is another quietly smouldering impetus for Brexit that many commentators have either failed to notice or chosen to ignore: after the economic crisis of 2008, one largely brought about by the wickedness and greed of bankers, it has been ordinary people who have borne the cost, in reduced services and savage cuts. Rightly or wrongly, the EU is seen as aligned to that protected cabal of affluent and seemingly untouchable financiers. Brexit was an attempt, however clumsy and misguided, to land a punch on them. (91)

Maconie aims to relate and legitimize the perspectives of 'ordinary' people by providing a counter narrative to a nominally divided and broken Britain in order to offer a different perspective than the simplistic dichotomies that mark contemporary political discourse in Britain. As explained in Anne-Julia Zwierlein and Joanna Rostek's categorization of realist and panoramic Brexit literature (132), *Long Road from Jarrow* is an attempt at creating panoramic representations of regional and demographic complexities. Maconie also uses the oft-deployed technique in Brexit literature of what Zwierlein and Rostek call "the testimonial or verbatim," by, at least notionally, talking with a diverse range of England's population "to produce or at least aim at multivocality and an equal distribution of representational space across the opposing parties" (129). Thus, Maconie's walk functions as a restorative, all-encompassing gesture against increased media reports of the social, class, generational, and familial fissures appearing since the referendum.

While Maconie's samples of the social flavour of England rest heavily on supping – eating, drinking, and social consumption – he finds the taste of Brexit overpowering and the media manipulation of it unsavoury. Maconie admits to his own fatigue in this regard when he comments that "Brexit takes up most of the front page" (*Long Road* 133) or remarks:

> As is now customary, the day's other news is uniformly 'Brexit,' an event which seems to have thrown every conversation and interaction, every

> normal daily event into an uncomfortable kind of relief and shine a strange, harsh new light that refracts the world differently. (144-45)

Maconie paints a picture of this Brexit-infused country as a new, estranged, even foreign land. The modern-day mirroring of the Jarrow March serves as comparative and reparative journey for the author, navigating (his) past and present in an attempt to comprehend the contemporary divide caused by Brexit. Indeed, he makes direct comparisons between now and 1936, informing us that

> [s]ome parallels between then and now suggest themselves immediately: A Conservative government recently returned to power with an increased majority. A Labour Party led into disarray by a leader widely seen as divisive and incompetent. The rise of extremism here and abroad fired by financial disasters, a wave of demagoguery and 'strong man' populism. Foreign wars driven by fundamentalist ideologies leading to mass displacement of innocent people. A subsequent refugee 'crisis.' The threat of constitutional anarchy with conflict between government, parliament and judiciary. Manufacturing and mass rallies resurgent as popular but questionable forums of political debate. Explosions of new forms of media. Inflammatory rhetoric stoked by a factionalised press. Football a national obsession, its wages, profits and morality constantly debated. (*Long Road* 11)

This enumeration, to which the impact of a pandemic disease could now be added, riffs on Juliet Gardiner's opening passage to *The Thirties* where she states that the thirties have come to represent a decade of "confusion, financial crisis, rising unemployment, scepticism about politicians, questions about the proper reach of Britain's role in the world" (xiii). Maconie's juxtaposition summarizes the key concerns he reiterates throughout his travel narrative which he describes as contributing to "the particularly weird, fissile state of England" (*Long Road* 11) which has culminated in the Brexit vote. In doing so, he creates a memory motif in his minding of the march that serves as a ruminative space to untangle a socio-political knot and, in parallel, assuage his personal apprehension with comprehension.

Maconie concludes his travelogue with a reflection on the wealth of experiences and insights he claims to have had on his journey, writing wistfully in his "Postscript":

> I walked from the top to the bottom and into the heart of England. I looked it in the eye from morning till night and I never grew tired of it. Like the marchers, I learned something from those long days, evenings and nights that no amount of TV news or opinion pieces or well-meant docu-

> mentaries could have given me. I learned about England now, about England then, and about England's secrets, its scraps and footnotes. I hope I have done it justice. Sometimes it baffled me, sometimes it irritated. But I came to know that, to quote that old maxim, yes it is my country right or wrong. It seems to be wrong about something almost every day now, but I understand some of its discontent, its bristling dissatisfaction with how it has been ignored, patronised and marginalised. (353)

Maconie's elegy to his journey foregrounds a newly found fascination which is also a trope in condition-of-England writing: a love for the land and the history of the country he has just traversed. Maconie suggests that by making the journey on foot, the pace affording a 'slower' engagement with people and places, he has been able to gain a more fundamental understanding for how and why the Brexit referendum was used as a protest vote. It is also a profound reckoning with his own sense of patriotism, which Maconie constructs as a realization attained along his journey. This is a common motive for travel writing set in the author-narrator's own country, since pride in the greatness of the country is paired with curiosity both in the historical roots of that greatness and its contemporary manifestations (Korte 67).

Even though Maconie's trip ends in the twenty-first century and his travelogue promises to make sense of the present condition of England, he cannot resist the nostalgic pull of looking back rather than addressing the future at the very end of his travelogue. Towards the end of the "Postscript," his tone of acceptance and consideration is tinged with unease and foreboding: "In 2016, for the first time for me, it was not glib chatter or student drivel to think that something very like fascism was arising again out of the depth of history, a rough beast slouching towards Bethlehem to be born" (*Long Road* 355). Drawing on the last two lines of William Butler Yeats's poem *The Second Coming* (1919), Maconie, like many other current social and political commentators (see O'Toole), re-employs Yeats' allegory of the menacing atmosphere of political disturbance and anxieties in inter-war Europe, culminating in the rise of fascism in Europe to the present day:

> Both countries, the England of 1936 and 2016, seemed to be in state of seizure, of quiet, twitchy convulsion, and jittery anticipation – dread even – of the next chapter in our national story. Both times, both moods, reflected our vexed relationship with the continent of Europe. (359)

In this way, Brexit, and the less readily observable undertones that it represents, haunt Maconie's trip down memory lane. Maconie's own allusion to the Jarrow March warns of the potentially shattering waves of a seismic socio-political shift that is emerging with uncertainty pervading national and international relationships. While his attempt to examine and propose a mode of reconciliation to Britain's (England's?) widening class and geographical rift is well meant, it also creates a sense of continuity and homogeneity between 1936 and 2016 that is not ultimately conducive to an accurate understanding of the complexities of the present day. Instead, looking back remains a national pastime.

References

Assmann, Aleida. *Cultural Memory and Western Civilization: Functions, Media, Archives*. Cambridge UP, 2012.

Assmann, Jan. "Communicative and Cultural Memory." *Cultural Memory Studies: An International and Interdisciplinary Handbook*, edited by Astrid Erll and Ansgar Nünning, De Gruyter, 2008, pp. 109-18.

Asthana, Anushka, et al. "UK Votes to Leave EU After Dramatic Night Divides Nation." *Guardian*, 24 June 2016, www.theguardian. com/ politics/2016/jun/24/britain-votes-for-brexit-eu-referendum-david-cameron.

Barthes, Roland. *Mythologies*. 1972. Hill & Wang, 2013.

Bignell, Jonathan. *Media Semiotics: An Introduction*. 1997. Manchester UP, 2002.

Blanton, Casey. *Travel Writing. The Self and the World*. Routledge, 2002.

Collette, Christine. "The Jarrow Crusade." *BBC History Online*, 3 March 2011, www.bbc.co.uk/history/british/britain_wwone/jarrow_01. shtml.

Cosslett, Rhiannon Lucy. "Family Rifts Over Brexit: 'I can barely look at my parents.'" *Guardian*, 27 June 2016, www.theguardian. com/lifeandstyle/2016/jun/27/brexit-family-rifts-parents-referendum-conflict-betrayal.

Davey, Kevin. *English Imaginaries: Six Studies in Anglo-British Approaches to Modernity*. Lawrence and Wishart, 1999.

Dorling, Danny. "Brexit: The Decision of a Divided Country." BMJ, 6 July 2016, pp. 1-2, www.bmj.com/content/354/bmj.i3697.full? ijkey=Qzh0MvExCSL1BkA&keytype=ref.

Drury, Colin. "Nigel Farage Won't Be Completing Brexit Betrayal March – After Weeks of Urging Supporters to Take Part." *Independent*, 16 March 2019, www.independent.co.uk/news/uk/home-news/brexit-march-leave-farage-betrayal-sunderland-london-a8826126.html.

Ehland, Christoph. *Thinking Northern: Textures of Identity in the North of England*. Rodopi, 2007.

Erlanger, Steven. "'Brexit' Aftershocks: More Rifts in Europe, and in Britain, Too." *New York Times*, 24 June 2016, www.nytimes. com/2016/06/25/world/europe/brexit-aftershocks-more-rifts-in-europe-and-in-britain-too.html.

Erll, Astrid, and Ansgar Nünning, editors. *Cultural Memory Studies: An International and Interdisciplinary Handbook*. De Gruyter, 2008.

Erll, Astrid, et al., editors. *A Companion to Cultural Memory Studies*. De

Gruyter, 2010.
Gardiner, Juliet. *The Thirties. An Intimate History*. Harper, 2010.
Habermann, Ina. *Myth, Memory and the Middlebrow: Priestley, du Maurier and the Symbolic Form of Englishness*. Palgrave Macmillan, 2010.
Ibbeson, Graham. *The Spirit of Jarrow*. 2001. Jarrow.
"Jarrow March." *Nexus Tyne and Wear*, 2019, www.nexus.org.uk/art/jarrow-march.
"Jarrow Song." The Official Charts Company 2019, www.officialcharts.com/search/singles/jarrow-song/.
Jorgenson-Murray, Stephen. "8 Reasons We Should Stop Assuming 'Northern' Means 'Pro-Brexit.'" *City Metric, New Statesman*, 6 March 2019, www.citymetric.com/politics/8-reasons-we-should-stop-assuming-northern-means-pro-brexit-4513.
Kensington, Mansfield and Meriden. "How Brexit Made Britain a Country of Remainers and Leavers." *Economist*, 20 June 2019, www.economist.com/briefing/2019/06/20/how-brexit-made-britain-a-country-of-remainers-and-leavers.
Kirk, Neville. *Northern Identities: Historical Interpretations of 'the North' and 'Northernness.'* Ashgate, 2000.
Korte, Barbara. *English Travel Writing: From Pilgrimages to Postcolonial Explorations*. Palgrave Macmillan, 2000.
Kumar, Krishan. *The Making of English National Identity*. Cambridge UP, 2003.
Leavenworth, Maria Lindgren. "Footsteps." *The Routledge Research Companion to Travel Writing*, edited by Alasdair Pettinger and Tim Youngs, Routledge, 2020, pp. 86-98.
——. *The Second Journey: Travelling in Literary Footsteps*. Umeå UP, 2010.
Maconie, Stuart. *Adventures on the High Teas: In Search of Middle England*. Ebury, 2009.
——. *Cider with Roadies*. Ebury, 2005.
——. "I'm a Marxist – We Are Misunderstood on Both the Left and Right." *New Statesman*, 31 July 2017, www.newstatesman.com/politics/uk/2017/07/i-m-marxist-we-are-misunderstood-both-left-and-right.
——. *Long Road from Jarrow: A Journey through Britain Then and Now*. Ebury, 2017.
——. *The People's Songs: The Story of Modern Britain in 50 Records*. Ebury, 2013.
——. *The Pie at Night: In Search of the North at Play*. Ebury, 2015.
——. *Pies and Prejudice: In Search of the North*. Ebury, 2008.
——. *The World This Weekend*, hosted by Mark Mardell, *BBC Radio 4*, 23

March 2019, Transcript, www.bbc.co.uk/programmes/m0003jp1.
"March to Leave." 27 Feb. 2019, marchtoleave.com.
Morton, David. "31 Things You Would Only Know If You Grew Up or Live in Jarrow." *Chronicle Live*, 13 May 2016, www.chroniclelive.co.uk/news/local-news/31-things-you-would-only-11326866.
Morton, H. V. *In Search of England*. Methuen, 1927.
"Nigel Farage Leads Pro-Brexit March to London." *DW*, 16 March 2019, www.dw.com/en/nigel-farage-leads-pro-brexit-march-to-london/a-47946402.
Olick, Jeffrey K., et al. *The Collective Memory Reader*. Oxford UP, 2011.
O'Neill, Maggie, and Brian Roberts. *Walking Methods: Research on the Move*. Routledge, 2020.
Orwell, George. *Road to Wigan Pier*. Gollancz 1937. Penguin Classics, 2001.
O'Toole, Fintan. "Fintan O'Toole: 'Yeats Test' Criteria Reveal We Are Doomed." *Irish Times*, 28 July 2018, www.irishtimes. com/opinion/fintan-o-toole-yeats-test-criteria-reveal-we-are-doomed-1.3576078.
Parkinson, Hannah Jane. "Farage's Brexit March: The Theatre of the Absurd Meets Storm-Hit Minion." *Guardian*, 18 March 2019, www.theguardian.com/commentisfree/2019/mar/18/march-to-leave-sorm-hit-minion-nigel-farage-brexit-protest.
Perry, Matt. *The Jarrow Crusade: Protest and Legend*. U of Sunderland P, 2005.
—. "The Myth of the Jarrow Crusade and the Making of a Local Labour Culture." *Radical Cultures and Local Identities*, edited by Krista Cowman and Ian Packer, Cambridge Scholars, 2010, pp. 129-48.
Picard, Tom. *Jarrow March*. Allison & Busby, 1981.
Price, Alan. "Jarrow Song." Warner Bros., 1974.
Priestley, J. B. *English Journey: Being a Rambling but Truthful Account of What One Man Saw and Heard and Felt and Thought during a Journey through England during the Autumn of the Year 1933*. Heinemann, 1934.
Rea, Vince. *Jarrow March*. 1984. Jarrow.
Robinson, George, and David Waller. "Tyne Built Ships: A History of Tyne Shipbuilders and the Ships That They Built." *Shipping & Shipbuilding Research Trust*, www.tynebuiltships.co.uk/Palmer2.html.
Rostek, Joanna, and Anne-Julia Zwierlein. Introduction: Brexit and the Divided United Kingdom. *Brexit and the Divided United Kingdom*, special issue of *Journal for the Study of British Cultures*, edited by Joanna Rostek and Anne-Julia Zwierlein, vol. 26, no. 1, 2019, pp. 3-16.
Rushton, Peter. "The Myth and Reality of Brexit City: Sunderland and the 2016 Referendum." 2017, sure.sunderland.ac.uk/id/eprint/

7344/.

Russell, Dave. *Looking North: Northern England and the National Imagination.* Manchester UP, 2004.

"Stuart Maconie." *PBJ Management*, 2019, www.pbjmanagement.co.uk/artists/stuart-maconie.

"Stuart Maconie Named as Our New President." *Ramblers*, 1 April 2017, www.ramblers.org.uk/en/news/latest-news/2017/april/stuart-maconie-named-as-our-new-president.aspx.

Taylor, Ros. "Leavers Have a Better Understanding of Remainers' Motivations Than Vice Versa." *London School of Economics and Political Science Blog*, 4 April 2018, blogs.lse.ac.uk/brexit/2018/05/04/leavers-have-a-better-understanding-of-remainers-motivations-than-vice-versa/.

Thompson, Carl. *The Routledge Companion to Travel Writing.* Routledge, 2015.

Wallace, Paul. "Commentary: May's Brexit Deal Ignores Leavers' Real Grievance." *Reuters*, 7 Dec. 2018, www.reuters.com/article/us-wallace-brexit-commentary/commentary-mays-brexit-deal-ignores-leavers-real-grievance-idUSKBN1O621M.

Wilkinson, Ellen. *The Town That Was Murdered: The Life-Story of Jarrow.* Gollancz, 1939.

Youngs, Tim. *The Cambridge Introduction to Travel Writing.* Cambridge UP, 2013.

Zwierlein, Anne-Julia, and Joanna Rostek. Literatures of Brexit: An Introduction. *Literatures of Brexit*, special issue of *Journal for the Study of British Cultures*, edited by Anne-Julia Zwierlein et al., vol. 26, no. 2, 2019, pp. 125-40.

The Cultural Topography of Rural Cinema-Going in the Post-War Highlands and Islands of Scotland

Ian Goode

This essay offers a historical view of cinema-going in the Highlands and Islands of Scotland. The Highlands and Islands Film Guild was formed in 1946 to deliver mobile film shows to areas that did not enjoy access to a cinema, to improve facilities, and to combat the depopulation of rural communities. It provided many young people with their first experience of film through shows delivered by operators who travelled to remote communities to exhibit film programmes in spaces not designed for this purpose. The improvised settings and the topography of the Highlands and Islands inform how the population experienced and remember the film shows. The cultural and historical significance of the Film Guild is confirmed by its successor, the Screen Machine, which provides isolated rural communities with a digital cinema experience. This popular form of cinema-going has profited from EU funding and underlines Scotland's and the EU's investments in civic provisions to remote areas in Europe such as the Highlands and Islands of Scotland.

Keywords: Film exhibition, rural cinema-going, Scottish communal identity, Highlands and Islands, European Union, England, cultural topography

The Scottish have a long tradition of going to the cinema. Trevor Griffiths remarks in *The Cinema and Cinema-Going in Scotland, 1896-1950* that "at a time, in 1950-1, when the British were the most inveterate cinemagoers in the world, visiting picture houses on average twenty-eight times a year, the average Scot went thirty-six times" (1). Cinema-going was

Brexit and Beyond: Nation and Identity. SPELL: Swiss Papers in English Language and Literature 39, edited by Daniela Keller and Ina Habermann, Narr, 2020, pp. 207-26.

made possible across the whole country and "[n]o community appeared truly complete without its own means of accessing the movies" (Caughie et al. 3-4). The cinema experience was and still is a fundamental part of Scottish communal life: in January 2020, the Highlands village of Cromarty, population 700, opened "[o]ne of the smallest cinemas in the UK" – it seats thirty-five people – a project that was primarily "made possible by EU and Creative Scotland funding" (BBC).

Not every community in Scotland has been lucky enough to receive its own fixed exhibition space but Scotland has been highly innovative in bringing the cinema experience to its remotest areas. This essay offers a historical insight into the tradition of rural cinema-going in the Highlands and Islands of Scotland after the Second World War. Oral history and archival research reveals how the specificities of the rural cinema-going experience and its exhibition practices contribute to the cultural topography of the Highlands and Islands as well as a sense of communal identity.

The Highlands and Islands Film Guild was formed in 1946 to deliver mobile film shows to areas that did not enjoy access to a cinema. These events required much effort from operators in transporting equipment to the remotest areas and the collaboration of community members to transform their village halls into temporary exhibition spaces. Today its successor, the Screen Machine, a fully-equipped "80-seat, air conditioned mobile digital cinema" (Regional Screen Scotland; see Figure 3), offers these communities a more modern and relaxed cinema experience.

The Screen Machine is run by Regional Screen Scotland – the institution dedicated to supporting community film exhibition for rural communities – and has profited from EU funding in the past, such as for the "North by Northwest – Films on the Fringe" project from 2014 (Creative Europe Desk UK). This cross-country collaboration between Ireland, Scotland, Iceland, Finland, and Norway served to "bring European Independent cinema to some of the remotest regions in North Western Europe" (Galway Film Centre, "North"). The manager of Ireland's mobile cinema (Cinemobile), Noreen Collins, described the necessity and uniqueness of the project as follows at the time:

> Each of the participating cinemas comes from countries with similar territory-types, geographically placed on the edge of Europe; each has a strong pride in the regions we are trying to reach and an understanding and knowledge of their demography. [...] The travelling nature of the venues gives the project an individuality and quirkiness that few other cinema projects in Europe have. (Galway Film Centre, "North")

Hence, the project enriched the cultural life of remote areas in Northern Europe, as well as encouraged a cultural exchange between these regions, strengthening a sense of European identity by highlighting what these regions have in common.[1]

The EU has played a significant role in improving the quality of life in remote regions such as the Highlands and Islands of Scotland. Neal Ascherson points out that

> Scotland is in many ways more closely linked to the EU than England has been, not least by the needs of its more dramatic geography. European funds helped to modernize and extend its difficult transport infrastructure, to maintain remote areas and communities and preserve the marginal agriculture of crofting and hill farming. (72)

Regional Screen Scotland announced in 2018 that it had secured funding through Creative Scotland until March 2021 (Jennings), but it remains to be seen how well the creative industry can sustain its programmes after Brexit.[2] The Highlands and Islands Film Guild and Regional Screen Scotland were/are major institutions in improving the cultural life and connectivity of the marginalized Scottish areas. Especially in areas where the visit of the Screen Machine constitutes a significant highlight as it belongs to one of very few cultural events in the respective communities. Hence, the following historical account of Scottish cinema-going in its scarcely populated regions illustrates why it is crucial that these regions not be forgotten after the UK has left the EU.[3]

---

[1] These regions not only share a cultural tradition of rural cinema-going but also a need to mitigate the effects of depopulation (see for instance Jernudd; Hjort and Lindqvist). Hence, these regions are dependent on migration and "[i]n a major contrast to England, immigration from Europe (Poland especially) has been deliberately encouraged by Scottish governments in order to balance an ageing population and correct Scotland's lamentable deficit in small service enterprises" (Ascherson 72).

[2] Sadly, Regional Screen Scotland's Irish equivalent, Cinemobile, was forced to stop serving its communities in July 2016 due to a lack of funding (Galway Film Centre, "Sad News").

[3] This essay is part of the research project *The Major Minor Cinema: The Highlands and Islands Film Guild (1946-71)* funded by the Arts and Humanities Research Council in the UK and carried out by a team from the Universities of Glasgow and Stirling. The project also invited creative writing to recognize the oral storytelling tradition that characterizes the recollection of the Film Guild and the cultural history of the area (Neely and Paul). The research is part of a recent turn in screen studies that, as Annette Kuhn observed, "seems increasingly to comprise a concatenation of sub disciplines, in which a focus on the historical, the local and the specific flourishes and any ambitions to create a totalizing theory are eschewed" (5). Part of this focus on the local sees a growing body

The Highlands and Islands Film Guild

The Highlands and Islands Film Guild was a non-commercial institution that delivered film shows on 16mm film to isolated communities in the crofting counties – an area in the north of Scotland where crofters would hold a small agricultural unit growing crops and rearing cattle – who did not enjoy easy access to permanent cinemas. The impetus for setting up the Film Guild as a civic necessity that would help improve cultural facilities and combat the long-standing problem of depopulation came from the Second World War when teachers implemented a mobile cinema scheme for evacuees who had been moved out of the cities to the safety of rural communities further north. This initiative spawned in Scotland was succeeded at a UK level by the more openly propagandist Ministry of Information (MOI) mobile cinema scheme. The MOI programmes consisted of mainly but not exclusively non-fiction films that had a specific message about how to support the war effort across the spheres of public and domestic life. More overtly propagandist films such as *London Can Take It!* (1940) documented the experience of the Blitz from the point of view of the people of London.

For the Highland and Island communities the provision of access to the visual medium of film had a significance beyond the wartime context, and education policy makers argued that it should be continued and developed for post-war audiences (The National Archives; Harding).[4] This appetite for mobile film shows also encouraged the Scottish Agricultural Organisation Society, which was primarily concerned about depopulation, to continue to provide mobile film shows for remote areas (The National Archives). The development of the scheme culminated in the formation of the Highlands and Islands Film Guild in 1946 and a group of mobile units with operators to deliver film shows to the crofting counties (Hunter).[5]

One of the research questions that the project, on which this essay is based, sought to address concerned the impact of the mobile cinema

---

of historical work that does not treat cinema as an exclusively urban form (Thissen and Zimmermann; Aveyard; Treveri Gennari et al.).

[4] The Film Guild was funded by a combination of the Scottish Education Department and the Education Authorities of the areas that wanted the institution to deliver film shows to their counties and could draw on the spaces necessary to accommodate the film shows and the prospective community audiences.

[5] At the height of its growth in the early 1950s the Film Guild ran fifteen mobile units that extended to the Shetland Isles in the north, the Outer Hebrides to the west and the Highland crofting counties between these areas.

upon the Highland and Island area, an area that was not uniformly covered by unifying media such as radio and television, and asked how surviving employees and members of the audience remembered it. Due to the effort that went into exhibiting the film shows in non-theatrical spaces, it is often these spaces and their environments that are integral to the memories of the audience and operators employed by the institution and less the actual films that were screened. The spatial and geographical challenges that the communities and operators faced had to be overcome collectively, a struggle that further strengthened a sense of community and solidarity.

The commitment of the Film Guild to reaching remote communities was made possible by a non-commercial and co-operative ethos where the well-attended shows in more populated areas contributed to covering the costs of the less well attended shows in thinly populated areas. This principle enabled the institution to deliver an experience of cinema to areas where the medium had not existed before such as the northern and western islands of Yell and Unst in the Shetland Islands or Lewis and Harris in the Outer Hebrides. A report published in 1950 states that the landmass occupied by the Highlands and Islands is 47% of the land surface of Scotland but contained less than 6% of the population (Scottish Home Department). Between 1950 and 1965, over half a million people left Scotland, roughly divided between those who moved overseas and those who settled in England (Devine 33). The extent of the space occupied by a decreasing number of people exposes the degree to which the Highlands and Islands were geographically marginalized in relation to the rest of Scotland and the rest of the UK. Viewed against this background, the Film Guild was a small cinema serving a large but underpopulated proportion of the landmass of the British Isles.

The Film Guild extended the geography of access to cinema-going in Britain through the mobility and versatility of the 16mm apparatus, and its vans and operators. It was referenced as an example of good practice in the 1949 UNESCO report concerning the *Use of Mobile Cinema and Radio Vans in Fundamental Education* (Goode, "UNESCO"). The use of the smaller gauge of 16mm expanded significantly in the UK during the Second World War, and the formation of the Highlands and Islands Film Guild, soon after the end of the war, occurred as the rest of the UK's mobile cinema was provided by an expansion of commercial operators looking to cater to more densely populated rural areas. The distribution of population meant that there was no equivalent to the Film Guild in the rest of the UK, which makes this institution deserving of a greater presence in the history of British cinema (Griffiths).

The purpose of the Film Guild to improve facilities for isolated communities through selective film programmes addressing a family audience, and the educational film shows that it also offered to schools in the daytime, gave the institution a legitimacy that the commercial cinema of the towns and cities did not have.[6] This legitimacy was bolstered by the spaces where the film shows were held; the village halls and similar exhibition spaces were a valued constituent of the social and cultural topography of the rural communities that had them. The combined efforts of the National Council of Social Service (NCSS) and the Carnegie UK Trust had facilitated loans and grants for the construction of more halls since the 1920s, but by the middle of the 1940s coverage was still far from comprehensive in the Highlands and Islands. Given this relative scarcity and social value, what the halls lacked in the iconography of cinema they compensated for in civic purpose and utility.

Jeremy Burchard argues that the village hall was the first secular and non-denominational public building in the post-medieval history of many villages (213). The transition of the hall from religious to secular space did not secure the approval of everyone in rural communities. Certainly in parts of the Isle of Lewis in the Outer Hebrides off the north-west coast of Scotland there was concerted opposition to the construction of new village halls. As early as 1946 the prospect of a new village hall and the activities that it would provide a space for, compelled some representatives of the Free Presbyterian Church to summon the authority of their faith to speak out in strong terms:

> Mr Macdonald remarked that the Trustees were proposing to lay out a site for a "dance hall" but he in the name of the whole of North Tolsta ratepayers was protesting against the scheme "for the reason that it won't be wholly used for dancing, but it will be used as orgy, and it will have a bad effect on the rising generation of this locality." (*Stornoway Gazette* 3)

The young people of the island were not put off by this type of pronouncement and registered their desire for more of the facilities that

---

[6] The feature films shown by the Film Guild tended to be provided by Hollywood and British production rather than the approved and growing body of European Art Cinema that was encouraged by specialist film societies in towns and cities. References to the rest of Europe and the wider world came mostly from newsreels and British films about the Second World War such as *The Cruel Sea* (1953) and *The Dambusters* (1955). One exception was a film about the northerly Shetland islands and their proximity to Norway that was the subject of *Shetlandsgjengen or Suicide Mission* (1954) that depicted the clandestine efforts of a special operation that transported agents between Shetland and occupied Norway during the Second World War (Goode, "Island Geographies").

Labour government policy deemed to be necessary for post-war renewal and improved leisure. The dialogue that took place on the Isle of Lewis confirms that there was some opposition to the prospect of a shift from communities mostly gathering in church, and from an ecclesiastical to a more secular topography; that would be confirmed by the emergence of the village halls and equivalent spaces in rural communities.

Fig. 1. c/o National Library of Scotland

This image of a Film Guild van arriving at a hall in the village of Kilmore in the west Highland county of Argyll demonstrates the functional, rustic construction and vernacular style of a village hall. Our findings reveal that although cinema audiences are usually fully immersed in the stories projected onto the screen, the halls where the films were exhibited and experienced significantly informed how the mobile film shows were remembered. Former relief operator Colin described the halls as

> very utilitarian, you could say dog-eared would probably be the correct description. The one in Shetland, in Yell, there was no heating or electric or anything else, it was just a tin roof, tin walls, two or three windows on the

> sides and a door. And there was no hot water, you took your own refreshment or whatever you needed to have. (Personal interview, 8 April 2019)

The basic rustic structure was more common than the elaborate stone structures of town halls, though the lack of comfort did not, in the early period of the service, deter the willing attendees or detract from the visiting attraction of the cinema. The prospect of the cinema visiting their area carried a strong appeal for the communities. However, towards the end of the 1950s, when the shows had become an established part of the culture of the Highlands and Islands and attendances were in decline, there is evidence to suggest that the lack of comfort in the halls did become more of a factor in the decision to attend the cinema shows (National Records of Scotland).

The halls were an important space in the cultural topography of rural communities. They were also used for activities that ranged from badminton and whist drives to meetings of community groups like the Scottish Women's Rural Institute. The multipurpose space of the halls suited the various uses that communities required of them. This was particularly true of the film show because the hall had to be transformed into a makeshift cinema. The preparation of the exhibition space created the opportunity for youngsters in the community to contribute to the assembly of an improvised cinema, and this with a greater degree of involvement and collaboration than was given by the conventional cinemas of towns and cities. The effort of having to improvise a cinema in spaces not constructed specifically for the purpose meant that the location was remembered with accurate detail and the common endeavour strengthened familial and communal ties with the institution. The annual reports of the Film Guild acknowledged the reliance on voluntary effort required by the operators to put on the shows (National Records of Scotland). Kathleen and Marion, the daughters of the operator Roddie Urquhart, remember helping him to set up the hall in Skeabost on the Isle of Skye:

> What I remember about Skeabost Hall in particular is going there and Dad would have to unlock it, then we would have to lay out the chairs, so we would have 20 or 30 chairs on that side and a gap, and the projectors would be in the middle at the gap, and then there'd be another set of chairs on this side. He took the money and everything, didn't he, I remember there being a table and a chair. (Personal interview, 12 November 2016)

Iain recalls the excitement he felt from contributing to the assembly of the cinema when the Film Guild visited his district of Point on the Isle of Lewis:

> And he [the operator] used to come every fortnight and we used to set up the hall, you had benches and chairs, you put them out and there was a stage in the hall as well. We used to put the screen, roll up the screen on the stage and the van came, roll up the gear and setting up the tripods and bringing their projectors on, and the spools. It was a big, big highlight for us you know, that was like massive for us. Like probably going to the Royal Albert Hall today, you know [laughs]. (Personal interview, 15 November 2016)

The opportunity to assist directly in the preparation of the space for the film show was clearly valued and contributed to a more open and intimate form of cinema in areas where permanent commercial cinema buildings were absent. Furthermore, members of a communal audience were much less anonymous to one another than those of an urban cinema audience. Inside the improvised exhibition arenas of the halls, the audience shared the space with the operator and the film apparatus, so that beyond seeing a film show, they also saw and heard it being projected by the operator who had arrived in their locality for the day of the show. This created a viewing environment where youngsters in the audience were recognized by their local peers and less likely to misbehave. Seating was not stepped but equally positioned at ground level, an arrangement that called for more considerate behaviour during the show. These conditions created an architecture of reception and cinema experience that contrasts with dominant understandings of cinema, but which for these rural audiences was still their cinema, and their means of going to the pictures. This combination of intimacy, community, and access to an experience of cinema that was shared across the Highlands and Islands was central to the recollection of the Film Guild, and often audiences remember the prospect of going to the film shows more than the actual films.[7]

---

[7] This investment in an institution that was providing a cultural service for rural communities can be contrasted with one of the recurring myths in films and literary fiction about the Highlands and Islands. The Kailyard tradition typically represents the sentimental idealization of village life and is described by Duncan Petrie as "the abdication of any engagement with the realities of the modern world" (3). The work of the Film Guild delivered a small part of the modern world to the Highlands and Islands and offers both a corrective to the myth, and a means of securing ongoing political support and legitimacy for a civic Scotland.

The operators personified the cinema delivered by the Film Guild and they represented the public face of the institution, occupying a mediating role between the community audiences located across the Highlands and Islands, and the central institution located farther south. There was an expectation that the operators' role would become extensive, and the relationships they cultivated with the communities were important to the standing of the Film Guild: "[T]he men who now are driver-projectionists may once have been bus-drivers, crofters, fishermen or bartenders, but one and all they are now film ambassadors, friends and confidantes of the people and general factotums" (Morris 30). Their work and travel across the Highlands and Islands connected remote areas not only physically but also culturally by turning rural cinema-going into a cross-regional, if not national, experience.

Part of the task of building relationships with isolated communities and meeting their expectations and anticipation of the mobile cinema's visit was predicated on the completion of the journeys undertaken by the operators in their vans. The landscape of the Highlands and Islands, the rudimentary road and sea transport infrastructure, plus winter weather, increased the pressure on the operators to reach the destinations of the shows allocated to their unit.

Fig. 2. Shetland Isles c/o Billy Williamson. During the height of the Film Guild's popularity in the 1950s the operator for the northern Shetland Isles had to transport equipment to islands such as Unst and Fetlar separately, and rely

on local helpers and transport to ensure that he reached his destination in time for the show. The next day he would have to make the same journey with the equipment in reverse back to his van.

The Film Guild vans driven by the operators signified a visiting attraction that would arrive in communities regularly and reliably. The vans were a combination of newly purchased vehicles and older ones inherited from the Ministry of Information; they represented solidity and reliability over comfort and speed, with operators also taking responsibility for their maintenance. People belonging to crofting communities did not necessarily live close to one another within a village, but were more widely scattered and therefore isolated across the landmass of the Highlands and Islands. Assisting these attendees became part of the operator's work, with the van functioning as a form of communal transport for the audience as well as the cinema equipment. Allan recalls being picked up by the operator during his childhood on the Isle of Skye:

> As we got a little bit older and we were entrusted to go to the Film Guild, or the "pictures" as we called them, on our own. Roddie would come along with this little Bedford van with the lettering on the side, *Highlands and Islands Film Guild* and it was absolutely packed with the equipment, he had two projectors and the film, the screen, all the bits and pieces, and he would stop and give us a lift. He would squeeze in three or four of us and in return we would then help offload stuff from the van into the hall and at the end of the evening we would reverse that process and Roddie would give us a lift back. (Personal interview, 24 August 2018)

Access to transport was one of a number of pressing issues, exacerbated by the geography of the area and a relatively meagre public transport service. Interviewees recall how seeing the Film Guild van parked in their areas confirmed that the mobile cinema and its operator had arrived to deliver a film show for them. This recognition affirmed their valued contribution to the cultural and social life of the community and its topography.

The operator's van transported the equipment required for the projection of the films but did not always contain the film reels. At certain points of the schedule the films had to be transported from the renters in London, or from other units in the Highlands and Islands, to the location of the next show. Ensuring that the films were where they were required at the right time required meticulous planning and organization from the centre. The films and the operators usually arrived at their destination on time, enabling the Film Guild to become a reliable and integral part of cultural life in the post-war Highlands and Islands, as they were able to overcome the handicaps presented by the terrain and its seasonal conditions.

The geography and physical topography of the area with its particular climate and environment regularly encroached on the cinema and how it was exhibited, experienced, and remembered. One of the most explicit examples of this is provided by the first secretary of the Film Guild, who narrates the actions taken by the community to ensure that the community of Eshaness, an exposed headland located on the west coast of the Shetland mainland, were able to receive their operator:

> Eshaness, craggy and isolated provides a rather special example of its appreciation. The hall there stands in the middle of what is almost a peat bog and there was no access road. The problem was a simple one – no road, no films. That was a challenge and the Shetlanders love a challenge: a common saying among these descendants of the hardy Vikings is "Say du nawthin," but that does not mean they do nothing. The men set to, carted stones and rubble, dumped it into the old track and so made their road, whilst the women, equally anxious and willing, forgot their knitting and attended to the refreshments. In a day and a night the job was done and George Horne, the Guild's first operator, drove his van up for the show. (Morris 30)

The narrative retelling of this intervention by the local community is typical of the stories that recollections of the Film Guild institution yield, albeit in this case with a very stereotypical account of gender roles. The oral tradition of the Highlands ensures that these types of memory are passed on to the following generations (Goode, "The Place of Rural Exhibition").

The ability of the communities to act collectively and voluntarily to ensure that the film shows were delivered to locations where cinema had not existed before was key to their early success and the longevity of the institution. The Film Guild benefited from the improvisational skills of local citizens who used local materials to furnish the halls. Examples of these enhancements include an operator making bespoke wooden boxes to hold admission money, the local community making cushions to make seating more comfortable, appropriating blankets left over from the war to use as blackout material, and taking oven-heated bricks wrapped in paper into the hall on winter nights to help keep warm – contributions that Philip Alperson described as spontaneous achievement within the constraints of the possible (274). These small investments in supporting and enhancing the cinema-going experience resulted from post-war austerity and geographical marginality.

The Film Guild reached the apex of its growth in the early 1950s, and although audiences did decline throughout this decade, the social functions of the institution had deepened since its formation. This enabled the management to maintain the argument for their contribution to the sustainability of small rural communities throughout the 1960s, when attendances dropped, and the necessity of the film shows were called into question by the funders. Its primary funder, the Scottish Education Department, assumed that the film shows had been replaced by television – a view that was fiercely contested by the Film Guild and educational studies (Blackburn). Despite this resistance and due to the end of post-war regeneration that came with the election of Conservative governments between 1951 and 1964 and the changes to leisure habits that emerged throughout the 1960s, the Film Guild declined until it was finally wound up in 1971.

The social qualities of accessibility and personification in tandem with the specificities of film exhibition in non-theatrical spaces, where geography and local material culture became intertwined with its operation, turned this cinema into a far more embodied experience that went beyond simply immersing oneself mentally in the stories projected onto the screen. These community spaces were located in places that were on the margin, and where regular cinema-going was not expected to be possible. The act of delivering film shows to these areas and their expectant audiences represents what Rob Shields has described as alternative geographies of modernity that enabled a distinctive experience of cinema that has, for a long time, been absent from its historical and theoretical configuration. The Film Guild made a significant contribution to the reach of British post-war cinema-going experience. Viewed in relation to the rest of British cinema exhibition, this was an exceptional cinema that depended on the financial support of the government and had no equivalent of the same scale showing films on a not-for-profit basis, for entertainment and education. Indeed, the Film Guild and the mobile cinema provided by its wartime precursor the MOI created an expectation amongst isolated communities that they should be able to see films in their areas. The historical impact of the Film Guild and its cultural legacy is evident in the resumption of organized provision of a cinema-going experience for the remote communities of the Highlands and Islands in the 1990s.

The Screen Machine

In 1998 a new version of mobile cinema was unveiled in the form of the Screen Machine, a purpose-built cinema vehicle that promised to deliver the latest films on 35mm to rural areas of the Highlands and Islands of Scotland. The idea of a wholly self-contained mobile cinema that removed the need for spaces that could accommodate a film show originated in France. A partnership of Highlands and Islands Enterprise, the Scottish Film Council and the then Highland Regional Council was formed to adapt and transfer the Cinemobile model from France. The consortium agreed to commission a Highland equivalent of the Cinemobile, financially supported by the National Lottery Fund. A body called HI-Arts was formed to take forward the commissioning process that would eventually lead to the launch of the Screen Machine (Livingston).

Fig. 3. The Screen Machine in Dornie with Eilean Donan Castle in the background c/o Regional Screen Scotland, David Redshaw

The Screen Machine is popular and has become well established in the Highlands and Islands. Its two (soon to become three) vehicles are now equipped with digital projection facilities and provide a genuinely theatrical cinema experience to rural communities that stands up to the offerings of the modern multiplex cinema and can even surpass the experience of watching television comfortably at home. It does not offer a commercial proposition for exhibiting films though it must be seen to be developing its potential audience as part of its remit. Like the Highlands and Islands Film Guild, it is borne out of the specific needs of the Highlands and Island communities who do not enjoy easy access to permanent cinemas. There is a growing community cinema sector in England and Wales providing a static and more intimate alternative to the multiplex cinema experience to rural areas, but there is no equivalent to the Screen Machine.

The size of the Screen Machine vehicles means that they cannot reach all of the Highlands and Islands, but there is a growing community cinema sector supported by Regional Screen Scotland that works to address this requirement. The popularity of the Screen Machine service with its latest feature films has not diminished with the increased use of streaming platforms, and this distinctive and communal mode of cinema-going experience remains a vital part of Scotland's cultural provision and cultural identity.

European Connections and Scottish Identity

The policy that supports the broadening of access to cinema in Scotland takes account of comparative contexts from the Continent that seek to ensure that access to a film experience is maximized and geographically equitable rather than left to the market and the size of the potential audience (Česálková). A recent report cited

> Norway as having a fantastic model of regional cinemas, with local people owning parts of community cinemas. People there are very well served, as they are in most of the Scandic countries, which have good models that give people access to films, including films from their own country. (Culture, Tourism, Europe and External Relations Committee 88)

The remote areas of Europe, such as Norway and Scotland, require sustained financial subsidy in the face of depopulation and limited opportunities. This has been termed "the Highland problem" in Scotland by historians of the area and there has been no shortage of enquiries by various types of government committees appointed to recommend potential solutions (Hunter; Burnett 109).[8] The initiatives that gave rise to the Screen Machine and its post-war predecessor are notable because they yielded tangible interventions with outcomes that genuinely improved the cultural life of the Highlands and Island communities and have, as mentioned above, also enjoyed support from the EU.

The EU has shown an understanding for marginalized areas in Europe and has also recognized the necessity to support the Scottish transportation system, agriculture, and culture (Ascherson 72). Furthermore, Gerry Hassan highlights how civic memory continues to be important to how Scotland sees itself and its increasing political difference to England (*Independence of the Scottish Mind*). Scotland can therefore be considered as stuck between a disunion with the EU that it regrets and a union with the UK it only half-heartily embraces.

England has shifted to the political right, helped by a first-past-the-post electoral system, and, in the wake of the vote for Brexit, has employed a more openly xenophobic and nationalist discourse. In contrast, Scotland's acceptance of, and requirement for, incoming migrants coupled with its refusal to see European Union institutions as an ontological threat to national sovereignty, mean that the distance between Scotland and the England represented by the current Conservative government and its allies has rarely been greater.[9] For Scotland the appetite for nationalism is derived less from an idea of blood and soil than from a claim to greater self-determination and a more socially progressive and open citizenship (Boyd; Hassan, *Independence of the Scottish Mind*). This difference is underlined by Nathalie Duclos, who has observed that whereas

> the phrases "the Scottish people" and "the people of Scotland" used to be interchangeable for the party, the latter phrase is now always preferred. It is argued that this is in keeping with the SNP's [Scottish National Party's] perception of Scottish citizenship as one that is based on residence, rather than

---

[8] The consultations with representatives of educational, social, and cultural institutions prior to the formation of the Film Guild underlined how important the attraction of cinema was to the area. One official stated that cinema was more important than electricity which would be arriving in the coming years through the hydro-electric scheme (National Archives). Access to cinemas was a cultural facility that was widely available in the towns and cities of Scotland and was viewed as a major improvement in remote communities, especially valued by the younger population.

[9] From the more than 20,000 students from across Europe who come to study in Scotland each year, to the 500 million bottles of whisky it exports throughout the EU, Scotland has had a long history of intellectual, cultural, literary, scientific, and economic contributions to Europe ("Scotland around the World").

> origins or ancestry, as well as with its claims to support a "civic" form of nationalism. (1-2)

The collective and historical agency of *the people* is important to the construction of the nation by the SNP and the sense of a movement towards a point of achieved self-determination and sovereignty (Hassan, "Scotland's Democratic Moment"). With the unionist meaning of Britishness under increasing pressure, the EU referendum campaign and subsequent debate demonstrated the propensity of Conservative governments to look backwards and inwards to the Second World War rather than forward to a renewed and cohesive Britain. England was giving clear signs that some of the electorate were uneasy with levels of immigration and the freedom of movement that underpins the meaning of Europe for many of its people and institutions. Scotland, in contrast, actively articulates a relationship with fellow European countries that does not undermine national sovereignty, but is considered a necessary part of it and essential to its future.

Projects such as the provision of rural cinema-going highlight Scotland's investments to improve communal life and culture and fight depopulation, as well as its similarities with other marginalized areas in Europe. David McCrone observes that "Scottish interest in Norway, Sweden, Finland, Denmark and Iceland can be explained by; their 'northern' position in relation to central Europe and the European Union; and their small populations and centre-left political dispensations" (209). These affinities between northern Europe and the history and cultural topography of Scotland reveal a relationship aligned with European cinema culture and policy.

This is a Scotland where the Scottish National Party has replaced the British Labour Party as the majority party, often constructed as more progressive and increasingly at odds with a British identity dominated by English, anti-European conservatism. While England remains locked on its current political course with left liberal alternatives unable to make a convincing impact, Scotland remains an exception to the conservative and imperial exceptionalism of England and Britain.

References

Alperson, Philip. "A Topography of Improvisation." *The Journal of Aesthetics and Art Criticism*, vol. 68, no. 3, Summer 2010, pp. 273-80.

Ascherson, Neal. "Scotland, Brexit and the Persistence of Empire." *Embers of Empire in Brexit Britain*, edited by Stuart Ward and Astrid Rasch, Bloomsbury Academic, 2019, pp. 71-78.

Aveyard, Karina. *The Lure of the Big Screen: Cinema in Rural Australia and the United Kingdom.* Intellect Books, 2014.

BBC. "Cromarty's New 35-Seat Cinema Opens Its Doors." 31 Jan. 2020, www.bbc.com/news/uk-scotland-highlands-islands-51325542.

Blackburn, John. *Pattern of Leisure: An Enquiry into the Place of Cinema and Television among Leisure Activities in the Scottish Highlands and Islands.* Scottish Educational Film Association and Scottish Film Council, 1961.

Boyd, Cat. "Radical Scotland Is Here to Stay." *Soundings: A Journal of Politics and Culture*, vol. 59, Spring 2015, pp. 32-36.

Burchard, Jeremy. "Reconstructing the Rural Community: Village Halls and the National Council of Social Service, 1919 to 1939." *Rural History*, vol. 10, no. 2, Oct. 1999, pp. 193-216.

Burnett, John. *The Making of the Modern Scottish Highlands 1939-1965: Withstanding the Colossus of Advancing Materialism.* Four Courts Press, 2011.

Caughie, John, et al. Introduction. *Early Cinema in Scotland*, edited by John Caughie et al., Edinburgh UP, 2018.

Česálková, Lucie. "'Feel the Film': Film Projectionists and Professional Memory." *Cinemagoing, Film Experience and Memory*, special issue of *Memory Studies*, vol. 10, no. 1, Jan. 2017, pp. 49-62.

Creative Europe Desk UK. "North by Northwest – Films on the Fringe." 2014, www.creativeeuropeuk.eu/funded-projects/north-northwest-films-fringe.

Culture, Tourism, Europe and External Relations Committee. "Making Scotland a Screen Leader 6th Report." Edinburgh, 2018, p. 88.

Devine, Tom. "The Sixties in Scotland: A Historical Context." *Sixties Scotland*, edited by Eleanor Bell and Linda Gunn, Rodopi, 2013, pp. 23-46.

Duclos, Nathalie. "The SNP's Conception of Scottish Society and Citizenship, 2007-2014. / La conception de la société et de la citoyenneté écossaises par le Scottish National Party: 2007-2014." *Revue Française de Civilisation Britannique / French Journal of British Studies*, vol. 21, no. 1, 2016, pp. 1-16.

Galway Film Centre. "North by North West – Films on the Fringe Launch." 23 Oct. 2014, www.galwayfilmcentre.ie/2014/10/23/north-by-north-west-films-on-the-fringe-launch/.

——. "Sad News for Galway's Cinemobile as It Is Set to Close." 16 July 2016, www.galwayfilmcentre.ie/2016/07/12/galways-cinemobile-to-close/.

Goode, Ian. "Island Geographies, the Second World War Film and the Northern Isles of Scotland." *Visual Culture in the Northern British Archipelago: Imagining Islands*, edited by Ysanne Holt et al., Routledge, 2018, pp. 51-68.

——. "The Place of Rural Exhibition: Makeshift Cinema-Going and the Highlands and Islands Film Guild (Scotland)." *Watching Films: New Perspectives on Movie-Going, Exhibition and Reception*, edited by Albert Moran and Karina Aveyard, Intellect, 2013, pp. 265-78.

——. "UNESCO, Mobile Cinema, and Rural Audiences: Exhibition Histories and Instrumental Ideologies of the 1940s." *Rural Cinema Exhibition and Audiences in a Global Context*, edited by Daniela Treveri Gennari et al., Palgrave Macmillan, 2018, pp. 219-35.

Griffiths, Trevor. *The Cinema and Cinema-Going in Scotland, 1896-1950.* Edinburgh UP, 2012.

Harding, Alan. *Evaluating the Importance of the Crown Film Unit, 1940-1952.* 2017. Nottingham Trent University and Southampton Solent University, PhD dissertation.

Hassan, Gerry. *Independence of the Scottish Mind: Elite Narratives, Public Spaces and the Making of a Modern Nation.* Palgrave Macmillan, 2014.

——. "Scotland's Democratic Moment." *Soundings: A Journal of Politics and Culture*, vol. 59, Spring 2015, pp. 23-27.

Hjort, Mette, and Ursula Lindqvist, editors. *A Companion to Nordic Cinema.* Wiley Blackwell, 2016.

Hunter, James. *The Claim of Crofting: The Scottish Highlands and Islands, 1930-1990.* Mainstream Publishing, 1991.

Jennings, Angie. "Creative Scotland Awards Regular Funding to RSS." *Regional Screen Scotland*, 25 Jan. 2018, www.regionalscreenscotland.org/creative-scotland-awards-regular-funding-to-rss/.

Jernudd, Åsa. "Youth, Leisure, and Modernity in the Film *One Summer of Happiness* (1951): Exploring the Space of Rural Film Exhibition in Swedish Post-War Cinema." *Rural Cinema Exhibition and Audiences in a Global Context*, edited by Daniela Treveri Gennari et al., Palgrave Macmillan, 2018, pp. 325-37.

Kuhn, Annette. "Screen and Screen Theorizing Today." *Screen*, vol. 50, no. 1, Spring 2009, pp. 1-12.

Livingston, Robert. "Screen Machine and Regional Screen Scotland: A Brief History." March 2016, www.screenmachine.co.uk/screen-machine-and-regional-screen-scotland-a-brief-history-2/.

McCrone, David. *Understanding Scotland: The Sociology of a Nation.* Routledge, 2001.

Morris, Tom. "The Men of the Wee Cinema." *Scotland's Magazine*, vol. 51, Dec. 1955, pp. 28-31.

The National Archives, D4/441, Report of Discussions at Conference at Inverness on 30/5/46 on the Society's Memorandum – "Film Shows for Rural Areas," 30 May 1946.

National Records of Scotland, ED27/252, Operators Conference Report December, 1952.

Neely, Sarah, and Nalini Paul. *Reel to Rattling Reel: Stories and Poems about Memories of Cinema-Going.* Cranachan Publishing, 2018.

Petrie, Duncan. *Screening Scotland.* British Film Institute, 2000.

Regional Screen Scotland. "The Screen Machine." 2020, www.regionalscreenscotland.org.

"Scotland around the World." *Brand Scotland*, 2019, www.scotland.org/about-scotland/scotland-around-the-world.

Scottish Home Department. *A Programme of Highland Development.* Her Majesty's Stationery Office, 1950, p. 5.

Shields, Rob. *Places on the Margin: Alternative Geographies of Modernity.* Routledge, 1992.

Stornoway Gazette, 1 March 1946, p. 3.

Thissen, Judith, and Clemens Zimmermann, editors. *Cinema beyond the City: Small-Town and Rural Film Culture in Europe.* Palgrave, 2016.

Treveri Gennari, Daniela et al., editors. *Rural Cinema Exhibition and Audiences in a Global Context.* Palgrave Macmillan, 2018.

Fractured Identities: How Brexit Threatens an Agreed Ireland

Maurice Fitzpatrick

Brexit has been exceptionally unsettling in Ireland, North and South. It has caused discord within Northern Ireland, exposed the highly contentious Irish border to fresh dilemmas, and strained Anglo-Irish relations more than any period since the 1980s. This essay explores the unique challenges that Brexit presents for Ireland and for Ireland's relations with the UK. As against narratives that localize the origins of Brexit to internal Conservative Party politics, this essay argues that the impetus of Brexit is also bound up with the instability that Northern Ireland has brought to the United Kingdom since the establishment of Northern Ireland in 1920. This analysis of Brexit is therefore situated in the *longue durée* of Anglo-Irish relations: historical perspectives are offered to problematize the radically different attitudes towards membership in the European community in Britain and Ireland. In the backdrop of Brexit's upheavals, this essay explores how Brexit has irreversibly reconstituted the interlocking 'three strands' of relationships – within Northern Ireland; between Ireland, North and South; between Great Britain and Ireland – that were essential to securing the Good Friday Agreement in 1998.

Keywords: Brexit, Unionism, United Kingdom, Good Friday Agreement, Northern Ireland

Brexit analysis is reminiscent of Sovietology: it is impossible to forget that the field of enquiry was created in the context of a highly capricious political development; and equally impossible to ignore that that politi-

Brexit and Beyond: Nation and Identity. SPELL: Swiss Papers in English Language and Literature 39, edited by Daniela Keller and Ina Habermann, Narr, 2020, pp. 227-49.

cal reality is susceptible to sudden disintegration, largely bringing the field of study down with it. Still, the transformative impact of Brexit socially, culturally, and constitutionally cannot be denied. Britain's project of exiting the EU, or indeed the UK's project of exiting the EU (each of the component parts of the UK leaving the EU together, and on the same terms) is so shambolic as to make it almost impossible to advance an analysis that does not require immediate revision. It is so hard to fully anticipate where Brexit is going mainly because, as the flailing attempts to effect it have shown, the planning behind it is so slipshod and the reasoning for it so absurd.[1]

Brexit has been the biggest political earthquake that England, Ireland, Scotland, and Wales (what Norman Davies has termed 'The Isles') have experienced so far this century. With any political earthquake comes a profound cultural unsettlement – in this case, a re-examination of identity across the Isles. As with the enormous Tōhoku earthquake in Japan in March 2011, the damage wrought by the UK's decision to leave the EU without adequate forethought as to its full implications spawned a tsunami in the manner in which negotiations have been conducted, and it could yet precipitate a meltdown in the fabric of the UK. Those realities will be keenly felt in Ireland, North and South. It is the effect on Ireland that is the focus of this essay, with particular attention to Brexit's impact on the delicate peace and stability brokered through the Good Friday Agreement in 1998, which was endorsed on both sides of the Irish border. That agreement was negotiated between the Irish and UK governments and by all of the main political parties (except the DUP) in Northern Ireland.[2] The Good Friday Agreement provided for

---

[1] I have, in some particulars, revised the text of the lecture delivered in Basel on 4 May 2019 to reflect current political realities such as the replacement of Theresa May by Boris Johnson as Prime Minister of the UK, the displacement of the Democratic Unionist Party (DUP) from its central position in the House of Commons as well as the agreement on the 'Northern Ireland Protocol' between the UK and the EU. Still, any updated analysis of Brexit is almost immediately dated. Suffice to say, as Benjamin the donkey in George Orwell's *Animal Farm* might have put it, Brexit has gone on as it has always gone on – that is, badly

[2] The cornerstone of Ulster Unionism since the foundation of Northern Ireland has been a non-negotiable 'guarantee' of Northern Ireland's position in the United Kingdom. Negotiating a new political settlement with nationalists was historically dogged by a perception that negotiation entailed the near-certainty of a diminution of that guarantee and thus was a threat to unionist political identity. The Anglo-Irish Agreement (1985) was negotiated between officials of the Irish and UK governments without the involvement of Northern Irish politicians precisely because of the refusal of unionist leaders to countenance alternatives to the constitutional position; as Dublin's lead negotiator of that agreement Michael Lillis wrote, "unionists were at that time […] immured

a Northern Irish Assembly, a power-sharing arrangement based on devolved power from the UK Parliament. Among its other provisions were an open border in Ireland; the right of Northern Irish people to be British, Irish, or both; and the right of the people of Northern Ireland to hold a plebiscite in the future on whether to unite with the rest of Ireland (commonly termed a 'border poll').

The June 2016 referendum's verdict registered profound differences of outlook in Britain, Scotland, and Northern Ireland, as reflected in the vote to leave in England and Wales and the vote to remain in Scotland and Northern Ireland. As the spheres widen – Britain, Great Britain, and the entire UK – the political fissures deepen. What is routinely referred to as 'Brexit' is in fact a misnomer. The difficulties in effecting a UKexit, as Brendan O'Leary has labelled it (vii), constitutes a central problem with the entire process from conception to implementation. The nub of UKexit's problems is Northern Ireland. When Britain sneezes, Northern Ireland catches a cold – which, in this case, has developed into pneumonia. Half a year after the UKexit referendum was held in June 2016, the Northern Ireland Assembly ceased to function.[3] This difficulty of governing Northern Ireland was exacerbated in June 2017 when Theresa May called an election to consolidate her majority in the House of Commons – losing it instead. Subsequently, in her search to form a government, she entered a confidence and supply pact with Northern Ireland's DUP which, from a Northern nationalist perspective, obliterated her government's credibility as a neutral co-guarantor of the Good Friday Agreement. Irish negotiator of the Anglo-Irish Agreement (1985) Michael Lillis has argued that Margaret Thatcher, by contrast, had "faced down the unionist hysteria that followed the Anglo-Irish Agreement of 1985. It is doubtful if she would have conceded what Mrs. May conceded to the DUP in 2017" ("John Hume").

The confidence and supply pact put the DUP in the cockpit where it steered (or, more accurately, obstructed) government policy on UKexit. The DUP leadership went to considerable lengths to present Ireland's European dimension as an encroachment upon their cultural and even

---

in their veto-proofed immunity from any other reality" ("Emerging"). Hard-line unionism's refusal to accommodate the nationalist identity in Northern Ireland was the central reason that the DUP repudiated the compromise that the Good Friday Agreement represented.

[3] Under the leadership of the adroit former Secretary of State for Northern Ireland Julian Smith and with the threat of an Assembly election in which the electorate could express its frustration, Sinn Féin and the DUP agreed on a deal to return to the Assembly after a three-year hiatus in January 2020.

religious identity – and this critique has a long tradition: DUP Euroscepticism dates to its stance on Ireland and the UK joining the European Economic Community in the early 1970s. The word 'ecumenism' appeared at the top of a list of nefarious effects of joining the common market on a DUP political poster at that time, urging against accession to the European Economic Community in the referendum held in 1975 to endorse the UK government's decision to join the EEC in 1973. Thus the DUP unblushingly campaigned for a culture premised upon sectarian division.

It is possible to trace the filiation of these quasi-religious objections of association with Europe to an identification with the Protestant Reformation. The political and religious leader principally responsible for conflating membership of the burgeoning European community with a betrayal of the purity of the Protestant Reformation was the then DUP leader, Ian Paisley. If these claims sound off the wall, that is because they do in fact exist as murals in East Belfast. One such mural references the 400th anniversary of Martin Luther's ninety-five Theses, which ironically originated in 'the continent' of Europe, and bears a putative quotation from The Book of Revelation 18:4 ("Come out of her [Babylon], My people, lest you share in her sins, and lest you receive of her plagues") rendered into the modern Northern Irish vernacular thus: 'Vote Leave EU.'

1972/1973 and the EEC

Enormous upheavals in the relationship between Northern Ireland and the UK had occurred the year before the UK and Ireland joined the EEC in 1973. In 1972 the UK Parliament had exercised its sovereignty over Northern Ireland by proroguing the Parliament of Northern Ireland and instituting direct rule of Northern Ireland from London. Throughout the period of direct rule – a period that closely mirrors the duration of the Northern Irish Troubles (1968-98) – Great Britain could, and did, negotiate with Europe, and with the Irish government, on matters of far-reaching concern to Ulster unionists without so much as consulting them.

1972 also saw the publication of a seminal pamphlet, *Towards a New Ireland: Proposals by the Social Democratic and Labour Party*. This new party, the SDLP, was pro-European, and it substantially emulated the politics of post-WWII German parties in its attempt to purge tribalism from Northern Irish politics, and replace it with an emphasis on practical politics. The concept of a New and Agreed Ireland existed in contradistinction to the catch-cry of a 'United Ireland' which was perceived by Unionists as a threat to their identity. In essence, the proposals for a New Ireland were:

1 That Britain declare it had no strategic interest in remaining in Ireland;
2 The creation of a power-sharing government within Northern Ireland (in contrast to The Parliament of Northern Ireland which had presided over half a century of discriminatory laws and rigged elections);
3 The need for the agreement and consent of the people of Ireland, North and South, as an essential precondition for constitutional change.

The union between Great Britain and Northern Ireland that existed throughout the Troubles was, on the face of it, similar to the union that existed from 1921-72. Yet in important particulars it was a diminution of union because after 1972, since Northern Ireland no longer had a parliament, unilateralism became the default mode of the UK government in its administration of Northern Ireland. Labour Leader Harold Wilson had even formulated what he termed a '16 point plan' in November 1971, to facilitate a total British withdrawal from Northern Ireland, which was extremely alarming from a unionist perspective, and helped to radicalize resistance towards London. Astute English observers of Northern Ireland have always understood that the ultimate face-off in Northern Ireland could see Northern Irish loyalism turn its aggression towards England should it violate the Union.

The UK and Ireland joining the EEC in 1973 was a necessary vaccination for the union of Great Britain and Northern Ireland to survive. It was a shot of reduced sovereign autonomy which helped to immunize the UK against the ideological contradictions of that Union and the deepening fragility of its economic and political commitment to Northern Ireland. UKexit, however, has exposed the burden of that commitment again, which had been alleviated by the UK joining a wider comity of nations since 1973.

Furthermore the act of the Republic of Ireland and UK together joining the EEC in 1973 helped to expunge a dilemma from Anglo-Irish relations in regard to Northern Ireland. Ireland and Britain began a process of pooling their sovereignty which, ultimately, was a necessary step towards stabilizing Northern Ireland. That enabled a series of agreements: the Sunningdale Agreement in 1973, the Anglo-Irish Agreement in 1985, and the Good Friday Agreement in 1998. Each agreement was fortified by its predecessor and inched closer towards a negotiated settlement. The moment that misalignment between the UK and the EU occurs, which is inevitable with UKexit, the degree of difficulty of realigning the intricacies of those agreements becomes clear.

The Union of Great Britain and Northern Ireland

Through the ingenuity of the Good Friday Agreement, the ultimate determination of the fate of the people of Northern Ireland lies with the people of Northern Ireland. The Good Friday Agreement enabled a glide towards a united political structure in Ireland, just as it provided for a retention of Northern Ireland for as long as its people decide. UKexit, by contrast, has unsettled these coexistent impulses and reinforced the binary relationships – unionist and nationalist – in which they had traditionally been cast: something that has caused a great deal of societal division and political antagonism. The impulse to reconfigure the relationship with the EU entails the UK first reconfiguring its relationship with Northern Ireland. UKexit has forced England to confront something that many in London had hoped was fully diffused and sectioned off: Northern Ireland. Denial of that fact constitutes the kernel of the disastrous handling of UKexit negotiations from the UK side during the 2016-19 period, and it begs the following questions: why was it so hard for the UK to acknowledge the centrality of Northern Ireland in negotiations? What was it that the UK cabinet and large swathes of politicians on both sides of the aisle in the House of Commons were so determined to avoid seeing?

Theresa May repeatedly stated that 'Brexit means Brexit,' a truism that was yet another avoidance strategy. What UKexit actually means is this. That Great Britain could, at high price, agree to a deal to self-regulate outside the EU, but not the entire United Kingdom. The reality of the choice between accepting two regimes in the UK instilled terror in proponents of UKexit. Theresa May was emphatic that "no British Prime Minister" ("PM Brexit") could sign up to such a compromise, and her effective coalition partner, DUP leader Arlene Foster, resorted to hundred-year-old rhetoric of the Solemn League and Covenant (1912) to invoke 'blood red lines' ("DUP Leader"). The difficulty of unyoking Northern Ireland from the EU in turn vitiated the possibility of Great Britain leaving the EU for as long as the UK refused to accept two regimes. The impact of such acceptance was magnified, and presented by the Conservative Party and the DUP almost as though the British state was being asked to amputate a limb or remove an organ from its constitutional body, and to do so in full knowledge that it still may not survive the surgery.

Ireland was (and is) so interlinked with the United Kingdom – the main binding element being Northern Ireland – that the UK can scarcely disengage from its union with Europe for as long as Ireland remains engaged to it. Theresa May's repeated insistence that *Britain* must regain control of its borders was a sleight-of-hand response to the fact that, after leaving the EU, the *UK*'s borders would have been uncontrollable while the Northern Irish state remains in the UK. This is substantiated in Article 49 of the Withdrawal Agreement negotiated by Theresa May on 8 December 2017: "In the absence of agreed solutions, the United Kingdom will maintain full alignment with those rules of the Internal Market and the Customs Union which, now or in the future, support North-South cooperation, the all-island economy and the protection of the 1998 Agreement" (European Union and the United Kingdom Government par. 49). This is known as 'the backstop.'[4]

Absent that condition, Theresa May may well have gained majority support for the Withdrawal Agreement. Instead, it was defeated in the House of Commons three times by historic margins. Agreement between the UK and the EU centred on the issue of the Irish border – and its implementation in the UK Parliament was blocked until it did a volte-face and accepted regulatory alignment in an all-island Irish economy.[5] Both Northern Ireland's particular constitutional status, as well as

---

[4] Boris Johnson, in an impressive political somersault, effectively activated the backstop by agreeing that Northern Ireland would be treated as a different customs regime to the rest of the UK and the customs border would move to the Irish Sea. Johnson and the then Taoiseach Leo Varadkar agreed on a customs border in the Irish Sea at a seminal meeting near Liverpool on 10 October 2019 which was the basis for a revised Withdrawal Agreement.

[5] Even two months after meeting Varadkar in Liverpool in October 2019 and after agreeing to a revised Withdrawal Agreement with the EU the following week, Johnson insisted that "[t]here will be no checks on goods from GB to Northern Ireland or Northern Ireland to GB" (Strauss et al.). Construction of customs infrastructure is currently underway in three of Northern Ireland's main ports: Warrenpoint, Larne, and Belfast. Northern Ireland will remain in the UK's customs territory but – alone among the constituent parts of the UK – Northern Ireland will be subject to the EU's customs code. Minister for the Cabinet Office Michael Gove published the UK's plans for the Northern Ireland Protocol in a May 2020 report. Article 34 acknowledges that "[e]xpanded infrastructure will be needed" (Cabinet Office 13) on goods entering

its location at the prospective EU-UK frontier, gave rise to the backstop.

Theresa May, on 14 January 2018, when proposing the Withdrawal Agreement to the House of Commons asked: "[W]hat would a no deal Brexit do to strengthen the hand of those campaigning for Scottish independence – or indeed those demanding a border poll in Northern Ireland? Surely this is the real threat to our Union." She proceeded to speak of "changes to everyday life in Northern Ireland that would put the future of our Union at risk" ("PM Statement in the House of Commons").

Similarly, DUP deputy leader Nigel Dodds said in the House of Commons on 15 November 2018, in response to the Withdrawal Agreement, that this would be the case if the Withdrawal Agreement were passed: "The choice is now clear: we stand up for the United Kingdom – the whole United Kingdom and the integrity of the United Kingdom – or we vote for a vassal state, with the break-up of the United Kingdom" (col. 441).

What Is It All About?

Many prominent advocates of leaving the EU have maintained that the UKexit is not about the EU. The question arises, then, what is it about? In David Hare's play *Time to Leave*, performed by Kristin Scott Thomas, the playwright attempts to identify the motive behind the UK's vote to leave the EU:

> [H]aving decided to leave, it doesn't feel any different, does it? I thought it would. I thought we'd be less angry. But we're not. You see, it's the anger, isn't it? That's what it's about. It's about the anger. [...] it's made me wonder: "What's the anger about?" But the other day I was in the garden, tying in the roses and suddenly I understood. From nowhere. I realised. "Oh that's why it hasn't worked. That's why we're all so unhappy. We voted to leave Europe. But that's not what we wanted. We wanted to leave England.

I would like to argue against the conclusion of *Time to Leave*: indeed it was not the EU that English Brexiteers were trying to leave, but neither, ultimately, was it England. The vote to leave was motivated in large part by a will to leave the United Kingdom of Great Britain and Northern

---

Northern Ireland from the rest of the UK. Article 35 pertains to the UK's proposals for implementing the same, which remains contentious in negotiations with the EU (14).

Ireland. Seen from this perspective, it is all the more comprehensible why a matter external to England, such as the Irish border, blocking Brexit became so neuralgic. When Theresa May spoke of spending money on "our priorities" ("PM Statement on EU Negotiations"), it was to the United Kingdom that she referred. Notwithstanding her repeated statements in defence of the 'precious union,' that steadfast commitment, even within her Conservative Party, is rapidly declining.

An Institute for Public Policy Research report, *The Dog That Finally Barked: England as an Emerging Political Community*, published in 2012, found an ongoing tension between devolved parliament and assemblies in Scotland, Northern Ireland, and Wales on the one hand, and the UK Parliament on the other:

> During the years since 1999 – and, indeed, at various points during the preceding decades when devolution was on the political agenda – more or less dire warnings have been issued about the likely impact of all this on opinion in England. The people of England, it was claimed, would become increasingly resentful of the anomalies that inevitably arise in the context of a system of asymmetric devolution. (Jones et al. 4)

Asymmetric devolution refers to Scotland, Wales, and Northern Ireland having a voice in both their own parliaments/assembly as well as in the UK Parliament where they can also determine policy for England,[6] whereas English MPs have a voice in the UK Parliament only. Another source of asymmetry is that per capita public spending is "higher in the devolved territories than in England itself" (4). These asymmetries, engendered or aggravated by the devolution of power, have created huge problems in the management of the UK political structure a generation after the Government of Wales Act in 1998, the Scotland Act in 1998, and the Good Friday Agreement in 1998.

Irish and UK Attitudes to the EU

English and Irish attitudes towards the EU are fundamentally different. That divergence antecedes the UKexit referendum; the referendum merely revealed it in an undeniable way, and placed it at the centre of Anglo-Irish relations. A Red C poll taken in May 2019 found that fully 93% of the Irish electorate endorse Ireland remaining in the European

---

[6] The Welsh Assembly, the Senedd, became the Welsh Parliament on 6 May 2020.

Union. Set against the June 2016 referendum, in which 46.6% of the English electorate voted to, Irish support for EU membership is exactly double that of England. Granted, there are variables: during the banking crisis a decade ago Irish support for the EU waned considerably. Still, the divergence is remarkable. Ireland is among the most fervid supporters of the EU, while England is among the most avowedly Eurosceptic. English separatism was the root of the UKexit vote while, conversely, Irish attachment to the European project makes an Irexit foredoomed. So in what lies the source of the disparity in attitudes?

As former Irish ambassador to the UK Bobby McDonagh has argued in the *Irish Times*:

> In Ireland and Britain, we increasingly perceive reality in quite different ways. The reasons a majority in the UK voted to leave the EU are, paradoxically, the very same reasons that an overwhelming majority in Ireland want to stay. This is true of each of the six main arguments of the Brexiteers.

McDonagh was referring to sovereignty, the taking back of control, immigration, expenditure, international trade, and independence. Arguably, the Irish state has similar objectives to England's when it comes to international trade, sovereignty, and independence. So, again, why is there such a difference in how each polity has resolved to deliver its objectives and advance its interests?

A clue to this conundrum comes from Irish playwright Brian Friel. In an interview before his play *Translations*, which explores how language is used to construct identity, opened in Derry in September 1980, Friel said:

> You and I could list a whole series of words, for example, that have totally different connotations for English people than they have for us. Words like loyalty, treason, patriotism, republicanism, homeland. So that in fact there are words that we think we share and which we think we can communicate with, which in fact are barriers to communication. (2:56-3:20)

We could now add the word 'Europe' to that list.

The prevailing narrative for the Irish in regard to Europe is that attaining a European identity did not come at the price of jettisoning Irish identity, and that out of the matrix of both identities has emerged a national narrative hospitable enough to accommodate the traditionally hostile micro narratives, particularly in the contested space of Northern Ireland. There has been a thoroughgoing failure on the part of Britain to grasp the full significance of Europe for the ongoing arrangements in

Northern Ireland, whereas almost ineluctably Ireland has viewed them within this configuration.

A political leader who understood the value of this new configuration intimately was John Hume, who continually referred to an epiphany early in his political life during a visit to Strasbourg. In a study of his political life I describe that when he walked across a bridge from Strasbourg in France into Kehl in Germany, he saw in Franco-Germany post-war construction a model for Northern Ireland:

> These two European nations had slaughtered each other for centuries until finally, through building post-war European institutions, they had found a way to make common cause: to "spill their sweat not their blood" as Hume put it. Through that partnership, crossing from France to Germany had become as simple as walking across a bridge. France and Germany had come to respect each other's culture, language and identity and agreed that they shared an overarching European identity which did not in the least impinge upon their regional or national identities. [...] In the shape of this successful bi-cultural environment, Hume found inspiration for the divided people of Northern Ireland. (155)

On 8 January 2019 German foreign minister Heiko Maas, speaking in Dublin, said, "we insisted, and still do, that a hard border dividing the Irish island is unacceptable. [...] It is a matter of principle, a question of identity for the European Union" (qtd. in Federal Foreign Office). Similarly, Emmanuel Macron told former Taoiseach Leo Varadkar on 2 April 2019 that "this solidarity is the very purpose of the European project" (qtd. in McCormack). New brooms such as Maas and Macron have perceived the overarching function of the European project in Ireland, and yet their British counterparts largely have not.

The Border

The Irish border generally means the boundary that demarcates the North from the South, which separates Derry from Donegal, wends past Tyrone and Fermanagh with Cavan to the South, abuts on Monaghan and flows into the sea in Louth. 'A hard border,' in UKexit negotiations, denotes a superstructure with tangible manifestations of a border (such as CCTV cameras, customs officers) which further delineates a division between the two jurisdictions in Ireland. Yet the idea of resisting the hard border is part of what makes the border hard. The groundswell of hostility towards a hardening of the Irish border, and the violence liable to be aimed at any tangible materiality delimiting the border, are constituent elements of the hard border itself. To adapt philosopher George Berkeley's immaterialism to political constructs such as a land border between two jurisdictions, the border itself is void of matter: it exists as an idea, and insofar as a critical mass of minds agree that they perceive that idea (Berkeley 407). Therefore the framing of the border as a matter of political arrangement, whether contested or consensual, only partially conveys the epistemological foundations of the border. The border did not cause the division in Ireland; the division helped to cause the border. Fear of the hardening of the border emanates from insecurity about the ability of people on the island of Ireland to coexist in peace.

The Irish border was instituted by fiat of the UK Parliament after Prime Minister Lloyd George threatened "immediate and terrible war" on Ireland lest the Irish negotiators agree to the Anglo-Irish Treaty (1921), and it forms part of a long history of Ireland being a bugbear of Britain's domestic politics and its parliament. As far back as the nineteenth century, Prime Minister of the UK William Gladstone, speaking in the Commons, maintained that "the Irish Question is the curse of this House. It is the great and standing impediment to the effective performance of its duties" (col. 1605). That impediment endures.

Given that UKexit makes the Irish border a European border, London has had, for the first time, to accept that the right of people in Northern Ireland to have rights qua citizens of the EU supersedes the UK's bid objective of 'taking back control.' The geographical anomaly that is Northern Ireland has made it so difficult to extricate from Europe: Northern Ireland is not in the Irish state, but it is on the island of Ireland; Northern Ireland forms part of the British state, but it does not form part of the island of Great Britain. The state is founded on a series of paradoxes, and EU membership has helped to modulate the political conflicts that they have engendered.

Theresa May's mantra, in the early phases of UKexit negotiations, that 'Brexit means Brexit' was countered with a more meaningful formulation on Sinn Féin signage throughout the North of Ireland: "Brexit means Borders." The liminal space known as the Irish border has been restive and troublesome since its inception. It has been the site of trade, both licit and illicit; the site of paradoxes (such as on the Inishowen Peninsula where the farther North one travels geographically the further South one gets politically); the border has been the site of contestation over boundaries which were inadequately settled by the Boundary Commission in 1925; it has been a refuge for evacuees from Bombay

Street in Belfast in 1969, when the crossing of it signified the release from their persecution; it has been an inspiration for writers, painters, poets, and film-makers, but a nightmare for governments to administer; the southern side of the border has been perceived, in Ian Paisley's weaselly designation, a sanctuary for terrorists.

In advocating a hard border, Jacob Rees-Mogg went even further than those in the DUP who covertly support it. He was not in Ireland, or at the Irish border, to hear the depth of scorn with which his ideas were greeted. Similarly, Nigel Farage, who said on 14 May 2017 that if Brexit does not proceed he will "don khaki, pick up a rifle and head for the front lines" (qtd. in Peck). Farage could claim that this comment was frivolous – coming from Farage, it cannot but be. Yet during 2016-19 there was a front opening up, and Farage would sooner have left the UK forever than patrol it. That front was the Irish border.

Irish Unity

Since the partition of Ireland nearly a century ago, the proposition of Irish unity has been weighted both by ideological commitments and by practical obstacles – ideological fervour has by far outstripped concrete action towards the realization of unity. Indeed, ideology in favour of a United Ireland has, ironically, undermined the practical cause. Today one of the central challenges of establishing an all-island Irish republic is to reclaim from ideologues the concept of a republic free from the sectarian connotations accruing from the Provisional IRA's campaign; to establish instead a consciousness of cultural and political commitment to a republican model of government and society. With the UKexit referendum, however, the perception of the practicality, and even the necessity, of increased Irish unification has entered the national discourse more definitively than at any time since the Irish Civil War (1922-23).

A corollary of the proposition of unity of the two states on the island of Ireland is Northern Ireland ceasing to be part of the UK, thereby potentially ending the UK. It is the DUP that has been chiefly responsible for lending prominence to the disintegration of the UK in UKexit discourse, one that borders – no pun intended – on maieutics: the latency of the political strain upon the UK and shift towards a United Ireland has become more actual through articulation. That the constituency which fears break-up of the union so much is apt to articulate it is deeply ironic. The DUP's pro-UKexit stance has become a harbinger of a unified political structure on the island of Ireland more than anything else in the past decades.

The prospect of a unified political structure on the island of Ireland presents multifarious challenges, not least a financial one. The annual subvention from the UK Exchequer to Northern Ireland runs higher than ten billion pounds sterling. Economists differ in their expectations of the financial shortfall in the event of a British severance of its political and economic responsibilities towards Northern Ireland; nobody disputes that there would be a shortfall. Europe would indubitably play a role in absorbing some of the costs of unification in Ireland, as it did when Germany reunified. Since the German Minister of Foreign Affairs, Heiko Maas, has referred to retaining an open border on the island of Ireland as a matter of European identity, it follows as a logical consequence of Maas's perspective that, in the eventuality of the majorities on both sides of the Irish border voting for the elimination of the border, European support (economic and political) would flow to consolidate the unification of Ireland as a performance of European unity. This potential role of the EU also informs the hardline unionists' distrust of the EU: if the EU were to supplant the UK as the source of essential finance for Northern Ireland, then the political argument against unification, which is already weakening, would lose its economic underpinning. Unionist distrust of the EU's support for Dublin's position on UKexit is thus enmeshed with an anxiety that the EU is colluding in a subversion of the unionist political identity by stealth.

The Good Friday Agreement and National Identity

The Good Friday Agreement in 1998 engendered a consensus, particularly south of the border, that the Irish border should remain untouched for several decades, in a hope that time itself might help to lessen the political divisions of Northern Ireland. Yet the temporal floor which the Good Friday Agreement provided – 1998 as a date for the new departure – is jeopardized by UKexit.

One of the essential advances for the citizens of Northern Ireland, acknowledged in the Good Friday Agreement, was liberation from a fixed identity. The fluidity of identity, as noted above, meant that, finally, the identity water table in Northern Ireland accorded with the tilt of the political topography; this enabled the cultural space in Northern Ireland to become more absorbent of its various elements. The futile and paradoxical attempt to force consent, which characterized so many of

London's policies vis-à-vis Northern Ireland during the Troubles, was jettisoned in favour of recognition that broad-based consent was a pre-condition for a stable settlement. This was liberating for Britain as well as for Northern Ireland. It was an acknowledgment that the historical basis for paranoia about the position of Northern Ireland had vanished, and part of what enabled its disappearance was the European project. As John Hume argued in 1993: "The Plantation of Ulster was England's reaction to the links with Spain. The Act of Union [1800] was England's reaction to the links with France. Ireland was the back door for England's European enemies. That's all gone in the new Europe of today" (Hume and McDonald).

The Good Friday Agreement considerably succeeded in transcending, or at least negotiating, the specificity of national identity. A difficult shift in perception of national identity from whereness to whatness enabled an essential relaxation of attitudes. As Fintan O'Toole has argued, the Good Friday Agreement "deterritorialises an idea of national identity" (42:07-11). The political language started to change and, as Seamus Deane put it, when political languages change "they herald a deep structural alteration in the attitudes which sustain a crisis" (14).

In the late 1990s, for the first time in its history, the Northern Irish state had a chance to attempt to discard the lenses imposed upon its vision of polarized history. The liberation that that view affords is the only clear pathway yet found towards an Agreed Ireland in which the people of Northern Ireland have a stake in their society. By contrast, as the UKexit negotiations descended into recrimination, the either/or bind calcified again during the 2016-19 period. On the politico-economic plane, the choice became either a customs barrier down the Irish Sea or at the border, which the two largest political parties in Northern Ireland, the DUP and Sinn Féin, portrayed as a zero-sum equation. Thus the attitudes in Northern Irish political commentary are increasingly redolent of the Troubles period more than the post-Troubles period, and the cultural attitudes that prevailed during the Troubles have resurfaced. Brexit revealed that dislodging Northern Ireland from its position in Europe vitiates the meta-identity that is, as is evident with the threatened severance from Europe, central to whatever stability it has achieved in the past twenty-one years.

On 31 March 2018 the *Economist* printed an illustration in which a young boy has his jumper, in EU colours, forcibly removed – leaving a T-shirt underneath with the Irish and Union Jack flags side by side. The headline read: "Identity Theft: Britain Underestimates Brexit's Damage to Northern Ireland – Those who won the referendum on the basis of culture and identity now seem deaf to such concerns." If, to adopt the *Economist*'s editorial language, an identity theft has occurred, it is worth specifying the essence of that identity. The reality of Northern Irish sovereignty being vested in people rather than in territorial claims or constitutional proclivities is much closer to Rousseau's concept of public sovereignty than the parliamentary sovereignty of the UK. It generated a discourse which helped to create the Good Friday Agreement. UKexit threatens to subsume the newer idiom with a reversion to the futile older discourse in Northern Ireland.

Moreover, cultural identification in Northern Ireland is underpinned by the law. As many as one quarter of Northern Ireland's 1.8 million population hold Irish passports, which automatically makes them citizens of the EU. The Charter of Fundamental Rights of the European Union is the fiat that extends to EU citizens the four defining freedoms of the single market – of goods, capital, services, and labour. That charter is as binding for Irish citizens in Northern Ireland as all other EU citizens. What authority, then, does *any* UKexit agreement have to abrogate the rights of Irish citizens in Northern Ireland as EU citizens? The EU has correctly acknowledged their case as being unique. Unsurprisingly, a lobby group dedicated to the matter of Irish citizens' rights in Northern Ireland has formed in Belfast, the Committee on the Administration of Justice (CAJ). The CAJ has argued that the December 2017 draft exit proposal by the British (agreed to by the Irish government) provided that "no diminution of rights is caused by its departure from the European Union" (European Union and United Kingdom Government par. 53, qtd. by CAJ). It is clear that the CAJ, and other groups in Northern Ireland besides, will militate against a de facto replacement of EU legal norms with British law, and hold the UK Parliament to the commitments it made when it passed the Good Friday Agreement into law.

Futures and Outcomes

One of the triumphs of UKexit – if such a sentence can be completed – is that after a very long and bitter history the people of Northern Ireland voted to remain in a modern, cosmopolitan, and future-orientated continental alliance of states. A majority (52%) of the Northern Irish voting electorate opted to join the EEC referendum in 1975, and a majority (56%) of the Northern Irish voting electorate reaffirmed their wish to be members of the EU in the 2016 referendum. A majority of the

Northern Irish electorate voted for a different future from the future for which a majority of the UK voted. That did not, nor does not, mean that they voted to leave the UK but it certainly prompts a new discussion about Northern Ireland's place within the UK.

A majority of people in Northern Ireland want to remain in the UK, while a majority of people in Northern Ireland voted to remain in the EU. Given that those two propositions are true, the pre-UKexit political reality reflected the wishes of the majority of people in Northern Ireland vis-à-vis the supranational structures that overarch the state, a consent that has heightened significance in a society so characterized by communities holding mutually exclusive constitutional objectives. The post-UKexit political reality, however, has not merely straitened political identity in Northern Ireland, and upset the interlocking set of associations that enabled power-sharing to occur in Northern Ireland; it has also taken those associations out of a sequence in which they stood some chance of working and placed them into a sequence in which their workability is considerably diminished. Brexiteers have tragically underestimated what the UK leaving the EU represents in the schema of Northern Ireland's delicate composition. By contrast, Lord Chris Patten, who chaired the commission that gave form to the new policing arrangements in Northern Ireland after the Good Friday Agreement, was not being alarmist when he likened the UK's flailing attempts to wade into Northern Irish politics as "blundering into the politics of Northern Ireland [...] with a can of petrol in one hand a box of matches in the other" (col. 2078).

UKexit may represent, for some Leave voters, a pristine possibility of utopia. However, the foundational myth for Ulster Unionists, particularly in times of political upheaval, is of an Edenic political origin, God-anointed and monarchally mandated. A political tabula rasa for England could potentially undermine the protections of the union, for which unionists fought and strove over the centuries. This point of divergence in English and Northern Irish unionist trajectories has brought nightmarish realities to Northern Ireland. In 2017 a group of people in Newtownards, presumably as a Halloween prank, placed a pig's head in front of the town's Islamic Centre. In 2019 a group of ten from the same community, dressed in Ku Klux Klan garb and masks, mustered in front of the same Islamic Centre, some making the Nazi salute. These particular emblems and signifiers are unprecedented in Northern Irish history. The lunge to embrace an authoritarian personality and evil cults is occurring against the backdrop of unionism losing its electoral majority for the first time in Northern Irish history: a desperate scapegoating of minorities to divert attention from unionism's political and cultural dilemmas.

In his resignation speech as Foreign Secretary, delivered in the House of Commons on 18 July 2019, Boris Johnson said: "[W]e allowed the question of the Northern Ireland border, which had hitherto been assumed on all sides to be readily soluble, to become so politically charged as to dominate the debate" (col. 448). It is hard to fit so many wrong assertions into one sentence. The Irish border ab initio is politically charged, and all sides should have assumed that it would dominate the debate on UKexit. One side did assume so from the inception – the Irish side. From small farmers on the border to politicians in Dublin, a relentless stream of warnings issued. If Brexiteers had been willing to listen, they might have averted the disaster.

Coda

On 24 July 2019 Boris Johnson became Prime Minister of the UK. Johnson gained what had eluded Theresa May: the support of the European Research Group (ERG), a fervid Brexiteer lobby group in Westminster. The ERG and Johnson adopted a new-found 'realism' in regard to Northern Ireland and the Irish border. As autumn 2019 wore on, the DUP, realizing that it had been played, began to vote against the government on Brexit motions – principally the new Withdrawal from the EU bill – and a UK general election became inevitable. Meanwhile, the leaders of the Irish and UK governments, Johnson and Varadkar, reached an understanding in Liverpool (see footnotes 4 and 5 above) about the position of Northern Ireland after Brexit. That understanding formed the basis of an amended Withdrawal Agreement from the EU on 17 October 2019, which comprised two documents: the Northern Ireland Protocol and a framework document outlining the future of the EU-UK relationship. Subsequently, in a development that comprehensively neutered the DUP's influence in Westminster, Boris Johnson led the Conservative Party to a landslide victory in the UK general election on 12 December 2019. DUP MPs (down from ten to eight) in the House of Commons at a stroke became powerless to block legislation and Johnson comfortably passed his Withdrawal Agreement through parliament.

Nationalists and moderates in Northern Ireland, who in the main voted Remain, are unhappy to leave the EU. Yet certain guarantees (above all, against a hardening of the Irish border) temper the impact of leaving, and they are assured of mechanisms to protect the rights of those who are Irish/EU citizens, albeit residents of the UK.

Neither unionists who voted to leave, nor unionists who voted to remain, are reconciled to the Northern Ireland Protocol since it establishes a customs border between Northern Ireland and Great Britain, which they fear will be an entering wedge for further division from 'the mainland.' Consequently, unionists are seething over the Conservative Party's betrayal and the way in which the DUP played its hand. When the DUP held the aces in the UK Parliament they systematically stymied Theresa May's Withdrawal Agreement. The result of their exertions is, from a unionist perspective, a considerably inferior deal being imposed upon them. May's warning in the House of Commons against blocking her Withdrawal Agreement ("PM Statement in the House of Commons") haunts them now.

A core concept of the Good Friday Agreement is the consent to constitutional change. Underpinning that concept is the role of the UK and Irish governments as protectors and guarantors of the consent principle. The crisis unionism now confronts is the deepening indifference of 'its' guarantor: the breaching of the union from without rather than within Northern Ireland.

The customs border down the Irish Sea is painful for unionists and awkward for everyone. Yet the re-establishment of a border in Ireland between the North and the South would have provoked immediate and enduring civil unrest. The negotiated outcome of Brexit constitutes the minimum justice that the people of Northern Ireland deserve.

References

Berkeley, George. *The Works of George Berkeley*. 1705-21. Vol. 1, *Gutenberg*, 20 May 2012, www.gutenberg.org/files/39746/39746-pdf.pdf.

Cabinet Office. "The UK's Approach to the Northern Ireland Protocol." May 2020, assets.publishing.service.gov.uk/government/uploads/system/uploads/attachment_data/file/887532/The_UK_s_Approach_to_NI_Protocol_Web_Accessible.pdf.

Committee on the Administration of Justice (CAJ). "Formal Complaint Lodged with European Ombudsman Over Post-Brexit Rights." 9 Oct. 2018, caj.org.uk/2018/10/09/formal-complaint-lodged-with-the-european-ombudsman-over-post-brexit-rights/.

Davies, Norman. *The Isles*. Macmillan, 1999.

Deane, Seamus. "Civilians and Barbarians." *A Field Day Pamphlet*, vol. 3, 1983, pp. 1-14.

Dodds, Nigel. "EU Exit Negotiations." UK Parliament, House of Commons, Hansard Online, vol. 649, cols. 431-82, 15 Nov. 2018, hansard.parliament.uk/commons/2018-11-15/debates/8595BA5C-B515-4BD3-A9FE-38345E6AE2B4/EUExitNegotiations.

"DUP Leader Arlene Foster: 'Our Red Line Is Blood Red.'" *Irish Times*, 3 Oct. 2018, www.irishtimes.com/news/politics/dup-leader-arlene-foster-our-red-line-is-blood-red-1.3650080.

Economist. "Identity Theft: Britain Underestimates Brexit's Damage to Northern Ireland." 31 March 2018, www.economist.com/leaders/2018/03/31/britain-underestimates-brexits-damage-to-northern-ireland.

European Union and the United Kingdom Government. "Joint Report." 8 Dec. 2017, ec.europa.eu/commission/sites/beta-political/files/joint_report.pdf.

Federal Foreign Office. "Maas in Ireland: 'A Strong Europe Needs Strong Foundations.'" *Auswärtiges Amt*, 9 Jan. 2019, www.auswaertigesamt.de/en/aussenpolitik/laenderinformationen/irland-node/maas-ireland/2175954.

Fitzpatrick, Maurice. *John Hume in America: From Derry to DC*. Irish Academic P, 2017.

Friel, Brian. Interview by Mary McAleese. "Friel's *Translations* at the Gate Theatre 1980." *Today Tonight*, 7 Oct. 1980, www.rte.ie/archives/2015/1002/731966-brian-friels-translations/.

Gladstone, William. "Second Reading." UK Parliament, House of Commons, Hansard Online, 6 April 1893, vol. 10, cols. 1597-1706, api.parliament.uk/historic-hansard/commons/1893/apr/06/second-reading-first-night.

Hare, David. "Time to Leave, A New Play by David Hare – Read the Script." *Guardian*, 19 June 2017, www.theguardian. com/stage/2017/jun/19/time-to-leave-a-new-play-by-david-hare-brexit-shorts.

Hume, John, and Sheena McDonald. "Interview with John Hume." *BBC – On The Record*, 17 Oct. 1993, www.bbc.co.uk/otr/intext93-94/Hume17.10.93.html.

Johnson, Boris. "Personal Statement." UK Parliament, House of Commons, Hansard Online, vol. 645, col. 448-50, 18 July 2019, hansard.parliament.uk/Commons/2018-07-18/debates/C59 9EEE1-D863-4AC9-87B3-35DA3A3EAFEE/PersonalStatement.

Jones, Richard Wyn, et al. *The Dog That Finally Barked: England as an Emerging Political Community*. London: Institute for Public Policy Research Report, 2012, www.ippr.org/files/images/media/files/publication/2012/02/dog-that-finally-barked_englishness_Jan2012_8542.pdf.

Lillis, Michael. "Emerging from Despair in Anglo-Irish Relations." *Dublin Review of Books*, www.drb.ie/essays/edging-towards-peace. Originally published in *Franco-Irish Connections: Essays, Memoirs and Poems in Honour of Pierre Joannon*, edited by Jane Conroy, Four Courts P, 2009.

——. "John Hume's Legacy." *Dublin Review of Books*, vol. 100, 1 May 2018, www.drb.ie/essays/john-hume-s-legacy.

May, Theresa. "PM Brexit Negotiations Statement." *UK Government*, 21 Sept. 2018, www.gov.uk/government/news/pm-brexit-negotiations-statement-21-september-2018.

——. "PM Statement in the House of Commons." 14 Jan. 2018, www.wired-gov.net/wg/news.nsf/print/PM+statement+in+the+House+of+Commons+14+January+2018+15012019142000.

——. "PM Statement on EU Negotiations." *UK Government*, 11 Dec. 2017, www.gov.uk/government/speeches/pm-statement-on-eu-negotiations-11-december-2017.

McCormack, Jayne. "Macron: EU 'Will Not Be Hostage to Brexit Crisis.'" *BBC News*, 2 April 2019, www.bbc.com/news/world-europe-47781254.

McDonagh, Bobby. "Ireland Loves Exactly What Britain Hates About Europe." *Irish Times*, 5 Jan. 2019, www.irishtimes.com/opinion/ireland-loves-exactly-what-britain-hates-about-europe-1.3747849.

O'Leary, Brendan. *A Treatise on Northern Ireland, Volume 3: Consociation and Confederation*. Oxford UP, 2019.

O'Toole, Fintan. "Borders and Belonging: British and Irish Identities in a Post-Brexit Era." Lecture delivered at Queen's University Belfast, 4 Oct. 2018, youtu.be/1SeadvWsn_k.

Patten, Chris. "European Union (Withdrawal) Bill." UK Parliament, House of Lords, Hansard Online, vol. 790, cols. 2073-2192, 2 May 2018, hansard.parliament.uk/Lords/2018-05-02/debates/28839055-F2B2-497C-A4DF-D797224BC747/EuropeanUnion(Withdrawal)Bill.

Peck, Tom. "Nigel Farage Would 'Pick Up a Rifle' If Brexit Is Not Delivered." *Independent*, 17 May 2017, www.independent. co.uk/news/uk/politics/nigel-farage-brexit-rifle-pick-up-uk-eu-withdrawal-ukip-leader-liberal-democrat-a7741331.html.

Strauss, Delphine, et al. "Boris Johnson Under Scrutiny Over Irish Sea Border Claims." *Financial Times*, 9 Dec. 2019, www.ft.com/content/790b5456-1a93-11ea-97df-cc63de1d73f4?shareType=nongift.

Unsettling Private Property in Linda Hogan's *Mean Spirit*

Cécile Heim

Private property is a crucial concept for the nation-building process of the United States as it transforms land into an extractive entity while defining citizenship according to capitalist ideals. This concept has been and still is forcibly imposed onto Indigenous peoples while, simultaneously, dismissing Indigenous ways of relating to the land. This essay examines how *Mean Spirit* (1990) by Chickasaw author Linda Hogan unsettles settler notions of private property by exploring and promoting an Indigenous way of relating to the land. This relationship is epitomized in Michael Horse's relationship to his horse and Belle's cultivating of corn. The essay begins with a discussion of the development and importance of private property in the nation-building process of the United States and proceeds to analyse the depiction and unsettling of private property in *Mean Spirit.*

Keywords: Private property, Linda Hogan, Indigenous Studies, Osage Reign of Terror, Oklahoma oil boom

Chickasaw activist, poet, and novelist Linda Hogan's first novel, *Mean Spirit* (1990), tells the story of Osage Elder Belle Graycloud and her community during the 1920 Reign of Terror.[1] The Osages and their allies have to negotiate between assimilating or, on the contrary, trying

[1] My heartfelt thanks to Daniela Keller, Ina Habermann, and Alexandre Fachard, as well as the reviewer for inspiring me to create the best possible version of this essay.

Brexit and Beyond: Nation and Identity. SPELL: Swiss Papers in English Language and Literature 39, edited by Daniela Keller and Ina Habermann, Narr, 2020, pp. 251-69.

to maintain their traditional lifeways. The novel starts with the murder of Grace Blanket, a young, wealthy Osage who is killed for her land allotment which hides a well of oil. Her daughter, Nola Blanket, is adopted by Belle, and the Osages try to understand who is killing their fellow community members. The novel ties together various narrative strands centring on multi-dimensional characters such as Belle Graycloud, Michael Horse, or Stace Red Hawk within the Indigenous community of Watona, Oklahoma, and the ending reveals that oil barons and their followers are eliminating Osages to obtain their land allotments and the oil contained in them, forcing the surviving Osage community to flee.

Hogan's poetic prose shifts narrative focalization and spins intricate metaphors allowing her to create a universe full of life and wonder. Her complex characters and humour (re-)humanize Indigenous people and examine the complexity of Indigenous and non-Indigenous relations in an increasingly oppressive settler state. While the novel explores multiple themes such as spirituality or writing and authority, I focus on the relationship between the notion of private property and the land that the novel lays out. I suggest that *Mean Spirit* unsettles extractive-capitalist practices toward the land that are exemplified by the oil business, while Indigenous relations with the land are epitomized by their way of growing corn, thus dislodging settler notions of private property.

Mean Spirit has generally received favourable reviews, except from Osage literary critics such as Robert Allen Warrior, who takes issue with Hogan's 'pan-Indianism': "Hogan uses a sort of pan-tribal New Age-ism with Southern Plains and Southeastern [...] features, presumably making it easier for her inter-tribal cast of characters to interact but losing the specificity of Osages in the process" (52). Hogan's use of non-nation-specific cultural heritage is problematic for scholars like Warrior who fight against stereotypical representations of Native Americans and for the sovereignty of Indigenous nations. For the mainstream public, however, the novel was a great success since it featured as 1991 Pulitzer Prize finalist. While heeding Warrior's criticism of the novel that this is not an accurate depiction of Osage culture, *Mean Spirit* is an important intervention in the representation of the Reign of Terror that forces its readers to question Western ways of relating to the land through private property.

Although Hogan's account is entirely fictional, the Reign of Terror in Osage country is a historical event. David Grann's non-fictional *Killers of the Flower Moon* (2018) documents these happenings and their influence on the development of the US police force and Federal Bureau of Investigation in great detail. The Reign of Terror took place in the 1920s after oil was discovered on Osage land. Oil companies rented land from Osages and paid them royalties which allowed them to become increasingly wealthy. Soon, however, Osages started to disappear or be killed; it is estimated that twenty-seven Osages died under suspicious circumstances between 1921 and 1925 (Cowan). Jon D. May, writing for the Oklahoma Historical Society, states that most crimes were "rarely investigated by local authorities; some were never solved" (n.p.). Three white men were suspected of these murders: Ernest Burkhart, who was sentenced to life for the murder of William E. Smith (Osage); William K. Hale (Burkhart's uncle) and John Ramsey (a local farmer), who were sentenced to life imprisonment in 1929 for the murder of Henry Roan (Osage).[2] All three were eventually paroled and Burkhart even received a full pardon in 1965 (May). Grann concludes in his book that Hale was the leader of the conspiracy to appropriate Osage land and, thus, the oil in it. His historical examination, however, does nothing to deconstruct racism, capitalist extraction of the land, or settler colonialism in general, and never mentions Hogan's novel. Yet *Killers of the Flower Moon* has received positive critical acclaim and even inspired Martin Scorsese to direct a movie on the topic, scheduled to be released in 2021. The movie will feature Leonardo DiCaprio and Robert De Niro and is shaping up to be another uncritical celebration of settler-colonial values and, therefore, a failed attempt at honouring Indigenous nations. Hogan's novel, then, serves as an important counter-narrative to current and future white cultural productions on the Reign of Terror against the Osage community since it addresses notions of property and extractive relations to the land.

That property is at the core of national US identity shows in past and ongoing struggles for territory. The fight for national territory initiated with colonization and perpetuated with such federal policies as the General Allotment Act continues today in Supreme Court cases such as *Tommy Sharp, Interim Warden Oklahoma State Penitentiary v. Patrick Dwayne Murphy*. As the podcast *This Land*, by Cherokee journalist Rebecca Nagle, explains, this case originates in a 1999 murder case where Patrick Murphy (Muscogee Creek) killed George Jacobs (Muscogee Creek). Murphy was arrested and sentenced to die by the state of Oklahoma, but he appealed on the grounds that the murder did not take place on state land, but on the Muscogee Creek Indian Reservation. The argu-

[2] Grann's *Killers of the Flower Moon* opens with a description of Mollie Kyle (Osage), Ernest Burkhart's wife, and her family, but focuses on the development of the police force and the Federal Bureau of Investigation.

ment runs that while the surface land has been sold to white farmers, the mineral rights still belong to the Muscogee Creek and Congress has never explicitly dissolved the reservation, which is why this land is still Muscogee Creek land. This argument, which applies not only to the Muscogee Creek reservation, but also includes the ones of the Cherokee, Chickasaw, Seminole, and Choctaw nations, was confirmed by the Tenth Circuit Court. The state of Oklahoma appealed, in turn, and the Supreme Court now has to decide whether the land of the above-mentioned five Indigenous nations, which constitutes about half the size of Oklahoma, is Reservation land, and thus subject to tribal sovereignty, or not. The Supreme Court was unable to reach a decision in this case because Justice Neil Gorsuch recused himself, thus leaving the case in a deadlock with a four to four opinion. However, the decision of the Tenth Circuit Court in favour of Murphy encouraged other people who were sentenced by the state to appeal their conviction based on the same arguments as Murphy. This is the case of Jimcy McGirt, who was sentenced for sex crimes against a child by the state even though this should have been a matter of tribal jurisdiction. The Supreme Court accepted McGirt's appeal and heard arguments on *Jimcy McGirt v. Oklahoma* in May 2020. It published its opinion in July 2020 ruling in favour of the petitioner with a five-to-four majority, thus confirming that the land of the Cherokee, Choctaw, Muscogee Creek, Seminole, and Chickasaw nations are Indigenous land and reverting jurisdiction of Indigenous citizens on this territory to tribal sovereignty. These cases illustrate the ongoing fight for ownership of the land, highlighting that colonialism is not a thing of the past.

These two Supreme Court cases and the Reign of Terror reveal how, even today, property and ownership dominate our relationship to the land and with each other.[3] Private property is one of the central concepts of settler-colonial discourse that shape the US nation.[4] It has been ratified as one of the fundamental rights of US citizens in the fourth and fifth amendments of the US Constitution in 1791. Especially the fifth amendment stipulates that "[n]o person shall [...] be deprived of life, liberty, or property, without due process of law; nor shall private property be taken for public use, without just compensation" (Arnheim 393).

---

[3] By 'our' I mean everybody who participates in capitalist practices, thinks in terms of private property, and/or does not conceive of the earth as a living being.

[4] Settler colonialism is a land-based project where, as Eve Tuck (Unangax) and K. Wayne Yang state, "settlers come with the intention of making a new home on the land, a homemaking that insists on settler sovereignty over all things in their new domain" (5). It is an ongoing form of colonialism.

Ownership is hence an inalienable right of US citizens and a crucial element of US citizenship and national consciousness. Yet, as I would argue, it is equally an economic and legal construct which serves the settler nation-building project that legitimates Indigenous land dispossession. For private property is inseparable from US settler colonialism, which is justified by the fraught idea that Indigenous nations do not own property, especially not real property, and do not tend to the land in what a capitalist society considers profitable ways. At the core of US nation-building, then, lies a reinforcement of the Euro-Western idea of possession over Indigenous ways of relating to the land. In the Indigenous epistemology, people belong to the land instead. The land is seen as the source of life, knowledge, and spirituality. In other words, all of creation in Indigenous ways of being springs from the land. Rather than owning it, Indigenous peoples guard and protect the land, which is why No Dakota Access Pipeline (NoDAPL) protestors, for instance, are called water protectors.[5] These competing ways of relating to the land become evident in contemporary Indigenous land protection movements such as the NoDAPL movement near Standing Rock, North Dakota, or the Mauna Kea sacred site protection by the Kanaka Maoli.[6] *Mean Spirit* intervenes precisely in these competing relations to the land by reinforcing Indigenous land-human relations that unsettle private property – a concept that wrongfully serves as justification for land dispossession and extraction.

Dispossession through Private Property

Private property is a legal concept in the nation-building process of Euro-Western nations that shapes socio-political relations, territory, and our relation to the land. The shift from commonly held lands to enclosure and the transformation of land into private property occurred in various waves in Europe, with a significant one in sixteenth-century England (Dunbar-Ortiz 34-36; Blomley "Territory"). It is especially John Locke's description of private property which was most influential

[5] The NoDAPL (No Dakota Access Pipeline) Standing Rock water protection movement led by Lakota and Dakota elders started in early 2016 and aims to protect the bodies of land and water which will be destroyed and contaminated by the construction of the Dakota Access Pipeline (see Faith; Standing Rock Water Protectors).

[6] Starting in 2018, the Kanaka Maoli (Native Hawaiians) fight the construction of one of the world's largest telescopes on their sacred mountain, Mauna Kea (see Goodyear-Ka'opua and Mahelona).

for the nation-building process of the United States. Property, according to Locke, already exists outside the state, as he claims in his *Two Treatises of Government*: "The great and chief end therefore of men's uniting into commonwealths and putting themselves under government is the preservation of their property" (2831). In this statement, Locke reasons that property is a concept which serves as primary motivation for the social contract as it needs to be protected and secured by the state. Hence, property is a concept around which socio-political relations are organized. This is maintained by contemporary property scholars, most emphatically by Nicholas Blomley, who defines property as "a right to some use or benefit of land. Such a right is necessarily relational, being held against others. [...] Property's 'bundle' of rights includes the power to exclude others, to use, and to transfer" ("Law" 121). More than this, property is the vector that defines citizenship on an individual level and sovereignty on the state level. As Robert Nichols emphasizes, "[f]or a Lockean, 'no property' equates to non-political, or 'no sovereignty'" ("Realizing" 48). For Locke, then, property serves as core entity around which the creation of the state is organized and alongside which citizenship is defined.

Locke's understanding of private property as a basic feature that delimits citizenship is adopted by the Founding Fathers for the purpose of nation-building as well as shaping the territory of the new nation of the United States of America. The counter-example of the 'civilized' state, that is, the Western European, for Locke is Native Americans. Nichols explains that "[b]ecause indigenous peoples did not till the soil or enclose the land, they could not exist in a civil society properly defined and thus could not claim political sovereignty" ("Realizing" 48). While the perception of Indigenous peoples as 'savages' does not emerge with Locke, he solidifies this notion in his political writings.[7] Thomas Jefferson admired Locke's writing and inherited his conception of private property as essential to a 'civilized' state and convenient justification for stealing land from Indigenous peoples. Nichols asserts that Jefferson "was the first person to translate Lockean thought into a systematic theory of 'savagism,' which founded U.S. Indian policy for decades" ("Realizing" 51). Locke's description of Native Americans as propertyless 'savages' and Jefferson's use of Locke to justify land grabbing

[7] As Lumbee lawyer Robert A. Williams, Jr., underlines: "His clichéd stereotypes and grossly inaccurate caricature of the Indian's savage, hunter-gatherer state defined a life of irredeemable hardship and irremediable want compared to the highly civilized state of humanity in an advanced agricultural society" (*Savage Anxieties* 205).

served as crucial tools for the settler-colonial nation-building process of the United States.[8]

To justify settler-colonial appropriation of land with the Lockean concept of property and to institutionalize it in the US Constitution and legal landscape is not only a territorial and/or socio-political enterprise, but it is, most of all, an imperial imposition. Paradoxically, settler colonialism turns land that is already home to a variety of Indigenous nations into private property. Seneca scholar Mishuana Goeman explains that "[p]rescribing the shape of land in colonial history was largely done with intent to claim land and make it readable as property" ("Land" 77). Land, which is "at the heart of indigenous identity, longing, and belonging" (73), is thus recoded into property. Instead of honouring the land as a source of life and knowledge, as Indigenous nations do, settler colonialism transforms land into property from which as much material and financial profit as possible has to be drawn. In other words, the land-turned-property becomes an extractable surface in the capitalist US nation. Contrary to the settler argument that Indigenous peoples did not tend to the land, which is why their taking it without consent is not theft, Nichols clarifies that

> [c]olonization entails the large-scale transfer of land that simultaneously *recodes* the object of exchange in question such that it appears *retrospectively* to be a form of theft in the ordinary sense. It is thus not (only) about the *transfer of* property, but the *transformation into* property. ("Theft" 14)

This process of land appropriation and its simultaneous transformation into property is called dispossession – a method that is inherent to settler colonialism. Nichols defines it as "a broad macro-historical process related to the specific territorial acquisition logic of settler colonization" ("Theft" 11). Not only is the invention of private property, therefore, a prerequisite for Indigenous land dispossession upon which the US nation is founded, but the transformation of land into property also creates the necessary conditions for the growth of US capitalism.

---

[8] Williams demonstrates how the savagery discourse continues even today in legal decisions: "The racist precedents and language of Indian savagery used and relied upon by the justices throughout this ongoing historical period of legalized racial dictatorship have most often worked [...] to justify the denial to Indians of important rights to property, self-government, and cultural survival. [...] Indians get treated legally by our 'present day' justices just as Indians were treated by the justices in the nineteenth century: as savages whose rights are defined according to a European colonial-era legal doctrine of white racial superiority over the entire North American continent" (*Like a Loaded Weapon* xxv).

Once the land of Turtle Island was claimed by the US government, it periodically attempted to assimilate Native Americans into its settler, capitalist society.[9] The most forceful attempt at assimilation and one of the most important moments of Indigenous land dispossession happened through the 1887 General Allotment Act, also called Dawes Act. This act was supposed to 'civilize' Native Americans by giving, initially, each individual 160 acres of land and was executed before the discovery of oil on these lands.[10] Kristen A. Carpenter explains: "The idea was that Indians would abandon traditional patterns of subsistence to become American-style farmers" (607). As a consequence of the General Allotment Act, Indigenous landholdings were reduced from 138 million acres in 1887 to 48 million acres in 1934 within two generations (Deloria and Lytle 10), 20 million acres of which were desert or semi-arid land. Part of the US nation-building process thus happens through the legal enforcement of private property, which enables the extractive economy of the United States because it grants exclusive access to the resources of the land. While Indigenous relations to the land determine their entire way of being as the land is a living source of all creation and knowledge, the settler relation to land reduces it to an entity from which profit needs to be extracted and, as such, produces the settler understanding of citizenship as capitalist.[11]

The Imposition of Private Property in *Mean Spirit*

Mean Spirit engages with the theme of private property and relates to the land in two ways. It embeds actual legislature and historical events into its narrative and it forces its readers to contemplate the earth as a living being which renders its fragmentation into private property an excessively violent, if not impossible, process. Featuring characters of the

---

[9] Turtle Island is the name for North America used by Indigenous nations on the eastern shores of the continent such as the Haudenosaunee.

[10] Dakota scholar Vine Deloria, Jr., and Clifford M. Lytle state the precise amount that the government gave to each Native American: "1. To each head of a family, one-quarter section; 2. To each single person over eighteen years of age, one-eighth section; 3. To each orphan child under eighteen years of age, one-eighth section; 4. To each other single person under eighteen years of age living, or who may be born prior to the date of the order to the president directing allotment of the lands, one-sixteenth section" (9).

[11] For a discussion on how white supremacy is included in the concept of private property, see Harris and Moreton-Robinson.

novel who comment on legislature is a strategy for Indigenous authors to reframe historical and political events from an Indigenous perspective. In other words, it is a way of (re)narrating history from a perspective that is not only continually obscured and silenced, but where, in addition, storytelling and literacy do not have the same status as in Euro-Western cultures.[12] Without reading novels such as *Mean Spirit* as historical documents, these fictitious texts still create a space which allows readers ephemerally to imagine the distress and confusion that actual historical processes, in this case the forceful implementation of private property, might have provoked. This is crucial for Indigenous nations who have consistently been dehumanized and written out of settler history, especially in such nations as the United States, Canada, and Australia where the national narrative is founded on Indigenous people's disappearance.

The forced transformation of land into private property is powerfully demonstrated when the narrator or various characters comment on actual laws. About the General Allotment Act, Hogan's omniscient narrator states that it

> seemed generous at first glance so only a very few people realized how much they were being tricked, since numerous tracts of unclaimed land became open property for white settlers, homesteaders, and ranchers. [...] No one guessed that black undercurrents of oil moved beneath that earth's surface. (8)

The General Allotment Act is treacherous as it turns Indigenous peoples into landowners while at the same time dispossessing them of more than half of their land. In addition, the narrator foreshadows the danger and conflicts that this notion of private property will bring to the Osages as soon as oil is discovered on their land. The fact that the narrator is voicing this warning while most characters seem unaware of the danger produces a structural irony which increases the reader's sympathy with the Indigenous characters of the novel.

When Hogan intertwines the law, oil-based capitalism, and private property in her novel, the latter becomes a way of determining who is included and excluded in the given settler economy. However, this inclusion is constantly regulated by the government as Hogan shows with regard to Belle's allotment: "Her land was 'without improvement,' as they called it when a person left the trees standing and didn't burn off

[12] For more information on Indigenous storytelling, see Archibald, Borrows, Justice, and Kovach.

the brush or put in a fence to contain their property" (80). Because Belle's land tenure is not considered civilized enough, it is taken over by the government and rented out to local farmers, an expropriation that Belle only realizes when a farm-hand comes to build a fence – a fence that represents the material transformation of land into property. When Belle complains to the Indian agent, his only answer is: "'You didn't improve it,' he said as he sat with his light gray eyes on her face. He'd seen it fit to strike up a deal with Hale [a white, wealthy farmer]. 'It's best not to leave the land lying idle,' he said" (213). It becomes evident in this response that the Indian agent executes and affirms contemporary property law enforcing the perception of land as a lifeless entity which is to be owned and exploited. Crucially, Indian 'ownership' is only respected as long as the land is visibly 'improved' according to Euro-Western standards of farming.

Accordingly, Indigenous people cannot simply own the land but are required to transform it into recognizable private property. This process, however, creates considerable confusion and upsets Osage Elder and water diviner Michael Horse's ability to read the land. He is responsible for keeping the fire of the community burning, helping them with any spiritual and existential questions, and finding water for his community members. But at the beginning of the novel, Horse has temporarily lost his gifts; instead of finding water, he discovers oil on Grace Blanket's allotment:

> He was worried. He didn't know how he had gone wrong. He had 363 wells to his credit. There was no water on Grace Blanket's land, just the thick black fluid that had no use at all for growing corn or tomatoes. Not even zucchini squash would grow there. (8)

Finding himself unable to rely on his traditional skills to understand the land, he discovers oil instead of water on Grace's land. While water is essential to the growth of plants and, thus, Osage subsistence, oil is the primary material extracted from the earth to make profit. The imposition of private property has thus rendered the land illegible for Horse, who continues to perform traditional Osage practices. Unfortunately, far from simply having "no use at all," this discovery has detrimental effects on the Osage community: Grace Blanket is murdered at the beginning of the novel by an oil rig company owner, to whom she had rented her land and who had made her wealthy. Thus, the novel depicts a loss of legibility of the land following the imposition of private property as well as the violent implications this transformation has on the local Indigenous communities.

Capitalist relations with the land are fatal and, perfidiously, capitalism additionally encourages the Osage community to inflict damage upon themselves. Hogan describes the shifting attitude of the Osages: "The Indians were happy to learn business ways, but before long they had no choice themselves but to become meat-eaters with sharp teeth, devouring their own land and themselves in the process" (54). Private property becomes innately violent and self-destructive. This description invokes the Anishinaabe, Algonquian, Cree, and Blackfeet figure of the weendigo – a cannibalistic creature that eats human flesh, who the more it eats, the more it craves this flesh. This singularly evil creature in Indigenous cosmologies is understood to be a personification of greed. Greed is a characteristic that is closely associated with settler colonialism as Anishinaabe Elder and author Basil Johnston shows: "Actually, the Weendigoes did not die out or disappear; they have only been assimilated and reincarnated as corporations, conglomerates, and multinationals. [...] But their cupidity is no less insatiable than that of their ancestors" (235). By invoking the weendigo, then, Hogan underlines the transformation of Osage community members into greedy capitalists – that is, into 'mean spirits' – alongside the transformation of land into private property. Native Americans have internalized settler practices that lead to unlimited land exploitation and self-destruction. Yellowknife Dene political theorist Sean Glen Coulthard points out that the internalization of settler-colonial values is inherent to settler colonialism as it

> operates through a circumscribed mode of recognition that structurally ensures continued access to Indigenous peoples' lands and resources by producing neocolonial subjectivities that coopt Indigenous people into becoming instruments of their own dispossession. (156)

Mean Spirit therefore powerfully demonstrates how the internalization of private property understood as a way of relating to the land imposed by the settler state leads Indigenous people to be defencelessly exposed to an insidious and harmful system that is profitable to others. The novel, however, equally reveals that these processes are far from smooth and met with resistance designed to unsettle private property.

Unsettling Private Property

More than testifying to the distress and precariousness caused by settler impositions and creating empathy for Indigenous characters, *Mean Spirit* forces its readers to reconsider our relations to the land. If the first half of the novel depicts how the Osage community endures oppressive policies and racism, the second half shows how the protagonists increasingly resist the assault on their community. The novel is, ultimately, pessimistic concerning the capacity for change since the Indigenous people of Watona have to flee from their lands while the earth is burning. Still, the sense of power emanating from the earth remains and some Indigenous characters such as Michael Horse, who appeared lost and confused at first, reconnect with their Indigenous values and ways of being. *Mean Spirit* unsettles the settler concept of private property by emphasizing that the earth is a living being, rewriting hierarchical human and nonhuman relations into kinship and by (re)mapping the land, which Goeman defines as a re-appropriation of space by re-claiming Indigenous relations to the land (*Mark My Words*).

Mean Spirit portrays the land as a living being throughout the novel even though most characters only realize this in its second part. The novel opens with a description of the hot summer nights that forced people to sleep outside:

> In that darkness, the white beds were ghostly. [...] A hand hung over the edge of a bed, fingers reaching down toward bluegrass that grew upward in fields. Given half a chance, the vines and leaves would have crept up the beds and overgrown the sleeping bodies of people. (3)

While the sleeping bodies are described as passive, empty shells, the earth, acting through plants, is alive attempting to embrace whoever lies on her. The beginning thus underlines the earth's liveliness and potential for growth. Moreover, the earth nurtures the Indigenous characters' power and resistance. For example, when Lettie, Belle's daughter, visits her secret lover in jail, "[h]er sorrow had turned to careless rage. It was as if the fiery land took the caution from deep inside the murmurings of her own skin" (186). Similar to the opening scene, the earth is assigned all the agency in this passage which, paradoxically, empowers Lettie to finally acknowledge her love for Benoit and help him prove his innocence. Thus, the land's agency, which is initially imperceptible and, therefore, confusing to some characters, builds the novel's sense of wonder and mystery by emphasizing its own power as living being.

The land's agency only becomes perceptible to all when it defends itself from excessive extraction. After an oil rig explosion,

> [t]he sweating men worked in the intense heat with steam rising from their reddened, flushed bodies. They dug a hole and plugged one side, and even as they worked, the snow beside China [one of Watona's inhabitants] melt-

> ed off the ground. It steamed upward, and the vision of it changed her. It was like watching hell rise up. She knew then, she knew that the earth had a mind of its own. She knew the wills and whims of men were empty desires, were nothing pitted up against the desires of earth. (186)

The oil rig workers are revealingly described as steaming, red bodies, as if they were swallowed by the ground and the earth was taking back control. The land acquires a "mind of its own," a living being with its own "desires." Like China, Horse recognizes the land's resistance and reads the quakes provoked by the explosion as "the rage of mother earth" (189). When the earth defends itself, not only does its agency become perceptible again to characters such as China and Horse, but also its strength and power, which are incomparable to humans' since "the wills and whims of men were empty desires." A sense of humility is thus inherent to the acknowledgement of the earth as living being.

The novel demonstrates through Horse's relationship with his horse and the use of corn that it is abusive and destructive to conceive of any living being, whether this concerns animals, plants, or the earth, as private property. Thus, the relationship between Horse and Redshirt is rewritten as one of kinship rather than possession, and corn is respected as a source of subsistence rather than a source of one-sided exploitation. Cherokee author Daniel Heath Justice broadly defines kinship as "an active network of connections, a process of continual acknowledgement and enactment" (41-42) which includes not only blood relations but "can also be about extra- or even non-biological cultural community relations, chosen connections and commitments" (75) with humans and other-than-human beings. He further calls it "the complex, embodied practice of sovereign belonging" (104). In other words, kinship describes a way of understanding the world that does not focus on the individual, but on the relational. Moreover, these relations among humans and/or between humans and other-than-human beings are based on mutual care, responsibilities, and respect. Indigenous kinship principles are therefore inherently connected to Indigenous ways of relating to the land, since the earth is seen as a powerful relative and source of life which defies Euro-Western conceptions of social organization including the heteronormative nuclear family or the individualist concept of private property.

The impossibility of turning a living being into private property is depicted in the relationship between Horse and his horse, Redshirt, as it embodies an Indigenous understanding of kinship. As discussed above, the role of Osage Elder Horse as water diviner and knowledge keeper is crucial in the Watona community. Throughout the first half of the novel, he can no longer rely on his divinations and keeps losing his horse. This could be read as Horse's loss of identity since he is named after the animal he keeps losing. However, instead of letting this irony stand for the sake of its tragicomic effect, Hogan elaborates on it: Horse is shown during a ceremony that Redshirt is near Sorrow Cave, which will become a crucial site of Indigenous resurgence in the novel. Throughout the second half of the novel, Horse regains his spiritual capacities and, simultaneously, learns to appreciate Redshirt's freedom. This mutual respect allows them to find an understanding at the end of the novel as Redshirt lets Horse ride him. To read Horse's relationship with Redshirt as one of loss and gain only works from a Euro-Western point of view where to have a horse is to own a horse; that is, to have it at one's disposal at the expense of its freedom. What Hogan offers instead is a vision of kinship. This kinship that defies the Western binary distinction between human and non-human is shown in Horse's and Redshirt's name. While Horse is called after the animal, the name Redshirt implies the human attribute of clothing. By thus deconstructing the human/non-human binary, the Western justification for Horse's ownership of Redshirt is undermined. Their relationship therefore illustrates the impossibility of turning another living being into private property while maintaining a mutually respectful relationship. Their story can thus be read as a model for how humans are to relate to any living being and respect it as sovereign being, whether this concerns a horse or the earth.

In a similar manner, Hogan (re)maps the land in and around Watona from an exploitable land of oil into an empowering land of corn. If the novel maintains that the earth is a living being, mapping is the process of rendering the land legible. In her monograph, *Mark My Words: Native Women Mapping Our Nations*, Goeman defines (re)mapping as

> the labor Native authors and the communities they write within and about undertake, in the simultaneously metaphoric and material capacities of map making, to generate new possibilities. The framing of 're' with parentheses connotes the fact that in (re)mapping, Native women employ traditional and new tribal stories as a means of continuation. (3)

It is therefore a process which aims to discursively and, ultimately, materially reclaim lands from which Indigenous nations have been dispossessed. Hogan does so by undermining settler perceptions of the land as a commodity and turning it into a source of strength and survival. The novel thus changes the legibility of the land from one that is based on capitalist practices to one that is based on Indigenous values.

Part II of *Mean Spirit*, which solidifies and amplifies Indigenous resurgence and resistance to settler colonialism, opens with Belle Graycloud's corn planting. Belle Graycloud, the matriarch of her community and a leading voice in Indigenous resistance, never lost any of the traditional ways and is closely associated with corn. She and other Osage Elders

> conditioned their fields with words and songs, first sprinkling sacred cornmeal that was ground from the previous year's corn, to foster the new life. The old corn would tell the new corn how to grow. [...] Some of the younger people made fun of her. They were embarrassed by the old ways and believed the old people were superstitious. [...] But after a few weeks, Belle's corn began to germinate and push upward while their fields remained bare, except for an occasional weed. Those few younger Indians who still planted corn stood by silently looking at their empty fields until finally they swallowed their pride and asked Belle if she'd come by and bless the crops. (209-10)

Corn thus represents traditional Indigenous culture, which Dunbar-Ortiz's historical reading of corn confirms as she states that "[s]ince there is no evidence of corn on any other continent prior to its post-Columbus dispersal, its development is a unique invention of the original American agriculturalists" (16). But more importantly, just as Belle plants old corn with the new one to teach the latter how to grow, Belle and other Osage Elders show their younger community members how to tend to the corn. While the oil pumps metonymically represent all forms of exploitative, capitalist relations to land, the planting and nurturing of corn preserve Indigenous ways and build bridges between Indigenous pasts, presents, and futures through the teachings of the land. Hogan counters Euro-Western capitalist logics with Indigenous land-based knowledge by highlighting the ways in which this relation to land strengthens Indigenous nations and kinship rather than enriching the community in a purely material manner.

Even some of the white characters sense the richness of corn without understanding it. Upon discovering that Calvin Severance, a white drunk, is the one digging holes in her cornfield, Belle asks him what he is looking for. He responds: "'I don't know.' He continued to dig. 'I just heard that there was a hidden treasure in a cornfield'" (250). While corn represents a form of power or richness, it is a richness that differs from the materialist-capitalist sense of the term and is, ironically, illegible to white settlers such as Calvin. Crucially, corn's richness is constructed through the reciprocity between the land and the people as they help each other grow and subsist, and is not recognized as farming or 'improvement' in a Euro-Western sense – contrary to oil extraction, which relates to the land in unequal and destructive ways. To turn corn into the symbol of the strength, richness, and wisdom of the Osage community, then, is to ground that strength and richness in the land and gain knowledge and wisdom from it. In sum, Hogan's novel unsettles private property and the capitalist relations it implies by offering an Indigenous model of relating to the living land and its human and non-human members.

Conclusion

Private property is essential to the US nation-building process as well as to its capitalist economy. It has been imposed on Indigenous peoples who do not relate to the land through ownership and capitalist extraction. Hogan's novel resists and unsettles this shift from land-based knowledge to the capitalist regime of private property by (re-)Indigenizing relations to the land. The unequal and dehumanized, capitalist relationship between owner and property becomes rewritten as mutual and reciprocal kinship between human and other-than-human beings in *Mean Spirit.* This transformation of property into kinship reconnects the Osage community to pre-colonial ways of subsistence. Thus, without giving all the responsibility or authority of cultivating and, maybe even, reinventing relations that are not based on private property to Indigenous nations, Indigenous artists, scholars, and activists such as Hogan offer visions of what non-property-based relationships can look like.

While this essay has focused on the Osages in Oklahoma, the way we relate to the land is constitutive of how we define citizenship, build our economy, and relate to one another across the globe. That the notion of private property is central to human relations, especially in the Euro-Western part of the world, is further emphasized by such contemporary social justice movements as Black Lives Matter or feminist protests, since we still fight against the legacies of belonging to groups of people who used to be property and who still suffer from the disenfranchisement that the status of humans-as-property produced. Considering the extractive, capitalist economy and society that private property generates, it hardly seems the most sustainable way of relating with the land and each other. We therefore need relations that are not based on ownership, profit, and extraction; instead, we must learn to decolonize our relationships.

References

Archibald, Jo-Ann (Q'um Q'um Xiiem). *Indigenous Storywork: Educating the Heart, Mind, Body, and Spirit.* UBC P, 2008.

Arnheim, Michael. *U.S. Constitution for Dummies.* For Dummies, 2018.

Blomley, Nicholas. "Law, Property, and the Geography of Violence: The Frontier, the Survey, and the Grid." *Annals of the Association of U.S. Geographers*, vol. 93, no. 1, 2003, pp. 121-41.

——. "The Territory of Property." *Progress in Human Geography*, vol. 4, no. 5, 2016, pp. 593-609.

Borrows, John. *Law's Indigenous Ethics.* U of Toronto P, 2019.

Carpenter, Kristen A. "Contextualizing the Losses of Allotment through Literature." *North Dakota Law Review*, vol. 82, 2006, pp. 605-26.

Coulthard, Sean Glen. *Red Skins, White Masks: Rejecting the Colonial Politics of Recognition.* U of Minnesota P, 2014.

Cowan, Lee. "Revisiting the 'Reign of Terror' on the Osage Nation." *CBS News*, 30 April 2017, www.cbsnews.com/news/killers-of-the-flower-moon-revisiting-the-reign-of-terror-on-the-osage-nation/.

Deloria, Vine, Jr., and Clifford M. Lytle. *U.S. Indians, U.S. Justice.* U of Texas P, 2004.

Dunbar-Ortiz, Roxanne. *An Indigenous Peoples' History of the United States.* Beacon P, 2014.

Faith, Mike, Jr. "Press Release." *Standing Rock Sioux Tribe*, 11 March 2019, www.standingrock.org/content/chairman-mike-faith-jr-standing-rock-sioux-tribe.

Goeman, Mishuana. "Land as Life: Unsettling the Logics of Containment." *Native Studies Keywords*, edited by Stephanie Nohelani Teves et al., The U of Arizona P, 2015, pp. 71-89.

——. *Mark My Words: Native Women Mapping Our Nations.* U of Minnesota P, 2013.

Goodyear-Ka'opua, Noelani, and Yvonne Mahelona. "Protecting Maunakea Is a Mission Grounded in Tradition." *Zora*, 5 Sept. 2019, zora.medium.com/protecting-maunakea-is-a-mission-grounded-in-tradition-38a62df57086.

Grann, David. *Killers of the Flower Moon: The Osage Murders and the Birth of the FBI.* Vintage, 2018.

Harris, Cheryl I. "Whiteness as Property." *Harvard Law Review*, vol. 106, no. 8, 1993, pp. 1707-91.

Hogan, Linda. *Mean Spirit.* Ivy Book, 1990.

Johnston, Basil. *The Manitous: The Spiritual World of the Ojibway.* Native Voices, 2001.

Justice, Daniel Heath. *Why Indigenous Literatures Matter.* Wilfried Laurier P, 2018.

Kovach, Margaret. *Indigenous Methodologies: Characteristics, Conversations, and Contexts.* U of Toronto P, 2009.

Locke, John. "From *Two Treatises of Government: An Essay Concerning the True Original, Extent, and End of Civil Government.*" *Norton Anthology of English Literature*, vol. I, edited by Stephen Greenblatt et al., W. W. Norton, 2006, pp. 2829-33.

May, Jon D. "Osage Murders." *The Encyclopedia of Oklahoma History and Culture*, www.okhistory.org/publications/enc/entry.php?entry=OS005.

Moreton-Robinson, Aileen. "Imagining the Good Indigenous Citizen: Race War and the Pathology of Patriarchal White Sovereignty." *Cultural Studies Review*, vol. 15, no. 2, 2009, pp. 61-79.

——. *The White Possessive: Property, Power, and Indigenous Sovereignty.* U of Minnesota P, 2015.

Nichols, Robert. "Realizing the Social Contract: The Case of Colonialism and Indigenous Peoples." *Contemporary Political Theory*, vol. 4, 2005, pp. 42-62.

——. "Theft Is Property! The Recursive Logic of Dispossession." *Political Theory*, vol. 46, no. 1, 2018, pp. 3-28.

Standing Rock Water Protectors. *#NoDAPL Archive*, www.nodaplarchive.com/.

This Land. Crooked Media, 2019, crooked.com/podcast-series/this-land/.

Tommy Sharp, Interim Warden Oklahoma State Penitentiary v. Patrick Dwayne Murphy, (17-1107) (2018-). *Legal Information Institute*, Cornell Law School, www.law.cornell.edu/supct/cert/17-1107.

Tuck, Eve, and K. Wayne Yang. "Decolonization Is Not a Metaphor." *Decolonization: Indigeneity, Education & Society*, vol. 1, no. 1, 2012, pp. 1-40.

Warrior, Robert Allen. "An American History by Dennis McAuliffe." Review of *The Deaths of Sybil Bolton*, by Dennis McAuliffe. *Wicazo Sa Review*, vol. 11, no. 1, 1995, pp. 52-55.

Williams, Robert A., Jr. *Like a Loaded Weapon: The Rehnquist Court, Indian Rights, and the Legal History of Racism in America.* U of Minnesota P, 2005.

——. *Savage Anxieties: The Invention of Western Civilization.* Palgrave Macmillan, 2012.

Nostalgia for a Fictive Past: Nation and Identity in a Post-Trump, Post-Brexit World

Shelley Fisher Fishkin

In an America ruled by Donald Trump (no less in a United Kingdom preoccupied by Brexit), we are witnessing a rise in nostalgia for a time when the nation could glory in being self-sufficient and independent of the rest of the world; a rise in nostalgia for a time when the supremacy of white, Anglo-Saxon protestants was unchallenged and when the world they had created was thought to be the bastion of civilization – its best and only hope. This nostalgia for a past that never was requires a calculated forgetting, and the construction of false memories. Central to both the rhetoric and policy of some key political leaders in the US and the UK, it is both xenophobic and racist – part of a disturbing upsurge in jingoistic nativism and ethnocentrism on both sides of the Atlantic. It is also false. For centuries, both the US and the UK have been – and still are – deeply influenced by people beyond their borders and people of colour beyond their borders and within them. 'Traditional' American culture has always been multicultural. Our teaching must take into account our increasingly complex understanding of what our common culture is and how it evolved.

Keywords: Nostalgia, ethnocentrism, racism, multiculturalism, travel, America

In an America ruled by Donald Trump (no less in a United Kingdom preoccupied by Brexit), we are witnessing a rise in nostalgia for a time when the nation could glory in being self-sufficient and independent of the rest of the world; a rise in nostalgia for a time when the supremacy

Brexit and Beyond: Nation and Identity. SPELL: Swiss Papers in English Language and Literature 39, edited by Daniela Keller and Ina Habermann, Narr, 2020, pp. 271-93.

white, Anglo-Saxon protestants was unchallenged and when the world they had created was thought to be the bastion of civilization – its best and only hope. This nostalgic vision, central to both the rhetoric and policy of some key political leaders in the UK and in the US – is both xenophobic and racist. It is part of a disturbing upsurge in jingoistic nativism and ethnocentrism on both sides of the Atlantic. It is also false.

Scholars in the academy on both sides of the Atlantic have long recognized what is wrong with this picture. They know that for centuries, many allegedly self-sufficient nations have been – and still are – in fact, deeply influenced by people beyond their borders and people of colour beyond their borders and within them. They have marshalled evidence of the distinctly uncivilized behaviour of so-called civilized nations vis-à-vis the allegedly benighted 'uncivilized' world those nations sought to bring into their orbit. They have documented efforts over centuries to challenge the legitimacy of the authority that white Anglo-Saxon protestants claimed for themselves, discrediting the idea of 'white supremacy' as anything other than a convenient fiction invoked to justify injustice and tyranny.

But we often have the sense today that what the academy has been uncovering for decades remains invisible to many political leaders who prefer to bury their heads in the sand, ostrich-like, rather than face these inconvenient truths head-on. Take the slogan of the Trump campaign for president in 2016 – "Make America Great Again." It mourns the passing of a putative time when Americans were completely independent of the rest of the world, and when someone who knew little about the world beyond America's shores could think of himself as an educated person. A time when English was the only language Americans needed to know. A time when white supremacy was widely accepted as an assumption based on scientific evidence that was a good organizing principle for society as a whole.

The nostalgia in which they prefer to indulge requires a calculated forgetting, and the construction of false memories. It is, in short, a nostalgia for a past that never was. But for those who prefer to embrace this false narrative of who we are and who we have been, culture itself poses a big problem. For American culture is increasingly coming to be understood as the product of a host of transnational nodes of connection stretching back to beyond the founding of the nation itself – nodes influenced by what writers read and by where they travelled. It is increasingly recognized as the complicated product of interpenetrating multilingual traditions, and as a culture shaped at its core by people of colour. Literature can be an antidote to this nostalgia for a fictive past. It can talk back to these myths and be a crucial corrective. For teaching and reading literature requires us to engage a present – and a past – that are infinitely more interesting and more complex.

Let us start by looking at the nostalgia for a time when the nation could glory in being self-sufficient and independent of the rest of the world, a time when it could be proudly nationalist and isolationist. Where do we find such a time? Nowhere. Whether we pay attention to the books writers read for inspiration, or the sites outside the US to which they travelled, transnational nodes of connection have shaped American literature and culture from the start.

Take what we learn, for example, from a remarkable book published in 2016 titled *The Islamic Lineage of American Literary Culture: Muslim Sources from the Revolution to Reconstruction* by Jeffrey Einboden. "Arguing that Muslim sources exercised a formative impact on U.S. literary origins," Einboden "traces a genealogy of Islamic influence that spans America's critical century of self-definition [...] from the 1770s to the 1870s" (xi). He adds: "Focusing on celebrated writers from the Revolution to Reconstruction, I excavate Arabic and Persian precedents that shaped U.S. authorial lives and letters," showing a previously overlooked "American literary engagement with Islamic texts and traditions" that stretches back to our founding era (xi). With Einboden as a guide, we come to recognize "early American authorship as a dynamic site of global exchange, rather than as an integral outcome of national exceptionalism" (xi). Furthermore, Muslim sources turn out to "permeate the personal lives and labors of iconic American writers" such as Washington Irving, Ralph Waldo Emerson, and Lydia Maria Child, as well as less well-known ones (xii). Extending work by Wai Chee Dimock, Einboden's chapter on Emerson focuses on Emerson's daily reading and translation of Persian poetry. It "reveals Emerson, an icon of American exceptionalism," as "America's most prolific translator of Islamic verse, rendering more than two thousand lines of Persian poetry from German sources" (xiv). For Einboden, "excavating archival sources that exhibit U.S. authors' adoption of Arabic and Persian idioms" allows us "to trace arcs in early America that anticipate our contemporary interests" in transnational American Studies (xv).

The impact of Asia on American literature and culture is equally revealing. It would be hard to find any moment in the history of the US when products, people, or ideas from Asia did not play a vital role (Fishkin, "Asian"). The American Renaissance? Thoreau and Emerson both were reading and learning from translations of Eastern texts (Hileman). American impressionism? The most famous works by painter

Mary Cassatt are indebted to lessons she learned from traditions of Japanese printmaking (Ives). How about *Adventures of Huckleberry Finn*, the book which Hemingway claimed gave birth to all twentieth-century American literature? Twain undertook his first experiments with using satire to attack racism when, as a young journalist in the 1860s, his direct exposés of racism towards the Chinese in San Francisco were censored (Fishkin, "Mark Twain" 69-72).

For over a century, scholars have noted the influence of East Asian poetic traditions on twentieth-century modernist American poets such as Ezra Pound, who adopted and adapted themes and forms of East Asian poetry in order to develop his own distinctive innovations in poetry in English (Jang; Qian; Huff; Williams). Scholars have also written broadly on the influence of Buddhist philosophical traditions on T. S. Eliot's poetry (Bruno).

While the influence of Asia on American modernist poets is not a new topic, the influence of Asia on the dean of Chicano letters in the US is. Américo Paredes, a writer from the Texas-Mexico borderlands, was the author of brilliant and innovative works of folklore and fiction. As Ramón Saldívar demonstrates in his book *The Borderlands of Culture*, it was Paredes's experiences as a journalist in occupied Japan that seminally shaped his ideas about citizenship and belonging. Saldívar argues that Paredes's encounter with "the borderlands of the postwar intercultural contact zones" (361) he was documenting in Japan impacted his understanding of the borderlands in which he had grown up in key ways (Fishkin, "Asian" 19-20).

While Emerson, Pound, Eliot, and other writers may have encountered cultures outside the US through their reading, for Herman Melville and Mark Twain no less than for Américo Paredes, travel was a particularly fruitful source of exposure to the world beyond America's shores. Lawrence Buell explores what Melville learned from his travels in an essay titled "Ecoglobalist Affects: The Emergence of U.S. Environmental Imagination on a Planetary Scale." He calls Melville "the first canonical U.S. author to have sojourned in the developing world, and to perceive the effects of gunboat diplomacy there from the standpoint of its indigenous victims" (239). An essay by Rüdiger Kunow shows how Melville's travels developed his respect for the native cultures he encountered and his deepened critique of missionaries. In a similar vein, Tsuyoshi Ishihara demonstrates how Twain's travels prompted him to re-examine his views on non-Western others, transforming his sense of himself and of Western civilization in the process.

My own work has looked at how Mark Twain's travels throughout the British Empire clarified his understanding of his native land in crucial ways, igniting what would become a lifelong rejection of American exceptionalism (Fishkin, "Mark Twain's Historical View"). "Travel," Twain wrote, "is fatal to prejudice, bigotry and narrow-mindedness, and many of our people need it sorely on these accounts" (*Innocents Abroad* 650). He knew whereof he spoke. Twain, who spent a third of his life living outside the United States, was one of America's first truly cosmopolitan writers, as at home in the world as he was in his own country, and his travels had a huge impact on his work (Fishkin, "Originally"). His journeys through India, for example, helped spark some of his most trenchant observations about the Slave South in which he had grown up. It is in *Following the Equator*, the record of his round-the-world lecture tour that he published in 1897, that Twain first expatiates – in print – on what racism at home and abroad have in common. Twain's encounters with exploitative, abusive power abroad set off trains of recollections stretching back to the slave-holding society in which he had spent his youth.

Before his trip to India, Twain had relegated to fiction the troublesome matter of coming to terms with the slave-holding world of his childhood. He had not explored this dimension of his world autobiographically before travelling to India. Then, one day in Bombay, a German's mistreatment of an Indian servant opened the floodgates, and memories of Twain's personal past came rushing in. The sight of a white man, a "burly German," giving a native servant "a brisk cuff on the jaw" without explaining what he had done wrong "flashed upon [him] the forgotten fact that this was the *usual* way of explaining one's desires to a slave" (*Following the Equator* 351). The scene brought back to him memories of his own father's mistreatment of "our harmless slave boy, Lewis, for trifling little blunders and awkwardnesses," and of a scene he witnessed when he was ten of "a man fling[ing] a lump of iron-ore at a slave-man in anger, for merely doing something awkwardly – as if that were a crime" (352). Twain marvels over

> the space-annihilating power of thought. For just one second, all that goes to make the *me* in me was in a Missourian village, on the other side of the globe, vividly seeing again these forgotten pictures of fifty years ago, and wholly unconscious of all things but just those; and in the next second I was back in Bombay, and that kneeling native's smitten cheek was not done tingling yet! (352)

Elsewhere in *Following the Equator*, in a manner so disarmingly subtle that it strikes the reader as virtually unconscious, Twain manages to invert the savage vs. civilized hierarchy establishing an equality between the races. His critique culminates in that volume in a highly memorable quip. "There are many humorous things in the world," he wrote, "among them the white man's notion that he is less savage than the other savages" (213). Twain's travels in India, Africa, Australia, and New Zealand led him to recognize with clarity and power the absurdity of the idea of white superiority – a recognition that would shape everything he wrote during the last decade and a half of his life.

Watching the supercilious German abuse a dark-skinned servant in imperial India brought it all home to Twain. It forced on Twain's recollection the underlying brutality of the so-called mild domestic slavery of his childhood. It also prompted him to ponder the question of how those in power justified such unjust arrangements to themselves. In other words, Twain's journeys allowed him to recognize the racism of his childhood as akin to the racist underpinnings of the imperialism he witnessed during his travels at the turn of the century as two sides of the same coin. Both were supported by one group's assumption that it was more civilized, virtuous, or admirable than everyone outside the group. It mattered little whether those who thought themselves superior hailed from Hannibal or Heidelberg, from Washington, DC, or Waganui, New Zealand. Unfailingly they were white, and they were insufferable. Those whom they despised and oppressed were non-white.

A Mark Twain who had long admired the Anglo-Saxon race and Anglo-Saxon civilization as the defenders of democracy and freedom now challenged the arrogance of the imperialist adventures of that race and that civilization in genres ranging from short story to essay to polemic. Initially, Twain had believed in the value of extending the power and influence of the United States into the Pacific when he thought that meant extending democracy; that was, as Twain put it, the American model. But to his dismay beginning in 1898, he saw his countrymen following what he referred to as the European model in foreign affairs, seeking to dominate another culture out of greed, selfishness, and arrogance masquerading as benevolence and altruism. That behaviour cast the US as the same sort of villain as the European nations that were rapaciously carving up Asia and Africa in the name of extending to these benighted regions the so-called blessings of civilization – but in reality to suit their own ends. Twain joined forces with the Anti-Imperialist League, becoming the most prominent anti-imperialist in the nation, connecting American policy in the Philippines with the behaviour of

American missionaries in China, and the behaviour of England, Belgium, Russia, France, and Germany in Africa and Asia (Twain, *Following the Equator*; Zwick, *Mark Twain's Weapons*; Zwick, "Mark Twain"; Fishkin, "Mark Twain and the Jews").

Twain's travels gave him the perspective to become America's most cogent and acerbic critic of what he would call "the lie of silent assertion" – "the silent assertion that nothing is going on which fair and intelligent men are aware of and are engaged by their duty to try to stop" (Twain, "My First Lie" 171). The concept helped him recognize how racist usurpations and hypocrisy crossed boundaries and cultures. He became, in the process, perhaps the most globally admired American writer of all time.

If American culture has been deeply shaped by transnational nodes of connection, sparked by writers' reading and by their travels, it has also been shaped by interpenetrating multilingual traditions. A number of books published in the last two decades have drawn our attention to American literature written in languages other than English, and to the transnational movements of people and culture that gave rise to a rich body of material (see for instance Sollors; Shell and Sollors; Yin; Wirth-Nesher; Bachman; Kanellos). Work like this is rooted in the assumption that American scholars need to be more attentive to voices that were previously largely redlined from the cultural conversation in the United States.

When I wrote my latest book, *Writing America: Literary Landmarks from Walden Pond to Wounded Knee* (2015), I featured a number of American writers who wrote American literature in languages other than English, from the early twentieth century to the present. Only limits of space prevented me from going back even earlier. For example, thanks to the pioneering work of Arturo Schomburg and its recovery by Werner Sollors, we now know that the earliest known work of fiction by an African American was a story written in *French* by a New Orleans-born African-American poet, playwright, and fiction writer named Victor Séjours – a story titled "Le mulâtre," which was published in *Revue des Colonies* in March, 1937.

In *Writing America*, I devoted significant attention to Gloria Anzaldúa, whose work has become widely taught not only in the US, but in Europe as well, and who is increasingly recognized as one of the great American writers of the twentieth century (Fishkin, *Writing America* 304-28). Anzaldúa's master work, *Borderlands/La Frontera* (1987), demonstrated more vividly than any work before it the interpenetrating multilingual traditions of the Southwestern region of the United States.

As a child in Hidalgo County, Texas, Anzaldúa was beaten in the schoolyard for speaking Spanish. But by the time she pens *Borderlands/La Frontera*, she is a confident writer who translates only when and how she chooses to. "I grew up between two cultures," she writes,

> the Mexican (with a heavy Indian influence) and the Anglo (as a member of a colonized people in our own territory). I have been straddling that *tejas*-Mexican border, and others, all my life. It's not a comfortable territory to live in, this place of contradictions. Hatred, anger and exploitation are the prominent features of this landscape. [...] The U.S.-Mexican border *es una herida abierta* where the Third World grates against the first and bleeds. And before a scab forms it hemorrhages again, the lifeblood of two worlds merging to form a third country – a border culture. (vii, 3)

While the border between the United States and Mexico may seem 'natural' from the standpoint of a culture that embraces the dominant version of US political and military history, from the perspective of the descendant of the ancient tribes that lived throughout the region, the border is a construct, dividing a people from itself. The story she tells about her cousin reminds us of the fear and danger that was a constant presence in the lives of her family members:

> In the fields, *la migra*. My aunt saying, "No *corran*, don't run. They'll think you're *del otro lao*." In the confusion, Pedro ran, terrified of being caught. He couldn't speak English, couldn't tell them he was fifth generation American. *Sin papeles* – he did not carry his birth certificate to work in the fields. *La migra* took him away while we watched. *Se lo llevaron.* [...] I saw the terrible weight of shame hunch his shoulders. They deported him to Guadalajara by plane. The furthest he'd ever been to Mexico was Reynosa, a small border town opposite Hidalgo, Texas, not far from McAllen. Pedro walked all the way to the Valley. *Se lo llevaron sin un centavo al pobre. Se vino andando desde Guadalajara.* (26)

While Anzaldúa wants to communicate the difficulties of living on linguistic borderlands, she also wants to communicate the richness it entails. Sometimes she achieves this through highly evocative, clear, and readable passages – like the story of her cousin – that move back and forth between Spanish and English in a seamless flow, giving the reader a sense of what it feels like to live in two languages. The book is also filled with slyly evasive 'non-translations' – passages that might appear, on the surface, to be translations, but which turn out, on closer view, to be instead paraphrases that reduce the passages that precede them. These passages underscore for the reader the poverty of one who does *not* have a mestiza consciousness of language.

Many of the 'approximate' translations occur when Anzaldúa is quoting colloquial speakers. She translates only the gist of what they say:

> Through our mothers, the culture gave us mixed messages: *No voy a dejar que ningún pelado desgraciado maltrate a mis hijos.* And in the next breath it would say, *La mujer tiene que hacer lo que le diga el hombre.* Which was it to be – strong, or submissive, rebellious or conforming? (40)

This is no translation; it is a summation. The English-speaking reader is motivated to figure out what exactly Anzaldúa's mother said. (What she said was, "I'm not going to let any miserable bum mistreat my kids." And "The woman has to do whatever the man says.") The English-only reader knows she is missing a lot by not understanding the Spanish. Anzaldúa will settle for nothing less than wrenching from her own experience as an outsider – as a Chicana, as a mestiza, and as a lesbian – the guideposts of a new way of being in the world. She makes a strong case for the idea that the sense of dislocation, ambiguity, uncertainty, and fear that living on cultural, social, linguistic, and sexual borders entails can be a positive force for the artist. For while living with constant fear of humiliation, deportation, and hundreds of unnamed terrors can paralyze, it can also produce a heightened sensitivity to one's environment. The individual who learns to manage those tensions develops extraordinary capacities to forge new creative syntheses (Fishkin, *Feminist Engagements* 15-17, 23-30).[1]

In *Writing America*, I also included writers whose English intentionally mimics the cadences of Yiddish, and writers who wrote in Yiddish themselves. Yiddish, of course, is the language spoken by Eastern European Jews who sought refuge in the US from the anti-Semitic persecution they faced in Europe from the nineteenth through the twentieth century – a language cherished fondly as the cultural heritage of their descendants. Abraham Cahan (*Imported*; *Rise*), Anzia Yezierska, Henry Roth, and Irena Klepfisz are just a few of the writers who sprinkle Yiddish words and phrases throughout their poetry and prose, creating

---

[1] Other writers who meld Spanish and English in their work include Tomás Rivera, author of *Y No Se Lo Tragó la Tierra…*; and Rolando Hinojosa, author of *The Valley*, both of whom hail from the US-Mexico Borderlands (Fishkin, *Writing America* 304, 308, 313-14, 329-30). Also Junot Díaz, who blends the Spanish spoken in the Dominican Republic of his early childhood with the hip and breezy English of urban centres in New Jersey where he spent his adolescence (Carpio; Díaz).

work that is both evocative and distinctive. The work of several writers who wrote American literature in Yiddish is being recovered and reappraised. The poet Morris Rosenfeld, for example, who worked long hours in a sweatshop all day, wrote poetry at night about the sweatshop and the toll it took on family life. His most famous poem is the poignant "*Mayn Yingele*," in which a father bemoans the fact that he sees his child at night only when he is asleep. He has to hear about how well the child played from his wife. Verses depict the father's sadness at not being able to hear his child begin to talk, at not being able to look into his eyes when he is awake. It ends with a thought the father cannot bear: "One morning, when you wake, my child / you'll find that I'm not there!" ("*Ven du vakst oyf amol, mayn kind, / Gefinst du mikh nit mer!*) (Rosenfeld 135-36; Fishkin, *Writing America* 206-08).[2]

If American literature and culture is the product of nodes of transnational connection and multilingual traditions, it has also been shaped at its core by people of colour. If "all modern American literature comes from one book by Mark Twain called *Huckleberry Finn*," as Ernest Hemingway declared (22), then all modern American literature comes, as well, from the African-American oral traditions that helped make that book what it is. In *Was Huck Black? Mark Twain and African-American Voices* (1993), I demonstrate, for example, that Twain drew on the speech of an engaging black child whom he had met to shape Huck's voice and that the rhetorical style of a slave acquaintance from Twain's childhood introduced him to the potential of satire as a tool of social criticism. I made the case that "the voice we have come to accept as the vernacular voice in American literature – the voice with which Twain captured our national imagination in *Huckleberry Finn*, and that empowered Hemingway, Faulkner, and countless other writers in the twentieth century" (4) – has its roots in the speech of specific African Americans Twain knew, and that Twain's satire also has African-American roots. Mark Twain appreciated the creative vitality of African-American voices and exploited their potential in his art. In the process, he taught his countrymen new lessons about the lyrical and exuberant energy of vernacular speech, as well as about the potential of satire and irony in the service of truth. Both of these lessons would ultimately make the culture more responsive to the voices of African-American writers in the twen-

[2] In *Writing America*, I also discussed the Chinese poetry inscribed on the walls of the Angel Island immigration centre in the San Francisco bay. These poems, carved into the wall by would-be immigrants from China in the early twentieth century who were detained at Angel Island while awaiting permission to enter the United States, are now recognized as some of America's earliest Asian-American literature (245-60).

tieth century. They would also change its definitions of what 'art' ought to look and sound like to be freshly, wholly 'American' (Fishkin, *Was* 5).

As I have claimed, "[s]omething new happened [in *Huckleberry Finn*] that had never happened in American literature before" (Fishkin, *Lighting* 112). It was a book that served as a declaration of independence from the genteel English novel tradition. I noted that "*Huckleberry Finn* allowed a different kind of writing to happen: a clean, crisp, no-nonsense, earthy vernacular kind of writing that jumped off the printed page with unprecedented immediacy and energy; it was a book that talked." African-American voices played a key role in making it what it was (112).

One critic notes that "the vernacular language ... in *Huckleberry Finn* strikes the ear with the freshness of a real boy talking out loud" (Albert Stone qtd. in Fishkin, *Was* 13). I have argued that the voice of an *actual* "real boy talking out loud" helped Twain recognize the potential of such a voice to hold an audience's attention and win its trust. On 29 November 1874, two years before he published *Tom Sawyer* and began *Adventures of Huckleberry Finn*, Mark Twain published an article called "Sociable Jimmy" in the *New York Times*. "Sociable Jimmy" is the first piece Twain published that is dominated by the voice of a child; this fact alone would seem to mark it as deserving of scholars' attention. I was therefore astonished to find, when I began looking into the matter, that it had been almost totally ignored. While Twain stopped at a hotel for the night during a lecture tour of the Midwest, he reports that a "bright, simple, guileless little darkey boy [...] ten years old – a wide-eyed, observant little chap" brought him his supper. The intensity of Twain's response to the child is striking. He notes that he wrote down what the child said, and sent the record home because he

> wished to preserve the memory of the most artless, sociable, and exhaustless talker I ever came across. He did not tell me a single remarkable thing, or one that was worth remembering; and yet he was himself so interested in his small marvels, and they flowed so naturally and comfortably from his lips, that his talk got the upper hand of my interest, too, and I listened as one who receives a revelation. I took down what he had to say, just as he said it – without altering a word or adding one. (Twain, "Sociable Jimmy" in Fishkin, *Was* 20)

Well, when I read that, I immediately thought of the "most artless, sociable and exhaustless talker" I had ever come across, and that, of course, was Huck Finn. Jimmy shares elements of grammar, syntax, and diction, cadences and rhythms of speech that critics have identified as central to the voice we know as Huck's. Jimmy and Huck both use adjectives in place of adverbs. Jimmy says, "[h]e's powerful sickly." Huck says, "I was most powerful sick." Jimmy says, "[s]ome folks say dis town would be considerable bigger." Huck says, "I read considerable to Jim about kings, dukes and earls and such" and "[t]his shook me up considerable." Jimmy says, "she don't make no soun' scacely," while Huck says "there warn't no room in bed for him, skasely." Both boys use the word "disremember" for "forget" in contexts that are virtually identical in the two texts. Jimmy says, "he's got another name dat I somehow disremember," while Huck says, "I disremember her name." Huck and Jimmy are both unpretentious, uninhibited, easily impressed, and unusually loquacious. They free-associate with remarkable energy and verve. And they are supremely self-confident: neither doubts for a minute that Twain (in Jimmy's case) or the reader (in Huck's) is completely absorbed by everything he has to say. Jimmy may have triggered Twain's recollection of the voices of playmates from his childhood, reminding him of the ease with which he could speak in that voice himself. As he put it in a letter to his wife Livy written shortly after he met Jimmy: "I think I could swing my legs over the arms of a chair & that boy's spirit would descend upon me & enter into me" (qtd. in Fishkin, *Was* 11-50).

If Huck's speech was inspired, in large part, by a black child, does that mean that Huck used language that would have been considered "black" at the time? During the 1880s, the period when the American Folklore Society came into being and the *Journal of American Folklore* was born, dialect scholars began to pay serious attention to what they called "negro English," and began collecting expressions that were common among blacks, rather than whites, in the South. On this list, as it turns out, are many expressions characteristic of Huck's speech. They include "by and by" meaning "after a while"; "powerful" and "monstrous" meaning "very"; "lonesome" meaning "depressed"; "I lay" meaning "I wager"; "warn't no use" meaning "there is no use in"; "to study" meaning "to meditate"; "sqush" meaning "to crush"; "if I'd a knowed" meaning "[i]f I had known," and "light out fer," meaning "to run for." These last two expressions, of course, appear in Huck's famous penultimate lines: "[I]f I'd a knowed what a trouble it was to make a book I wouldn't a tackled it and aint't agoing to no more. But I reckon I got to light out for the Territory ahead of the rest, because Aunt Sally she's going to adopt me and sivilize me and I can't stand it. I been there before" (Twain, *Adventures* 366; Fishkin, *Was* 11-50).

What happened between Twain's first encounter with Jimmy in 1871 and his decision to let a voice very much like Jimmy's be the narrator of a novel some four years later, when he began *Huck Finn*? For one thing Mary Ann Cord told her story. Mary Ann Cord was a former slave who worked as the cook at Quarry Farm, the home in Elmira, New York, belonging to Twain's sister-in-law, where the Clemens family spent summers during Twain's most productive and creative years. One evening, in the summer of 1874, Mary Ann Cord told Twain, his wife, and others assembled, the powerful and moving story of her being forcibly separated from her youngest child on the auction block, and eventually being miraculously reunited with him after the war. Twain wrote that he found the story she told "a shameful tale of wrong & hardship," but also "a curiously strong piece of literary work to come unpremeditated from lips untrained in literary art" – a comment that shows his awareness of the close relationship between speaking voices and literature. Throughout his career as a lecturer and as a writer, Twain aspired to have the effect upon listeners and readers that speakers like Mary Ann Cord had upon him (Fishkin, *Was* 8-9). For while Jimmy's vernacular speech had intrigued Twain, Mary Ann Cord showed Twain the possibilities of combining vernacular speech with accomplished narrative skill. Her story, which would become Twain's first contribution to the *Atlantic Monthly*, was another key step on the road to *Huck Finn*. Mary Ann Cord's storytelling underlined for Twain the fact that serious, compelling emotions could be communicated in the vernacular, and that the vernacular could be artfully structured into a compelling narrative (30-50).

It was another black speaker – a brilliant satirical slave named Jerry who Twain thought of as "the greatest man in the country" – who introduced Twain to satire as a tool of social criticism. The book that changed all of American literature that followed is now recognized as a sly satirical critique of the nation's retreat from black rights in the years that followed the end of the Civil War. The captivity of Jim in the final portion of the novel takes on new meaning when we understand it in the context of the time in which Twain wrote, a time when the nation was re-enslaving its black citizens by law and by force (51-76).

Ralph Ellison observed that "[t]he spoken idiom of Negro Americans" was "absorbed by the creators of our great nineteenth-century literature even when the majority of blacks were still enslaved. Mark Twain celebrated it in the prose of *Huckleberry Finn*" (qtd. in Fishkin, *Was* 128-29). But the role of "the spoken idiom of Negro Americans" in shaping the language of Americans was doggedly denied by scholars throughout the twentieth century. As late as the 1960s, folklorists and ethnographers still resisted the idea that the terms "OK," "wow," "uh-huh," and "unh-unh" were African-American contributions to the American language – which they are (Holloway, "What" 59). A paradigm shift began to happen in the 1990s, one which I charted in publications including an article titled "The Multiculturalism of 'Traditional' Culture" and another called "Interrogating 'Whiteness,' Complicating 'Blackness': Remapping American Culture." I noted over a hundred books and articles published by scholars in literary criticism, history, cultural studies, anthropology, popular culture, communication studies, music history, art history, humour studies, linguistics, and folklore that all lent support to this pithy comment by Robert Farris Thompson: "To be white in America is to be very black. If you don't know how black you are, you don't know how American you are" (n.p.; see also Fishkin, "Interrogating 'Whiteness'" 429). Traditional American culture turns out to be less 'white' than was previously thought.

Just as such 'minority' traditions are key to understanding Mark Twain, so are African traditions essential to understanding the work of Herman Melville – as historian Sterling Stuckey and literary critics Eric Sundquist and Viola Sachs have shown. They have demonstrated Melville's deep interest in African customs, myths, languages, and traditions and have pointed out the African influence on works such as *Moby Dick* and the short story "Benito Cereno." Sachs has uncovered numerous references to the Yoruba god Legba in *Moby Dick*, while Stuckey and Sundquist have examined the use of Ashanti drumming and treatment of the dead in "Benito Cereno," suggesting that the treatment of the corpse of the rich slaveholder Aranda in "Benito Cereno" was not a racist allusion to African savagery, as critics have argued, but rather evidence of Melville's insight into Ashanti rituals and the shrewd political use his characters made of those traditions.

In popular culture, as well, familiar artefacts generally accepted as 'white' are now recognized as having more complicated roots. Howard L. Sacks and Judith Rose Sacks have argued cogently in their book, *Way Up North in Dixie: A Black Family's Claim to the Confederate Anthem*, that "Dixie," the song that became the anthem of the Confederacy, was written by a black family in nineteenth-century Ohio, and not, as had been thought, by the white minstrel performer who appropriated the song and presented it as his own. Historians Christopher P. Lehman (63-72) and David Roediger (48) reveal the African and African-American roots of that staple of American popular culture, Bugs Bunny. Roediger notes that the verb "bug," meaning to annoy or vex someone, has its roots partly in Wolof, the West-African language spoken by the largest group of Africans to arrive in this country in the seventeenth century (48). Moreover, he writes, "the fantastic idea that a vulnerable and weak rabbit could be tough and tricky enough to menace those who menace him enters American culture" largely through tales that were told among various ethnic groups from West Africa and further developed by American slaves (48). Mel Watkins tracks comedian Lenny Bruce's hip, irreverent satire to the wit of black musicians and entertainers with whom he associated (485). Joseph E. Holloway has traced to African languages the roots of many familiar American words and expressions. These include – in addition to "OK, wow, uh-huh and unh-unh" – "banana," "yam," "banjo," "bad-mouth," "bodacious," "bogus," "bronco," "coffee," "cola," "guff," "guy," "gumbo," "diddle," "dirt," "honkie," "hoodoo," "jamboree," "jazz," "Jiffy," "Jive," "kooky," "phony," "rap," "tote," "yam," "you all," and "zombie" (Holloway, "Africanisms" 82-110). And John Edward Philips provides an illuminating overview of multidisciplinary research on African influences on 'white' American culture in his essay "The African Heritage of White America." And although there is not space here to examine the ways in which British culture has also been shaped at its core by people of colour, this is a topic that scholars have been increasingly exploring in recent years in work that resonates with research American scholars have done (see for instance Julia Sun-Joo Lee; Fisch).

'Traditional' American culture has always been multicultural. Our teaching must take into account our increasingly complex understanding of what our common culture is and how it evolved. Doing so will "force us to examine how an unequal distribution not of talent but of power permitted a blatantly false monocultural myth to mask and distort the multicultural reality" (Fishkin, "Reclaiming" 86). This new vision of our culture will be more accurate than any that we have had before – and more stimulating. It will also provide a healthier base on which to build for the future. Forging this vision may not be easy, but it is a challenge we must embrace.

Contemporary cultural productions, no less than key works of the last two centuries, require that we engage these issues, as a brief closing discussion of one recent American novel will make clear. Transnational nodes of connection, multilingual traditions, and the centrality of people of colour all come together in the celebrated 2017 novel *Pachinko*, by Min Jin Lee, a National Book Award finalist, and a book recognized with many other awards. Lee is an American born in Korea who has lived in both America and Japan and is married to a Japanese American.

With its evocation of the language of characters speaking Korean, Japanese, and English as well as combinations of all three, her book is the complicated product of interpenetrating multilingual traditions. These transnational nodes shape the book at its core. And given that the book is profoundly influenced by Lee's awareness of the history of the Civil Rights movement in America, as well as of the history of Asians in America, it is a novel shaped at its core by people of colour. *Pachinko* is a book that defies borders. It is a book about Koreans in Japan that only an American could have written. *Pachinko* is the product of Lee's empathetic, border-crossing generosity of spirit. It is a book that makes me proud to call Min Jin Lee a friend and a fellow American – as well as a marvellous writer.

Coda

Many Americans are taken aback by the ignorance, self-importance, braggadocio, self-satisfied provincialism, and knee-jerk nationalism on display by the current occupant of the White House. But it is important to remind ourselves that these attitudes and behaviour are nothing new. Consider Mark Twain's 1869 book, *The Innocents Abroad*, a satirical record of the first sizeable cohort of middle-class, middle-American tourists' visit to Europe. "The people of those foreign countries are very, very ignorant," Twain wrote. "In Paris they just simply opened their eyes and stared when we spoke to them in French! We never did succeed in making those idiots understand their own language" (645). He notes that throughout the trip,

> [w]e always took care to make it understood that we were Americans – Americans! When we found that a good many foreigners had hardly ever heard of America, and that a good many more knew it only as a barbarous province away off somewhere, that had lately been at war with somebody, we pitied the ignorance of the Old World, but abated no jot of our importance. (645)

Or a half century later, consider the prologue that opens *Main Street* (1920) by Sinclair Lewis:

> Main Street is the climax of civilization. That this Ford car might stand in front of the Bon Ton Store, Hannibal invaded Rome and Erasmus wrote in Oxford cloisters. What Ole Jenson the grocer says to Ezra Stowbody the banker is the new law for London, Prague, and the unprofitable isles of the sea; whatsoever Ezra does not know and sanction, that thing is heresy, worthless for knowing and wicked to consider. Our railway station is the final aspiration of architecture. ([i])

George Babbitt, in Lewis's novel *Babbitt* (1922), is proud of living in Zenith, a fictional Midwestern city that is truly "great" (a ubiquitous word in speeches and tweets by the leader of the free world today). He brags that the city has "an unparalleled number of miles of paved streets, bathrooms, vacuum cleaners, and all the other signs of civilization" – clear signs of its "all-round unlimited greatness" (187). The ignorance and self-importance of the self-satisfied provincialism, knee-jerk nationalism, and braggadocio emanating from the Oval Office today may infuriate us, but before we despair, let us remember that the US is also a nation that has produced gifted writers able to unmask these traits, often with wit, with humour, and with a faith that recognizing these alarming flaws is a first step towards becoming the kind of society that rejects them (Fishkin, "America's"). Recognizing the boldness and brilliance of these writers' critiques of our society – and embracing a vision of our world that welcomes these critiques and learns from them – is the task of literary scholars today.

References

Anzaldúa, Gloria. *Borderlands/La Frontera: The New Mestiza*. 1987. 25th Anniversary 4th ed. Introduction by Norma Cantú and Aida Hurtado, Aunt Lute Books, 2012.

Bachman, Merle. *Recovering "Yiddishland": Threshold Moments in American Literature*. Syracuse UP, 2007.

Bruno, Tim. "Buddhist Conceptual Rhyming and T. S. Eliot's Crisis of Connection in *The Waste Land* and 'Burnt Norton.'" *Asian Philosophy*, vol. 23, no. 4, 2013, pp. 365-78.

Buell, Lawrence. "Ecoglobalist Affects: The Emergence of U.S. Environmental Imagination on a Planetary Scale." *Shades of the Planet: American Literature as World Literature*, edited by Wai Chee Dimock and Lawrence Buell, Princeton UP, 2018, pp. 227-48.

Cahan, Abraham. *The Imported Bridegroom and Other Stories of the New York Ghetto*. Introduction by Gordon Hutner, Signet, 1996.

——. *The Rise of David Levinsky*. 1917. Introduction by John Higham, Harper, 1966.

Carpio, Glenda. "Now Check It: Junot Díaz's Wondrous Spanglish." *Junot Díaz and the Decolonial Imagination*, edited by Monica Hanna et al., Duke UP, 2016, pp. 257-90.

Díaz, Junot. *The Brief Wondrous Life of Oscar Wao*. Riverhead Books, 2007.

Dimock, Wai Chee. "Hemispheric Islam: Continents and Centuries for American Literature." *American Literary History*, vol. 21, no. 1, 2009, pp. 28-52.

Einboden, Jeffrey. *The Islamic Lineage of American Literary Culture: Muslim Sources from the Revolution to Reconstruction*. Oxford UP, 2016.

Fisch, Audrey A. *American Slaves in Victorian England: Abolitionist Politics in Popular Literature and Culture*. Cambridge UP, 2000.

Fishkin, Shelley Fisher. "America's Politics and the Antidote to Despair." *Times Literary Supplement* (TLS Online), 5 Oct. 2017, www.the-tls.co.uk/articles/public/american-literature-trump-twain-lewis/.

——. "Asian Crossroads/Transnational American Studies." *The Japanese Journal of American Studies*, no. 17, 2006, pp. 5-52, www.jaas.gr.jp/jjas/PDF/2006/No.17-005.pdf.

——. *Feminist Engagements: Forays into American Literature and Culture*. Palgrave Macmillan, 2009.

——. "Interrogating 'Whiteness,' Complicating 'Blackness': Remapping American Culture." *American Quarterly*, vol. 47, no. 3, Sept. 1995, pp. 428-66, www.jstor.org/stable/2713296?seq=1#page_scan_tab_contents.

——. *Lighting Out for the Territory: Reflections on Mark Twain and American Culture.* Oxford UP, 1997.

——. "Mark Twain." *From Fact to Fiction: Journalism and Imaginative Writing in America.* Oxford UP, 1988, pp. 53-84.

——. "Mark Twain and the Jews." *The Arizona Quarterly*, vol. 61, no. 1, Spring 2005, pp. 137-66.

——. "Mark Twain's Historical View at the Turn of the Twentieth Century." *Proceedings of the 1999 Kyoto American Studies Summer Seminar.* Ritsumeikan University, 2000.

——. "The Multiculturalism of 'Traditional' Culture." *Chronicle of Higher Education*, 10 March 1995, www.chronicle.com/article/The-Multiculturalism-of/84008.

——. "'Originally of Missouri, Now of the Universe': Mark Twain and the World." *Developing Transnational American Studies*, edited by Nadja Gernalzick and Heike C. Spickermann, Winter, 2019.

——. "Reclaiming the Black Presence in 'Mainstream Culture.'" *African Roots/American Cultures: Africa in the Creation of the Americas*, edited by Sheila S. Walker, Rowman and Littlefield, 2001, pp. 81-88.

——. *Was Huck Black? Mark Twain and African American Voices.* Oxford UP, 1993.

——. *Writing America: Literary Landmarks from Walden Pond to Wounded Knee.* Rutgers UP, 2015.

Hemingway, Ernest. *Green Hills of Africa.* Charles Scribner's Sons, 1935.

Hileman, Bryan. "Transcendental Forerunners." *American Transcendentalism*, archive.vcu.edu/english/engweb/transcendentalism/roots/rootsintro.html.

Hinojosa, Rolando. *The Valley.* Bilingual P/Editorial Bilingue, 1983.

Holloway, Joseph E. "Africanisms in African American Names in the United States." *Africanisms in American Culture*, edited by Joseph E. Holloway, Indiana UP, 2005, pp. 82-110.

——. "'What Africa Has Given America': African Continuities in the North American Diaspora." *Africanisms in American Culture*, edited by Joseph E. Holloway, 2nd ed., Indiana UP, 2005, pp. 39-64.

Huff, AdriAnne. *The Flow of Absence: Asian Influence from Ezra Pound to Gary Snyder.* VDM Verlag, 2008.

Ishihara, Tsuyoshi. "Mark Twain's Travel Books and Empire: The Transformation of Twain's Views on Non-Western Others and the Western Self." *Waseda University Faculty of Education Academic Research*, vol. 54, no. 19, Feb. 2006, core.ac.uk/download/pdf/46865133.pdf.

Ives, Colta. "Japonisme." *Heilbrunn Timeline of Art History*. New York: The Metropolitan Museum of Art, Oct. 2004, www.metmuseum.org/toah/hd/jpon/hd_jpon.htm.

Jang, Mi-Jung. "The East Asian Influence in Ezra Pound's Pre-Cathay Poetry." *American Studies*, vol. 34, 2011, pp. 233-55, s-space.snu.ac.kr/bitstream/10371/88675/1/10.%20Articles%20%20%20The%20East%20Asian%20Influence%20in%20Ezra%20Pound%60s%20Pre-Cathay%20Poetry.pdf.

Kanellos, Nicolas. *Herencia: The Anthology of Hispanic Literature of the United States*. Oxford UP, 2003.

Klepfisz, Irena. *A Few Words in the Mother Tongue: Poems Selected and New, 1971-1990*. Eighth Mountain P, 1991.

Kunow, Rüdiger. "Melville, Religious Cosmopolitanism and the New American Studies." *Journal of Transnational American Studies*, vol. 3, no. 1, 2011, escholarship.org/uc/item/8n55g7q6.

Lee, Julia Sun-Joo. *The American Slave Narrative and the Victorian Novel*. Oxford UP, 2010.

Lee, Min Jin. *Pachinko*. Grand Central Publishing, 2017.

Lehman, Christopher P. *The Colored Cartoon: Black Representation in American Animated Short Film*. U of Massachusetts P, 2009.

Lewis, Sinclair. *Babbitt*. Harcourt, Brace, 1922.

——. *Main Street*. Harcourt, Brace, and Howe, 1920.

Philips, John Edward. "The African Heritage of White America." *Africanisms in American Culture*, edited by Joseph E. Holloway, 2nd ed., Indiana UP, 2005, pp. 372-96.

Qian, Zhaoming, editor. *Ezra Pound and China*. U of Michigan Press, 2003.

Rivera, Tomás. *Y No Se Lo Tragó la Tierra.... [And the Earth Did Not Devour Him...]*. Translated by Evangelina Vigil-Piñon, Arte Público P, 1992.

Roediger, David. *History Against Misery*. Charles Kerr Publishing Co., 2006.

Rosenfeld, Morris. "Mayn Yingele/My Little Son." Translated by Aaron Kramer. *Jewish American Literature: A Norton Anthology*, edited by Jules Chametzky et al., W. W. Norton, 2001, pp. 135-36.

Roth, Henry. *Call It Sleep*. 1934. Introduction by Alfred Kazin and afterword by Hana Wirth-Nesher, Farrar, Straus, and Giroux, 1991.

Sachs, Viola. *L'Imaginaire Melville: A French Point of View*. UP of Vincennes, 1992.

Sacks, Howard L., and Judith Rose Sacks. *Way Up North in Dixie: A Black Family's Claim to the Confederate Anthem*. Smithsonian Institution P, 1993.

Saldívar, Ramón. *The Borderlands of Culture: Américo Paredes and the Transnational Imaginary*. Duke UP, 2006.

Séjours, Victor. "Le mulâtre/The Mulatto." Translated by Andrea Lee. *The Multilingual Anthology of American Literature*, edited by Marc Shell and Werner Sollors, New York UP, 2000, pp. 156-67.

Shell, Marc, and Werner Sollors, editors, *The Multilingual Anthology of American Literature: A Reader of Original Texts with English Translations*. New York UP, 2000.

Sollors, Werner, editor. *Multilingual America: Transnationalism, Ethnicity, and the Languages of American Literature*. New York UP, 1998.

Stuckey, Sterling. *African Culture and Melville's Art: The Creative Process in Benito Cereno*. Oxford UP, 2008.

Sundquist. Eric. "Ashantee Conjurers. Africanisms and Africanization." *To Wake the Nations: Race in the Making of American Literature*. Harvard UP, 1994, pp. 163-74.

Thompson, Robert Farris. "The Kongo Atlantic Tradition." Lecture presented at the University of Texas, Austin, 28 Feb. 1992.

Twain, Mark. *Adventures of Huckleberry Finn*. 1885. Oxford UP, 1996.

——. *Following the Equator and Anti-Imperialist Essays*. 1897. Oxford UP, 1996.

——. *The Innocents Abroad*. 1869. Oxford UP, 1996.

——. "My First Lie and How I Got Out of It." 1899. *The Man That Corrupted Hadleyburg and Other Stories and Essays*. 1900. Oxford UP, 1996, pp. 167-80.

Watkins, Mel. *On the Real Side: Laughing, Lying, and Signifying – The Underground Tradition of Humor That Transformed American Culture from Slavery to Richard Pryor*. Simon and Schuster, 1995.

Williams, R. John. "Modernist Scandals: Ezra Pound's Translations of 'the' Chinese Poem." *Orient and Orientalisms in US-American Poetry and Poetics*, edited by Sabine Sielke and Christian Kloeckner, Peter Lang, 2009, pp. 102-24.

Wirth-Nesher, Hana. *Call It English: The Languages of Jewish American Literature*. Princeton UP, 2008.

Yezierska, Anzia. *Bread Givers*. 1925. Introduction by Alice Kessler Harris, Persea Books, 1975.

Yin, Xiao-huang. *Chinese American Literature since the 1850s*. U of Illinois P, 2000.

Zwick, Jim. "Mark Twain and Imperialism." *A Historical Guide to Mark Twain*, edited by Shelley Fisher Fishkin, Oxford UP, 2002, pp. 227-55.

——. *Mark Twain's Weapons of Satire: Anti-Imperialist Writings on the Philippine-American War*. Syracuse UP, 1992.

Notes on Contributors

VICTORIA ALLEN is a doctoral researcher at the Christian-Albrechts-Universität, Kiel, Germany. She is currently completing her PhD in Media and Cultural Studies on the representations of northernness articulated in industrial myths and memories produced in Tyne and Wearside popular culture. Her research interests encompass semiotic analysis, cultural and critical theory, Gender Studies, and collective and cultural memory.

JO ANGOURI is Director of Undergraduate Studies in Applied Linguistics and the University-level Academic Director for Education and Internationalization at the University of Warwick. Her research involves three interrelated strands: leadership and teamwork in high-pressure, high-risk professional settings; language, politics, and ideology; and migration, mobility, and multilingualism. Jo is co-directing two international research networks, one on Migration Identity and Translation and one on Migrants in Working Life. She is the founding editor of the Language at Work series (Multilingual Matters) and she is also co-editing Discourse Approaches to Politics, Society, and Culture for John Benjamins. She has strong presence and involvement in research policy and works for the UK Economic and Social Research Council and the Arts and Humanities Research Council. In the last ten years, she has published over seventy refereed papers, three special issues, two books, three edited volumes, and two conference proceedings. She has been a visiting scholar in different institutions in New Zealand, Australia, and Europe, and she is currently a Visiting Distinguished Professor at Aalto University, School of Business, Finland.

CHRISTINE BERBERICH is Reader in Literature at the University of Portsmouth, UK. Her main areas of specialism are literatures of national identity, in particular Englishness, and Holocaust Literatures, especially perpetrator writing. Her monograph *The Image of the English Gentleman in*

20th Century Literature: Englishness and Nostalgia was published in 2007. She is co-editor of *These Englands: Conversations on National Identity* (2011), *Land & Identity: Theory, Memory, Practice* (2012), and *Affective Landscapes in Literature, Art and Everyday Life* (2015), as well as editor of *The Bloomsbury Introduction to Popular Fiction* (2014). She is currently working on a monograph on *Nazi Noir*, a public-interest book on P. G. Wodehouse and his time in a Nazi internment camp, as well as an edited collection on the migrant voice and Brexit.

MATTHIAS D. BERGER studied English and German languages and literatures with a focus on medieval English literature and culture in Bern and Aberdeen. In 2020, he successfully defended his PhD thesis, entitled *Unique Continuities: The Nation and the Middle Ages in Twenty-First-Century Switzerland and Britain*, in which he explores contemporary cultural, social, and political invocations of the Middle Ages in negotiations of national identity. He has published two essays: "Roots and Beginnings," on neo-Whiggish medievalism in Brexiteer Daniel Hannan's writings (in the *Anglistentag Proceedings 2016*); and "This Most Historic of Locations," on recent battlefield commemorations in England and Switzerland (in *Studies in Medievalism* XXVII).

SHELLEY FISHER FISHKIN is the Joseph S. Atha Professor of Humanities, Professor of English, and Director of American Studies at Stanford University. She is the author, editor, or co-editor of 47 books and over 100 articles and essays. A past president of the American Studies Association, she is a founding editor of the *Journal of Transnational American Studies*. In 2019 the American Studies Association created an award in her honour: The Shelley Fisher Fishkin Prize for International Scholarship in Transnational American Studies.

MAURICE FITZPATRICK is a lecturer, film director and an author from Ireland. A graduate of Trinity College Dublin, he was a recipient of the Ministry of Education of Japan scholarship 2004-07 and a lecturer at Keio University, Tokyo (2007-11), at Bonn University (2011-12) and at the University of Cologne (2012-16). He has made two documentary films for the BBC: *The Boys of St. Columb's* (also an Irish public television, RTÉ, production) and *Translations Revisited*. In 2017, he wrote, directed, and produced a documentary feature film, *In the Name of Peace:*

John Hume in America, on the political life of Nobel Peace Prize laureate John Hume, which has screened in over thirty countries. He is also the author of a book entitled *John Hume in America: From Derry to DC* (University of Notre Dame Press, 2019) which has been welcomed by Speaker of the House of Representatives Nancy Pelosi as "a wonderful reminder of the strength in diplomacy and the close relationship between the United States and Northern Ireland" and by the *Sunday Business Post* as one of the "20 Vital Books [...] about the Northern conflict." He was a Poynter Fellow at Yale University in 2019 and is the 2020 Heimbold Chair of Irish Studies at Villanova University.

IAN GOODE is Senior Lecturer in Film and Television Studies at the University of Glasgow. His current research interests concern the histories of rural cinema-going and the specificities of its exhibition and experience. He is working on a monograph arising from the project *The Major Minor Cinema: The Highlands and Islands Film Guild (Scotland 1946-71)*, funded by the Arts and Humanities Research Council in the United Kingdom and carried out by a team from the Universitites of Glasgow and Stirling.

INA HABERMANN is Professor of English Literature at the University of Basel and acted as Director of the Centre of Competence Cultural Topographies from 2009 to 2017. Her publications include *Myth, Memory and the Middlebrow: Priestley, du Maurier and the Symbolic Form of Englishness* (Palgrave Macmillan, 2010) and, as editor with Daniela Keller, *English Topographies in Literature and Culture: Space, Place, and Identity* (Brill Rodopi, 2016). She ran the Swiss National Science Foundation project British Literary and Cultural Discourses of Europe (2014-17) and is the editor of *The Road to Brexit. A Cultural Perspective on British Attitudes to Europe* (Manchester UP, 2020). Her research interests include middlebrow writing, Britishness and Englishness, literary otherworlds, and Anglo-European Studies.

CÉCILE HEIM is a doctoral candidate in North American Studies and Gender Studies at the University of Lausanne. Her dissertation examines the representation and dismantling of violence against Indigenous women and girls in the novels of four contemporary Indigenous writers: Louise Erdrich (Anishinaabe), Frances Washburn (Lakota/

Anishinaabe), Edén Robinson (Haisla/Heiltsuk), and Katherena Vermette (Métis/Anishinaabe). Her latest publication is an entry on Stephen Graham Jones in the *Literary Encyclopedia.*

DANIELA KELLER is a Postdoctoral Teaching and Research Fellow at the University of Basel. She completed her PhD thesis, entitled *Germany and Physics in English Fiction after 1960: A Diffractive Reading of Anglo-German Entanglements*, in 2019. She co-edited the essay collection *English Topographies in Literature and Culture: Space, Place, and Identity* (Brill Rodopi, 2016) with Ina Habermann and has recently written an essay entitled "Sensing I and Eyes in Ali Smith's *How to Be Both*" for a collection on diffractive reading edited by Kai Merten (Rowman & Littlefield, 2021).

MARTIN MIK is Director of Student Experience in the School of Life Sciences and Sessional Teacher in the School for Cross-faculty Studies at the University of Warwick. He has been researching European Institutions since 2006; his previous research has looked into the impact of EU membership on individual member states, in particular in relation to the Court of Justice of the European Union. His further research interest in the British political system focuses on the evolving role of the Monarchy. These interests feed into his teaching. Martin has always been committed to multidisciplinary work and works with students to excite and empower them to understand complex historical and political issues.

HARALD PITTEL is a post-doctoral lecturer at the University of Potsdam. He was a visiting scholar at Delhi University (2018-19). His PhD thesis is entitled *Romance and Irony – Oscar Wilde and the Political.* His areas of interests include political affect studies, comparative film studies, genre theories, and materialist theories of culture. His second book project explores how the crises of the present might effect a new understanding of world literature.

BARBARA STRAUMANN is Assistant Professor with tenure track at the English Department of the University of Zurich. Her research interests include the long nineteenth century, gender, film, visuality, multimediality, economic criticism, celebrity culture, queenship, and royalty.

She is the author of *Figurations of Exile in Hitchcock and Nabokov* (2008), *Female Performers in British and American Fiction* (2018), and the co-author of *Die Diva: Eine Geschichte der Bewunderung* (2002). Her current research projects focus on debt in the Victorian novel and the emergence of celebrity in nineteenth-century culture.

NORA WENZL studied English and American Studies and obtained her PhD in applied linguistics from the Department for English Business Communication at Vienna University of Economics and Business, Austria. Her PhD thesis entitled *"This is about the kind of Britain we are": Brexit, British Identity, and Nation Branding in Conservative Discourses* combines approaches from linguistics, cultural studies, and marketing to explore Conservative Leave and Remain discourses in the run-up to the EU referendum. Her work has been published in the 2019 volume *Discourses of Brexit*, as well as an upcoming volume on *Language and Country Branding*.

MICHELLE WITEN is Junior Professor of English and Irish Literature in the Seminar für Anglistik und Amerikanistik at the Europa-Universität Flensburg. She received her doctorate from the University of Oxford and has also held an Oberassistentin position at the University of Basel. Her first monograph, *James Joyce and Absolute Music* (Bloomsbury, 2018), looks at Joyce's use of fugal structure through the lens of nineteenth-century musical debates and his drafting process. Her second book examines the incorporation of news and serialization practices in nineteenth-century periodicals.

Index of Names

Abulafia, David, 31, 32, 36
Æthelred, 29
Aitchison, Martin, 154n2
Albert von Sachsen-Coburg und Gotha (Prince Albert), 43, 44, 44n4, 45, 46, 50, 51
Alderson, Brian, 154n2, 165
Alperson, Philip, 218, 224
Anderson, Benedict, 46, 58, 101, 118
Angouri, Jo, 64, 65, 67, 83n14, 93
Anthony, Laurence, 103, 118
Anzaldúa, Gloria, 277, 278, 279, 289
Archibald, Jo-Ann, 259n12, 268
Armistead, Claire, 154n2, 155, 164
Armitage, David, 112, 118
Arnheim, Michael, 254, 268
Arnott, Jake, 179, 181
Arthur (King), 191
Ascherson, Neal, 10, 20, 209, 209n1, 222, 224
Assmann, Aleida, 191, 191n5, 202
Assmann, Jan, 191, 202
Asthana, Anushka, 196, 202
Avery, Gillian, 150, 164
Aveyard, Karina, 210n3, 224
Bachman, Merle, 277, 289
Baird, Julia, 48n8, 58
Baker, Paul, 100, 102, 118
Baldwin, Stanley, 190
Ballantine Perera, Jennifer, 10n3, 20
Barber, Tony, 162, 164
Barker, Thomas Jones, 56, 60
Barthes, Roland, 26, 36, 193, 202
Baxendale, Helen, 14, 20
Beauregard, Devin, 13n7, 20
Bechhofer, Frank, 13, 21
Bell, Steve, 147, 164
Berberich, Christine, 149, 164, 170, 181
Berger, Matthias, 36
Berkeley, George, 238, 247
Bhatia, Vijay, 65, 65n3, 93
Bignell, Jonathan, 193, 202
Billig, Michael, 102, 118
Blackburn, John, 219, 224
Blaikie, Andrew, 124, 143
Blair, Tony, 52n12
Blanton, Casey, 196, 202
Blomley, Nicholas, 255, 256, 268
Blunt, Emily, 43n1
Blyton, Enid, 145, 146, 147, 148, 149, 164
Boer, Pim den, 24, 36
Bogdanor, Vernon, 9, 10, 20
Borrows, John, 259n12, 268
Bosse, Abraham, 47
Boty, Pauline, 131
Bourne, Ryan, 100, 118
Bowie, David, 150
Boyd, Cat, 222, 224

Boyle, Danny, 51
Brown, John, 50, 51
Brownlie, Siobhan, 33, 36
Bruce, Lenny, 285
Bruno, Tim, 274, 289
Buell, Lawrence, 274, 289
Burchard, Jeremy, 212, 224
Burkhart, Ernest, 253, 253n2
Burnett, John, 221, 224
Butterfield, Herbert, 28, 36
Byers, Sam, 167, 181
Cable, Vince, 162
Cahan, Abraham, 279, 289
Calhoun, Craig, 12, 15, 16, 20
Cameron, David, 25, 81, 82, 93, 170
Campbell, James, 28
Cannadine, David, 48, 48n8, 49, 50, 58
Carpegna, Falconieri, 25, 36
Carpenter, Kristen A., 258, 268
Carpio, Glenda, 279n1, 289
Carrell, Severin, 11n4, 20
Carroll, Leavis (alias Lucien Young), 145, 149, 150, 151, 164
Carroll, Lewis, 145, 146, 149, 150, 151, 164
Cartwright, Anthony, 146, 167, 181
Cassatt, Mary, 274
Caughie, John, 208, 224
Cavell, Edith, 49
Česálková, Lucie, 221, 224
Chambre, Agnes, 33, 36
Chapman, James, 42, 45, 45n5, 58
Chapman, Kate, 26n4, 36
Cheyette, Bryan, 172, 174, 181
Child, Lydia Maria, 273
Churchill, Winston, 71, 93, 161
Clark, Malcolm, 152, 153, 154, 154n2, 164
Clarke, Harold D., 122, 143
Clegg, Nick, 147, 164
Clinton, Hillary, 150
Cockburn, Patrick, 25, 36
Coe, Jonathan, 167, 168, 175, 176, 177, 181
Coleman, Jenna, 43n1
Collette, Christine, 193n6, 202
Colley, Linda, 100, 109, 118
Collins, Noreen, 208
Colman, Olivia, 52n12
Conrad, Joseph, 172
Cook, James, 153, 153n1, 154
Corbyn, Jeremy, 149
Cord, Mary Ann, 283
Cornwell, Bernard, 146
Cosslett, Rhiannon Lucy, 196n9, 202
Coulthard, Sean Glen, 261, 268
Cowan, Lee, 253, 268
Craig, Daniel, 51
Crane, Walter, 56, 60
Cummings, Dominic, 147, 163
D'Arcens, Louise, 24, 36
Daddow, Oliver J., 115, 118
Dante, Alighieri, 137
Davey, Kevin, 184n1, 202
Davies, Norman, 228, 247
Day, Helen, 152, 154n2, 157n4, 158, 164
de Gaulle, Charles, 73, 74
De Niro, Robert, 253
Deacon, David, 159, 164
Deane, Seamus, 241, 247
Deloria, Vine, Jr., 258, 258n10 268
Dench, Judi, 41, 43, 50, 50n11,

52, 53, 54, 55, 57
Derrida, Jacques, 30, 136, 143
Devine, Tom, 211, 224
Díaz, Junot, 279n1, 289
DiCaprio, Leonardo, 253
Dickens, Charles, 136
Dimock, Wai Chee, 273, 289
Dinan, Desmond, 71, 80, 93
Dodds, Nigel, 234, 247
Donington, Katie, 9, 14, 20
Dorling, Danny, 12, 20, 55, 58, 146, 164, 188, 202
Drury, Colin, 194n8, 202
Du Garde Peach, L., 162, 164
Du Gay, Paul, 101, 118
Duclos, Nathalie, 222, 224
Dunbar-Ortiz, Roxanne, 255, 265, 268
Duthie, Peggy Lin, 151, 165
Eaglestone, Robert, 10, 20, 145, 163, 165
Edgar (King), 30
Edward VIII, 45, 49, 161
Ehland, Christoph, 188, 202
Einboden, Jeffrey, 273, 289
Eldridge, John, 132, 143
Eldridge, Lizzie, 132, 143
Elgar, Edward, 46
Eliot, T. S., 274
Elizabeth I, 50
Elizabeth II, 51, 52, 52n12, 62, 67n6
Elliott, Andrew B. R., 25, 25n3, 36
Ellison, Ralph, 283
Else, Nicole, 154n2
Emerson, Ralph Waldo, 273, 274
Erlanger, Steven, 196n9, 202
Erll, Astrid, 191, 191n5, 202
Etherton, Sir Terence, 149
Evans, Margaret, 159, 165
Evans, R. J. W., 24, 37
Fairclough, Norman, 101, 118
Faith, Mike, Jr., 255n5, 268
Farage, Nigel, 33, 147, 149, 194, 194n8 195, 197, 239
Fawkes, Guy, 135
Fazal, Ali, 51
Ferguson, Donna, 159, 165
Fielding, Steven, 43n2, 48n7, 58
Fisch, Audrey A., 285, 289
Fishkin, Shelley Fisher, 273, 274, 275, 277, 279, 279n1, 280, 281, 282, 283, 284, 285, 288, 289
Fitzpatrick, Maurice, 247
Ford, Elizabeth A., 45, 50, 58
Foster, Arlene, 232
Fox-Leonard, Boudicca, 155, 156, 163, 165
Foy, Claire, 52n12
Frears, Stephen, 41, 43, 50, 52, 52n12, 55, 56, 57
Freud, Lucian, 172
Friel, Brian, 236, 247
Frye, Northrop, 137, 138, 139, 140, 143
Gardiner, Juliet, 199, 203
Geary, Patrick J., 25, 37
George VI, 48, 49, 52, 161
George, Lloyd, 238
George, Stephen, 77, 94
Gibbins, Justin, 115, 118
Gilleard, Christopher, 125, 143
Gilliam, Terry, 121, 122
Gladstone, William Ewart, 44, 238, 247
Goeman, Mishuana, 257, 262, 264, 268

Goode, Ian, 211, 212n6, 218, 225
Goodwin, Daisy, 43n1
Goodwin, Matthew J., 100, 118
Goodyear-Ka'opua, Noelani, 255n6, 268
Gorsuch, Neil, 254
Gove, Michael, 29n7, 147, 149, 233n5
Grann, David, 252, 253, 253n2, 268
Grant, Linda, 167, 168, 177, 178, 179, 181
Gregor, Neil, 31, 32, 37
Griffiths, Trevor, 207, 211, 225
Groebner, Valentin, 24, 37
Gullette, Margaret M., 125, 129, 131, 143
Habermann, Ina, 10, 10n3, 12, 20, 184n1, 186n2, 203
Hale, William K., 253, 260
Hall, Stuart, 101, 118
Halliday, M. A. K., 99, 100, 102, 103, 118
Hampson, Frank, 154n2
Hannan, Daniel, 15, 27, 27n5, 28, 29, 29n6, 29n7, 30, 30n8, 30n9, 31, 31n10, 32, 34, 37
Harding, Alan, 210, 225
Hare, David, 234, 248
Harris, Cheryl I., 258n11, 268
Harrison, Melissa, 146
Hassan, Gerry, 222, 223, 225
Hazeley, Jason A., 145, 155, 156, 159, 160, 165
Hazell, Robert, 13, 13n6, 21
Heath, Edward, 74, 77, 78
Heath, Oliver, 100, 118
Hegel, Georg Wilhelm Friedrich, 30
Hemingway, Ernest, 274, 280, 290
Henderson, Alisa, 9, 10, 15, 21
Henley, Jon, 170, 181
Henneböhl, Dennis, 123, 144
Henry VIII, 31
Higgs, Paul, 125, 143
Hileman, Bryan, 274, 290
Hinojosa, Rolando, 279n1, 290
Hitler, Adolf, 161
Hjort, Mette, 209n1, 225
Ho, Don, 102, 118
Hobbes, Thomas, 47, 58
Hobsbawm, Eric, 48, 58
Hogan, Linda, 18, 251, 252, 253, 259, 261, 264, 265, 266, 268
Holloway, Joseph E., 284, 285, 290
Homans, Margaret, 43n1, 54n14, 58
Hood, Robin, 191
Hopkins, Nick, 99, 100, 102, 119
Horne, George, 218
Howarth, David, 64, 94
Huff, AdriAnne, 274, 290
Hughes, Stuart, 156, 165
Hume, John, 229, 237, 241, 248
Humphris, Frank, 153, 154, 165
Hunter, James, 210, 221, 225
Ibbeson, Graham, 192, 203
Inglehart, Ronald, 122, 143
Irving, Washington, 273
Ishihara, Tsuyoshi, 274, 290
Islam, Gazi Nazrul, 101, 118
Islentyeva, Anna, 111, 118
Ives, Colta, 274, 291
Jacobs, George, 253
James II, 29

Jang, Mi-Jung, 274, 291
Jefferson, Thomas, 256
Jennings, Angie, 209, 225
Jennings, Will, 63, 64, 94
Jernudd, Åsa, 209n1, 225
John (King), 33
John, Peter, 63, 64, 94
Johnson, Amy, 50
Johnson, Boris, 11, 11n4, 33, 84, 147, 149, 159, 170, 222, 228n1, 233n4, 233n5, 244, 245, 248
Johnson, Lorraine, 154n2, 165
Johnston, Andrew James, 28, 37
Johnston, Basil, 261, 268
Jones, Cynan, 167, 168, 172, 181
Jones, Richard Wyn, 235, 248
Jorgenson-Murray, Stephen, 188, 203
Justice, Daniel Heath, 259n12, 263, 269
Kanellos, Nicolas, 277, 291
Kantorowicz, Ernst H., 42n1, 58
Karim, Abdul, 16, 41, 51, 52, 53, 54n14, 55, 57
Keating, Michael, 10, 21
Kelly, Angela, 51, 58
Kenny, Michael, 10, 13, 14, 15, 21
Kensington, Mansfield, 196n9, 203
Kensington, Meriden, 203
Kingman, David, 122, 143
Kirk, Neville, 188, 203
Klepfisz, Irena, 279, 291
Knapp, Andrew, 31, 37
Knight, Sam, 27, 29n7, 37
Koller, Veronika, 101, 118
Korte, Barbara, 195, 196, 200, 203
Kovach, Margaret, 259n12, 269
Kreis, Georg, 34n13, 37
Kuhn, Annette, 209n3, 225
Kumar, Krishan, 34, 38, 184n1, 185, 203
Kunow, Rüdiger, 274, 291
Kyle, Mollie, 253n2
Lady Diana, 52n12
Lanchester, John, 167, 181
Leavenworth, Maria Lindgren, 184, 187, 203
Lee, Julia Sun-Joo, 285, 291
Lee, Min Jin, 285, 286, 291
Leerssen, Joep, 33, 38
Lehman, Christopher P., 284, 291
Levy, Andrea, 169, 181
Levy, David A. L., 169, 170, 181
Lewis, Sinclair, 287, 291
Lillis, Michael, 228n2, 229, 248
Lindqvist, Ursula, 209n1, 225
Livingston, Robert, 220, 226
Locke, John, 255, 256, 269
Lotman, Yuri M., 142n3, 143
Lowbridge, Caroline, 154, 154n2, 155, 165
Luther, Martin, 230
Lynch, Andrew, 24, 36
Lynn, Vera, 51
Lytle, Clifford M., 258, 258n10, 268
Maas, Heiko, 237, 240
Macdougall, Norman, 135, 143
Macmillan, Harold, 72
Maconie, Stuart, 17, 183, 184, 185, 186, 186n2, 186n3, 187,

188, 189, 189n4, 190, 191, 192, 193, 195, 196, 196n9, 197, 198, 199, 200, 203
Macron, Emmanuel, 237
Madden, John, 50
Mahelona, Yvonne, 255n6, 268
Mammone, Andrea, 31, 38
Mansfield, Katherine, 133, 139
Marchal, Guy P., 24, 37
Marra, Meredith, 65, 93
Martinson, Jane, 159, 160, 165
Marx, Karl, 30
Marzocchi, Ottavio, 170, 181
Matthiessen, Christian, 99, 100, 102, 103, 118
May, Jon D., 253, 269
May, Theresa, 11, 12n5, 33, 82, 84, 149, 179, 222, 228n1, 229, 232, 233, 234, 235, 238, 245, 248
McCormack, Jayne, 237, 248
McCrone, David, 13, 21, 223, 226
McCulloch, Derek, 157, 165
McDonagh, Bobby, 236, 248
McDonald, Russ, 50, 50n11, 58
McDonald, Sheena, 241, 248
McGirt, Jimcy, 254
McNeil, Rob, 171, 181
Melville, Herman, 274, 284
Miller, Vaughne, 79, 94
Milton, John, 137
Milward, Alan, 73, 94
Minois, Georges, 125, 143
Mirren, Helen, 52n12
Mitchell, Deborah C., 45, 50, 58
Mole, Richard C. M., 101, 119
Mollin, Sandra, 99n1, 119
Montfort, Simon de, 26, 28
Moody, Ian, 162
Moreton-Robinson, Aileen, 258n11, 269
Morris, Chris, 9n2, 21
Morris, Joel P., 145, 155, 156, 160, 165
Morris, Tom, 216, 218, 226
Morton, David, 188, 204
Morton, H. V., 185, 186n2, 204
Moss, Sarah, 146
Mulderrig, Jane, 104n3, 119
Murphy, Patrick, 253, 254
Murray, W., 161, 165
Nagle, Rebecca, 253
Namusoke, Eva, 14n8, 21
Neagle, Anna, 41, 43, 43n3, 45, 45n5, 46, 47, 49n9, 50, 50n10, 52, 53, 56
Neely, Sarah, 209n3, 226
Newbigin, Eleanor, 162, 165
Nichols, Robert, 256, 257, 269
Nightingale, Florence, 49
Nora, Pierre, 24, 38
Norris, Pippa, 122, 143
Nünning, Ansgar, 191, 191n5, 202
O'Carroll, Lisa, 11, 21
O'Leary, Brendan, 229, 248
O'Neill, Maggie, 194, 204
O'Rourke, Kevin, 147, 165
O'Toole, Fintan, 11, 12n5, 14, 21, 25, 25n2, 33, 34, 38, 168, 169, 171, 177, 181, 200, 204, 241, 249
Olick, Jeffrey K., 191n5, 204
Orestano, Francesca, 153n1, 166
Orwell, George, 185, 186, 186n2, 204, 222, 228n1
Osborne, George, 147

Ovid, 136
Paisley, Ian, 230, 239
Palmer, Charles, 188, 189
Paredes, Américo, 274
Parkeh, Bhikhu, 112, 119
Parkin, Tim, 125, 143
Parkinson, Hannah Jane, 194, 204
Pater, Walter, 125
Patten, Christopher Francis, Baron Patten of Barnes, 243, 249
Paul, Nalini, 209n3, 226
Pearce, Nick, 14, 15, 21
Peck, Tom, 239, 249
Perry, Matt, 190, 192, 194, 194n7, 204
Petrie, Duncan, 215n7, 226
Philip II, 33
Philips, John Edward, 285, 291
Piao, Scott, 102, 119
Picard, Tom, 190, 204
Pine, Richard, 130, 143
Pompidou, Georges, 74
Ponsonby, Sir Henry, 53, 56
Potter, Beatrix, 151
Pound, Ezra, 274
Powell, Enoch, 30, 30n8, 169, 176
Price, Alan, 193, 204
Priestley, J. B., 185, 186, 186n2, 189, 204
Prince, 150
Prince Frederick of Prussia, 44
Qian, Zhaoming, 274, 291
Radcliffe, Mark, 185
Ramsey, John, 253
Ranger, Terence, 58
Rasch, Astrid, 14, 22
Rau, Petra, 123, 143
Rea, Vince, 192, 204
Redford, Duncan, 11, 21
Redshaw, David, 220 fig. 3
Rees-Mogg, Jacob, 26, 33, 239
Reicher, Stephen, 99, 100, 102, 119
Reisigl, Martin, 101, 119
Reisz, Karel, 172
Richards, Jeffrey, 49n9, 58
Rickman, Alan, 150
Ridley, Jane, 48n8, 58
Riihimäki, Jenni, 115, 119
Rilke, Rainer Maria, 133, 139
Risbridger, Eleanor, 148, 166
Rivera, Tomás, 279n1, 291
Roan, Henry, 253
Roberts, Andrew, 31, 31n10
Roberts, Brian, 194, 204
Robinson, George, 188, 204
Roediger, David, 284, 291
Rosaldo, Renato, 55, 58
Rosenfeld, Morris, 280, 291
Rostek, Joanna, 12n5, 21, 196, 198, 204, 205
Roth, Henry, 279, 291
Rousseau, Jean-Jacques, 242
Rushdie, Salman, 174
Rushton, Peter, 194, 205
Russell, Dave, 188, 205
Sabater, Albert, 123, 144
Sachs, Viola, 284, 291
Sacks, Howard L., 284, 292
Sacks, Judith Rose, 284, 292
Saldívar, Ramón, 274, 292
Sales, Philip James, Lord Sales, 149
Samson, Odette, 50
Sanchez, M. G., 10n3, 22
Sartre, Jean-Paul, 30
Schomburg, Arturo, 277

Schulte, Regina, 42n1, 58
Scorsese, Martin, 253
Scott Thomas, Kristin, 234
Scott, Edward, 82, 97
Séjours, Victor, 277, 292
Sellar, Walter Carruthers, 33, 38
Selvon, Sam, 169, 181
Shakespeare, William, 136
Shaw, Kristian, 16, 146, 163, 166, 171, 181
Shell, Marc, 277, 292
Shields, Rob, 219, 226
Shipman, Tim, 25, 38, 147, 166
Siddle, W. D., 158, 166
Simpson, Wallis, 45
Slembrouck, Stef, 99n1, 119
Smith, Ali, 12, 17, 121, 123, 124, 125, 127, 128, 129, 130, 131, 132, 133, 134, 135, 136, 137, 138, 141, 141n2, 142, 144, 146, 167, 182
Smith, Julian, 229n3
Smith, William E., 253
Sollors, Werner, 277, 292
Spiering, Menno, 109, 110, 115, 119
Spongberg, Mary, 28, 38
Starkey, David, 31
Stevenson, Robert Louis, 147
Stewart, Heather, 33, 38
Stone, Albert, 281
Strauss, Delphine, 233n5, 249
Street, Sarah, 43n3, 45, 49, 50, 58
Stuckey, Sterling, 284, 292
Sumption, Jonathan, 31n9, 38
Sundquist, Eric, 284, 292
Sutherland, John, 33, 38
Swales, John, 65, 65n3, 97
Tajfel, Henri, 101, 102, 119
Taylor, Miles, 54n15, 58
Taylor, Ros, 196n9, 205
Tenniel, John, 150
Thatcher, Margaret, 78, 122, 229
Thissen, Judith, 210n3, 226
Thomas, John, Baron Thomas of Cwmgiedd, 149
Thompson, Carl, 205
Thompson, Dorothy, 48n8, 59
Thompson, Geoff, 103, 119
Thompson, Robert Farris, 284, 292
Thoreau, Henry David, 273
Thunberg, Greta, 140
Tomkins, Adam, 15
Tomlinson, Sally, 55, 58, 146, 156n3, 164, 166
Tönnies, Merle, 123, 144
Treveri Gennari, Daniela, 210n3, 226
Trump, Donald, 271, 272
Tuck, Eve, 254n4, 269
Tuite, Clara, 28, 38
Twain, Mark, 274, 275, 276, 277, 280, 281, 282, 283, 284, 287, 292
Umunna, Chuka, 123, 144
Urquhart, Roddie, 214
Utz, Richard, 29, 38
Vallée, Jean-Marc, 43n1
Varadkar, Leo, 233n4, 233n5, 237, 245
Victoria (Queen), 16, 41, 42, 43, 43n1, 43n2, 44, 44n4, 45, 46, 47, 48, 48n7, 48n8, 49, 49n9, 50, 50n10, 51, 52, 53, 54, 54n14, 54n15, 55, 55n15, 56, 57
Vincent, Bruno, 145, 166

Walden, George, 147, 166
Wall, Stephen, 77, 97
Wallace, Paul, 196n9, 205
Waller, David, 188, 204
Ward, Stuart, 14, 22
Warrior, Robert Allen, 252, 269
Watkins, Mel, 285, 292
Weight, Richard, 169, 182
Wellings, Ben, 14, 20
Wenzl, Nora, 104n3, 109, 111, 114, 116, 119
Wesker, Arnold, 172
White, Hayden, 138, 139, 144
Wilcox, Herbert, 41, 43, 43n3, 45, 45n5, 46, 49n9, 50, 52, 56
Wilde, Oscar, 125
Wilkinson, Ellen, 189, 189n4, 190, 205
William III (William of Orange), 29
Williams, R. John, 274, 292
Williams, Raymond, 123, 132, 144
Williams, Robert A., Jr., 256n7, 257n8, 269
Williamson, Billy, 216 fig. 2
Williamson, David, 25, 38
Wilson, A. N., 48n8, 59
Wilson, Harold, 74, 77, 78, 79, 231
Winder, Robert, 25, 39
Wingfield, Harry, 153, 154
Wirth-Nesher, Hana, 277, 292
Wodak, Ruth, 64, 83n13, 84, 93, 97, 101, 118, 119, 120
Wohlbrück, Adolf Anton Wilhelm, 44n4
Wood, Ian N., 24, 39
Wood, James, 136, 144
Worsley, Lucy, 48n8, 59
Wring, Dominic, 170, 182
Yang, K. Wayne, 254n4, 269
Yeatman, Robert Julian, 33, 38
Yeats, William Butler, 200
Yeo, Colin, 179, 182
Yezierska, Anzia, 279, 292
Yin, Xiao-huang, 277, 292
Young, Hugo, 77, 97
Young, Lola, Baroness Young of Hornsey, 172, 182
Youngs, Tim, 184, 186, 205
Zeegen, Lawrence, 146, 151, 152, 154, 154n2, 163, 166
Zimmermann, Clemens, 210n3, 226
Zwick, Jim, 277, 293
Zwierlein, Anne-Julia, 12n5, 21, 196, 198, 204, 205

Swiss Papers in English Language and Literature (SPELL)

Edited by
The Swiss Association of University Teachers of English (SAUTE)

General Editor: Lukas Erne

Already published:

1
Anthony Mortimer (ed.)
Contemporary Approaches to Narrative
1984, 129 Seiten
€[D] 16,–
ISBN 978-3-87808-841-7

2
Richard Waswo (ed.)
On Poetry and Poetics
1985, 212 Seiten
€[D] 21,–
ISBN 978-3-87808-842-4

3
Udo Fries (ed.)
The Structure of Texts
1987, 264 Seiten
€[D] 26,–
ISBN 978-3-87808-843-1

4
Neil Forsyth (ed.)
Reading Contexts
1988, 198 Seiten
€[D] 21,–
ISBN 978-3-87808-844-8

5
Margaret Bridges (ed.)
On Strangeness
1990, 239 Seiten
€[D] 23,–
ISBN 978-3-8233-4680-7

6
Balz Engler (ed.)
Writing & Culture
1990, 253 Seiten
€[D] 24,–
ISBN 978-3-8233-4681-4

7
Andreas Fischer (ed.)
Repetition
1994, 268 Seiten
€[D] 34,–
ISBN 978-3-8233-4682-1

8
Peter Hughes / Robert Rehder (eds.)
Imprints & Re-visions
The Making of the Literary Text, 1759-1818
1995, 241 Seiten
€[D] 34,–
ISBN 978-3-8233-4683-8

9
Werner Senn (ed.)
Families
1996, 282 Seiten
€[D] 36,–
ISBN 978-3-8233-4684-5

10
John G. Blair / Reinhold Wagnleitner (eds.)
Empire American Studies
Selected papers from the bi-national conference of the Swiss and Austrian Associations for American Studies at the Salzburg Seminar, November 1996
1997, 275 Seiten
€[D] 36,–
ISBN 978-3-8233-4685-2

11
Peter Halter (ed.)
Performance
1998, 226 Seiten
€[D] 36,–
ISBN 978-3-8233-4686-9

12
Fritz Gysin (ed.)
Apocalypse
2000, 130 Seiten
€[D] 29,–
ISBN 978-3-8233-4687-6

13
Lukas Erne / Guillemette Bolens (eds.)
The Limits of Textuality
2000, 204 Seiten
€[D] 34,–
ISBN 978-3-8233-4688-3

14
Martin Heusser / Gudrun Grabher (eds.)
American Foundational Myths
2002, 224 Seiten
€[D] 39,–
ISBN 978-3-8233-4689-0

15
Frances Ilmberger / Alan Robinson (eds.)
Globalisation
2002, 193 seiten
€[D] 39,–
ISBN 978-3-8233-4690-6

16
Beverly Maeder (ed.)
Representing Realities
Essays on American Literature, Art and Culture
2003, 228 Seiten
€[D] 39,–
ISBN 978-3-8233-6040-7

17
David Spurr / Cornelia Tschichold (eds.)
The Space of English
2004, 322 Seiten
€[D] 58,–
ISBN 978-3-8233-6122-0

18
Robert Rehder / Patrick Vincent (eds.)
American Poetry
Whitman to the Present
2006, 238 Seiten
€[D] 49,–
ISBN 978-3-8233-6271-5

19
Balz Engler / Lucia Michalcak (eds.)
Cultures in Contact
2007, 210 Seiten
€[D] 49,–
ISBN 978-3-8233-6272-2

20
Deborah L. Madsen (ed.)
American Aesthetics
2007, 241 Seiten
€[D] 49,–
ISBN 978-3-8233-6372-9

21
Martin Heusser / Andreas Fischer / Andreas H. Jucker (eds.)
Mediality / Intermediality
2008, 170 Seiten
€[D] 49,–
ISBN 978-3-8233-6457-3

22
Indira Ghose / Denis Renevey (eds.)
The Construction of Textual Identity in Medieval and Early Modern Literature
2009, 222 Seiten
€[D] 49,–
ISBN 978-3-8233-6520-4

23
Thomas Austenfeld / Agnieszka Soltysik Monnet (eds.)
Writing American Women
2009, 232 Seiten
€[D] 49,–
ISBN 978-3-8233-6521-1

24
Karen Junod / Didier Maillat (eds.)
Performing the Self
2010, 196 Seiten
€[D] 49,–
ISBN 978-3-8233-6613-3

25
Guillemette Bolens / Lukas Erne (eds.)
Medieval and Early Modern Authorship
2011, 323 Seiten
€[D] 49,–
ISBN 978-3-8233-6667-6

26
Deborah L. Madsen / Mario Klarer (eds.)
The Visual Culture of Modernism
2011, 265 Seiten
€[D] 49,–
ISBN 978-3-8233-6673-7

27
Annette Kern-Stähler / David Britain (eds.)
English on the Move
Mobilities in Literature and Language
2012, 171 Seiten
€[D] 49,–
ISBN 978-3-8233-6739-0

28
Rachel Falconer / Denis Renevey (eds.)
Medieval and Early Modern Literature, Science and Medicine
2013, 256 Seiten
€[D] 49,–
ISBN 978-3-8233-6820-5

29
Christina Ljungberg / Mario Klarer (eds.)
Cultures in Conflict/Conflicting Cultures
2013, 209 Seiten
€[D] 49,–
ISBN 978-3-8233-6829-8

30
Andreas Langlotz /
Agnieszka Soltysik Monnet (eds.)
Emotion, Affect, Sentiment:
The Language and Aesthetics of Feeling
2014, 268 Seiten
€[D] 49,–
ISBN 978-3-8233-6889-2

31
Elisabeth Dutton / James McBain (eds.)
Drama and Pedagogy in Medieval and Early Modern England
2015, 304 Seiten
€[D] 49,–
ISBN 978-3-8233-6968-4

32
Ridvan Askin / Philipp Schweighauser (eds.)
Literature, Ethics, Morality: American Studies Perspectives
2015, 238 Seiten
€[D] 49,–
ISBN 978-3-8233-6967-7

33
Ridvan Askin / Philipp Schweighauser (eds.)
Literature, Ethics, Morality: American Studies Perspectives
2017, 238 Seiten
€[D] 49,–
ISBN 978-3-8233-6967-7

34
Antoinina Bevan Zlatar / Olga Timofeeva (eds.)
What is an Image in Medieval and Early Modern England?
2017, 300 Seiten
€[D] 49,–
ISBN 978-3-8233-8150-1

35
Lukas Etter / Julia Straub (eds.)
American Communities: Between the Popular and the Political
2017, 250 Seiten
€[D] 49,–
ISBN 978-3-8233-8151-8

36
Margaret Tudeau-Clayton / Martin Hilpert (eds.)
The Challenge of Change
2018, 267 Seiten
€[D] 49,–
ISBN 978-3-8233-8241-6

37
Annette Kern-Stähler / Nicole Nyffenegger (eds.)
Secrecy and Surveillance in Medieval and Early Modern England
2019, 216 Seiten
€[D] 49,–
ISBN 978-3-8233-8326-0

38
Cécile Heim / Boris Vejdovsky /
Benjamin Pickford (eds.)
The Genres of Genre: Form, Formats, and Cultural Formations
2019, 178 Seiten
€[D] 49,–
ISBN 978-3-8233-8327-7

39
Daniela Keller / Ina Habermann (eds.)
Brexit and Beyond: Nation and Identity
2021, 312 Seiten
€[D] 49,–
ISBN 978-3-8233-8414-4